Hiking
Northern California

Ron Adkison

Published in cooperation
with the

**American
Hiking
Society**

FALCONGUIDES®

GUILFORD, CONNECTICUT
HELENA, MONTANA
AN IMPRINT OF THE GLOBE PEQUOT PRESS

FALCONGUIDES®

All photos by Rod Adkinson unless otherwise noted.
Cover photo by Larry Prosor

Library of Congress Cataloging-in-Publication Data
Adkison, Ron.
    Hiking northern California / by Ron Adkison ; all text and maps by the author, photos by the author except as noted.-- 3rd ed.
        p. cm. -- (A Falcon guide)
    Rev. ed. of: Hiking California. 1997.
    ISBN 978-1-56044-701-6

    1. Hiking--California--Guidebooks. 2. California--Guidebooks. I. Title. II. Series. III. Adkison, Ron. Hiker's guide to California.
GV199.42.C2 A25 2000
917.94'0453 21--dc21

                                                                99-042149

Printed in the United States of America.
First Edition/Third Printing

♻ Text pages printed on recycled paper.

To buy books in quantity for corporate use
or incentives, call **(800) 962–0973**
or e-mail **premiums@GlobePequot.com**.

The author and The Globe Pequot Press assume no liability for accidents happening to, or injuries sustained by, readers who engage in the activities described in this book.

Contents

Acknowledgments

Wild country may change imperceptibly during a human lifetime, but each passing year brings changes to trails and trailheads, access roads, and backcountry regulations. As a result, keeping a guidebook up-to-date is an endless process.

This book, *Hiking Northern California*, represents a third and new edition of the original book, *Hiking California*. To keep the book as accurate and as up-to-date as possible, I re-scouted many of the trails and added 19 new hikes. I returned to California in 1998 after a long absence; that visit rekindled the deep feelings I hold for California's wildlands, the stomping grounds of my childhood.

Although far too numerous to name individually, I wish to extend my sincere thanks and gratitude to the dozens of employees of the Forest Service, Bureau of Land Management, and Park Service, for helping me to attain the goal of keeping this guide accurate and up-to-date. Rising far beyond the call of duty, their generous contributions included reviewing the text, helping me make sense of new regulations, and making important corrections and suggestions to ensure the hike descriptions are accurate and easy to follow. These people are truly public servants and deserve great credit for the fine work they do.

My family also made it possible for me to undertake this project, while I was in the field and behind the keyboard at home. Special thanks go out to my family—Lynette, Ben, and Abbey.

Finally, the first edition would never have been possible without the unflagging support and generous help of my parents, who encouraged and nurtured my passion for wild country since my childhood. My father, in particular, shared my enthusiasm for the backcountry and unselfishly made it possible for me to follow my dreams. It is to his memory I wish to dedicate this book.

In Memoriam
George Bruce Adkison
(1923–1998)

Map Legend

Interstate	00	Campground	▲
U.S. Highway	00	Picnic Area	
State or Other Principal Road	00 000	Cabins/Buildings	▪
Forest Road	22512	Peak	9,782 ft.
Interstate Highway	═══⟹	Dome	
Paved Road	▬▬⟹	Mine	≺
Gravel Road	══⟹	Elevation	9,782 ft. ✕
Unimproved Road	===⟹	Gate	•——•
Trailhead	◯	Mine Site	✕
Alternate Trailhead	◌	Town	◯
Main Trail(s)/Route(s)	▬ ▬ ▬	Pass	⌣
Alternate/Secondary Trail(s)	▬ ▬ ▬	Meadow	↯
Cross-country Route	··········	Powerline	•——•——•
Parking Area	Ⓟ	National Forest/Park/ Wilderness Boundary	
River/Creek/Falls		Map Orientation	N
Intermittent Stream		Scale	0 0.5 1 Miles
Spring	⌀		
Glacier			
Lake			

Overview Map

Introduction

California! The mere mention of the name conjures up images of Spanish ranches, of Franciscan missions, of the Gold Rush, of vast and fertile farmlands, of rugged and spectacular coastlines, of superb, mild weather, of large cities, of parched deserts, and of mountains and wilderness.

California, our nation's most populous state, means different things to each of us, but to hikers it can be expressed in one word—Paradise! Yes, California has it all, and you can hike here in virtually every month of the year. In summer, heat-oppressed lowlanders flee to the cool high country; as winter tightens its grip, hikers descend into the more hospitable environs of the foothills, the coast, or the desert.

The slow pace of hikers allows them to experience firsthand the changing face of nature in this incredibly diverse land. Backcountry travelers can revel in the magnificent energy of a high-mountain thunderstorm or enjoy the mellow morning sun reflected on shimmering pine needles. They can spend hours watching fluffy cumulus clouds roll by on invisible rivers in the sky or experience the excitement of a large trout rising to a fly, momentarily interrupting a perfect reflection in the glassy water. Hikers are rewarded with the exhilaration and satisfaction of finally scaling mountain crags, where the unspoiled landscape stretches from horizon to horizon; they are lulled to sleep by the chuckling waters of a clear, cold mountain stream.

Nowhere else in the world does a land of such infinite diversity and contrast exist. From the summit of Mount Whitney, the highest point in the lower 48 states, you can stand within 100 miles of the lowest point in North America. Immediately to the east and more than 10,000 feet below lies the deepest valley on the continent, Owens Valley. Directly across that valley rise the Inyo-White Mountains, hosting one of the oldest living species on earth, the bristlecone pine. West of Mount Whitney, within the heavily forested western slope of the Sierra Nevada (the country's longest unbroken mountain chain), stand the largest living things on earth, the giant sequoia. As you soon discover, though, this incredible diversity and contrast is not limited to a few well-known features.

Moreover, by exploring these backcountry trails and marveling at the variety of landforms, flora, and fauna, you may also journey inward. Through a wilderness of profound questions, you hike toward deeper insights into the workings of the natural world, where every plant, animal, and rock has its place and function, all seemingly separate, but all intricately related.

No single guidebook, of course, could possibly log every potential hike in a state as vast and diverse as California. But each hike described here provides an introduction to innumerable hiking opportunities nearby, be they trail walks or rugged cross-country scrambles.

As you gain the ability, knowledge, and confidence necessary for safe exploration, your backcountry adventures are limited only by your imagination. *Hiking Northern California* can only whet your appetite for exploring the Golden State—exploration that could, indeed, encompass many lifetimes of adventure.

Winter camping in the High Sierra requires knowledge of the special hazards associated with winter conditions. RICK MARVIN PHOTO.

Using this book

HIKES

For the most part, the hike descriptions are self-explanatory. A few points, however, require some discussion to help you get the most from each hiking trip.

The **General location** indicates geographical location, wilderness area (if any), which government agency manages the area, mileage in a straight line, and direction from major towns and cities.

Four basic **Types of hikes** are described in this guide: *round trips*, where you hike to a particular destination, then retrace your route back to the trailhead; *loop trips*, where you hike in on one trail and hike out to the same trailhead via a different route, perhaps retracing as much as 1 mile of trail; *semi-loop trips*, where you negotiate a small loop but retrace a portion of your route; and *point-to-point* or *shuttle trips*, where you begin at one trailhead and hike out to another. This last type of trip requires that you leave another car at the opposite trailhead, have someone pick you up, or divide your group, hiking from opposite trailheads and exchanging car keys in the backcountry.

Hikes strictly classified as day hikes are too short for backpacking or do not have adequate water or campsites available. Classification of hikes as suitable for either day or backpack hikes indicates that they can be completed in one strenuous day or can be taken at a slower pace, with nights spent camping in the backcountry.

Generally, backpack hikes are those trips that cover too much distance to be finished comfortably in one day. A backpack hike may also be classified because the attractions of an area, such as the fishing or magnificent scenery, warrant a leisurely pace for a more enjoyable trip.

Occasionally, a hike is listed as suitable for backpacking if water is carried along. Packing water, however, is usually practical only for one-night camping or if snow patches are available from which you can melt the water you need. But if lugging pounds of water for miles doesn't sound appealing, remember that dry camps are usually insect-free, more remote, and less used than campsites near water. Many solitude-seeking hikers find that the advantages of dry camps far outweigh any inconvenience of packing a supply of water. One gallon of water per person for each night at a dry camp is usually adequate.

Hikes listed as cross-country or partially cross-country should be attempted only by hikers experienced in off-trail hiking and routefinding. Many of these hikes are straightforward, but some require skills that novice hikers have not yet developed. A few of these cross-country hikes include routes classified as class 2 or class 3. Class 2 routes are essentially scrambles over rough terrain, often involving boulder-hopping or scrambling along steep, and occasionally unstable, slopes—you must use your hands sometimes to maintain your balance or latch onto a hold. Most hikers with some cross-country experience should have no trouble on class 2 routes, but lug-soled boots are recommended.

Class 3 routes entail basic rockclimbing skills where hand and foot holds come into play. These routes are often quite exposed, and the unsteady or novice climber may need to be roped up on class 3 routes. No hike described in this guide involves class 3 climbing, but nearby peaks that are suggested for side trips often do.

Distance figures list the *total* distance of a hike.

The **Difficulty** rating is based on the average hiker's ability and may vary depending on your physical condition, weather conditions, and trail or route conditions.

Elevation gain and loss figures are approximations, accurate to within 50 feet. These figures are composites based on altimeter readings. For example, a one-way hike that ascended 1,000 feet, descended 750 feet, ascended another 1,000 feet, and then descended 500 feet, would have an elevation gain of 2,000 feet and an elevation loss of 1,250 feet. Especially in rugged terrain, such figures often indicate the strenuous nature of a hike more accurately than would the simple difference between the elevation gain and loss (in this example, 750 feet).

For round trips, elevation gain and loss figures are listed for the hike in— simply reverse those figures for the return trip. For example, if you gain 1,500 feet and lose 150 feet for the hike into a particular destination, you then would lose 1,500 feet and gain 150 feet for the hike back to the trailhead. Only one figure is listed if the hike only gains elevation or only loses elevation from the trailhead to the destination. For example, if the elevation gain figure is listed as "1,200 feet," then you gain 1,200 feet of elevation from the trailhead to the destination. On the return trip, you would lose that 1,200 feet going back to the trailhead. Such a listing indicates that a hike is all uphill to the destination; if only an elevation loss figure is listed (indicated by a minus sign), then the hike is downhill all the way to the destination.

Occasionally, the text refers to a mountain peak or lake as "Peak 11,071" or "Lake 6,730." This title refers to unnamed peaks or lakes and indicates the elevation of such a feature.

Best season listings are designed to indicate the optimum season in which to take a given hike. Since conditions can vary on a yearly basis, however, these listings are certainly not decisive. Thus, for high-country hikes, the season indicated is the most snow- and storm-free period of the year; for lower elevation or desert hikes, the ideal season is the coolest time of year. For some hikes, the season indicated is "all year." During the storm season (from about November through March), however, you should stay updated on weather forecasts and avoid stormy periods.

Knowing the **Water availability** is critical for a safe and enjoyable hike in the backcountry. Places where reliable water sources are known to exist are generally listed for the benefit of backpackers taking extended hikes. Day hikers are always advised to bring their own water, since few day hikers carry water filters to purify backcountry water sources. Day hikers should always carry *at least* 1 quart of water per person.

MAPS

Three types of **Maps** are commonly listed in *Hiking Northern California:* national forest maps, United States Geological Survey (USGS) topographic quadrangles, and specific wilderness maps.

Each national forest is covered by its individual map, which is most useful for locating the general area of a given hike and can be invaluable in locating the trailhead. The cost of such maps is modest, and they are available at the U.S. Forest Service (USFS) ranger station closest to the described hike.

USGS topographic quadrangles (referred to as quad(s) for each hike) are preferred by most hikers. These maps have contour lines that help hikers visualize the landscape and identify landmarks and landscape features such as lakes, streams, and peaks.

California is now covered by 7.5-minute quadrangles, which usually have contour intervals of 40 feet, cover an area of about 9 miles by 7 miles, and are on a scale of 1:24,000. (In other words, 1 inch on the map is equivalent to 24,000 inches on the ground.)

Most trails and roads are depicted accurately on the new topographic quadrangles. The maps used in *Hiking Northern California* show the correct location and configuration of trails and roads, and are designed to complement the listed quadrangles.

Topographic maps are available at most backpacking and sporting goods stores and at some national forest and most national park visitor centers, or they can be ordered directly from the USGS. Standard topographic quadrangles are currently $4 each when ordered from the USGS, with a $3.50 handling charge per order. To order, simply list the name of the map(s) needed in alphabetical order, how many of each are needed, the product identification number, the state (all maps needed for this guide are California quadrangles unless otherwise indicated), the scale desired, and the price. Send orders to U.S. Geological Survey Information Services, Box 25286, Denver, Colorado 80225. To order by fax, call (303) 202-4693. It is advisable to request a Map Index Kit for California from the USGS prior to mailing any order. This kit includes a map index for the state, order forms, and a list of map dealers.

Many, but not all, wilderness areas in California are covered by topographic wilderness maps produced by the Forest Service. In addition to showing trails and trailheads, these excellent maps provide much useful information about each wilderness, as well as tips on zero impact practices and wilderness regulations. These maps are available by mail or in person from the appropriate Forest Service District Ranger office.

Also, for some of the desert areas covered in this book, Bureau of Land Management (BLM) maps are listed. These maps are on a scale of 1:2,500,000 and cover an area of about 50 miles by 30 miles. They are invaluable for finding your way on remote desert roads in eastern California and are available at all eastern California BLM offices.

WILDERNESS PERMITS

The wilderness permit system in northern and central California has been greatly simplified since the 1980s, and few wilderness areas have permit requirements today. The **Permits** heading tells you which areas require permits and where to obtain them. In many areas that require wilderness permits, you can reserve them in advance by contacting the appropriate District Ranger office (see Appendix A).

The California Campfire Permit is required for the use of open fires and backpack stoves outside of developed campgrounds anywhere in California. These permits are free-of-charge and are good for one year. They can be obtained at any USFS office in the state.

TRAILHEADS

Trailheads listed in this guide under Finding the trailhead will vary—some are located alongside major state highways, others are found in very remote backcountry locations. Consistent with highway signs, state highways in this book are referred to as "California Highway 299" or "CA 299." Forest roads (abbreviated "FR") are labeled on Forest Service maps, if not on the road or at road junctions, with a multiple number-letter designation (e.g., FR 14N11).

To locate the hikes in this book, use the general location maps in this guide in tandem with a good California road map and USFS, USGS, BLM, or National Park Service (NPS) maps.

TRAIL MARKERS

Backcountry hikers occasionally encounter ducks or blazes, and these trail markers are often referred to in this book. Ducks—small stacks of rocks—are most common in timberline or alpine areas and mark obscure or cross-country routes. Avoid building ducks when traveling cross-country, however. They are usually unnecessary and always detract from the wilderness experience. Other hikers can find their own way, and you do no one a favor by lining a possible cross-country route with ducks. Hikers who need ducks to find their way shouldn't be traveling cross-country in the first place.

Blazes, usually the letter *i* carved into the bark of trees, are found along most wilderness trails. Often, blazes are the only clues to the location of an obscure or abandoned trail, and they become invaluable when the trail is buried in snow. Still, never blaze trees in the backcountry. Keep in mind that most trail signs are semipermanent fixtures at best, and may be unreliable. The detailed hike descriptions in this guide, on the other hand, will get you where you want to go, trail signs or not.

Finally, remember that you don't need to hike each described route in its entirety, or in the described direction, to enjoy a particular hiking area. Simply choose an area that appeals to you, and let your ability and desire dictate how far to go or which trail to take. After all, enjoyment is what hiking is all about!

Author's Hike Recommendations

Easy day hikes suitable for hikers with limited time, novice hikers, and parents with small children	1 Pfeiffer Falls, Valley View Loop; hike to Pfeiffer Falls 7 Big Meadow to the Domeland; hike to Manter Meadow 8 West Meadow to Stony Meadow, Rincon Trail; hike to Schaeffer or Stony Meadows 10 Albanita Meadows 11 Blackrock Gap to Kern Peak; hike to Casa Vieja Meadows area 12 Cottonwood Loop; hike to Horseshoe Meadow or Cottonwood Creek area 14 Jordan Peak 16 Rowell Trailhead to Williams and Comanche Meadows; hike to Rowell Meadow environs) 18 Boole Tree Loop Trail 24 North Fork Big Pine Creek; hike to Second Falls 30 Rock Creek to Upper Morgan Lake; hike to Little Lakes Valley 32 Duck Pass Trailhead to Tully Lake; hike to Mammoth Creek Lakes 37 White Mountain Sampler 43 Saddlebag Lake to McCabe Lakes; hike around Saddlebag Lake	44 Green Creek to Summit Lake; hike to Green Lake 46 Highway 108 to Sardine Falls 48 Blue Canyon; hike the first mile or so of the canyon 50 Gianelli Trailhead to Upper Relief Valley; hike to Burst Rock 53 Carson Pass to Frog, Winnemucca, and Round Top Lakes; hike to Frog or Winnemucca Lakes 59 Lakes Basin; hike to Round or Big Bear Lakes 61 Frazier Falls 62 Silver Lake to Gold Lake 63 Hay Meadow to Long Lake; easy access to Caribou Wilderness lakes) 64 Warner Valley to Boiling Springs Lake and Terminal Geyser; hike to Boiling Springs Lake 67 Butte Lake to Snag Lake Loop; hike to south end of Butte Lake 70 Pine Creek Basin 75 Elk Prairie to Fern Canyon and Gold Bluffs Beach via the James Irvine Trail; hike to Fern Canyon via Davison Road and Gold Bluffs Beach 77 Long Gulch to Trail Gulch Loop; hike to Long Gulch Lake
Moderate day hikes	4 Pinnacles National Monument 5 Big Basin Redwoods State Park 9 Jackass Peak 17 Lookout Peak 19 Big Baldy 20 Redwood Mountain Loop 22 Twin Lakes 25 Lake Sabrina to Hungry Packer Lake; hike to Blue Lake 26 Lake Sabrina to Tyee Lakes; hike to George Lake	27 North Lake to the Lamarck Lakes; hike to Grass or Lower Lamarck Lakes 28 North Lake to Pine Creek; hike to Loch Leven 30 Rock Creek to Upper Morgan Lake 31 Rock Creek to Pioneer Basin; hike to Ruby Lake 34 Lillian Lake Loop; hike to Vandeberg Lake

Moderate day hikes (continued)	35 Isberg Trailhead to Hemlock Crossing; hike to Cora Lakes	56 Alpine Meadows Road to Five Lakes
	36 Piper Mountain	57 Grouse Ridge to Glacier Lake
	42 Saddlebag Lake Road to Gardisky Lake	58 Feather Falls National Recreation Trail
	45 Emma Lake	64 Warner Valley to Boiling Springs Lake and Terminal Geyser
	48 Blue Canyon	
	49 Dardanelles Loop	66 Crags Lake
	51 Ebbetts Pass to Nobel Lake	71 Mount Wittenberg
	52 Sandy Meadow Trailhead to Wheeler Lake	72 Summit Springs Trailhead to Snow Mountain
	53 Carson Pass to Frog, Winnemucca, and Round Top Lakes	74 Lightning Trailhead to Kings Peak
	54 Schneider Camp to Showers Lake	75 Elk Prairie to Fern Canyon and Gold Bluffs Beach via the James Irvine Trail
	55 Luther Pass to Freel Meadows	79 South Kelsey Trail to Bear Lake, Little Bear Valley

Strenuous day hikes	2 Mount Carmel	39 Hetch Hetchy Reservoir to Rancheria Falls
	6 Walker Pass to Morris Peak	40 Tioga Road to Ten Lakes
	15 Alta Peak	41 Tioga Pass to Mount Dana
	24 North Fork Big Pine Creek; hike to First, Second, or Third Lakes	47 Sonora Peak
		59 Lakes Basin
	27 North Lake to Lamarck Lakes; hike to Upper Lamarck Lake	60 Mount Elwell Loop
		65 Lassen Peak
	28 North Lake to Pine Creek; hike to Piute Lake or Piute Pass	73 North Yolla Bolly Mountains Loop
	29 South Lake to Dusy Basin; hike to Saddlerock Lake	77 Long Gulch to Trail Gulch Loop
	31 Rock Creek to Pioneer Basin; hike to Mono Pass	78 Forest Road 39N48 to Bingham Lake
	38 Desert Creek to Mount Patterson	

Easy to moderate short backpacks	10 Albanita Meadows	53 Carson Pass to Frog, Winnemucca, and Round Top Lakes
	20 Redwood Mountain Loop	
	22 Twin Lakes	57 Grouse Ridge to Glacier Lake
	30 Rock Creek to Upper Morgan Lake	63 Hay Meadow to Long Lake
	42 Saddlebag Lake Road to Gardisky Lake	68 Tamarack Trailhead to Everett and Magee Lakes
	45 Emma Lake	72 Summit Springs Trailhead to Snow Mountain
	48 Blue Canyon	74 Lightning Trailhead to Kings Peak
	51 Ebbetts Pass to Nobel Lake	
	52 Sandy Meadow Trailhead to Wheeler Lake	79 South Kelsey Trail to Bear Lake, Little Bear Valley

| Moderate to strenuous short backpacks | 3 Pine Valley
15 Alta Peak
16 Rowell Trailhead to Williams and Comanche Meadows
21 Courtright Reservoir to Dinkey Lakes
24 North Fork Big Pine Creek
25 Lake Sabrina to Hungry Packer Lake
26 Lake Sabrina to Tyee Lakes
27 North Lake to the Lamarck Lakes
29 South Lake to Dusy Basin
34 Lillian Lake Loop
39 Hetch Hetchy Reservoir to Rancheria Falls
40 Tioga Road to Ten Lakes
43 Saddlebag Lake to McCabe Lakes | 44 Green Creek to Summit Lake
50 Gianelli Trailhead to Upper Relief Valley
67 Butte Lake to Snag Lake Loop
69 Patterson Lake via the Summit Trail
73 North Yolla Bolly Mountains Loop
76 Canyon Creek Lakes
77 Long Gulch to Trail Gulch Loop
78 Forest Road 39N48 to Bingham Lake
80 Shackleford Creek to Summit Lake |
| **Extended backpacks of three or more days** | 7 Big Meadow to the Domeland
8 West Meadow to Stony Meadow, Rincon Trail
11 Blackrock Gap to Kern Peak
12 Cottonwood Loop
13 Horseshoe Meadow to Rocky Basin Lakes
23 Onion Valley to Whitney Portal
28 North Lake to Pine Creek | 29 South Lake to Dusy Basin
31 Rock Creek to Pioneer Basin
32 Duck Pass Trailhead to Tully Lake
33 Agnew Meadows to Devils Postpile
35 Isberg Trailhead to Hemlock Crossing |

Backcountry Rules and Wilderness Regulations

All users of backcountry lands in California have a responsibility to become familiar with and abide by the rules and regulations governing the use of those lands. Many backcountry areas have specific restrictions regarding the use of campsites, open fires, stoves, etc., for reasons as diverse as preserving solitude for visitors, protecting delicate environments such as riparian zones and alpine areas, or allowing damaged campsites to recover from overuse. These specific regulations, attached to wilderness permits, are in addition to the regulations listed below. Visitors should become familiar with *all* regulations, including those described below, before venturing into California's wilderness backcountry; there is no better way to ensure a safe, enjoyable trip that minimizes disturbance of the land and other visitors.

In state park, national park, and national monument backcountry:

- Firearms, loaded or unloaded, are prohibited.

- Pets are prohibited on backcountry trails.

- The collection of natural features, such as wildflowers, antlers, and rocks, is prohibited. Fishing is allowed under California state fishing regulations, but hunting, shooting, molesting, or disturbing (with the intent to harm) wildlife is prohibited.

- Backcountry permits are required for all overnight use of backcountry areas.

In national forest wilderness only:

- The discharging of firearms is permitted in national forest wilderness areas only for emergencies and the taking of wildlife as permitted by California game laws. However, some wilderness areas are also game refuges where firearms are prohibited.

- Dogs are permitted in national forest wilderness, but are not encouraged. They can pollute water sources, harass wildlife and other hikers, and endanger their owners by leading an angry bear back to camp. If you must bring your dog into national forest wilderness, please keep it under restraint as much as possible, particularly on trails and near other hikers and campers.

- The use of a trail, campsite, or other area in any wilderness by a group larger than 25 people is prohibited.

- A valid wilderness permit is required to enter or use the Trinity Alps Wilderness.

- A valid wilderness permit is required to camp in the Ansel Adams, Dinkey Lakes, John Muir, Hoover, Kaiser, and Golden Trout Wilderness areas.

- A valid wilderness permit is required to camp in the Emigrant, Carson-Iceburg, and Mokelumne Wilderness areas between April 1 and November 30 each year.

In both national forest and national park backcountry:

- Where terrain permits, locate campsites at least 100 feet from trails, streams, lakeshores, meadows, and other campers. When damaged, fragile lakeshore and streamside vegetation may take generations to recover.

  Campsites located away from water are comparatively insect-free and are often considerably warmer. To avoid continually trampling delicate streamside and lakeshore vegetation, carry a supply of water to your camp for drinking, cooking, and washing.

- Shortcutting switchbacks and walking outside of established trails is prohibited. Such shortcutting creates an erosion problem that contributes to the deterioration of the existing trail. Besides, hikers save little, if any, time by shortcutting trails, and the additional energy required to negotiate rugged country makes this practice unproductive.

- Any destruction, defacement, or removal of natural features is prohibited. Avoid disturbing wildflowers, trees, shrubs, grasses, etc., which are important segments of the ecological community. Don't chop, drive nails or carve initials into, cut boughs from, or otherwise damage live trees or standing snags. Damaged trees are vulnerable to insects and disease.

- Pack out all unburnable refuse. Aluminum foil and plastics do not burn and must be packed out along with cans, bottles, and leftover food scraps—not buried. Many foods carried by backpackers are packaged in airtight foil-lined containers that will not burn—pack them out. Even if buried, leftover food scraps will attract hungry animals. As wild animals become accustomed to eating human food, their natural foraging habits are disrupted, creating problems for future campers at the site.

- Do not litter the trail. Put all trash, including cigarette butts, gum, orange peels, and candy wrappers in your pocket or pack while traveling.

- Stop to smoke. Smoking while traveling is not only hazardous, it is also against the law. Locate a safe spot in a cleared or barren area, free of flammable material, such as a large rock or a sandy area. Never crush out a cigarette on a log or stump. Be sure all matches, ashes, and burning tobacco are fully extinguished before leaving the area.

- Protect water quality. Bury body waste in a shallow hole, 5 to 8 inches deep, in the biologically active layer where bacteria and fungi will help decompose waste fairly rapidly. It is helpful to carry a small, lightweight garden trowel. Locate a spot at least 200 feet from campsites, trails, and existing or potential watercourses, so that rain and snow runoff will not carry pollutants to lakes and streams. Fish entrails should be burned whenever possible and should never be thrown into water sources.

- Keep all washwater at least 100 feet from water sources. Do not use any type of soap or detergent in or near water sources or potential watercourses. Even biodegradable soaps contain ingredients that can pollute water. Usually, sand or gravel can clean pots more effectively than soap.

- A California fishing license is required by anyone over sixteen years of age who plans to fish. California fishing regulations apply in wilderness areas.

- All mechanized and motorized equipment, including bicycles, motorcycles, chain saws, and snowmobiles, are prohibited in wilderness areas. Some roadless areas which are not officially designated as wilderness may also have restrictions regarding the use of motorized equipment. Some state parks allow bicycles on trails, but they are prohibited in other backcountry areas.

- Yield the right-of-way to pack and saddle stock on trails. Stand well off the trail until the animals have passed. Simple-minded pack animals are easily spooked by sudden noises and movements, so talk to the packer in a normal tone of voice to let the animals know you are there.

- Collecting plant and animal life, minerals, or other natural and historical objects is permitted for scientific study only. Special written authorization is required and must be obtained in advance from either a park superintendent or forest supervisor. These permits are not issued for personal collections. Please do not pick the wildflowers; leave them for others to enjoy. Allow them to complete their life cycles so they can perpetuate the beauty of the area.

- The construction of rock walls, large fireplaces, fire rings, benches, tables, shelters, bough beds, rock or wood bridges, trenches, or other similar structures alters the natural character of the land and is not permitted. Make an effort to leave the least possible trace of your passing.

- Wilderness Visitor's Permits are required all year for entry into some national forest and all national park wilderness areas in California. A Wilderness Visitor's Permit is free to anyone who agrees to abide by the regulations listed above and any special restrictions applying to a travel area. They are issued at the ranger station nearest to the point of entry and can be obtained in person or by mail (in some wilderness areas).

There are certain advantages to obtaining a permit in person. Doing so often provides the only contact with Forest Service or National Park Service personnel who are quite knowledgeable on many aspects of the wilderness. They are more than happy to answer any questions, particularly about regulations, trail conditions, snowpack, problem bears, weather forecasts, etc.

Only one permit is required for each group traveling together, and that permit is issued for only one trip. It must be in the possession of a group member while traveling in the backcountry. If that trip crosses into adjacent wilderness areas, the permit will be honored in those areas. Remember, Wilderness Visitor's Permits are required for both day hikes and overnight hikes in some national forest wilderness areas, while in other areas, they may only be required for overnight camping. In national parks, permits are only required for overnight camping.

A permit system allows the issuing agency to obtain information on where, when, and how a particular area is used. This valuable information enables the agency to make important management decisions, such as whether limited use is required to preserve the wilderness qualities of a particular area. Information recorded on wilderness permits may also aid in locating lost or injured hikers.

In most California wilderness areas, the maximum group size is 25 people, but that number is lower in some areas. Any large number of people traveling and camping together inevitably has an adverse impact on the land. If you plan on hiking with a large group, be sure to check with the ranger station closest to your trailhead about group size limits.

At many of the most heavily used wilderness trailheads, particularly in the High Sierra, a quota system has been implemented. This system allows the managing agency to limit the number of backpackers entering the wilderness on a daily basis. Such quota systems have become necessary to protect the area's solitude and to prevent the continued degradation of campsites and trails. Quota systems allow a maximum number of people to use a given area while maintaining the qualities of wilderness that visitors seek. The following wilderness areas described in *Hiking Northern California* have seasonal entry quotas in effect: Ansel Adams, John Muir, Yosemite, and Sequoia–Kings Canyon Wilderness areas. To assure entry into these areas, consider obtaining your wilderness permit in advance.

A wilderness permit also allows the building of campfires where permitted. If you plan to build a campfire or use a backpack stove outside of wilderness areas, you must obtain a California Campfire Permit. For the Los Padres National Forest in central California, however, a Special Campfire Permit is required. This permit must be obtained in person at a Forest Service ranger station and requires that applicants have at least a small shovel available for use at the campfire site.

To obtain a wilderness permit by mail, contact the District Ranger office or NPS office for reservation information (see Appendix A for addresses and telephone numbers).

Zero Impact

If the preceding list of wilderness rules and regulations seems confusing, or overwhelmingly restrictive, it shouldn't. In most cases, these regulations simply embody common sense. They represent the choice between the degradation or preservation of California's vanishing wilderness resources.

The National Wilderness Preservation Act of September 3, 1964, defines wilderness as "an area of undeveloped federal land retaining its primeval character and influence without permanent improvements or human habitation . . . where the earth and its community of life are untrammeled by man . . . where man is a visitor who does not remain . . . and is protected and managed so as to preserve its natural condition . . . " The USFS, BLM, and NPS manage wilderness areas in accordance with this act, striving to maintain their primitive character by protecting native plants and animals and preserving healthy watersheds, while at the same time providing the public an opportunity to use the wilderness and to benefit from the wilderness experience.

With increasingly heavy use in California's roadless areas, such wilderness qualities and experiences are becoming more rare. The regulations applied to California's wilderness areas simply attempt to maintain those qualities that we, as backcountry visitors, seek.

In addition to the rules and regulations listed earlier, other simple practices can help hikers leave no trace of their passing upon the wilderness:

- Respect the right of other visitors to enjoy solitude. Loud voices and clanging pots destroy the peaceful qualities inherent to the wilderness. Allow plenty of room between your party and other campers to assure privacy and solitude.

- The use of backpack stoves is highly recommended. In some areas, wood fires are prohibited. Never build a fire in subalpine or timberline areas where dead wood is scarce and lends aesthetic value to an austere landscape. It is difficult to justify a few hours of meager warmth in a timberline environment as you burn wood from trees that have withstood the ravages of icy winds and deep snows for hundreds or even thousands of years. Moreover, campfires leave an indelible mark upon the landscape and should be built only in emergencies, or when dead and downed wood is in abundance and the fire danger is low. If you must build a fire, choose a site with an existing fire ring—don't build a new one.

- Avoid creating new campsites. Camp on existing sites whenever possible. Unfortunately, too many existing campsites are either badly overused or too close to water sources or trails. If you must camp on a previously unused site, choose a durable spot, such as a sandy or pine needle–covered area. If you clear your sleeping area of rocks, twigs, or pinecones, be sure to scatter them back over your site before you leave. Never uproot or damage vegetation or perform any excavation at your campsite. Leave it as primitive as you found it.

The rest after a long day's hike to a scenic campsite more than compensates for the exertion required to get there. RICK MARVIN PHOTO.

During your travels through California's wilderness areas, you may occasionally meet a backcountry ranger. He or she will be glad to answer questions concerning the wilderness. Unfortunately, however, too much of a ranger's time is spent cleaning up after careless hikers, dismantling fire rings, and offering reminders or issuing citations to those visitors who forget or refuse to abide by the regulations. Minimize this unpleasant burden of backcountry rangers by doing your part to protect our precious wilderness areas.

THREE FALCON PRINCIPLES OF ZERO IMPACT

- Leave with everything you brought.
- Leave no sign of your visit.
- Leave the landscape as you found it.

Leave no trace—and put your ear to the ground and listen carefully. Thousands of people coming behind you are thanking you for your courtesy and good sense.

Details on these guidelines and recommendations of zero impact principles for specific outdoor activities can be found in the guidebook *Leave No Trace*. Visit your local bookstore or call Falcon Publishing at (800)582-2665 for books on zero impact principles, guidelines, and recommendations for specific outdoor activities.

Hazards in the Backcountry

It seems that there are as many reasons for seeking wild places as there are hikers. One thing, above all, that hikers have in common is the desire for a safe and enjoyable outdoor experience.

City life takes its toll on many hikers, and a long weekend in the wilderness may be a yearlong focus of anticipation. In their haste to escape the rat race, to "get away from it all," some hikers forget the potential hazards that exist in those wild areas.

The following list addresses the kinds of hazards typical in the backcountry. No matter what the situation, good judgment—an awareness of potential hazards and how to deal with them—is your best insurance.

- A good first-aid kit, and a working knowledge of the use of its components, is essential.

- Before venturing into the backcountry, gather as much information as possible about the area you will visit. Study maps and read as much as you can about the area. Contact the ranger station nearest to your hike for information about swollen streams, problem bears, snow on the route, carnivorous insects, etc. The ideal time to gather this information is before you leave home; otherwise, ask for information when you obtain your wilderness permit.

- Before departing, leave a detailed travel plan with a responsible person and stick to that plan religiously. If you fail to return at the designated time, that person should contact a county sheriff or district ranger in your travel area so that a search and rescue operation can be activated. If you return later than planned, be sure to notify the above-mentioned agencies so search operations can be discontinued.

- Always be prepared when entering any wild area. Carry a topographic map and check it frequently as your hike progresses. A topographic map in combination with a compass, or a Global Positioning System unit, and a working knowledge of their use, will help you stay oriented.

- When traveling cross-country (which should only be attempted by experienced hikers), observe landmarks and locate them on your map as you go along. Remember that terrain looks quite different from opposite directions.

- Proper equipment selection is also important. Good, sturdy footwear (preferably lug-soled boots), dependable shelter, warm clothing (wool, synthetic pile, and other fabrics that retain insulation when wet are best), and plenty of food are basic items for your pack. Gear should be light-weight, with as little bulk as possible. Excellent books are available which offer help in the selection of proper outdoor gear.

- Choose a hike within the capability of the members of your group, and stay together on the trail, particularly toward nightfall.

- If a storm develops or darkness is descending, make camp as soon as possible. Never hike at night. Keep in mind that darkness comes quickly to the mountains and desert.

- When hiking in hot, dry country, particularly the desert, always carry ample water. At least 1 gallon of water per person per day is required for strenuous activities in hot weather. Don't ration your water—simply drink whenever you are thirsty.

- It is never wise to hike alone. Solo cross-country hiking is especially dangerous.

- Never take unnecessary chances. Don't be afraid to turn back or end your trip if someone in your group becomes ill, if swollen streams or snow block your route, or if inclement weather encroaches. The wilderness will always be there—make sure you are able to return and enjoy it.

- Know the limitations of your body, your equipment, and the members of your group. Don't exceed those limits.

- If you think you are lost, or become injured, stop traveling at once, stay calm, and decide upon a course of action. Study maps and try to locate landmarks that will help orient you. Do not continue until you know where you are. If you left a travel plan with a responsible person, and if you followed that plan, a search party will look for you and should have no trouble finding you.

    In some areas, following a creek downstream will lead you out of the mountains. In larger wilderness areas, this practice may lead you farther into the wilderness and compound the problem.

    A series of three signals, such as whistles, shouts, or light flashes, is universally recognized as a distress signal. Only contemplate starting a signal fire in emergencies, and even then, make sure it can be done safely. Rescuers will be directed to you by smoke, not flames.

- Beware of fast water. Some of the most frequently encountered hazards in the backcountry are swiftly running streams or rivers. Although many large backcountry streams in California are bridged, those that are not require special precautions, especially during periods of spring snowmelt or after heavy rains. The power of a swiftly running mountain stream is as easy to underestimate as it is impressive.

    Take no chances when crossing swift streams. Search upstream and downstream for a crossing via logs or boulders, but remember that they can be very slippery. If you can't find a crossing, your only choice is to ford the stream. During spring runoff, creeks will be at their lowest level in the early-morning hours before the sun begins melting the snowpack once again.

    Before entering the water, plan exactly what you will do. Never ford a stream above a cascade or waterfall. Look for a level stretch of water, perhaps where the stream has divided into numerous channels. Choose a spot where you and your gear will wash onto a sandbar or shallow area in the event you lose your footing.

Try to cross at a 45-degree angle downstream. Some hikers use a pole or staff on their upstream side to aid in crossing swift waters. Remove your pants (bare legs create less friction) and socks, but put your boots back on for better footing on the slippery stream bottom. Unhitch the waist strap on your pack so that you can dump it if you lose your footing.

- Allow plenty of time to let your body adjust. The majority of California hikers travel from low elevations to the high country and must acclimate themselves to the reduced oxygen in the atmosphere. A rapid rise to high altitudes often produces headache, loss of appetite, fatigue, nausea, shortness of breath, and insomnia in people unaccustomed to the thin air. Rest, as well as consumption of liquids and high-energy foods such as candy and dried fruit should help alleviate these symptoms. If they persist, however, descend to a lower elevation. At any elevation, take it easy during your first few days on the trail.

- Take shelter during thunderstorms. California hikers are fortunate to live in a state that enjoys such a mild climate. More often than not, you are treated to fine weather in the backcountry. Even in summer, though, storms can develop quickly. Although they are usually of short duration, the high winds, lightning, and intense precipitation accompanying them create hazards not to be taken lightly.

HYPOTHERMIA

First and foremost, you must stay dry. A wet, tired hiker exposed to the wind is in danger of developing hypothermia, an abnormal lowering of the body's internal temperature.

Hypothermia, sometimes called "exposure," can occur at relatively mild temperatures. Symptoms of hypothermia include shivering, slurred speech, fumbling hands, stumbling, and drowsiness. If you or members of your group develop any of these symptoms, immediate treatment is required. Hypothermia can be fatal if left untreated.

To help you become familiar with hypothermia and its causes, symptoms, and treatments, the Forest Service offers a wealth of free literature on the subject.

In general, wet clothing should be removed from a hypothermic victim immediately. Warm drinks—but not coffee or tea—should be given to internally warm the victim; external warming, preferably by body-to-body contact, should begin as soon as possible.

Cold, unsettled weather is common in spring and fall, while summer storms are largely characterized by afternoon and evening thundershowers. Backcountry travelers should always anticipate storms and carry a reliable tent, effective rain gear, and clothing that will remain insulating when wet. Be sure to obtain extended weather forecasts before heading into wild country, and be alert to changing weather conditions.

Although most summer storms are brief, occasionally a tropical storm hits the state, usually in August or September, and can dominate the weather for days. Still, it is better *not* to panic and hastily attempt to flee the wilderness. Just pitch camp and stay put—chances are excellent that it will be over by morning.

LIGHTNING AND FLASH FLOODS

Lightning is perhaps the most dangerous and frightening aspect of summer storms. Don't be caught on a ridge or mountaintop, under large, solitary trees, in the open, or near open water during a lightning storm. Try to seek shelter in a low-lying area, ideally in a dense stand of small, uniformly sized trees. Stay away from anything that might attract lightning, such as metal tent poles, pack frames, or fishing rods.

In the desert, where summer thunderstorms are more common, avoid hiking, and never camp, in a wash or canyon bottom. It doesn't have to rain where you are for a flash flood to occur; one can emanate from heavy rainfall several miles away.

INSECTS

Don't let insects bug you! They are unavoidable—but not unbeatable—in the backcountry, especially during June and July at higher elevations. The most common nuisance to hikers is the persistent mosquito. Your best line of defense is to anticipate annoying insects on any hike and to carry a good insect repellent. Consider using a natural insect repellent. Products containing citronella are quite effective and can make forays into bug-infested terrain tolerable, even enjoyable.

Ticks are fairly common throughout the wooded, brushy, and grassy areas of California. They are most active from March until early summer. All ticks are potential carriers of Rocky Mountain spotted fever, Colorado tick fever, and tularemia (rabbit fever). The western black-legged tick, only 1/8-inch long, transmits Lyme disease, a bacterial infection named for the Connecticut town where it was first recognized. These diseases are transmitted to humans and other mammals by the bite of an infected tick.

Your best defense against hosting a tick is to avoid areas infested by ticks, which, of course, is not always possible or practical when hiking in wild country. If you must be in an area infested with ticks, wear clothing with a snug fit around the waist, wrists, and ankles. Layers of clothing are most effective in keeping ticks from reaching the body. Since ticks don't always bite right away (they often crawl around on a potential host for several hours before deciding where to feed on a victim's blood), a strong insect repellent can also be an effective deterrent. There are products available that are formulated specifically for ticks.

Examine yourself and your pets frequently while in tick country. Ticks should be removed as soon as possible. It is wise to let a physician extract a tick to avoid the risk of a secondary infection (if the head is left under the skin). If you must remove a tick yourself, protect your hands with gloves, cloth, or a piece of paper. Specially designed tick-extractor tweezers work best, but ordinary tweezers can also be used with a steady pulling motion.

Always avoid crushing the tick. The application of a tincture of iodine may induce the tick to let go and may prevent infection. If the tick's head remains imbedded in the skin, see a physician to have it removed. Always wash your hands and apply antiseptic to the bite.

The majority of Lyme disease infections have occurred in the coastal counties of Marin, Sonoma, Mendocino, and Humboldt, all north of San Francisco. Initial reactions include a red, circular rash at the location of the bite and flu-like symptoms. If caught early enough, a variety of antibiotics usually cure the disease; if it goes undetected and progresses, heart complications, facial paralysis, and arthritis could develop. Symptoms of the diseases transmitted by ticks generally appear between two days and two weeks after the bite and include severe headache, fever, chills, nausea, and pain in the lower back and legs. If you notice these symptoms after being bitten by a tick, see a physician immediately.

In addition to remaining tick-free, do not rest or camp near rodent colonies or burrows. These locations can be infested with fleas that are potential carriers of the bubonic plague.

RATTLESNAKES

Never kill rattlesnakes unnecessarily. Rattlesnakes are an important segment of the ecosystem. Given a chance, a rattler sunning itself on the trail will often attempt to escape. Be wary, though. Rattlers don't always give warning before striking.

The most abundant California rattler, the western diamondback, delivers a painful and dangerous bite, but healthy individuals rarely succumb to its bite. Rattlers are common near water sources below 6,000 feet, and sometimes are found at elevations as high as 8,000 feet. Watch where you put your hands and feet in snake country, especially when stepping over logs or climbing in rocky areas, and wear good boots. The majority of snakebites occur to the lower limbs. Always carry a snakebite kit and familiarize yourself with its use.

POISON OAK

Learn to recognize and avoid poison oak. This plant is quite common in most areas of California (except the desert) below 5,000 feet. The green leaves of poison oak are divided into three leaflets, which are lobed and shiny. The plant has a white or greenish white berry and grows as a shrub or vine. The leaves turn bright red in summer and fall, and drop off the plant in winter.

Contact with any part of the plant can produce an irritating rash. Avoid touching clothes, pets, or equipment that have come into contact with poison oak. If you do make contact with this plant, wash the area with cold water and soap as soon as possible. Also wash all clothes that touched the plant. An itch-relieving ointment is a wise addition to any first-aid kit. Some fortunate people seem immune to poison oak, but most of us will be forced to terminate our hikes when the trail becomes overgrown with this common member of the Sumac family. Squaw bush, which does not cause a rash, is nearly identical to poison oak, and the two are often confused. Nevertheless, beware of any plant you suspect might be poison oak.

BEARS

Take precautions against bears. Black bears inhabit most mountainous regions of California. Although seldom seen in wilder areas, they have become a problem in places where they have grown accustomed to easily attainable food. Yosemite, Sequoia–Kings Canyon National Parks, and their surrounding areas are particularly known as problem-bear habitats.

If you suspect there are bears in your travel area, keep your food supply from becoming the main course for a hungry bear. In all national parks and in some national forest areas, the law requires that you store your food properly. Keep your camp clean of food scraps and keep food odors away from your gear. Never leave dishes dirty, especially overnight. Always carry about 50 feet of cord with you for hanging food in a tree.

The counterbalance method of suspending food from a tree is one method to protect your food supply. Put all food and any other items having an odor that might attract bears (such as toothpaste, soap, or trash) into two evenly weighted stuff sacks and hang them from a sturdy tree limb at least 15 feet above the ground and 10 feet from the tree trunk. Food should hang about 5 feet below the tree limb. Leave packs on the ground with all flaps and zippers open so that a curious bear won't damage them while nosing around.

The most effective way to protect food from curious and hungry bears are bear-resistant food-storage canisters. These virtually indestructible canisters are lightweight and store about one week's supply of food for one person. Although the canisters are expensive, they will pay for themselves by keeping your food safe over the course of a few backcountry trips—the canisters are 100 percent effective at protecting your food supply. In some backcountry areas, you are required to use these canisters if food-storage boxes are unavailable. The canisters can also be rented from most national park visitor centers and from some national forest ranger stations.

Keep your distance from all bears, especially bear cubs. Don't even consider recovering food from a bear—just chalk it up to experience.

Not all black bears are black, but you can be sure there are no grizzly bears left in California. The state's last grizzly sighting occurred in 1924 in Sequoia National Park.

GIARDIA

Assume that all backcountry water is contaminated. There's nothing like drinking from a clear, cold mountain stream after a long, hot day on the trail. After all, mountain water is the purest, safest water source available, right?

Most people who drink untreated backcountry water will not contract any symptoms of intestinal illness. As the culprit cited in increasing reports of intestinal disease among backcountry users, *Giardia lamblia*, a single-celled microscopic parasite, has earned a lot of attention in recent years. Moreover, there are other germs in California surface water which can also cause intestinal diseases.

All hikers should take appropriate steps to ensure that their water is pure. Boiling water for at least five minutes is the surest way to kill Giardia and other waterborne microorganisms. Since water boils at a slightly cooler temperature at higher elevations, maintain the boil for at least ten minutes to be safe. Other purification methods involve adding a tincture of iodine or a saturated solution of iodine; various water-purification tablets are readily available at backpacking and sporting goods stores. Although these products are not as effective against Giardia as boiling water is, they are quite effective against most other waterborne organisms.

Of course, the best protection is to pack water from home, but this option is impractical for extended hikes. If you do use backcountry water, draw it upstream from trail crossings or from springs (the safest of backcountry waters, especially at their source). If you become intestinally ill within three weeks of a backcountry visit, see a physician.

Wherever you obtain water in the backcountry, it *must* be purified before drinking, or even brushing your teeth. It is also recommended that you treat water obtained from melting snow. The surest way to safely purify water is to use a pump-type water filter. Filters such as Katadyn, Pūr, First Need, Sweetwater, and MSR have been proven to eliminate most waterborne organisms. For added insurance, choose a filter that removes viruses as well. Also choose one that can be easily cleaned and maintained in the field. These filters are widely available at most outdoor and sporting goods stores.

FIRES

Exercise extreme caution when using any form of fire. California, with its dense blankets of chaparral and forests that are tinder dry in summer and fall, has the greatest fire danger of any place on earth. You are responsible for keeping your fire under control at all times and will be held accountable for the costs of fighting any fire and for any damage resulting from your carelessness. These costs can be enormous, not to mention the destruction fire causes to vegetation and wildlife habitat, as well as to human life and property.

California typically has long, hot, very dry summers, making fire danger acute at this time. Open fires are prohibited in many areas during this period. Certain national forest areas, primarily the lower-elevation areas with an abundance of brush, are closed to entry during the fire season, usually from about July 1 until the first substantial rains of fall. Other areas may also be closed periodically due to high or extreme fire danger. Fire restrictions and periods of closure vary on a yearly basis, so check with the appropriate agency in advance of your trip.

If you plan to build a campfire or use a backpack stove, you must obtain a California Campfire Permit (see Backcountry Rules and Wilderness Regulations). If you must have a campfire, it is important that you keep it small, build it on bare mineral soil, never leave it unattended, and drown it—don't bury it—before you leave, making sure it is cold and completely extinguished.

DRIVING TO THE TRAILHEADS

Drive carefully in the mountains. Driving to trailheads often involves negotiating rough, dirt-surfaced mountain roads, and people unfamiliar with mountain driving must use caution and common sense. When driving to any trailhead via long, winding, and often narrow dirt or paved roads, stay on your side of the road and watch for cattle, logging trucks, and other vehicles. Mishaps can be avoided by driving with care and attention.

When driving in remote locations, either in the desert or the mountains, always be sure your vehicle is in good condition. Check your brakes, make sure you have plenty of fuel, and carry basic emergency equipment. A shovel, axe, saw, at least 5 gallons of water, and extra food and clothing should help you deal with a variety of unforeseeable problems and may be your only hope in some remote areas. Also, if you have a cellular phone, bring it with you. Most high points in the state offer the possibility of obtaining a signal for your phone. Don't hesitate to check ahead with the appropriate agency regarding road conditions before setting out for the trailhead.

TEN ESSENTIALS

Always carry the "ten essentials." The following is a list of items every hiker should carry into the backcountry to ensure safety and survival:

1. a topographic map of the area and a compass (a compass, however, is useless unless you familiarize yourself with its use in tandem with a topographic map);

2. water and means of purification (at least 1 gallon per person per day in hot weather);

3. good footwear and extra clothing;

4. a signal mirror;

5. dark glasses and sunscreen;

6. a pocket knife;

7. waterproof matches and a fire starter;

8. a first-aid kit;

9. a tent, tarp, or something that can be rigged for emergency shelter;

10. food.

Most importantly, don't forget your common sense—the bottom line in the backcountry is safety.

For an in-depth look at backcountry hazards, their causes, and how to deal with them, many hikers take courses in first aid and outdoor survival. All hikers should read at least one of a number of excellent books available on these subjects.

HIKING WITH CHILDREN

With the birth of a child, some new parents might think their hiking and backpacking days are over, at least until Junior is old enough to walk several miles and carry a pack. Parents who forego hiking trips during a child's formative years are not only missing out on some of the most rewarding and memorable experiences to be enjoyed as a family, but the kids also miss a tremendous learning experience in which they can gain confidence and a growing awareness of the world around them.

Kids can enjoy the backcountry as much as their parents, but they see the world from a different perspective. It's the little things adults barely notice that are so special to children: bugs scampering across the trail, spiderwebs dripping with morning dew, lizards doing push-ups on a trailside boulder, splashing rocks into a lake, watching sticks run the rapids of a mountain stream, exploring animal tracks on sand dunes. These highlights are but a few of the natural wonders kids enjoy while hiking backcountry trails.

To make the trip fun for kids, let the young ones set the pace. Until they get older and are able to keep up with you, forget about that 30-mile trek to your favorite backcountry campsite. Instead, plan a destination that is only a mile or two from the trailhead. Kids tire quickly and become easily side-tracked, so don't be surprised if you don't make it to your destination. Plan alternative campsites en route to your final camp.

Help children to enjoy the hike and to learn about what they see by pointing out special things along the trail. Encourage them to anticipate what is around the next bend—perhaps a waterfall or a pond filled with wriggling tadpoles. Make the hike fun; help kids stay interested and they will keep going.

Careful planning that stresses safety will help make your outing an enjoyable one. Young skin is very sensitive to the sun, so always carry a strong sunscreen and apply it to your kids before and during your hike. A hat helps keep the sun out of sensitive young eyes. A good bug repellent, preferably a natural product, should also be a standard part of your first-aid kit. Consider a product that helps take the itch and sting out of bug bites. Rain gear is also an important consideration. Kids seem to have less tolerance to cold than adults, so ample clothing is important. If your camp will be next to a lake or large stream, consider bringing a life vest for your child.

Parents with young children must, of course, carry plenty of diapers. Be sure to pack them out when you leave. Some children can get wet at night, so extra sleeping clothes are a must. A waterproof pad between the child and the sleeping bag should keep the bag dry, an important consideration if you stay out more than one night.

Allow older children who can walk a mile or two to carry their own packs. Some kids will want to bring favorite toys or books along. They can carry these special things themselves, learning at an early age the advantages of packing light.

Kids may become bored once you arrive in camp, so a little extra effort may be required to keep them occupied. Imaginative games and special foods they don't eat at home can make the camping trip a new and fun experience for both kids and parents. Have the kids help with camp chores, such as gathering firewood and helping maintain the campfire.

Set up a tent at home and consider spending a night or two in it so your child can grow accustomed to your backcountry shelter. Some kids will be frightened by dark nights, so bring along a small flashlight to use as a night-light. Kids seem to prefer rectangular sleeping bags that allow them freedom of movement. A cap for those cool nights will help keep the young ones warm.

Parents of very young children can find an alternative to carrying baby food in jars. There are lightweight and inexpensive dry baby foods available; all you do is add water.

Children learn from their parents by example. Hiking and camping trips are excellent opportunities to teach young ones to tread lightly and minimize their imprint upon the environment. Important considerations to keep in mind when hiking with the kids are careful planning, stressing safety, and making the trip fun and interesting. There may be extra hassles involved with family hiking trips, but the dividends are immeasurable. Parents gain a rejuvenated perspective of nature, seen through their child's eyes, that rewards them each time they venture out on the trail.

See the Author's Hike Recommendations for a list of day hikes and overnight hikes that are suggested for the entire family. Carefully read each description, study the maps, and prepare for any hazards that may be present.

A typical High Sierra trail leads hikers through alpine terrain, with jagged, snowy peaks constantly visible in all directions. JOHN RIHS PHOTO.

South Coast Ranges

The South Coast Ranges rise abruptly from the rugged central California coast south of the San Francisco Bay Area and provide a mountainous backdrop west of the semiarid San Joaquin Valley. Aligned northwest to southeast, the parallel ranges that comprise this mountainous region have been uplifted and severely folded and faulted along the very active San Andreas Rift Zone. Although these mountains are not very high by California standards, they rise high enough, up to 5,862 feet, to capture significant moisture from Pacific storms and to create a marked rain shadow effect on their eastern slopes and in the San Joaquin Valley.

The South Coast Ranges are thickly mantled in chaparral, oak woodlands, and stands of bay, sycamore, white alder, and buckeye. Isolated conifer groves occur in the highest elevations, including Douglas-fir, ponderosa pine, and rare stands of Santa Lucia fir and knobcone pine. California's southernmost coast redwoods occur in isolated groves in some of the region's coastal canyons.

Hundreds of miles of hiking trails traverse this well-vegetated country of the Los Padres National Forest, various state parks, and both national forest and national monument wilderness areas. The crown jewel of the South Coast Ranges' wild areas is the Ventana Wilderness, which boasts about 200 miles of backcountry trails throughout its 200,000 acres.

The South Coast Ranges offer exceptional recreational opportunities, affording hikers the option to extend their outdoor season year-round. When typical high-country hiking destinations are cloaked by winter's snowpack, the South Coast Ranges can be enjoyed in their most inviting seasons, from October through May.

1   Pfeiffer Falls/Valley View Loop

Highlights:	This short hike leads through a forest of towering coast redwoods to a beautiful waterfall and an excellent viewpoint of the Big Sur coast.
General location:	Foothills of the Santa Lucia Range, Pfeiffer-Big Sur State Park, 2 miles southeast of Big Sur.
Type of hike:	Semi-loop, half-day hike.
Distance:	1.7 miles.
Difficulty:	Easy.
Elevation gain and loss:	500 feet.
Trailhead elevation:	310 feet.
High point:	Valley View, 800 feet.
Best season:	All year (avoid stormy weather).

Pfeiffer Falls/Valley View Loop

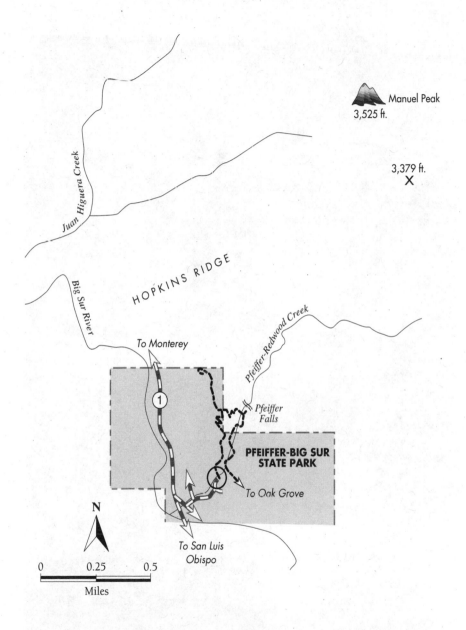

Water availability: Bring your own.
Maps: Los Padres National Forest map; USGS Big Sur 7.5-minute quad (part of trail not shown on quad).
Permits: Not required.

Pfeiffer Falls.

Key points:

0.0   Pfeiffer Falls Trailhead.

0.4   Junction below Pfeiffer Falls; bear right
       and ascend to falls, then return to junction
       and turn right (west).

0.7   Junction with Valley View Trail; bear right
       (west).

1.0   Valley View; return to junction and turn right (south).

1.7   Return to trailhead.

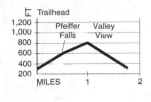

Finding the trailhead: From California Highway 1, 2 miles south of Big Sur and 112 miles north of San Luis Obispo, turn southeast and enter Pfeiffer-Big Sur State Park. A modest day-use fee is collected at the entrance booth. Turn left at the stop sign just beyond the booth and quickly bear right where a sign on the left-hand side of the road indicates "Lodging." Adequate parking is available 0.1 mile beyond, just before reaching an "Authorized Vehicles Only" sign.

The hike: Pfeiffer-Big Sur State Park encompasses a small region of the lower Big Sur River about 5 miles upstream from where it empties into the Pacific Ocean. The park protects some of the southernmost coast redwoods in California. This leisurely stroll is well suited for families with children or anyone else in the Big Sur area wishing a break from highway driving and a chance to stretch their legs.

From the parking area, walk northeastward across the road to locate the sign indicating Pfeiffer Falls, Valley View, and Oak Grove. Proceeding northeast along Pfeiffer-Redwood Creek, you soon pass a northwestbound trail on your left that descends from Valley View. You will return via that trail.

Stay right at the junction where the sign points to Pfeiffer Falls and Oak Grove and continue your course along the small creek and beneath the shade of coast redwood, tanbark-oak, California sycamore, and California bay trees. Redwood sorrel is the dominant ground cover here.

A short climb up a redwood stairway brings you to a junction with the southeastbound Oak Grove Trail, where you bear left. In 0.4 mile, after passing the upper end of the left-branching Valley View Trail, cross the creek and ascend a series of redwood stairs. You will soon reach the base of the 35-foot precipice of Pfeiffer Falls, over which Pfeiffer-Redwood Creek plunges.

From this pleasant locale, descend the redwood stairway and turn right onto the Valley View Trail. This trail quickly climbs out of the redwoods and enters a tanbark-oak forest. As you continue to gain elevation, coast live oaks begin to dominate the scheme of the forest. At the point where your trail begins to descend, turn right (northwest) where the sign points to Valley View. The trail climbs northwest along a small ridge shaded by coast live oaks. This stretch of trail also has poison oak and ends at a loop in an oak grove. The panoramic views from this point easily justify the effort.

Thickly forested Pfeiffer Ridge blocks your view immediately to the west, but to the northwest, the Pacific coast is visible where Point Sur's surf-battered knob juts into the ocean. Directly below to the west lies the narrow valley draining the Big Sur River, a major drainage on the west slope of the Santa Lucia Range.

From this viewpoint, return to the previously mentioned junction and turn right, descending back toward Pfeiffer-Redwood Creek. Near the canyon bottom, you re-enter a coast redwood and tanbark-oak forest. Cross the creek via a wooden bridge and retrace your steps a short distance to your car.

2 Mount Carmel

Highlights:	This interesting trip follows the high ridges in the western reaches of the Santa Lucia Range and leads to a dramatic vista overlooking the rugged interior of the Ventana Wilderness.
General location:	Santa Lucia Range, Ventana Wilderness (Los Padres National Forest), 20 miles southeast of Monterey.
Type of hike:	Round-trip day hike.
Distance:	9.8 miles.
Difficulty:	Strenuous.
Elevation gain and loss:	+2,767 feet, -400 feet.
Trailhead elevation:	2,050 feet.
High point:	Mount Carmel, 4,417 feet.
Best season:	October through May.
Water availability:	Bring your own.
Maps:	Los Padres National Forest map; Ventana Wilderness map (topographic); USGS Big Sur and Mount Carmel 7.5-minute quads.
Permits:	Wilderness permits are not required. A National Forest Recreation Pass is required for each vehicle ($5 per day or $30 per year), and is obtainable at any Los Padres National Forest ranger station. A California Campfire Permit is required to use open fires and backpack stoves.

Key points:

0.0 Bottchers Gap Trailhead; take the Skinner Ridge Trail.

3.0 Junction with Turner Creek Trail; bear right (northeast) and begin ascending.

4.1 Trail junction on Devils Peak; turn left (north).

4.9 Mount Carmel.

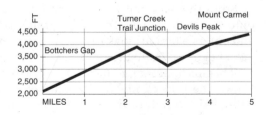

Finding the trailhead: From California Highway 1, 11.5 miles south of Carmel and 14 miles north of Big Sur, turn east onto Palo Colorado Road. Follow this

Mount Carmel

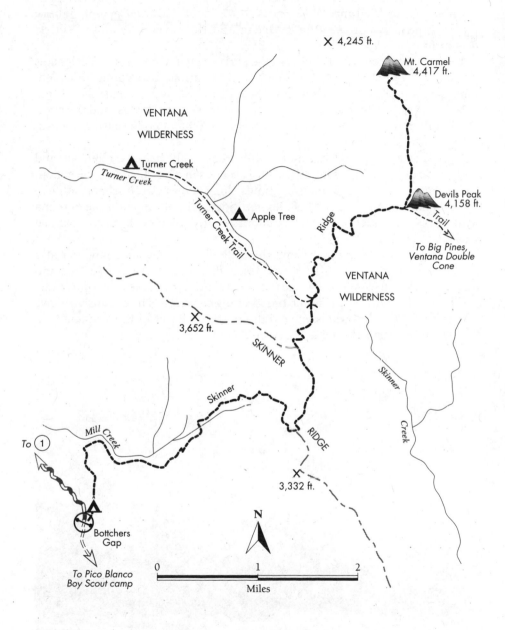

X 4,245 ft.

Mt. Carmel
4,417 ft.

VENTANA

WILDERNESS

Turner Creek

Turner Creek

Turner Creek Trail

Apple Tree

Ridge

Devils Peak
4,158 ft.

Trail

To Big Pines,
Ventana Double
Cone

VENTANA

WILDERNESS

X
3,652 ft.

SKINNER

Skinner

Skinner Creek

Mill Creek

To ① 1

RIDGE

X
3,332 ft.

Bottchers
Gap

N

To Pico Blanco
Boy Scout camp

0   1   2

Miles

paved, but sometimes steep and narrow, road for 7.4 miles to the trailhead and campground at Bottchers Gap.

The hike: This moderately strenuous hike takes you to the northwestern sentinel of the Ventana Wilderness, 4,417-foot Mount Carmel, where magnificent views of the Pacific Ocean and the rugged Ventana Wilderness unfold.

Your trail proceeds northeast from the parking area, where a sign designates the route as the Skinner Ridge Trail and lists various backcountry destinations. You soon begin a 0.4-mile northward traverse over chaparral-covered, west-facing slopes. Enjoy the occasional ocean views to the west and the over-the-shoulder views of Pico Blanco's massive 3,709-foot cone soaring majestically into the sky to the south.

The route soon approaches upper Mill Creek, well shaded by live oak and madrone. For the next 1.8 miles, the trail ascends in a northeasterly direction, sometimes near the creek and sometimes along slopes clad in chaparral, live oak, and madrone, to the crest of Skinner Ridge, where you enter the Ventana Wilderness. This section of trail is intermittently lined with poison oak, so pass with caution.

A shady, northward jaunt along this ridge brings you to a junction at a 3,200-foot saddle. The left-hand trail descends northwest to Apple Tree and Turner Creek trail camps. Continue northeastward from the saddle; your route, the Skinner Ridge Trail, wastes no time gaining elevation. The expansive views of the Pacific Ocean to the west and the rugged interior of the Ventana Wilderness to the east help make the steep ascent pass quickly.

Ventana Double Cone and the rugged interior of the Ventana Wilderness dominate the vistas from the slopes of Mount Carmel near the central California coast.

After climbing 900 feet in 1 mile, you finally reach the open ridge just west of Devils Peak's black oak–covered summit. You soon reach a sign reading Palo Colorado, pointing back to the way you came. Leave the Skinner Ridge Trail and proceed northward on a faint trail that begins just west of the high point of Devils Peak. The Skinner Ridge Trail continues eastward into the Ventana Wilderness. Just north of Devils Peak, leave the shade behind and proceed north along the sometimes brushy ridgeline trail. After 0.8 mile, you reach the small stack of boulders crowning Mount Carmel's summit.

From the peak, a magnificent, all-encompassing vista unfolds. To the northwest sprawls Monterey Bay. To the west, the Santa Lucia Range plummets more than 4,000 feet into the Pacific Ocean in just 5.5 miles. To the east and southeast stands the rugged interior of the Ventana Wilderness, beckoning adventurous hikers with its network of trails, lovely creeks, and backcountry experiences.

Return to the trailhead via the way you came. Backpackers will want to continue east on the Skinner Ridge Trail, where several trail camps and more remote mountain scenery await.

3 Pine Valley

Highlights:	This fine trip, one of the most scenic in the Ventana Wilderness, follows high ridges en route to the lovely pine-encircled meadows of Pine Valley.
General location:	Santa Lucia Range, Ventana Wilderness (Los Padres National Forest), 15 miles southwest of Soledad and 25 miles southeast of Monterey.
Type of hike:	Semi-loop backpack, 2 to 3 days.
Distance:	12.8 miles.
Difficulty:	Moderately strenuous.
Elevation gain and loss:	3,660 feet.
Trailhead elevation:	4,350 feet.
High point:	4,750 feet.
Best season:	October through May.
Water availability:	Available only in Pine Valley at 7.4 miles; carry an ample supply.
Maps:	Los Padres National Forest map; Ventana Wilderness map (topographic); USGS Chews Ridge and Ventana Cones 7.5-minute quads.
Permits:	Wilderness permits are not required. A National Forest Recreation Pass is required for each vehicle ($5 per day or $30 per year), and is obtainable at Los Padres National Forest ranger stations. A California Campfire Permit is required to use open fires and backpack stoves.

Key points:

0.0   Pine Ridge Trailhead.
3.5   Junction at Church Creek Divide; bear left (west) staying on Pine Ridge Trail.
5.7   Junction with northwestbound trail to Pine Valley; turn right.
6.2   Junction with southwestbound trail to Bear Basin; stay right (northwest).
7.5   Junction with Carmel River Trail in Pine Valley; turn right (southeast).
9.3   Return to Church Creek Divide; turn left onto Pine Ridge Trail.
12.8   Return to Pine Ridge Trailhead.

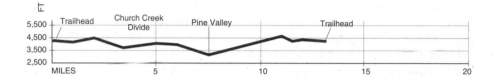

Finding the trailhead: From US Highway 101 in Greenfield, 59 miles north of Paso Robles and 39 miles south of Salinas, turn west onto Monterey County Road G16. Proceed west on this paved road, following signs pointing to Carmel Valley. After driving west from Greenfield for 29.3 miles, turn south onto the signed Tassajara Road. Bear left after 1.3 miles at the junction with westbound Cachagua Road. The pavement ends after another 1.6 miles. Reach the trailhead after another 7.5 miles, just beyond the turnoff to China Campground. Parking is limited to about six to eight vehicles.

The Tassajara Road can also be reached by following CR G16 east from Carmel for about 23 miles.

The hike: The Santa Lucia Range, part of the South Coast Ranges of California, rises abruptly eastward from the Pacific coast to a region of 4,000- and 5,000-foot peaks and ridges. The heart of this extremely rugged, often brush-choked range is protected within the boundaries of the Ventana Wilderness.

More than 200 miles of trails crisscross this interesting area, offering easy access into its remote and scenic interior. The area is especially enjoyable when the high-elevation wilderness areas are rendered inaccessible by deep winter snowpack.

The Marble Cone Fire of August 1977 consumed a great portion of the vegetation in the Ventana Wilderness. Chaparral is the primary vegetation in this wilderness and is adapted to periodic fires, which are actually beneficial to this type of vegetation. Fires help to germinate seeds that can only be released from their hard coverings by very high temperatures. Fire also eliminates dead and diseased vegetation and adds beneficial nutrients to the soil upon which renewed growth can flourish.

Summers can be hot in the Ventana Wilderness, and snow sometimes dusts the higher peaks and ridges in winter. Nevertheless, with careful planning, the area can be enjoyed throughout the year.

The numerous springs in the area are seasonal, so be sure to carry an adequate water supply.

Pine Valley

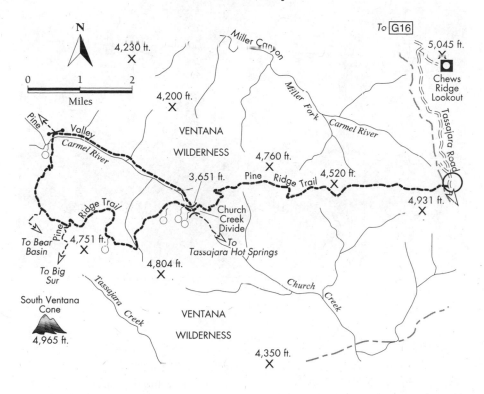

In some years, fire conditions can be severe enough that all fires, including backpack stoves, may be prohibited at any time. Be sure to check with the ranger station in King City prior to embarking on your trip.

Your hike begins on the west side of the Tassajara Road where the signed Pine Ridge Trail heads west. The trail soon enters a "ghost" forest of pine and oak, destroyed by the Marble Cone Fire. As is often the case in chaparral plant communities, that rapidly spreading blaze destroyed existing plants but did not kill their root systems. The increasingly dense growth you see today is a result of "crown-sprouting," an adaptation many plants in this community have developed to re-establish themselves immediately after a fire.

Hikers often find the regrowth in the wilderness to be quite vigorous. You may need to thrash through the sometimes dense chaparral that is only occasionally cleared by Forest Service trail crews. Beware that in spring, you may host a tick or two during your first 3.5 miles along the Pine Ridge Trail. During this undulating stretch of trail to Church Creek Divide, you pass through sections of burned forest alternating with open, grassy hillsides that offer sweeping views into the rugged interior of the Ventana Wilderness.

The tall pines and rich meadows of Pine Valley in the Ventana Wilderness offer a refreshing change of pace from the brush-covered slopes of the Santa Lucia Range.

As you begin the final descent via switchbacks to Church Creek Divide, ponderosa pine, black oak, and madrone begin to mix with the mostly Coulter pine and tanbark-oak forest. Upon reaching the 3,651-foot Church Creek Divide, you are confronted with a four-way junction. The northwestbound Carmel River Trail descends into Pine Valley, forming the return leg of your loop. To the left, the southeastbound trail descends to a trailhead on Tassajara Road near Tassajara Hot Springs. Continue west on the Pine Ridge Trail, indicated by a sign pointing to Big Sur Ranger Station and California Highway 1.

You pass through cool stands of black and live oak, ponderosa and Coulter pine, and madrone. The understory primarily consists of a species of ceanothus. Ceanothus (more commonly known as the California lilac) is a shrub that is often found in the lower elevations of California's mountains, ranging from the foothill areas to the montane forests. Its bright panicles of flowers, usually blue or white, add fragrance to the warming spring air.

The forest along the initial stretch of the Pine Ridge Trail west of Church Creek Divide was largely untouched by the Marble Cone Fire and remains a pleasant, shady walk. After walking 0.4 mile, pass above the camping area labeled Divide Camp on the quad. Situated below the trail in a fern- and grass-covered opening, a seasonal stream provides water for campers using this seldom-occupied site.

As you near the next trail junction, you pass back into a "ghost" forest. This fairly open hillside provides westward views to the rugged summits of 4,727-foot Ventana Cone and 4,853-foot Ventana Double Cone.

At a point 2.2 miles west of Church Creek Divide, you reach a hard-to-spot junction with a northwestbound trail. A sign indicating this junction lies just above the trail in overgrown brush. Turn right here, leaving the Pine Ridge Trail, and begin to descend through a recovering stand of oak under stark ponderosa pine snags. During this descent, glimpse the meadowland expanse of the Pine Valley floor below and to the north. This sometimes faint trail descends for 0.5 mile to another junction. Stay alert during this descent; the trail may be overgrown and can easily be lost.

At this trail junction, the sign points southwest to Bear Basin, but that faint trail becomes difficult to follow within 0.5 mile. Bear right at the junction—the sign points to Pine Valley. This segment of trail is much easier to follow than the previous 0.5 mile and steadily descends for 1.3 miles to the floor of lush Pine Valley. Upon reaching the valley, first pass through Pine Valley Camp and then hop across the Carmel River. Pine Valley Camp is a superb location for an overnight stay. There are two picnic tables and fireplaces here, along with a cold-piped spring. The camp is shaded by tall ponderosa pines, and lush ferns and grasses complete the setting. A 0.75-mile jaunt downstream from the camp leads to impressive Pine Falls, offering a fine diversion for overnight campers.

After crossing the willow- and alder-clad Carmel River, the trail approaches a fenceline and a gate. The Carmel River Trail heads northwest through the gate, soon passing a cabin on private property. But you turn right and follow the trail southeast, paralleling the fenceline.

The north side of this aptly named valley is bounded by some intriguing rock outcrops, providing a backdrop that contrasts with the mellow character of the valley. Pine Valley was fortunately spared the destructive fury of the Marble Cone Fire. Thus, its environs provide a vivid change of pace from the surrounding scorched hillsides.

The trail generally follows the course of the Carmel River as you leave the ferns, grasses, and pine forest. Hop across two small tributary creeks and then step across the infant Carmel River four times. After hiking 1.8 miles from Pine Valley Camp to Church Creek Divide, turn left onto Pine Ridge Trail and retrace your steps for 3.5 miles back to the trailhead.

4 Pinnacles National Monument

Highlights:	This hike tours the Pinnacle Rocks, the eroded remnants of an ancient volcano, in the heart of Pinnacles National Monument.
General location:	Gabilan Range, Pinnacles National Monument, 30 miles southeast of Salinas.
Type of hike:	Loop day hike.
Distance:	4.5 miles.
Difficulty:	Moderate.
Elevation gain and loss:	1,450 feet.
Trailhead elevation:	1,270 feet.
High point:	2,600 feet.
Best season:	October through May.
Water availability:	Bring your own.
Maps:	Pinnacles National Monument map; USGS North Chalone Peak 7.5-minute quad.
Permits:	Not required. An entry fee is required.

Key points:

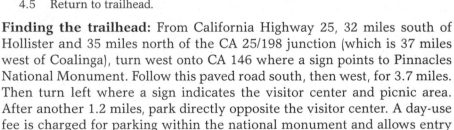

- 0.0   Bear Gulch Trailhead.
- 0.3   Junction with High Peaks Trail above picnic area; bear right onto High Peaks Trail.
- 1.75   Junction with south end of Tunnel Trail; bear right (north).
- 2.6   Junction with north end of Tunnel Trail; bear right (northeast) again.
- 3.1   Junction with eastbound trail to Chalone Creek Campground; bear right (south).
- 4.5   Return to trailhead.

Finding the trailhead: From California Highway 25, 32 miles south of Hollister and 35 miles north of the CA 25/198 junction (which is 37 miles west of Coalinga), turn west onto CA 146 where a sign points to Pinnacles National Monument. Follow this paved road south, then west, for 3.7 miles. Then turn left where a sign indicates the visitor center and picnic area. After another 1.2 miles, park directly opposite the visitor center. A day-use fee is charged for parking within the national monument and allows entry for seven consecutive days.

The hike: The Pinnacle Rocks, remnants of an ancient volcano, are the highlight of this moderately easy hike in the Gabilan Range. The region is semiarid, receiving the bulk of its annual precipitation during the cool winter months. Long, hot, and dry summers are the rule here, as they are throughout most of California. The vegetation, adapted to California's Mediterranean-type climate, consists primarily of chaparral. Digger pines,

Pinnacles National Monument

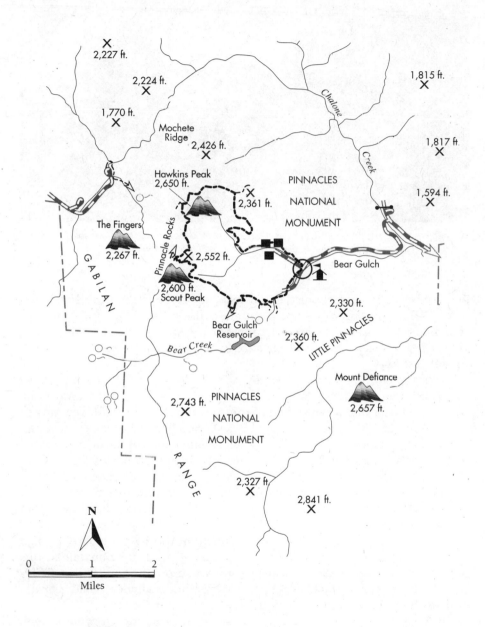

The aptly named Pinnacle Rocks, remnants of an ancient volcano, are continually visible to hikers along the High Peaks Trail in central California's Pinnacles National Monument.

endemic to California, clothe the upper slopes in stands almost thick enough to be called forests. Views are panoramic along the ridgetop segment of this hike, where hikers are surrounded by strange fingers and crags composed of volcanic breccia. Be sure to carry plenty of water and watch for rattlesnakes.

From the parking area opposite the visitor center, some very impressive cliffs and crags are seen along the northwestern skyline; you will soon be scrambling over and around them. From this point, walk southwest up the road for about 150 feet to the signed Bear Gulch Trailhead. Follow the trail through the picnic area to a large sign displaying a map of the area. The trail then begins ascending Bear Gulch through vegetation consisting of California buckeye, toyon, coast live oak, and blue oak. Boulders and cliffs soon make an appearance across the canyon to your north; as they begin to enclose the canyon bottom in shade, poison oak and monkey flower join the understory.

After reaching the first of many trail junctions, bear right where the sign points to High Peaks. (You will stay right at all trail junctions along this hike.) The High Peaks Trail descends slightly to cross the almost-always-dry Bear Gulch, passing a stack of moss-encrusted boulders under a shady canopy of coast live oak before negotiating a few gentle switchbacks.

Digger pines and volcanic boulders seem to proliferate as you ascend, until both are quite numerous atop the Pinnacle Rocks ridge. Following each right-branching trail, the High Peaks Trail continues its steady, yet gentle, ascent toward the Pinnacle Rocks. The dry, sunny slopes this trail traverses are dominated by chemise and include specimens of manzanita and buckbrush (a ceanothus species).

As the trail nears the jagged crags that comprise Scout Peak, it begins a series of switchbacks across chaparral-covered slopes. The sparse stand of digger pines that cling to this rocky slope casts only minimal shade for hikers. The trail, wedged between Scout Peak and a group of impressive, finger-like rocks, surmounts the crest of the Pinnacle Rocks ridge about 1.75 miles from the trailhead. From this ridge, view the spectacular crags of The Fingers, just 0.5 mile west.

Turning north at the ridgetop junction, continue your hike along the High Peaks Trail. Grand vistas await you along this pinnacle-ridden stretch of trail. Turkey vultures are quite common along this ridge and are frequently seen soaring among the crags. To the west across the broad Salinas River valley rises the Santa Lucia Range, capped by mile-high peaks. To the north and south, your view is filled by the rounded, grass- and chaparral-covered slopes of the Gabilan Range. The Pinnacles are part of this range, but provide a stark contrast to the rounded topography typical of the range.

The trail bypasses some of the most rugged crags; where no bypass is possible, it ascends these rugged rocks directly via steep steps that have been cut into solid rock, with handrails provided for your safety. From this point, you can frequently glimpse the lookout-topped North Chalone Peak to the south. At an elevation of 3,304 feet, it is the highest point in this national monument.

As you near the end of this exhilarating section of trail, notice the dramatic pinnacle-crowned dome of the Balconies across Chalone Creek Canyon to the north. Leaving the bulk of the pinnacle formations behind, your trail descends past the last left-branching trail. Your route, presently the Condor Gulch Trail, begins descending southeastward and offers good views of the south walls of Hawkins Peak. Its slopes are clothed in chemise, with the abundant digger pines doing little to shade hikers on this sun-drenched mountainside.

The trail contours above a spur road and some outlying national monument buildings and then descends a short distance to complete your loop at the trailhead.

5 Big Basin Redwoods State Park

Highlights:	This scenic trip leads hikers through oak woodlands, Douglas-fir forests, and one of California's southernmost coast redwood forests on the west slopes of the Santa Cruz Mountains.
General location:	Santa Cruz Mountains, Big Basin Redwoods State Park, 22 miles southwest of San Jose.
Type of hike:	Loop day hike.
Distance:	6.2 miles.
Difficulty:	Moderate.
Elevation gain and loss:	1,320 feet.
Trailhead elevation:	1,000 feet.
High point:	1,350 feet.
Low point:	500 feet.
Best season:	All year (avoid stormy weather).
Water availability:	Bring your own.
Maps:	Big Basin Redwoods State Park map No. 2; USGS Big Basin and Franklin Point 7.5-minute quads (trail not shown on quads).
Permits:	Not required. An entry fee is required.

Key points:

- 0.0 Big Basin Trailhead.
- 0.1 Junction with Skyline-to-the-Sea Trail; turn left (south).
- 0.3 Bear right (west) at junction with southbound trail.
- 0.8 Five-way junction on ridge; proceed straight ahead (northwest), downhill.
- 1.1 Junction with northwestbound shortcut trail to Sunset Trail; stay left (west).
- 2.4 Junction with northbound Timms Creek Trail; turn right (north).
- 3.3 Junction with Sunset Trail; turn right (north).
- 5.2 Junction with southeastbound shortcut trail leading to Skyline-to-the-Sea Trail; continue straight ahead (east).
- 5.4 Junction with Middle Ridge Fire Road; stay straight (east).
- 5.5 Junction with northbound Ridge Fire Trail; stay right (east).
- 5.9 Junction with Skyline-to-the-Sea Trail; turn right (south).
- 6.1 Junction with connector trail leading back to trailhead; turn left (east).
- 6.2 Return to trailhead.

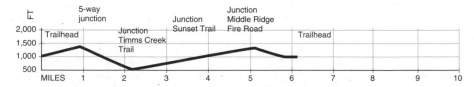

Finding the trailhead: The trailhead lies directly west of the Big Basin Redwoods State Park Headquarters on the west side of California Highway 236. To reach Big Basin, head north from Santa Cruz for 13 miles via CA 9, then turn left and follow CA 236 to Big Basin.

Big Basin Redwoods State Park

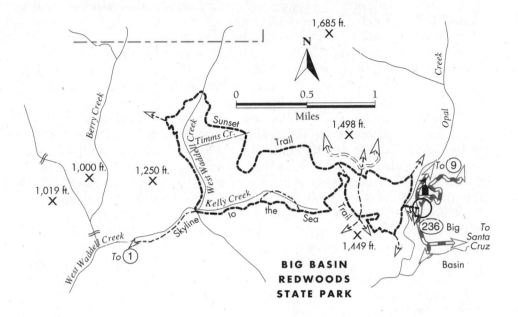

Big Basin can also be reached by following Interstate 280 south from San Francisco for about 20 miles. Then turn south onto CA 35 and proceed south for about 25 miles. Turn west onto CA 9 and after 6 miles turn west again onto CA 236, proceeding 8 miles to Big Basin.

Directly across the highway from the headquarters, proceed through the entrance station, pay the day-use fee, and park in the large parking area on the left.

The hike: This trip takes hikers through California's first redwood state park. The trail leads through magnificent coast redwood forests while traversing the often-steep terrain of the Santa Cruz Mountains. Although fairly rigorous, the hike is suitable for most hikers.

Several backcountry trail camps in the state park offer visitors a rare opportunity to camp amongst impressive coast redwoods. If you plan to camp in the backcountry, check with the visitor center in Big Basin for details. Be sure to carry an adequate supply of water.

Begin this hike at a large sign indicating the Redwood Trail and proceed west. You soon meet a southbound trail leading to the Blooms Creek Campground and a northbound trail leading to the Campfire Center. Proceed straight ahead to the Skyline-to-the-Sea Trail.

The Redwood Trail branches left at the junction near the restroom. Go straight ahead, crossing Opal Creek via a wooden bridge, and intersect the Skyline-to-the-Sea Trail. The northbound segment of this trail forms the return leg of your loop.

Turn left and begin hiking southward under massive coast redwoods and tanbark-oaks. After 0.2 mile, turn right where the sign points to Berry Creek Falls. Begin a 0.5-mile ascent, dwarfed by the gigantic coast redwoods and Douglas-firs. At the top of this climb, you reach a five-way ridgetop junction. The forest at this point consists of Douglas-fir and tanbark-oak. This change in forest type reflects the drier, warmer conditions that prevail on this ridge, conditions that are unsuitable to host a coast redwood forest.

Proceed northwest from this junction, staying on the Skyline-to-the-Sea Trail. Your trail contours west-facing slopes, thickly forested once again with large coast redwoods, as it descends toward Kelly Creek. Within 0.3 mile, you reach another junction, with a right-branching trail that leads up to the Sunset Trail (the return leg of your loop). Stay left and continue descending into the depths of Kelly Creek. Hikers without the time or energy required for this 6-mile hike may elect to utilize this short connector trail to loop back to the trailhead via the Sunset Trail, forming only a 2.1-mile loop.

After another 0.6, mile you reach a junction in Kelly Creek Canyon. You can take either fork; they both rejoin within 0.5 mile. As you descend farther into this shady canyon, sword fern, redwood sorrel, and trillium increase in abundance in the evergreen huckleberry–dominated understory. About 1.6 miles below the five-way ridgetop junction, you meet the northbound Timms

Coast redwoods, among the earth's tallest trees, dominate the forest in Big Basin Redwoods State Park along the central California coast.

Creek Trail, marked by a 4-inch, square wooden post. Although all trail junctions in this state park are well marked, these small posts can easily be missed by a hiker striding along, fully absorbed in the area's quiet beauty.

Upon leaving the Skyline-to-the-Sea Trail, turn right onto the Timms Creek Trail and immediately cross Kelly Creek on a redwood log. Your trail begins a gentle ascent along the shady environs of West Waddell Creek. This trail is noticeably much less used than the Skyline-to-the-Sea Trail.

After a pleasant upstream jaunt, negotiate a few switchbacks and reach the Sunset Trail, 0.9 mile from Kelly Creek. Turn right onto this trail and begin a gentle descent; after 0.25 mile, cross West Waddell Creek via a wooden bridge. Look for small trout in the pool just above the bridge.

The trail then begins a gentle, generally southeastward ascent. Douglas-firs dominate the drier, mostly south-facing slopes and ridgetop sites, while the coast redwoods favor the lower, moister, and more shady environments.

After hiking 1.6 miles from the crossing of West Waddell Creek, pass a right-branching connector trail and 0.2 mile beyond, reach a junction with the Middle Ridge Fire Road. Cross the road and descend eastward; the sign indicates that park headquarters is 0.9 mile ahead.

You soon pass the northbound Ridge Fire Trail after another 0.1 mile. After the next 0.4 mile, you intersect the Skyline-to-the-Sea Trail just above a picnic area along Opal Creek. Turn right (south) and walk 0.2 mile to a sign indicating Jay Trail Camps and park headquarters. Turn left (east) here and retrace your steps to the trailhead.

Southern Sierra Nevada

Although geologists and geographers have extensively subdivided the Sierra Nevada, this book, for simplicity, divides the range into north and south. The part of the range located south of the Yosemite National Park boundary is considered the Southern Sierra Nevada. Much of this part of the Sierra Nevada is popularly known as the "High" Sierra.

Stretching from the broad Kern Plateau in the south to the southern peaks of Yosemite in the north, the Southern Sierra is a land of superlatives. Boasting more than 2.2 million acres of contiguous wilderness, thousands of miles of backcountry trails, more than 1,000 wilderness lakes, some of the highest peaks and the largest contiguous landmass above 10,000 feet in the lower 48 states, rare tree species such as the giant sequoia and foxtail pine, and the mildest weather of any major mountain range in the nation, the Southern Sierra Nevada is a hiker's paradise unrivaled in the United States.

This region is California's most well known and frequently visited recreation destination. Within the Southern Sierra are such renowned landmarks as Mount Whitney, Kings Canyon, the Mammoth Lakes area, and the Minarets. The Southern Sierra conjures up images of popular places like Sequoia–Kings Canyon National Parks, the John Muir Wilderness, Bishop Creek, Rock Creek, Horseshoe Meadow, Huntington Lake, Lake Edison, and Evolution Valley. Yet there are also little-known destinations where, in a region that can often seem overcrowded, hikers enjoy utter solitude and the inspiration and freedom only the Sierra Nevada backcountry can provide. Places such as the Kern Plateau, the upper Kern River basin, the headwaters of the South and North Forks of the San Joaquin River, and the lonely basins lying at the headwaters of the Kings River offer adventurous backpackers a brief, yet memorable, escape from the constraints of civilization. There are ample opportunities for day hikers and weekend backpackers to enjoy popular or lonely places.

The trails of the Southern Sierra generally open by June in elevations below 7,500 to 8,000 feet, while the high country often remains sealed by winter's snowpack until early to mid-July. Snowfields often linger in the high country throughout much of the summer. More and more backcountry enthusiasts are extending their outdoor season in the Southern Sierra by touring the backcountry on skis and snowshoes from November through May. I have taken many of the trips described below on snowshoes during the winter months. Only those explorers skilled in winter travel, cold-weather survival, and navigation over snow-covered terrain, and with a familiarity of avalanche hazards should attempt backcountry travel during the snow season.

6 Walker Pass to Morris Peak

Highlights:	This view-packed hike follows the Pacific Crest Trail (PCT) across the high desert slopes of the Southern Sierra and ends with a scramble to one of the range's southernmost peaks, where broad vistas of desert and mountains unfold.
General location:	Southern Sierra Nevada, Owens Peak Wilderness (BLM, Ridgecrest Resource Area), 60 miles northeast of Bakersfield and 25 miles west-northwest of Ridgecrest.
Type of hike:	Round-trip day hike.
Distance:	8.8 miles.
Difficulty:	Moderately strenuous.
Elevation gain and loss:	1,965 feet.
Trailhead elevation:	5,250 feet.
High point:	Morris Peak, 7,215 feet.
Best season:	April through November.
Water availability:	None available; bring your own.
Maps:	USGS Walker Pass 7.5-minute quad.
Permits:	Not required.

Key points:

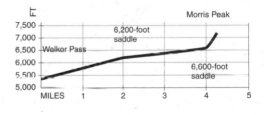

0.0   PCT Trailhead; take trail northeast from Walker Pass.

2.1   Reach 6,200-foot saddle.

3.9   Crest 6,600-foot saddle; leave the trail here and ascend the ridge to the northeast.

4.4   Morris Peak.

Finding the trailhead: The trailhead lies on the north side of California Highway 178 at Walker Pass, across the road from the historical marker. Walker Pass is about 8.7 miles west of Freeman Junction on CA 14 and 74 miles east of Bakersfield via CA 178.

The hike: The crest of the extreme Southern Sierra Nevada contrasts markedly with the heavily forested Greenhorn Mountains and the Great Western Divide to the west. These high ridges capture the bulk of the moisture from Pacific storms. Thus, the Sierra crest south of Olancha Peak is semiarid. Only sparse forests exist on the highest slopes of this segment of the Sierra Nevada crest, consisting primarily of pinyon pine. These drab, sometimes monotonous forests do have their advantages, though. In autumn, for example, many people visit stands of pinyon pine to harvest their delicious nuts.

When deep snowpack bars hikers from High Sierra trails in winter, they can view that same High Sierra from a fairly comfortable vantage point atop

Walker Pass to Morris Peak

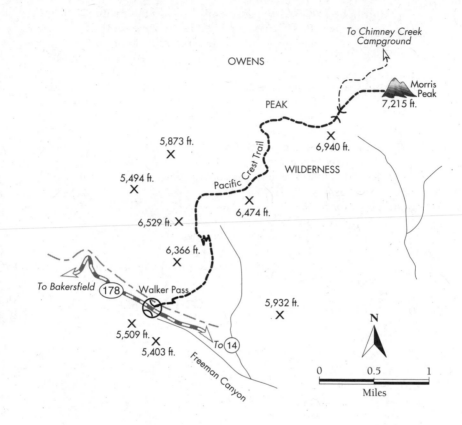

Morris Peak; its ramparts are rarely visited by deep snow.

The trail leads northeast from the pass, rising moderately at first before leveling off on a gentle grade. You soon pass above scattered clumps of Joshua trees and enjoy excellent eastward views from down into Freeman Canyon to Indian Wells Valley and beyond to the El Paso Mountains. The steadily ascending trail jogs northward after you encounter rabbitbrush on the open slopes. You have good views to the south, from across the gap of Walker Pass to the pinyon-forested Scodie Mountains, the southernmost extension of the Sierra Nevada.

The numerous side-hill cattle trails you pass at one point attest to the BLM's policy of leasing public lands to individuals for grazing purposes. You eventually pass a PCT marker and a "No Motorcycles" sign and enter the realm of pinyon pines. Here you begin a series of switchbacks that ascend east-facing slopes, until you resume a northbound traverse and quickly cross to the west side of the Sierra Nevada crest.

After hiking 2.1 miles from Walker Pass, you reach a pinyon-shaded campsite situated on a 6,200-foot saddle just west of Peak 6,474. Beyond the campsite, good views are available northwest to High Sierra peaks, with the fascinating Domeland country in the foreground. These vistas are especially exciting when the Southern Sierra sits under its annual blanket of snow.

After hiking 1.8 miles from the campsite, you reach a Sierra crest saddle at 6,600 feet, just north of the conical Peak 6,940. At this point, leave the PCT and ascend the steep, boulder- and pinyon pine-covered Sierra Nevada crest to the northeast. You soon level off on a false peak; continue east on this level before rising steeply once again. Climb over a few minor hills and find yourself standing atop the 7,215-foot summit of Morris Peak, where a superb vista unfolds.

Peakbaggers may wish to follow the PCT north toward Owens Peak and the Spanish Needles. The PCT stretches for 17.5 miles through the Owens Peak Wilderness to the Chimney Creek Campground. Water and camping are available in the canyon of Spanish Needle Creek, 10 miles northwest of Morris Peak, allowing for an extended stay in this rugged portion of the Sierra crest. Most hikers will retrace their steps back to the trailhead.

7 Big Meadow to the Domeland

Highlights:	This memorable backpack is a grand tour of Domeland's unique landscapes, ranging from its high divides to sprawling meadows, and passes by a multitude of granitic spires and domes.
General location:	Southern Sierra Nevada, Domeland Wilderness (Sequoia National Forest), 55 miles northeast of Bakersfield.
Type of hike:	Loop backpack, 3 to 4 days.
Distance:	21.9 miles.
Difficulty:	Moderate.
Elevation gain and loss:	4,750 feet.
Trailhead elevation:	7,840 feet.
High point:	9,580 feet.
Best season:	Late May through October.
Water availability:	Abundant between 7.4 miles and 11 miles (between Machine Creek and Trout Creek), at 12.2 miles, at 13.1 miles, and from Manter Creek at 18.5 miles.
Maps:	Sequoia National Forest map; Domeland Wilderness map (topographic); USGS Sirretta Peak and Rockhouse Basin 7.5-minute quads.
Permits:	Wilderness permits are not required. A California Campfire Permit is required to use open fires and backpack stoves.

Key points:

0.0	Main Summit Trailhead; walk northward along Salmon Creek.
0.4	Junction with Main Summit Trail; bear right (northeast).
2.6	Crest 9,580-foot saddle east of Sirretta Peak.
7.4	Junction with Machine Creek Trail; stay right (northeast).
9.7	Junction with northbound Dark Canyon Trail; bear right (east).
10.1	Junction with northbound doubletrack; stay right (east).
10.2	Leave the doubletrack and follow the southeastbound trail down to the ford of Trout Creek.
11.0	Ford Trout Creek.
16.0	Junction with Domeland Trail branching northeast; continue straight ahead (southwest).
17.5	Junction at north end of Manter Meadow; bear right (southwest).
18.5	Junction at west end of Manter Meadow; turn right (west).
21.1	Reach Manter Meadow Trailhead at Big Meadow; turn right (north) and follow Forest Road 23S07 back to trailhead.
21.9	Return to trailhead.

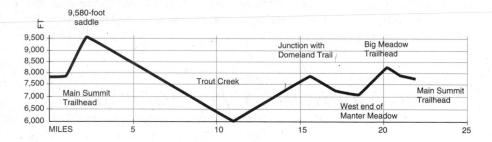

Finding the trailhead: From Kernville, proceed north along the Kern River Road for about 19 miles, then turn right (east) onto the Sherman Pass Road. Do not take the left-forking road that immediately crosses the Kern River and ascends into the Great Western Divide country.

After driving about 5.7 miles from the river, turn right (south) where a sign indicates Big Meadow. Follow this dirt road as it ascends southeastward; avoid turning onto the numerous signed spur roads. After driving 9.8 miles from the Sherman Pass Road, you reach a junction. The right-hand (southeast) fork, FR 22S0l, leads southward along the western margin of Big Meadow, as indicated by the sign. Take the left-hand fork, FR 23S07 (it rises steeply at first), for 0.7 mile to the north end of Big Meadow and turn left (north) where the sign indicates the Main Summit Trail. Follow this spur road for about 100 yards to its end and park here.

The hike: Occupying the southern end of the Kern Plateau are the awe-inspiring domes, spires, and crags of the Domeland Wilderness that rise out of a dark-green conifer forest. This trip encompasses a wide variety of Domeland scenery, including subalpine forests of foxtail pine, picturesque meadows, and some of the most intriguing rock formations in the entire wilderness.

Campsites abound in the thickly forested terrain of the Domeland Wilderness. Water becomes increasingly scarce, though, by late summer.

Big Meadow to the Domeland

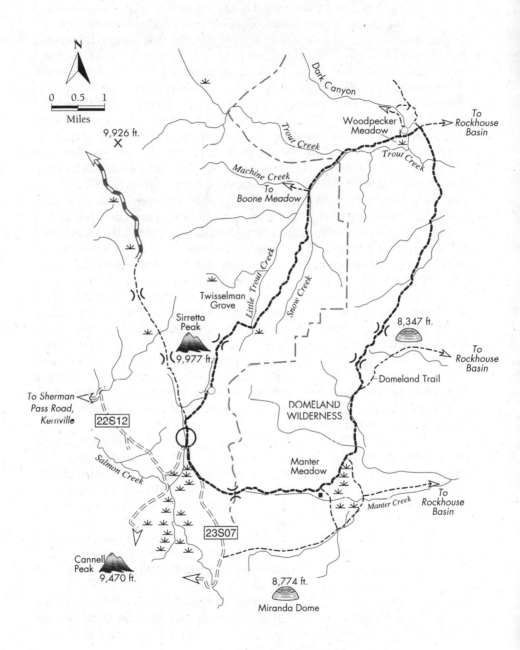

N

0   0.5   1
Miles

9,926 ft.
X

Dark Canyon

Trout Creek

Woodpecker
Meadow

To
Rockhouse
Basin

Trout Creek

Machine Creek
To
Boone Meadow

Little Trout Creek

Snow Creek

Twisselman
Grove

Sirretta
Peak

9,977 ft.

8,347 ft.

To
Rockhouse
Basin

Domeland Trail

To Sherman
Pass Road,
Kernville

22S12

DOMELAND
WILDERNESS

Salmon Creek

Manter
Meadow

To
Rockhouse
Basin

Manter Creek

23S07

Cannell
Peak
9,470 ft.

8,774 ft.

Miranda Dome

Cattle can be seen grazing in Manter Meadow and in the forks of Trout Creek, usually from about July through September.

From the trailhead, walk northward along the course of the small Salmon Creek under the shade of Jeffrey and lodgepole pines and white firs. After 0.4 mile, the Main Summit Trail continues straight ahead, while your trail branches right. The trail ascends along an intermittent tributary of Salmon Creek and soon passes a small, sloping meadow. Splash through the runoff of a cold, reliable spring, the least-suspect source of water on the entire hike.

After leaving the lodgepole pines and red firs behind, ascend the final steep slopes to a pass at 9,580 feet that is shaded by the southernmost stand of foxtail pines in California. Foxtail pines grow in the timberline forests of the Southern Sierra Nevada, northward from here to near the southeastern boundary of Kings Canyon National Park. They are also found in isolated stands in the Klamath Mountains of northwestern California. This tree is readily identifiable by its bundles of five needles, arranged densely around the ends of its branches. With a little imagination, these branches resemble a fox's tail. This pine is nearly identical to the bristlecone pine of the Great Basin and the southern Rockies. The primary difference is that the scales on the cones of bristlecone pines have an obvious, slender, in-curved prickle, or bristle; the foxtail pine has a minute, unnoticeable prickle on the scales of its cones.

From the pass, the trail descends into the upper reaches of Little Trout Creek, which you hop across just below a lodgepole pine–encircled meadow. A brief traverse then leads you to a steep, northeast-trending ridge. This ridge treats you to red fir–framed vistas, including the Great Western Divide in the northwest and the Sierra crest, as far north as 12,123-foot Olancha Peak, in the northeast. Your trail descends steeply along this ridge and then levels off along the often-dry course of Snow Creek. The open Jeffrey pine forest in this area reflects a decrease in precipitation as compared to the high ridge you crossed earlier.

Step across Little Trout Creek once again and meet a westbound trail ascending Machine Creek; cross this creek and proceed downstream. The trail soon crosses Trout Creek (where the fishing is fair). Then, with brushy slopes closing in, it climbs steeply over a low hill, descending briefly to reach an old, closed doubletrack. Stroll eastward along this road for 0.7 mile, where the Dark Canyon Trail branches north.

The green expanse of Woodpecker Meadow lies a short distance south of your doubletrack, seemingly out-of-place in this arid, brushy region. From this point you get your first glimpse of the majestic Domeland country, lying on the southeastern horizon.

Beyond the Dark Canyon Trail, continue eastward and pass a piped spring, crossing Dark Canyon's creek. About 0.4 mile beyond the Dark Canyon Trail, another doubletrack branches north; soon thereafter, turn right (south) at a signed junction, leaving the doubletrack.

The trail heads south through dense brush and enters a stand of Jeffrey pine after 0.75 mile. It then descends to the rockbound course of Trout Creek, which you immediately ford. The trail climbs steeply through the brushy terrain above the creek's south bank and then continues southward along slopes covered with buckthorn, mountain mahogany, oak, and manzanita. The trail approaches spectacular vertical rock formations that will excite even the most seasoned hiker. You soon cross a small creek, re-enter forest cover, and climb 500 feet to another small creek that flows over solid rock in the shadow of impressive, near-vertical rock walls.

The trail crosses the creek and begins a steep ascent under the shade of Jeffrey pines and white firs to a saddle at an elevation of 8,000 feet. From this saddle, a highly recommended side trip to Dome 8300 (about 0.3 mile northeast) begins. A short cross-country jaunt northeast along the ridge leads you to the open, rocky summit area of this dome, where all the Domeland and much of the Southern Sierra is visible. This vista is, perhaps, the finest viewpoint in the entire wilderness. Many peaks of the Kern Plateau meet your gaze, including much of the alpine crest of the Great Western Divide and the Sierra Nevada crest as far north as Mount Whitney. To the south lies the Domeland plateau, where granite rock formations of virtually every type soar above the thickly forested landscape.

From the saddle, hike southward through a park-like forest to another saddle. Descend past the northeast-branching Domeland Trail that leads across the Domeland plateau to Rockhouse Basin and the South Fork Kern River to the east. Continue your southward course and parallel a small creek for 0.5 mile. Striking rock formations rise directly above the creek to your east, and walls and crags dot the slopes of the high ridge to the west.

After leaving the creek behind, cross over a low ridge and then stroll through open, Jeffrey pine–covered ground. You'll soon cross another small creek that's usually dry by September. The trail then crosses a low, boulder-stacked ridge

A typical Domeland Wilderness trail traverses open forests of Jeffrey pine.

and descends to a junction with a southbound trail that skirts the eastern margin of Manter Meadow, one of the most scenic camping areas in the wilderness. Hikers who choose to camp near the meadow will find several sites below its outlet creek.

A small spring that feeds Manter Creek just below the meadow offers relatively safe drinking water. For safety's sake, though, this source should be purified, as should any water obtained in the wilderness. Hikers should be especially careful to purify water from Manter Creek since it drains the summertime home of a large herd of cattle that graze in the wilderness as part of the Forest Service's multiple-use land management policy.

Bear right at that trail junction, proceed southwest, and manage occasional glimpses of the large meadow through openings in the forest. Step across a muddy gully below the grassy opening and then parallel a fenceline, passing another trail junction and an old cabin on your left. The trail now heads westward along a Manter Creek tributary and begins the the final ascent of your hike through a shady pine and fir forest.

Exit the Domeland Wilderness after surmounting another saddle, this one at 8,300 feet, and then descend westward along an old bulldozer track created when the forest in this area was selectively cut. About 0.8 mile from the saddle, you emerge onto a dirt road just east of Big Meadow. Turn right (north) and follow this road for 0.8 mile to your car at the Main Summit Trailhead.

8   West Meadow to Stony Meadow, Rincon Trail

Highlights:	This fine backpack along the western edge of the Kern Plateau leads hikers from cool subalpine forests and meadows to oak woodlands and pine groves along the Kern Canyon Fault above the Kern River.
General location:	Southern Sierra Nevada, Sequoia National Forest, 55 miles northeast of Bakersfield and 20 miles north of Kernville.
Type of hike:	Point-to-point backpack, 2 to 3 days.
Distance:	14.6 miles.
Difficulty:	Moderate.
Elevation gain and loss:	+1,400 feet, -5,450 feet.
Trailhead elevation:	8,720 feet.
High point:	8,790 feet.
Low point:	4,700 feet.
Best season:	Early June through early November.
Water availability:	Abundant between 0.8 mile and 3.2 miles, and between Stony Meadow and Durrwood Creek from 4.8 miles to 8.6 miles.

Maps: Sequoia National Forest map; USGS Durrwood Creek and Fairview 7.5-minute quads.

Permits: A California Campfire Permit is required to use open fires and backpack stoves.

Key points:

0.0   West Meadow Trailhead; head west.
0.8   Junction at Corral Meadow; stay right (west).
2.0   Junction with southbound trail to Sherman Peak; bear right (northwest).
4.8   Junction at Stony Meadow; turn left (west) and descend into Cedar Canyon.
8.5   Turn left at junction and descend to Durrwood Creek.
9.7   Junction with Rincon Trail; turn left (south).
14.6   Rincon Trailhead.

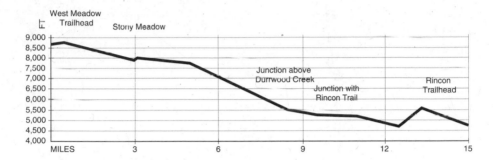

Finding the trailhead: The Sequoia National Forest map is highly recommended to navigate the roads leading to this trailhead. From Kernville, follow the Kern River Road north for about 19 miles, then turn right; the left fork crosses the Kern River and ascends to the Great Western Divide country. The paved road climbs steadily eastward, crossing over Sherman Pass (at an elevation of 9,200 feet) after 14.4 miles, and then proceeds on an undulating northeast course across the Kern Plateau. After driving 5.6 miles from Sherman Pass, you reach a junction at the north end of the small, narrow Paloma Meadows. Turn left (north) onto the dirt Forest Road 22S41, passing Bonita Meadows and traveling across thickly forested terrain. Bear right after 3.4 miles where southbound FR 22S41A branches left. You reach the road's end after another 1.1 miles, where adequate parking space is available along the north edge of West Meadow.

The turnoff from the Sherman Pass Road (FR 22S05) can also be reached from US Highway 395 via the Kennedy Meadows Road. After driving about 37 miles west from US 395, turn south at Blackrock Junction and follow FR 22S05 south for 10.7 miles to the Paloma Meadows junction.

Be sure to leave another vehicle at the signed Rincon Trailhead, 2.8 miles east of the Kern River on the Sherman Pass Road. If you don't, hitchhiking back to West Meadow will be difficult, at best.

The hike: This backpack trip, downhill almost all the way, surveys a variety of Kern Plateau scenery on trails seldom used by hikers. Combining isolated

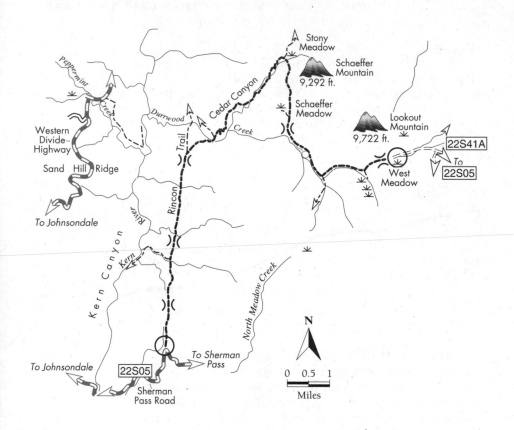

camping experiences in the deep forest with wide panoramas obtained while traversing open hillsides, this easy and memorable hike allows newcomers to the Kern Plateau to gain appreciation for a fine land that sees few visitors.

Wildlife is plentiful, and water is usually close at hand, except along the Rincon Trail, where you pass several small but unreliable creeks. Hikers may want to avoid the area between June and late August, when grazing cattle are present.

Begin this hike by walking west from the trailhead on a good trail through a lodgepole pine forest. You soon cross over a low ridge and descend to the long, narrow Corral Meadow, reaching a junction after 0.8 mile. Turn right and begin descending along the grassy banks of the small creek.

About 1.2 miles from Corral Meadow, a signed trail branches left (south), heading for Sherman Peak. Bear right here and continue descending along Durrwood Creek through dense lodgepole pines and small meadows. After another 1.2 miles, you reach the sagebrush-clad clearing labeled "Schaeffer Meadow" on the quad.

Here the trail leaves Durrwood Creek and passes through a low gap to the north, shaded by a Jeffrey and sugar pine and white fir forest. Cross two more saddles along your northbound course and, 1.6 miles from Durrwood Creek, reach the small, grassy clearing of Stony Meadow. An icy creek slices through the meadow, emanating from the steep west slopes of 9,292-foot Schaeffer Mountain, whose near-vertical cliffs provide an exciting 800-foot backdrop to the meadow.

Proceed through the meadow to a mauled trail sign. Straight ahead, a faint, unmaintained trail leads over the ridge into Rattlesnake Creek. Turn left and begin a protracted descent into Cedar Canyon. Partway down the canyon, incense-cedar increases in frequency among the other forest trees, joining a ground cover of gooseberry, currant, and the fragrant kit-kit-dizze.

The trail leaves the conifer forest at an elevation of 6,400 feet, crosses Cedar Canyon's creek, and continues descending along the north side of the creek. Beyond this ford, enjoy good eastward views into the extremely rugged middle reaches of Durrwood Creek. The route quickly becomes hemmed in by chaparral, including mountain mahogany, ceanothus, fremontia, live oak, and Brewers oak. During this descent, you have superb views down into and across Kern Canyon to Slate Mountain, the Needles, and the Great Western Divide. As you begin a series of switchbacks down into Durrwood Creek, the alpine peaks of the southern Great Western Divide briefly meet your gaze in the northwest.

Turn left after hiking 3.7 miles from Stony Meadow; the main trail descends westward above Durrwood Creek. Your trail, however, drops 0.1 mile to a boulder-hop ford of Durrwood Creek, much larger here than where you left it in Schaeffer Meadow. The creek is shaded by Jeffrey and ponderosa pines and white alders. A few fair campsites can be found near this ford.

Proceed over a low, brushy ridge on a southwesterly course, intersecting the north-south Rincon Trail after 1.1 miles. You will follow the course of the Kern Canyon Fault on the southbound Rincon Trail from here to the end of the hike. Along this route, you cross over five low saddles and four intermittent creeks, sometimes in chaparral and sometimes in a forest of ponderosa pine, incense-cedar, and Brewers oak. The forest puts forth a brilliant golden display with the onset of autumn.

The final saddle involves a steep, sustained ascent of 750 feet. Before beginning this ascent, avoid a westbound trail leading down to the Kern River. Just before topping this saddle, you will be treated to unobstructed views northward up Kern Canyon to the Great Western Divide. Upon reaching the saddle at 5,540 feet, relish the excellent southward view along the Kern Canyon Fault, which cuts a deep V-notch into the ridge across Brush Creek. From here, glide down the moderately steep trail to the Rincon Trailhead.

9   Jackass Peak

Highlights:	This short, partly cross-country hike leads through cool forests to an exhilarating scramble (class 2) up the granodiorite crag of Jackass Peak, where far-ranging vistas of the wild Kern Plateau unfold.
General location:	Southern Sierra Nevada, Sequoia National Forest, 70 miles northeast of Bakersfield and 45 miles northwest of Ridgecrest.
Type of hike:	Round-trip day hike.
Distance:	2.4 miles.
Difficulty:	Moderate.
Elevation gain and loss:	645 feet.
Trailhead elevation:	8,600 feet.
High point:	Jackass Peak, 9,245 feet.
Best season:	Late June through October.
Water availability:	Bring your own.
Maps:	Sequoia National Forest map; USGS Monache Mountain 7.5-minute quad.
Permits:	Not required.

Key points:

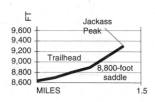

0.0   Trailhead at the end of Forest Road 35E06.
0.3   Junction with Albanita Trail; bear left (southeast).
0.5   Saddle at 8,800 feet; leave the trail and proceed northeast, cross-country.
1.2   Jackass Peak.

Finding the trailhead: Drive to the Blackrock Ranger Station on the Kern Plateau (described in Hike 11), 37 miles west of US Highway 395 and 51 miles north of Kernville. From the ranger station, drive north on the paved FR 21S03 for 3.8 miles, then turn right (northeast) onto FR 21S36 where a semipermanent sign indicates the Monache Jeep Road. Follow this dirt road for 3.6 miles, then bear right where the Monache Jeep Road departs to the left (north). Stay left, turning onto FR 35E06 after another 1.3 miles at its junction with southbound FR 21S36A. Continue another 0.8 mile to the trailhead at the end of the road.

The hike: The Kern Plateau offers hikers exceptional backcountry experiences in both designated and non-designated wilderness areas. The wide swath of plateau country visible from Jackass Peak's easily attainable summit will entice hikers to further investigate this fascinating and seldom-visited region of the Sierra Nevada.

From the trailhead, hike southeast on the old abandoned logging trail for 0.3 mile through a forest of Jeffrey pine and red fir to the junction with the Albanita Trail where you turn left (southeast). This trail is rarely used, except by deer and black bear.

Jackass Peak • Albanita Meadows

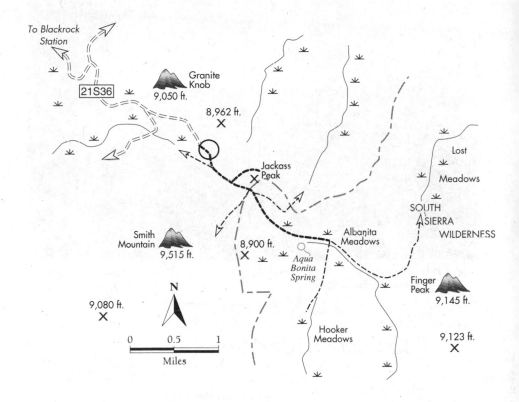

After hiking another 0.2 mile, you reach a saddle on a ridge at 8,800 feet. From this point, get your first glimpse of Jackass Peak's granite crag. Leave the trail here and hike cross-country in a northeasterly direction. Pass through another small saddle just west of the peak and work your way around to the northeast side, where you can scramble more easily up the granitic rock to the summit.

To the north, the Kern Plateau's two outstanding features make themselves apparent from your rocky viewpoint: Monache Meadows, the largest meadow in the Sierra Nevada, and Olancha Peak. At an elevation of 12,123 feet, it is the highest point on the Kern Plateau. Also view the Sierra crest as far north as the Mount Langley-Mount Whitney region, with the Great Western Divide's sawtooth ridge lining the western horizon.

From the peak, carefully retrace your route back to the trailhead.

Jackass Peak affords memorable vistas of the remote Kern Plateau, including Manache Meadows, the largest grassland in the Sierra.

10 Albanita Meadows

See Map on Page 59

Highlights:	This easy hike leads through peaceful forests to a seldom-visited subalpine meadow on the Kern Plateau.
General location:	Southern Sierra Nevada, South Sierra Wilderness (Sequoia National Forest), 70 miles northeast of Bakersfield and 45 miles northwest of Ridgecrest.
Type of hike:	Round-trip day hike or overnighter.
Distance:	4.4 miles.
Difficulty:	Easy.
Elevation gain and loss:	+200 feet, -200 feet.
Trailhead elevation:	8,600 feet.
High point:	8,800 feet.
Best season:	Mid-June through October.
Water availability:	Available at Aqua Bonita Spring at 2 miles. If day hiking, bring your own.
Maps:	Sequoia National Forest map; South Sierra and Golden Trout Wilderness areas map (topographic); USGS Monache Mountain 7.5-minute quad.
Permits:	A California Campfire Permit is required for use of open fires and backpack stoves.

Key points:

- 0.0 Trailhead at the end of Forest Road 35E06.
- 0.3 Junction with Albanita Trail; bear left (southeast).
- 0.5 Saddle at 8,800 feet.
- 0.8 Junction on saddle at wilderness boundary; continue straight ahead (southeast).
- 0.9 Junction with left-branching trail; stay right (southeast) and begin descending.
- 2.0 Aqua Bonita Spring.
- 2.2 Junction with southbound Hooker Trail.

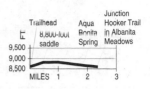

Finding the trailhead: Follow driving directions for Hike 9.

The hike: Several peaceful subalpine meadows dot the conifer-clad landscape of the South Sierra Wilderness. These grasslands are seldom visited and the trails to them are often faint or nonexistent, but the going is easy and the camping is pleasant. Elevation gain in this area is negligible, making a hike in this part of the South Sierra Wilderness an ideal choice for novice hikers or parents with children. Since this is bear country, backpackers must make an effort to keep a clean camp and to store food properly.

Follow Hike 9 for 0.5 mile to the 8,800-foot saddle, then continue walking east on the trail, entering the South Sierra Wilderness as you crest a low ridge and meet the southbound Jackass National Recreation Trail on your right. Continue southeast through thick conifers, avoid a left-branching trail, and drop down into a bowl containing the spreading Albanita Meadows. The trail here is often faint; simply follow the main trunk of the meadow eastward toward the craggy Finger Rock massif on the eastern skyline.

You will soon pass the fenced-in Aqua Bonita Spring along the southern margin of this lodgepole pine–encircled spread. This spring is your best source of water in the area, but wise hikers will still purify it.

About 0.2 mile east of the spring, a faint tread—the Hooker Trail—branches south, leads over a low ridge, and then drops into the infrequently visited upper reaches of Hooker Meadow after 0.75 mile. Boasting one of the most extensive aspen stands on the Kern Plateau, this remote locale is especially impressive after the first frosts of autumn have turned the aspens' shimmering leaves into a brilliant show of yellows and oranges.

The upper reaches of the small stream draining Hooker Meadow tend to dry up as summer wears on, so a downstream jaunt will probably be necessary to obtain water.

Back at the trail junction in Albanita Meadows, you may either return to the trailhead or continue eastward, following the north side of the small stream that drains the meadow and forms the headwaters of Lost Creek.

Where the meadow-bordered creek bends south, a trail branches left and briefly heads east into the forest. This rarely used path soon turns north and crests a low ridge, entering an open forest of pine and fir. After a brief and gentle descent, you reach the upper (south) end of the long and narrow Lost Meadows after 1.5 miles. Capture an inspiring view of Olancha Peak to the north, with a green expanse of meadow in the foreground, framed by trailside lodgepole pines.

Potential camping areas around Lost Meadows are plentiful, but the creek draining the meadow may dry up as the summer progresses. It would be wise to pack water the short distance from Aqua Bonita Spring after late July.

11   Blackrock Gap to Kern Peak

Highlights:	This fine backpack features rich meadows and cool forests and the chance to scale one of the Kern Plateau's highest peaks, where superb, far-ranging vistas of the Southern Sierra unfold.
General location:	Southern Sierra Nevada, Golden Trout Wilderness (Inyo National Forest), 75 miles northeast of Bakersfield.
Type of hike:	Round-trip backpack, 3 to 5 days.
Distance:	26.6 miles.
Difficulty:	Moderate.
Elevation gain and loss:	+3,920 feet, -1,350 feet.
Trailhead elevation:	8,940 feet.
High point:	Kern Peak, 11,510 feet.
Best season:	Late June through mid-October.
Water availability:	Abundant at Casa Vieja Meadows at 2.3 miles, Long Canyon Creek at 4.7 miles, Long Stringer at 6.4 miles, River Spring at 7.2 miles, and from Redrock Creek between 8.3 miles and 9 miles.
Maps:	Sequoia National Forest map; Golden Trout and South Sierra Wilderness areas map (topographic); USGS Casa Vieja Meadows and Kern Peak 7.5-minute quads.
Permits:	A wilderness permit is required; obtain at the Cannell Meadow Ranger District office in Kernville or at Blackrock Ranger Station.

Key points:

0.0	Blackrock Trailhead.
1.7	Junction with eastbound trail at Casa Vieja Meadows; stay left (northwest).
2.2	Junction with southwestbound trail along west margin of Casa Vieja Meadows; bear right (north).
2.3	Junction with descending trail leading to Jordan Hot Springs; bear right (northeast).
4.7	Long Canyon Creek.
5.6	Beer Keg Meadow.
7.2	River Spring.
8.3	Junction at Redrock Meadows; turn right (east-northeast).
11.2	Crest Toowa Range at 10,250 feet; leave the trail here and follow crest northwest, cross-country.
13.3	Kern Peak.

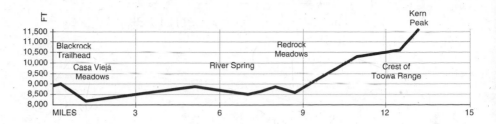

Finding the trailhead: From Kernville, drive about 19 miles up the Kern River Road and turn right (east) onto the Sherman Pass Road (Forest Road 22S05). This road quickly climbs eastward out of Kern River Canyon and begins a steady ascent through the Brush Creek drainage. After 3.1 miles, pass a gate that is usually closed between late November and late May. The road surmounts Sherman Pass 14.4 miles from the river. Continue east, then north, and avoid the numerous signed spur roads.

After driving 17.2 miles beyond Sherman Pass, you reach a four-way junction. The east-branching road, FR 22S05, leads to Kennedy Meadows and to US Highway 395. Continue straight ahead (north) and the paved road now bears the number FR 21S03. Pass the seasonal Blackrock Ranger Station and continue north for 8.1 miles. Avoid several signed spur roads on your way to the Blackrock Trailhead at the road's end, 59.2 miles from Kernville.

Or, from US 395, about 9 miles north of its junction with California Highway 14 and 56 miles south of Lone Pine, turn west where a large sign indicates that Kennedy Meadows is 25 miles ahead. Follow this steadily climbing paved road up to the crest of the Sierra Nevada and across the rolling Kern Plateau. After 25 miles, you reach a junction. Turn left; the northbound road ends in 3 miles at the Kennedy Meadows Campground. Immediately pass the Kennedy Meadows General Store and cross the South Fork Kern River via a bridge. This road leads west for another 12 miles to Blackrock Junction, where you turn right (north), and drive 8.1 miles to the trailhead.

The hike: This pleasant backpack through a red fir and lodgepole pine forest, occasionally interrupted by verdant, wildflower-filled meadows, leads hikers to the best viewpoint on the Kern Plateau, the remote alpine summit of Kern Peak. In addition to being one of the most isolated and seldom-visited mountains on the Kern Plateau, Kern Peak offers superb, awe-inspiring vistas that encompass hundreds of square miles of lonely, relatively unknown wilderness—undoubtedly, one of the finest wilderness viewpoints in California. Hikers certainly won't be beating a path to its summit, though. Few hikers even know about the area, and getting to the trailhead involves driving many miles of confusing (but paved) forest roads.

Solitude-seekers should be more than satisfied after leaving the last vestiges of hikers behind at Redrock Meadows and ascending the slopes of the Toowa Range, with no company other than mule deer, black bear, and Clark's nutcrackers. Hikers uncomfortable without the guidance of a trail should

Blackrock Gap to Kern Peak

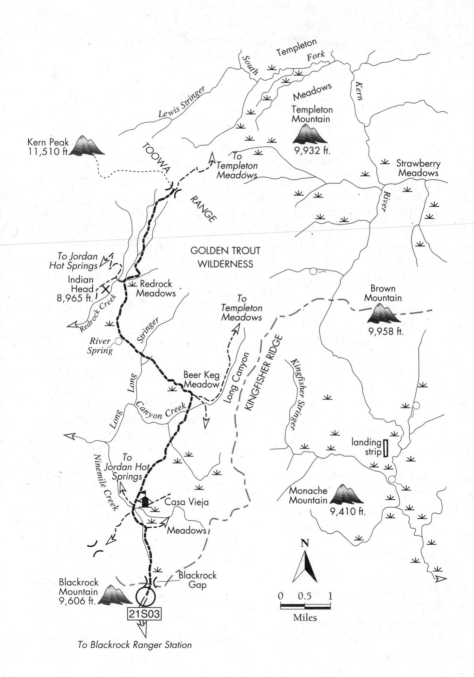

Kern Peak
11,510 ft.

Templeton Fork

South

Lewis Stringer

Meadows
Templeton
Mountain
9,932 ft.

Kern

Strawberry
Meadows

TOOWA

To
Templeton
Meadows

RANGE

River

GOLDEN TROUT
WILDERNESS

To Jordan
Hot Springs

Indian
Head
8,965 ft.

Redrock
Meadows

Brown
Mountain

9,958 ft.

Redrock Creek

Stringer

River
Spring

To
Templeton
Meadows

Long Canyon

KINGFISHER RIDGE

Long

Beer Keg
Meadow

Kingfisher Stringer

Long

Canyon Creek

landing
strip

To
Jordan Hot
Springs

Ninemile Creek

Monache
Mountain

9,410 ft.

Casa Vieja

Meadows

N

Blackrock
Mountain
9,606 ft.

Blackrock
Gap

0   0.5   1

Miles

21S03

To Blackrock Ranger Station

64

avoid the final 2 miles to the peak, which require some moderate routefinding.

Campsites abound on the thickly forested terrain of the central Kern Plateau, and water is plentiful. Cattle will be found grazing in some of the meadows along this hike, usually from early July through September, and water purification is always a must. Fishing for pan-sized golden trout is fair in Ninemile Creek and in Long Canyon Creek.

Since the first road on the Kern Plateau opened the area to logging in the late 1950s, a good portion of the plateau has been penetrated with roads. One advantage to this construction is the easy access that's resulted to the best of the Kern Plateau, those portions protected as the Golden Trout and South Sierra Wilderness areas. This vast area is good hiking country, where walking is easy and the scenery is pleasant and sometimes spectacular. Signs of overuse are minimal—the area isn't as popular with hikers as are regions of the High Sierra, but it certainly is no less attractive.

From the road's end, walk north past a corral for 0.2 mile to Blackrock Gap, where you enter the Golden Trout Wilderness. The route then descends along a tributary of Ninemile Creek for 1.7 miles under the shade of towering red firs to a junction with an eastbound trail. Continuing northwest; your trail skirts the western margin of the sloping Casa Vieja Meadows and soon passes a southwest-branching trail immediately before bypassing a snow survey cabin on your left.

Casa Vieja Meadows is one of the many rich grasslands in the Golden Trout Wilderness.

A short distance beyond the cabin, you emerge from a lodgepole pine forest to ford Ninemile Creek at the lower end of Casa Vieja Meadows. Immediately beyond the ford, you meet a westbound trail that leads to Jordan Hot Springs, a small enclave of civilization that is the destination of the majority of hikers in this region.

Resume your northerly course and pass a closed, eastbound doubletrack that leads past the seasonal ranger station (visible 0.1 mile east). Leaving the grasslands of the meadows behind, the trail passes over a low gap and descends to a ford of Lost Trout Creek. It then traverses lodgepole pine–shaded slopes to the grassy banks of Long Canyon Creek, about 2.4 miles from Casa Vieja Meadows.

After fording this noisy stream, a short uphill stretch brings you to another junction. The eastbound trail continues ascending Long Canyon, but you turn left (west), climb over a low hill, and enter Beer Keg Meadow where the trail becomes faint. Continue your northwestward course and cross two branches of Long Stringer, where open, grassy environs offer good views southwestward to the heavily forested hill of 9,121-foot Manzanita Knob. About 0.5 mile beyond the last ford of Long Stringer, you pass the unusual River Spring. Here a large stream emerges from between two small boulders just below the trail. This spot is the purest source of water encountered on this hike and shouldn't be contaminated by any cattle that might be in the area. This is the finest spring I have seen in over 8,000 miles and 30 years of hiking.

Beyond the spring, pass through a small meadow and then traverse the slopes shaded by lodgepole pine and red fir. Before beginning a short descent into Redrock Meadows, glimpse the copper-colored crag of Indian Head, its 500-foot face rising precipitously above Redrock Creek. Upon entering the first of Redrock Meadow's grassy clearings, bear right where a westbound trail departs to your left. The sometimes faint trail ascends the easternmost fork of Redrock Creek, curves in a northwesterly direction through dense lodgepole pine forest, crosses another small creek, and begins the steep ascent to the crest of the Toowa Range in red fir shade.

Leave the trail at the crest of the Toowa Range, at 10,250 feet, a major east-west ridge dividing the waters of the Kern River from its south fork. Your route, now cross-country, leads westward along the crest of this ridge through a thick forest of lodgepole and foxtail pine. After walking 1 mile along the gentle crest, the steep east slopes of Kern Peak confront you, rising abruptly out of a small cirque. Stay just north of the crest and jog southwestward; a short, but steep, scramble up to the low point on the cirque's headwall brings you to the summit's ridge. Ascend this ridge through a sparse forest of foxtail pine. The expanding vistas lure you onward to the barren summit of Kern Peak, where a breathtaking view of the Kern River drainage is revealed. Little remains of the long-abandoned fire lookout tower that once capped this peak. Topographic quads may be helpful in identifying distant landmarks.

From the peak, carefully retrace your cross-country route back to the trail and then backtrack to the trailhead.

12 Cottonwood Loop

Highlights:	This memorable, view-packed trip crosses two high Sierra crest passes and features long timberline traverses, and side trip options, leading to dozens of alpine lakes.
General location:	Southern Sierra Nevada, Golden Trout Wilderness, Sequoia-Kings Canyon Wilderness, and John Muir Wilderness, 12 miles southwest of Lone Pine.
Type of hike:	Loop backpack, 3 to 5 days.
Distance:	21.2 miles.
Difficulty:	Moderate.
Elevation gain and loss:	3,400 feet.
Trailhead elevation:	9,950 feet.
High point:	New Army Pass, 12,400 feet.
Best season:	July through mid-October.
Water availability:	Available at Horseshoe Meadow, from springs at Poison Meadow at 3.1 miles, Chicken Spring Lake at 7.1 miles, between 12.1 and 13.6 miles, abundant between High Lake at 15.8 miles and South Fork Cottonwood Creek at 20.2 miles.
Maps:	Inyo National Forest map; Sequoia-Kings Canyon and John Muir Wilderness areas map (two sheets, topographic); USGS Cirque Peak, Johnson Peak, Mt.Whitney, and Mt. Langley 7.5-minute quads.
Permits:	A wilderness permit is required. Trailhead quotas are in effect. Obtain permit from the Mt. Whitney Ranger Station in Lone Pine. Reservations for permits can be made up to six months in advance (see Appendix A for information).

Key points:
0.0	Cottonwood Lakes Trailhead; walk back down road and turn right (west).
0.8	Reach Cottonwood Pass Trailhead at the road's end.
1.0	Junction with Trail Pass Trail; turn left (south).
2.3	Junction with Pacific Crest Trail (PCT) at Trail Pass; turn right (west) onto PCT.
3.6	Poison Meadow.
6.5	Cottonwood Pass, junction with Cottonwood Pass Trail; continue ahead (west) on PCT.
7.1	Chicken Spring Lake.
10.1	Enter Sequoia National Park.
10.9	Junction with Siberian Pass Trail; turn right (north), leave the PCT and descend toward Rock Creek.
12.1	Junction with New Army Pass Trail; turn right (east).
14.4	New Army Pass.
17.4	Junction with northbound trail to upper Cottonwood Lakes; continue straight ahead (east).

17.8	Junction with trail to South Fork and Cirque Lakes; stay left (northeast).
18.7	Junction with westbound trail to Muir Lake; stay right (east).
19.6	Junction with old Cottonwood Creek Trail; bear right (southwest) and ascend away from Cottonwood Creek.
20.2	Junction with old trail leading southwest to Horseshoe Meadow; stay left (southeast).
21.2	Return to Cottonwood Lakes Trailhead.

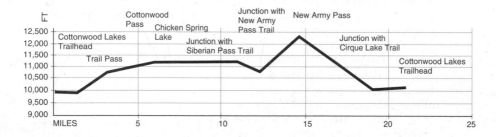

Finding the trailhead: From US Highway 395 in Lone Pine, turn west onto the signed Whitney Portal Road. Follow this road westward along Lone Pine Creek and through the boulder-covered Alabama Hills for 3.5 miles to the signed Horseshoe Meadow Road and turn left (south). Ahead you can see the switchbacks of your road ascending the great eastern escarpment of the Sierra Nevada. Follow this good, paved road for about 19 miles to a junction. Bear right here and ascend 0.5 mile to the Cottonwood Lakes Trailhead, the terminus of this hike.

The hike: Stated simply, the Sierra Nevada is a huge westward-tilting block of the earth's crust uplifted along major faults at its eastern base. The eastern escarpment is abrupt, rising as much as 10,000 feet in 10 miles from the floor of Owens Valley and sloping gently westward into the Central Valley from a crest of high peaks. This range is California's largest and most spectacular, spanning more than 400 miles in length and as much as 80 miles in width in some places. It includes perhaps the most dramatic mountainous terrain in the nation. Combine this majestic scenery with a mild climate and easy access into its remote backcountry, and the result is perhaps the most exceptional hiking country on earth.

At the southern end of the High Sierra, the range's glorious alpine peaks dissolve into the rounded, gentle terrain of the forested Kern Plateau. Generally less spectacular (but no less worthy of exploration), the Kern Plateau sees few hikers. The numerous large grasslands and the few alpine peaks that dot this landscape offer a refreshing change of pace from the mostly forest terrain. The Kern Plateau is home to grazing cattle during the summer months, but these semipermanent bovine residents are rarely more than a slight inconvenience to hikers.

This fine hike is an introduction to this transitional region of the Sierra, including the crossing of a 12,400-foot pass, a 14,000-foot peak within easy

Cottonwood Loop

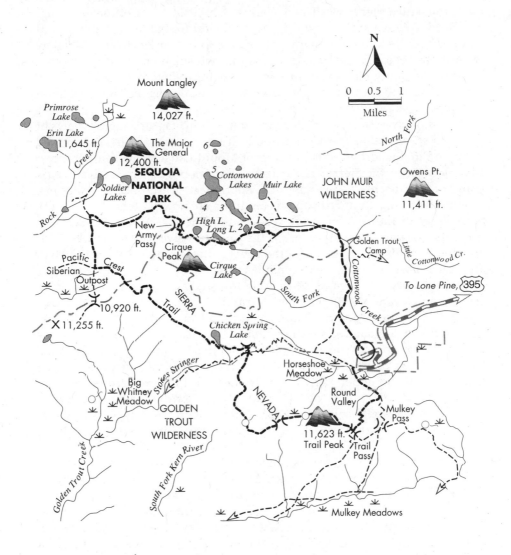

walking distance (easy for experienced hikers), access to remote alpine lakes, and a timberline traverse on the PCT. It offers hikers a chance to escape civilization while basking in endless horizons of wilderness, refreshing to both mind and body.

From the Cottonwood Lakes Trailhead, stroll down the pavement for 0.5 mile, then turn right (west) and walk 0.3 mile to the Cottonwood Pass Trailhead. Follow the Cottonwood Pass Trail west for 0.2 mile, then turn left and head south across the sandy and grassy spread of Horseshoe Meadow toward Trail Pass. En route, hop across the two small creeks draining that spread. The sandy margins of this and other Kern Plateau grasslands are a result of excessive overgrazing by sheep and cattle during the late nineteenth century. These meadows have not since recovered.

As you proceed southward along the sandy trail, capture superb views of the peaks encircling the Cottonwood Creek drainage. The flat-topped mountain in the northwest is 14,027-foot Mount Langley, the southernmost 14,000-footer in the Sierra. The barren upper slopes of conical Trail Peak, rising out of the heavy timber to the southwest, were once the site of a proposed ski area. Trail Peak and its environs are now protected within the boundaries of the Golden Trout Wilderness. The low, forested ridge that wanders eastward from Trail Peak is the unimpressive Sierra Nevada crest, which begins its steady climb to the spectacular alpine peaks of the High Sierra just north of Trail Peak's alpine crown.

Soon you begin to ascend the densely forested north slopes of the Sierra crest to an elevation of 10,500 feet at Trail Pass, where there is a four-way junction, 1.5 miles from the Cottonwood Pass Trailhead.

Straight ahead (south), a trail descends into Mulkey Meadows. Mulkey Creek was the original source of golden trout planted in Cottonwood Creek. Golden trout, California's state fish, originally existed in only a few tributaries of the upper Kern River drainage until they were introduced into Cottonwood Creek in the 1870s. Today, Cottonwood Lakes 1, 2, 3, and 4 are the state's only source of pure-strain golden trout eggs. All four of the Cottonwood Lakes are closed to fishing to protect the golden trout population.

At Trail Pass, turn right (west) onto the PCT, and traverse north-facing slopes after a few short switchbacks. As you approach Poison Meadow and the first adequate campsites along the hike, pass a northwest-trending spur trail that offers access to a corral and possible campsites. Immediately beyond the spur trail, splash through the waters of an icy spring cascading down from above your trail; this spring is the last reliable source of water until Chicken Spring Lake, more than 4 miles ahead.

Your route traverses the foxtail pine–shaded slopes above the sagebrush margin of Poison Meadow on its westward ascent and soon surmounts the crest of the Sierra Nevada at a 10,800-foot saddle. From this point, you begin a view-filled 3-mile traverse, first heading west and then north to Cottonwood Pass. About 0.75 mile beyond the saddle, you pass just below the wildflower-speckled environs of an early-season spring that is the source of the South Fork Kern River. Just beyond the spring, glimpse the South

The Cottonwood Lakes in the John Muir Wilderness are the state's only source of pure-strain golden trout eggs. JOHN REILLY PHOTO.

Fork Meadows to the southwest, as well as the numerous other Kern Plateau grasslands and Kern Peak's alpine summit to the south.

Upon reaching Cottonwood Pass, at 11,180 feet, you are confronted with another four-way junction. The eastbound trail descends back down to Horseshoe Meadow and to your trailhead, while the westbound trail switchbacks down into the Big Whitney Meadow 1,400 feet below. Stay on your northbound trek along the PCT and cross the often-dry outlet stream draining Chicken Spring Lake. This lake, sometimes heavily used, depends upon aerial transplants to maintain a golden trout population. The trail climbs above the lake and begins a protracted timberline traverse along the sandy southwestern slopes of the Sierra crest. The vast green, sand-rimmed expanse of Big Whitney Meadow to the southwest provides a vivid contrast to the dark-green forested hills that surround it. The extensive, snowy crags of the Great Western Divide stand boldly on the western skyline, creating an impressive view that accompanies you for miles.

The trail soon contours into a small cirque, rounds a ridge, and passes a sign informing you that you are entering Sequoia National Park. As the trail begin to descend, capture glimpses of the jagged crest of the Kaweah Peaks Ridge between the trailside foxtail pines. You can also see the flower-dotted spread of the Siberian Outpost's subalpine meadow sloping away to the west. After hiking less than 1 mile from the park boundary, part company with PCT hikers and turn right (north).

After a short climb, the trail begins a forested descent into the headwaters of Rock Creek. Gaze ahead northward to the awe-inspiring peaks encircling the upper Rock Creek drainage. A few miles to the northwest, Joe Devel Peak soars out of the heavily forested landscape, the southern-most 13,000-foot peak in the Sierra Nevada. After hiking 1.25 miles from the PCT, you reach a junction along a Rock Creek tributary where there are several convenient, but overused, campsites.

A highly recommended side trip begins here, following the northbound trail to the Soldier Lakes, crossing the low ridge just west of The Major General, and then ascending into the headwaters of Rock Creek. The Mount Whitney and Johnson Peak 7.5-minute USGS quads are recommended for this cross-country route. The alpine basin at the head of this drainage abounds with beautiful fish-filled lakes and is surrounded by a host of impressive peaks, all rising well above 13,000 feet.

From the above-mentioned junction, your trail turns right (east) and ascends along a meadow-lined creek toward the massive granite hills that form the crest of the Sierra. Rising above the timberline, the trail makes a few switchbacks, angles toward a low gap in the crest, suddenly veers southeast, and then ascends sandy, alpine slopes to New Army Pass. The vistas from this high pass are far-reaching, extending as far eastward as Telescope Peak in the Panamint Range. To the west, view much of the Great Western Divide, while to the north, see the high peaks girdling upper Rock Creek. The relatively gentle south slope of Mount Langley, 2 miles to your north along the undulating crest of the Sierra Nevada, offers an easy opportunity for hikers with some cross-country experience to break the 14,000-foot barrier; superb vistas accompany this trek as well.

From the pass, the trail switchbacks down the steep headwall of a cirque and levels off on the basin floor. Stunted timber begins to appear as you pass High Lake and descend to forested Long Lake. Long Lake and the South Fork Lakes sometimes offer good fishing but have been known to freeze out fish populations during hard winters. Remember that Cottonwood Lakes 1, 2, 3, and 4 are closed to fishing, but the remainder of the basin's lakes are open to fishing from July 1 through October 31, with a limit of five trout. Only artificial flies with single barbless hooks may be used.

From Long Lake, your route descends eastward toward upper South Fork Lake and then jogs northeastward to skirt the southern shore of Cottonwood Lake No. 2. Just beyond this lake, you meet a northbound trail leading to the upper Cottonwood Lakes. Continue east, bypass the grass-rimmed shore of Cottonwood Lake No. 1, and then switchback down a foxtail pine–covered slope to meet the right-branching trail leading to South Fork and Cirque Lakes.

Continue downstream and meet another trail in less than 1 mile, immediately after hopping across Cottonwood Creek. Turn right and proceed downstream along the sometimes meadow-fringed creek. You soon re-cross to the creek's south bank and pass the fenced-in private property of Golden Trout Camp (also known as Thacher School).

You reach a signed trail leading to the Cottonwood Lakes Trailhead, about 1.1 miles below the last stream crossing. Turn right onto that trail and briefly skirt a long meadow. A pleasant 0.6-mile stroll through the forest leads to an easy crossing of the grassy-banked South Fork Cottonwood Creek. Shortly thereafter, bear left onto the newer trail, traversing among foxtail and lodgepole pines, for 1 mile until you reach the road's end and your car.

13 Horseshoe Meadow to Rocky Basin Lakes

Highlights:	This very scenic backpack leads into a remote lake basin on the northern edge of the Kern Plateau and features far-ranging vistas and good fishing for golden trout.
General location:	Southern Sierra Nevada, Golden Trout Wilderness (Inyo and Sequoia National Forests), 12 miles southwest of Lone Pine.
Type of hike:	Round-trip backpack, 4 to 6 days.
Distance:	27 miles.
Difficulty:	Moderate.
Elevation gain and loss:	+2,700 feet, -1,900 feet.
Trailhead elevation:	9,950 feet.
High point:	Cottonwood Pass, 11,180 feet.
Best season:	Mid-July through early October.
Water availability:	Available just east of Cottonwood Pass, from Stokes Stringer, Golden Trout Creek in Big Whitney Meadow, Barigan Stringer, and at Rocky Basin Lakes.
Maps:	Inyo and Sequoia National Forests map; Golden Trout Wilderness map (includes South Sierra Wilderness); USGS Cirque Peak and Johnson Peak 7.5-minute quads.
Permits:	Required for overnight use; obtain at the Mt. Whitney Ranger Station in Lone Pine. Reservations for permits can be made up to six months in advance (see Appendix A for information).

Key points:

0.0   Cottonwood Pass Trailhead.
0.2   Junction with southbound Trail Pass Trail; continue straight ahead (west).
1.0   Junction with northeastbound trail to Cottonwood Creek; stay left.
3.8   Cottonwood Pass, junction with Pacific Crest Trail (PCT); continue straight ahead (southwest).
7.5   Junction with northwestbound trail in Big Whitney Meadow; continue straight ahead.

8.1 Junction with Siberian Pass Trail at western margin of Big Whitney Meadow; turn left (southwest).

8.3 Junction with Little Whitney Trail; turn right (southwest).

10.8 Junction with Rocky Basin Lakes Trail alongside Barigan Stringer; bear right (northwest).

13.5 Rocky Basin Lakes.

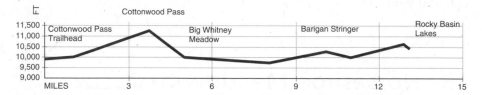

Finding the trailhead: See driving directions for Hike 12 and follow the paved Horseshoe Meadow Road for about 19 miles to a junction. The right-branching road leads to the Cottonwood Lakes Trailhead parking area. Follow the left (west) fork straight ahead for 0.3 mile to the Cottonwood Pass Trailhead parking area at the road's end.

The hike: Horseshoe Meadow is an easily accessible and justifiably popular portal into the backcountry of Sequoia National Park and the Golden Trout Wilderness. From the road's end at nearly 10,000 feet, the high country of the southern High Sierra is only a few hours away by trail.

This fine trip crosses the Sierra crest via its southernmost 11,000-foot pass, drops into the expansive spread of Big Whitney Meadow, and then ascends deeper into the backcountry until you reach a small chain of timberline lakes. The trip combines subalpine forests, timberline environments, vast meadows, and fish-filled lakes in a unique Sierra landscape, where the Kern Plateau fades into the peaks and basins of the High Sierra.

Begin hiking west from the spacious Cottonwood Pass Trailhead, following the sandy trail that skirts the northern margin of overgrazed Horseshoe Meadow. Avoid the southbound Trail Pass Trail (see Hike 12) after 0.2 mile, and proceed through an open forest of lodgepole and foxtail pine. Good views from this stretch of the trail reach far above, to the rocky cone of Trail Peak rising south of the meadow and to the barren granite crest of the Sierra to your northwest.

After passing a faint northeastbound trail leading to Cottonwood Creek, leave Horseshoe Meadow behind and begin a gradual ascent through the forest. Jump across a small, grass-fringed tributary stream and then climb to the foot of the steep slope that rises to the notch of Cottonwood Pass. The trail then begins a series of switchbacks that ascend along the course of a small, tumbling stream. The tight switchbacks rise to a willow-clad opening, followed by another series of longer switchbacks that top out on the Sierra crest at 11,180-foot Cottonwood Pass, 3.8 miles from the trailhead. Large snowdrifts, and perhaps a cornice, often block your last several yards to the pass until early July.

The vistas that open up from the pass easily justify your efforts. They are

Hikers en route to Rocky Basin Lakes traverse the vast spread of Big Whitney Meadow, seen here sprawling out below the Pacific Crest Trail.

ample rewards for day hikers as well. Westward, gaze across the vast Kern Plateau to the distant Great Western Divide, a long crest of 12,000- and 13,000-foot peaks rising 20 miles from your perch. You are looking across a portion of the largest expanse of wilderness in California, stretching 30 miles west from Horseshoe Meadow to the Kaweah River in Sequoia National Park, 30 miles south to Kennedy Meadows on the South Fork Kern River, and 100 miles north to California Highway 120 at Tioga Pass.

From the four-way junction atop the rocky pass, follow the southwestbound trail that descends into the sloping meadow at the head of Stokes Stringer and leads you deeper into the vast wilderness that spreads out before you. *Stringer* is a moniker common to small, meadow-bordered streams on the Kern Plateau. There are fair campsites inside the forest above the west end of the sagebrush-clad meadow that lies about 0.5 mile west of the pass. Descend 700 feet via more than two dozen switchbacks and hop across small Stokes Stringer to find a few more fair campsites. The trail ahead descends via more switchbacks to the eastern arm of Big Whitney Meadow at 9,900 feet, where the grade levels out.

The trail leads southwest, turns west, again crosses sluggish Stokes Stringer, and ascends gradually over a low ridge studded with lodgepole pines. A gradual, 150-foot descent leads you into Big Whitney Meadow, a 2-square-mile expanse of grass, where you are likely to find either cattle or horses, or both, grazing during the summer. After crossing one of several sluggish

75

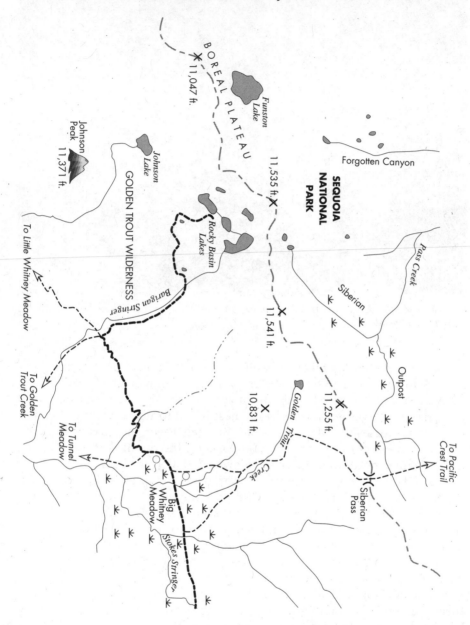

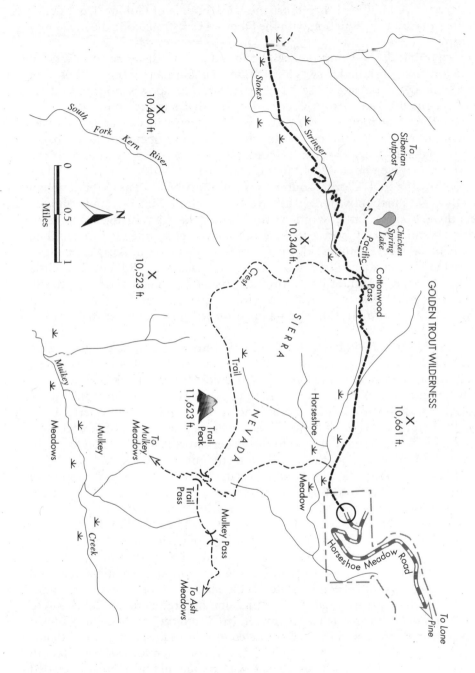

streams draining the meadow, pass a northwestbound shortcut trail leading to the Siberian Pass Trail at 7.5 miles. Continue west for 0.6 mile, skirting a lodgepole-clad hill, and then cross the main branch of Golden Trout Creek before reaching the junction with the Siberian Pass Trail along the meadow's western margin.

Good, but dusty, campsites can be found a short distance southwest of this junction, with better sites located farther south along the west edge of the meadow. Campsites also sit alongside the meadow's northwest arm, with a small Golden Trout Creek tributary that supplies more appealing water than that found in the meadow. Fine views reach across this vast spread to blocky granite ridges that are mantled in open forests of foxtail and lodgepole pine. Especially memorable is the view northeast to the towering rubble pile of 12,900-foot Cirque Peak.

Follow the trail 0.2 mile southwest from the Siberian Pass Trail junction to the next junction, where you leave Big Whitney Meadow and continue southwest on the Little Whitney Trail toward Barigan Stringer. You must first ascend 550 feet over 2 gradual miles to a broad, pine-clad ridge. Then descend 300 feet from the ridge in 0.5 mile to the banks of Barigan Stringer, situated in a broad, shallow valley at 10.8 miles and 10,080 feet. The Little Whitney Trail continues its southwest, up-and-down course for 5 miles to reach its namesake meadow. The Barigan Stringer Trail turns southeast and descends into the valley to its junction with the Siberian Pass Trail in 1.7 miles.

Bear right at the junction leading toward Rocky Basin Lakes, ascending past lovely meadows and through the lodgepole and foxtail pine forest alongside Barigan Stringer's small creek. This creek drains the lakes above until late summer, when the lower lake's outlet usually dries up. The uphill grade increases as you work your way up the stringer and through increasingly rocky terrain. Hop across the creek and make a final ascent of 500 feet to a low ridge. From there, descend to the easternmost lake in the Rocky Basin chain, resting just below the 10,800-foot contour.

The three largest lakes (out of the four in the basin) offer good camping in an open timberline forest of foxtail pines, as well as productive fishing for golden trout. Keep in mind that campfires are not allowed at the Rocky Basin Lakes. The basin can't claim to be the most beautiful in the area. It is a raw, rocky landscape backed up by a 700-foot headwall of highly fractured granite. No great peaks rise above, only the gentle ridgeline of the Boreal Plateau. This area's remoteness, good camping, great fishing, and side trip opportunities compensate for the lack of alpine splendor, though.

Side trips to Johnson Lake, the depression of large Funston Lake, and to the Boreal Plateau are highly recommended. From the southernmost lake in Rocky Basin, proceed southwest (cross-country) to a low, rocky notch that is 300 feet above you and 0.5 mile away. From that notch, descend 500 feet in 0.3 mile to Johnson Lake at 10,620 feet, where you will find good, uncrowded camping and golden trout fishing.

You can also ascend north from the notch onto the broad, gentle expanse of the Boreal Plateau. Featuring magnificent vistas of the southern peaks of the High Sierra crest and the Great Western Divide, the plateau also boasts a colorful display of the fragrant blooms of myriad alpine cushion plants. Particularly delightful to your olfactory senses are the dwarf lupine and phlox. A gentle ascent for 0.8 mile up to the plateau yields views down to the deep, blue Funston Lake at 10,840 feet. This lake lies within Sequoia National Park, where wood fires are not allowed above 10,400 feet. It is easily reached from the plateau crest via a steady 0.7 mile, 500-foot descent through open, alpine fell fields.

There is an alternate 11.7-mile route for returning to the trailhead that will appeal to more adventurous hikers. From the lower, northernmost lake in the basin, Lake 10,745, ascend cross-country for 400 feet to a narrow notch at 11,200 feet, on the boundary of Sequoia National Park. From there, leave the Golden Trout Wilderness and enter the park while descending 400 feet into the long timberline spread of lonely Siberian Outpost. This foxtail-fringed meadow affords superb solitude in the isolated camping areas around its margins.

Follow the meadows of Siberian Outpost first northeast and then ascend eastward to the head of the meadow beneath Cirque Peak. As you approach the head of the meadow, you will intercept the Siberian Pass Trail a short distance north of the pass and 3.5 miles from Rocky Basin Lakes. You can either turn left (north) onto this trail for 0.4 mile to the PCT or continue cross-country for about 0.75 mile and pick up the PCT just below timberline on the shoulder of Cirque Peak.

From your junction with the PCT, proceed southeast on that trail, following a lengthy, view-filled traverse. After about 3.5 miles, you reach the overused Chicken Spring Lake with the only water and suitable campsites along that traverse. Continue past the lake for another 0.6 mile to Cottonwood Pass, turn left (east), and retrace your steps for 3.8 miles to the trailhead.

14 Jordan Peak

Highlights:	This rewarding trip leads to a lookout-capped peak on the Great Western Divide, where memorable vistas of the southern High Sierra unfold.
General location:	Southern Sierra Nevada, Sequoia National Forest, 30 miles northeast of Porterville.
Type of hike:	Round-trip day hike.
Distance:	1.6 to 4 miles.
Difficulty:	Easy.
Elevation gain and loss:	715 to 915 feet.
Trailhead elevation:	8,200 or 8,400 feet.
High point:	Jordan Peak, 9,115 feet.
Best season:	Mid-June through October.
Water availability:	Bring your own.
Maps:	Sequoia National Forest map; USGS Camp Nelson 7.5-minute quad.
Permits:	Not required.

Key points:

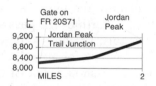

- 0.0 Gate on Forest Road 20S71; follow road uphill (west).
- 1.2 Junction with Jordan Peak Trail; turn right (west) onto trail.
- 2.0 Jordan Peak.

Finding the trailhead: There are two ways to locate the beginning of this remote hike: (1) from Porterville via the tortuously twisting and turning California Highway 190; or (2) from Kernville via the Kern River Road and the Western Divide Highway.

(1) Follow CA 190 east from Porterville for about 40 miles to a junction with northbound FR 21S50. This junction is marked by a sign pointing north to Golden Trout Wilderness Pack Trains, 7.5 miles ahead. There is also a highway sign at this point indicating Johnsondale, California Hot Springs, and Kernville, with mileage listings to each of these points. Turn left (north) here. The pavement ends after 4.5 miles; turn left where a sign points to Clicks Creek Trailhead. Continue northwest on FR 21S50 and bear right 1.2 miles from the end of the pavement, where a sign points to Clicks Creek Trailhead, Jordan Peak Lookout, and Summit Trailhead. After driving another 1.7 miles, turn left at the Jordan Peak Lookout sign. This westbound road, FR 20S71, is closed annually from November 1 through June 1. If you intend to take this hike at a leisurely pace, park here; if you are in a hurry, drive west on FR 20S71 for 1.2 miles to the signed trailhead.

(2) From Kernville, drive north up the Kern River on the locally signed Sierra Way. After driving about 19 miles along the Kern River, bear left where the Sherman Pass Road branches right and cross the river via a two-lane bridge. After driving 4 miles from the river, avoid a left-branching road

Jordan Peak

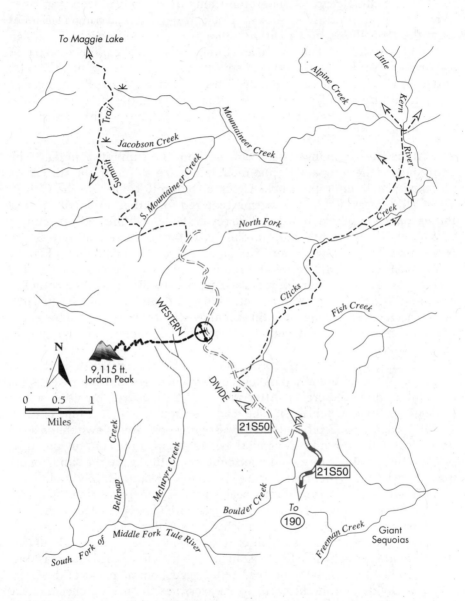

that leads to the abandoned lumbermill town of Johnsondale; just 0.6 mile farther, avoid a right-branching road that leads to Camp Whitsett and beyond. Turn left where the sign points left to the Western Divide Highway. Avoid the left-branching road to Thompson Camp after 8 miles from the river, where the sign indicates California Hot Springs. After driving 11.2 miles from the Kern River, turn right onto the Western Divide Highway; a sign here points to CA 190, Ponderosa, and Camp Nelson. Follow this good paved road north, avoiding several signed spur roads. At a point about 15.2 miles from the previous junction and 26.5 miles from the Kern River, make a sharp right turn onto FR 21S50, just beyond a sign listing mileage to Camp Nelson, Springville, and Porterville. From here, follow the first description to reach the trailhead.

The hike: The sweeping vistas available from the summit of Jordan Peak easily justify the long and scenic mountain drive to the trailhead. Hikers planning a trek along the Clicks Creek or Summit Trails into the Golden Trout Wilderness (wilderness permit required for either) are urged to take this easy warm-up hike for a grand survey of the terrain they will encounter.

As you will see while atop Jordan Peak, the extreme southern Sierra Nevada was largely unglaciated. This landscape, especially the Kern Plateau to the east, clearly illustrates the rounded, plateau-like character of the region that existed millions of years ago, before the Sierra Nevada batholith began uplifting to its present height. Many lofty, alpine peaks in the High Sierra escaped glaciation, standing far above the rivers of ice. So they, too, are remnants of the broad, gentle surfaces that characterized the region in ancient times.

From the gate on FR 20S71, proceed west on a gentle grade through a red fir forest. You occasionally pass logged-over openings and the road passes over a few spring-fed creeks. After strolling 1.2 miles, you meet the signed Jordan Peak Trail on your right. The road ends at a turnout, 0.1 mile beyond.

The Jordan Peak Trail leads southwest and soon begins switchhbacking up a selectively cut red fir–covered slope. As you near the summit, chinquapin, mountain whitethorn, and manzanita begin to invade the sunny openings. A few final switchbacks bring hikers to the summit. Silver pines (or western white pines) grow on the peak's north slope, preferring the colder microclimate that prevails there. These trees are closely related to the five-needled sugar pine, but are distinguished by smaller cones.

Upon surmounting the summit of Jordan Peak, you immediately understand why this peak hosts a fire lookout tower—the view is truly far-reaching, and splendid as well. To the northeast, the jagged, alpine peaks of the Great Western Divide line the horizon. To the west lies the gaping chasm of the North Fork of the Middle Fork Tule River, more than 5,000 feet below. Moses Mountain, at 9,331 feet, soars westward from the depths of that canyon, and 10,042-foot Maggie Mountain and its satellite summits rise to the east.

Far to the east lies the Kern Plateau, punctuated on the eastern horizon by the 12,123-foot Olancha Peak. Kern Peak is also visible on the northeastern skyline. The massive flanks of Slate Mountain rise steadily to the

After an easy ascent to Jordan Peak, far-ranging vistas unfold, stretching across the forested landscape of the Southern Sierra to the alpine peaks of the Great Western Divide.

south above Camp Nelson and the South Fork of the Middle Fork Tule River until they peak at 9,302 feet. On the southwest horizon, the Mount Pinos region can be seen, and on a clear day, you can gaze across the broad plain of the San Joaquin Valley to the South Coast Ranges on the western horizon. These truly inspiring vistas will cause hikers to linger. The lookout is occupied during fire season, usually from June through October.

From the peak, retrace your route to the trailhead.

After completing the easy jaunt to Jordan Peak, you may decide to descend the Clicks Creek Trail to the Little Kern River (wilderness permit required, contact the Sequoia National Forest supervisor in Porterville or the Kernville Ranger Station). This well-marked trail heads northeast from Log Cabin Meadow, about 1.2 miles south of the Jordan Peak turnoff on FR 21S50. The trail descends for 6 miles through conifer forest, following Clicks Creek most of the way, to good campsites along the Little Kern River where fishing can be good for Little Kern golden trout.

15 Alta Peak

Highlights:	This rigorous hike features an exciting ascent to a superb alpine vista point on the western slope of the Sierra Nevada.
General location:	Southern Sierra Nevada, Sequoia National Park, 35 miles northeast of Visalia.
Type of hike:	All-day hike or overnighter.
Distance:	13 miles.
Difficulty:	Strenuous.
Elevation gain and loss:	3,844 feet.
Trailhead elevation:	7,360 feet.
High point:	Alta Peak, 11,204 feet.
Best season:	Late June through mid-October.
Water availability:	Wolverton Creek at 1.8 miles and seasonally at Mehrten Meadow at 4.3 miles. If day hiking, bring your own.
Maps:	Sequoia–Kings Canyon National Parks map; Sequoia–Kings Canyon and John Muir Wilderness areas map (two sheets, topographic); USGS Lodgepole 7.5-minute quad.
Permits:	Required for overnight use. Obtain permit at the Lodgepole Visitor Center, 2 miles northeast of the trailhead turnoff.

Key points:

0.0	Wolverton Trailhead.
1.7	Junction with northbound Lakes Trail; bear right (southeast).
2.6	Junction with Alta Trail at Panther Gap; turn left (east).
4.3	Mehrten Meadow.
4.7	Junction with Alta Peak Trail; turn left (north).
6.5	Alta Peak.

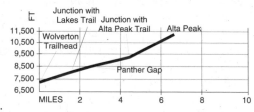

Finding the trailhead: From Visalia, follow California Highway 198 east for 53.5 miles and turn right (east) where a large sign indicates Wolverton. This turnoff is about 3 miles northeast of Giant Forest. Turn east onto Wolverton Road and drive 1.5 miles to the large turnaround at the trailhead. Avoid the road branching right to the Wolverton Corrals, 0.25 mile from the highway.

From Fresno, follow CA 180 east for 55.5 miles to its junction with the General's Highway at the Wye; turn southeast and drive 26 miles to the trailhead.

The hike: Most ascents of alpine peaks in the Sierra Nevada involve at least some scrambling or basic rock climbing, and are accessible only to those

Alta Peak

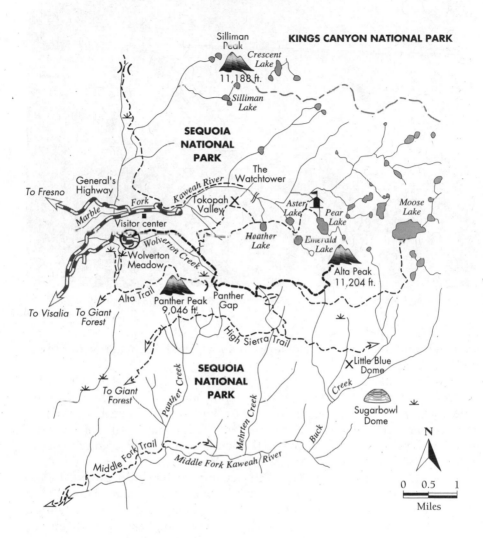

hikers with the skills and conditioning required to attain their summits. By taking advantage of a good trail, though, anyone in good physical condition who takes this hike has the opportunity to stand upon the alpine summit of Alta Peak and enjoy an all-encompassing vista, rivaling the best Sierra viewpoints. This trip surveys west-slope scenery ranging from red fir forests to the lichen-encrusted granite slabs atop Alta Peak.

The trail begins near the eastern edge of the large parking area, where a large sign identifies various backcountry destinations. After a short climb, turn right (east); the westbound trail descends to the Marble Fork Kaweah River. Your gentle ascent through a red fir forest leads you on an easterly, then southeasterly course. After 1.7 miles, the Lakes Trail comes in on

A vast landscape of ice-scoured granite peaks spreads across the vista from Alta Peak.

your left and leads to several overused subalpine lakes where camping is strictly regulated.

Continue your ascent through the fir forest along Wolverton Creek for 0.9 mile to the low saddle of Panther Gap at 8,480 feet, where your route intersects the Alta Trail coming from the Giant Forest. From this point you can see the high peaks of the Great Western Divide to the east. The fantastic jumble of spires and crags visible to the south, across the deep trench of the Middle Fork Kaweah River, are the Castle Rocks.

Proceeding east along the Alta Trail, accompanied by ever-expanding vistas, begin a 1-mile traverse across mostly open south-facing slopes, with Jeffrey and sugar pine affording occasional shade. At the junction with a southbound path descending to the High Sierra Trail, bear left and contour into the bowl that contains Mehrten Meadow and the first adequate campsites on the hike. The cliffs and crags associated with Alta Peak, and the granite dome of Tharps Rock that looms above the meadow combine with the excellent views to make this a highly scenic camping area. Water is usually available from the small creek until late summer.

Near the east side of the Mehrten Meadow bowl, turn left onto the Alta Peak Trail. The Alta Trail continues eastward, leading to Moose Lake and providing access to the alpine expanse of the Tableland. Your trail crosses an avalanche chute emanating from Alta Peak and climbs the steep slopes under the imposing Tharps Rock. Views are good across Mehrten Meadow to the western Sierra Nevada foothills and even to the San Joaquin Valley on clear days.

As the trail emerges onto more open, rocky slopes, western white pine makes its debut and quickly dominates the forest. After crossing a small creek, negotiate a single switchback and then climb the very steep rock and gravel slopes, passing a few solitary, weather-tortured foxtail pines. The trail fades out just before reaching the summit, so scramble up the granite slabs to attain Alta Peak.

The view from the peak takes in a large slice of the Sierra Nevada, from the Mount Goddard region in the north to the peaks of the Great Western Divide rising out of Mineral King valley in the south. Mount Whitney's sloping summit plateau is unmistakable on the eastern horizon. To the west lies the vast haziness of the San Joaquin Valley, with the South Coast Ranges forming the western horizon, visible only on clear days.

From the peak, retrace your route back to the trailhead.

16 Rowell Trailhead to Williams and Comanche Meadows

Highlights:	This short backpack trip surveys pleasant meadow and forest country on the western slopes of the Southern Sierra Nevada, high above Kings Canyon.
General location:	Southern Sierra Nevada, Jennie Lake Wilderness (Sequoia National Forest), and Sequoia–Kings Canyon Wilderness, 60 miles east of Fresno.
Type of hike:	Loop backpack, 2 to 3 days.
Distance:	13.3 miles.
Difficulty:	Moderate.
Elevation gain and loss:	3,070 feet.
Trailhead elevation:	7,830 feet.
High point:	Kanawyer Gap, 9,600 feet.
Best season:	July through mid-October.
Water availability:	Abundant.
Maps:	Sequoia National Forest map; Sequoia–Kings Canyon National Parks map; Jennie Lake and Monarch Wilderness areas map (topographic); USGS Mount Silliman and Muir Grove 7.5-minute quads.
Permits:	A wilderness permit is required for overnight camping in Kings Canyon National Park and can be obtained at the Grant Grove visitor center, located 1.4 miles north of the junction of California Highway 180 and the General's Highway at the Wye. This junction is 1.6 miles east of the Big Stump Entrance to Kings Canyon National Park.

Key points:

- 0.0   Rowell Trailhead.
- 2.4   Junction with Jennie Lake Trail; bear left (east).
- 2.6   Junction at Rowell Meadow; bear left (north) toward Marvin Pass.
- 3.6   Junction at Marvin Pass; turn right (east).
- 4.2   Junction with Mitchell Peak Trail; stay right (east).
- 4.7   Kanawyer Gap.
- 6.4   Williams Meadow.
- 7.6   Junction at Comanche Meadow; turn right (west) and begin ascending.
- 9.5   Pond Meadow Gap.
- 10.7   Return to junction at Rowell Meadow, turn left (west), and backtrack to trailhead.
- 13.3   Rowell Trailhead.

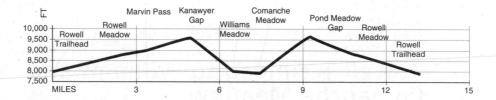

Finding the trailhead: Drive to the signed Big Meadows turnoff from the General's Highway—the main road leading through Sequoia National Park that connects CA 180 and CA 198. This turnoff is about 63 miles east of Fresno via CA 180 and the General's Highway, and 72.5 miles east of Visalia via CA 198 and the General's Highway.

Upon locating this turnoff, turn east and follow the paved road toward Big Meadows, indicated by signs at numerous junctions. After driving 4.75 miles from the highway, bear right where the sign indicates Kings Canyon Pack Station and Horse Corral Meadow. After driving 9.1 miles from the General's Highway, turn right immediately before the paved road crosses Horse Corral Creek, where a sign indicates Rowell Trailhead and the Horse Corral Pack Station. Follow this fairly rough dirt road, Forest Road 13S14, generally south for 2 miles to its end at the trailhead parking area, high above Boulder Creek canyon.

The hike: Access to remote backcountry and good fishing streams awaits hikers who negotiate this fine loop through an uncrowded, meadow-dotted and forest-covered landscape. Far-flung panoramas reward hikers who take the short side trip to Mitchell Peak, where the snowy battlements of jagged High Sierra summits contrast with the heavily forested terrain lying in the foreground.

The trail begins on the east side of the road, just north of the parking area. From here, the trail heads east through a forest of red and white fir. It soon jogs south and begins traversing the rocky and forested slopes high above Boulder Creek canyon. After hiking 1.4 miles, the trail bends northeast across the sunny, rockbound slopes above Gannon Creek, a noisy Boulder Creek tributary.

Rowell Trailhead to Williams and Comanche Meadows

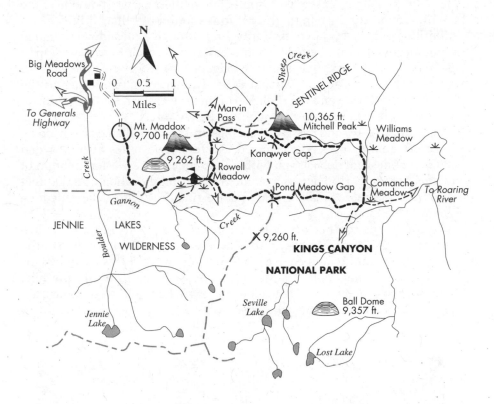

The trail eventually approaches a small creek and begins ascending along its course under a canopy of lodgepole pines. Leaving that small creek behind, the trail levels off on a meadow-floored, wildflower-brightened, lodgepole-shaded plateau, passing just north of the Rowell Meadow snow survey shelter. A wilderness ranger uses this cabin as a base camp during the summer season.

The trail continues east from the cabin, passing a southbound trail that leads to JO Pass, Gannon Creek, and Jenny Ellis Lake. Continue eastward through the lodgepole pine forest, passing several excellent campsites, to an easy small creek crossing just below a pool filled with small trout. At the trail junction on the east bank of the creek, turn left (north) toward Marvin Pass. The right-branching trail forms the return leg of your loop.

Your trail leads north through a meadow-carpeted lodgepole forest, crosses a small creek, and enters a drier forest of red fir and lodgepole pine while ascending to Marvin Pass. After hiking 1 mile from the previous junction, you reach the pass and a trail junction at an elevation of 9,050 feet. Turn right (east) here onto the Kanawyer Gap Trail and climb moderately for 0.6 mile to the old Mitchell Peak Trail, which branches left (north) from your trail. This unsigned junction is difficult to locate, obscured by an overgrown clump of chinquapin. Hikers who appreciate endless views should take the 2.25-mile round-trip hike to the 10,365-foot summit of Mitchell Peak.

Continue east and find yourself traveling through a meadow dominated by shoulder-high corn lilies; shortly thereafter you reach Kanawyer Gap at 9,600 feet, shaded by a predominantly lodgepole pine forest on the western boundary of Kings Canyon National Park. The jagged alpine peaks of the Great Western Divide and the High Sierra line the eastern skyline; unfortunately, they are barely visible through the heavy forest.

Descend eastward and pass a few springs and two small creeks; the lodgepole forest quickly blends into mixed conifers. Two miles of hiking and 1,600 feet of descent deposit you within 0.25 mile of the western margin of Williams Meadow. Hop across a small creek at an elevation of 8,000 feet and cross three more small streams before finally reaching the mile-long Williams Meadow.

The trail turns south, skirting the western edge of this beautiful lodgepole-rimmed grassland. An easy ford is necessary near the lower end of the meadow. Your southbound course continues just west of this meadow-bordered creek draining Williams Meadow. The best campsites on the hike (except for those in the Rowell Meadow area) will be found west of the trail, between Williams and Comanche Meadows.

Williams Meadow makes a fine destination in the forested western reaches of Kings Canyon National Park.

About 1 mile below Williams Meadow is the small, wet Comanche Meadow. Your trail briefly approaches this meadow before veering away from it into the lodgepole pine forest. Just west of the meadow lies a trail junction. The left-branching (eastbound) trail leads past Sugarloaf Valley to the Roaring River and beyond. Anglers will want to sample the sometimes excellent fishing in the Roaring River, which can be reached after 6 miles of pleasant, forested, eastbound hiking.

For this hike, though, turn right at the junction and begin a steady, moderate-to-steep, westward ascent. White firs begin to replace the lodgepole pines on these well-drained slopes, becoming the dominant forest tree. As you gain elevation, enjoy the occasional views southward to the broken granite crowning the Silliman Crest and eastward to the 12,000- and 13,000-foot peaks of the Great Western Divide.

En route, cross a small, cold creek, then ascend the final 0.5 mile to the lodgepole pines and red firs of Pond Meadow Gap. Here you re-enter lands administered by Sequoia National Forest. A westward descent of 1.4 miles, under a shady canopy of pine and fir, brings you to a junction with a southeastbound trail leading to Seville Lake and other glacial tarns nestled beneath the Silliman Crest.

Continue straight ahead and reach the junction with the northbound Marvin Pass Trail. Retrace your route through Rowell Meadow back to the trailhead.

17 Lookout Peak

Highlights:	This short, rewarding hike leads to a panoramic vista point, featuring dramatic views of Kings Canyon and the great peaks of the southern High Sierra.
General location:	Southern Sierra Nevada, Sequoia National Forest, 60 miles east of Fresno.
Type of hike:	Round-trip half-day hike.
Distance:	1.2 miles.
Difficulty:	Moderately easy.
Elevation gain and loss:	531 feet.
Trailhead elevation:	8,000 feet.
High point:	Lookout Peak, 8,531 feet.
Best season:	Late June through October.
Water availability:	None available; bring your own.
Maps:	Sequoia National Forest map; Monarch and Jennie Lake Wilderness areas map (topographic); USGS Cedar Grove 7.5-minute quad.
Permits:	Not required.

Key points:

0.0 Don Cecil Trailhead; Don Cecil Trail descends northeast into Kings Canyon National Park; follow Lookout Peak Trail north.

0.6 Lookout Peak.

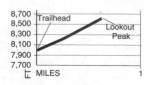

Finding the trailhead: Follow the driving directions for Hike 16, but instead of turning south after driving 9.1 miles from the General's Highway, continue straight ahead on Forest Road 14S11.

After 9.5 miles, the pavement ends at the junction with the southbound road leading to the Marvin Pass Trailhead. Continue straight ahead at this junction. Stay right at the junction at 11.4 miles and bear left at an unsigned junction with a graded dirt road after 11.5 miles. After 13.2 miles, you approach a saddle immediately south of Lookout Peak and reach another junction. Turn left (east) here and drive the final few yards to a spacious parking area at the Don Cecil Trailhead. In addition to ample parking, there are undeveloped campsites in a park-like forest of pine and fir.

The hike: Lookout Peak, a boulder-stacked granite crag, lies just outside of the Monarch Wilderness boundary on the western edge of Kings Canyon National Park. Its 8,531-foot summit stands more than 4,000 feet above Kings Canyon, one of the Sierra Nevada's most profound gorges. The short but fairly rigorous hike to the summit rewards hikers with stunning vistas into Kings Canyon, and beyond, to the lofty crags of the High Sierra.

From the saddle at the road's end, the only signed trail you will find is the Don Cecil Trail, descending 3,500 feet in 6.5 miles to Kings Canyon near Cedar Grove. Your trail, faint at first, leads north across the broad saddle, behind the trail sign, toward the cone of Lookout Peak. Blazes on tall pines help show the way. An obvious single track soon appears.

Follow this trail, gradually ascending through an open forest of ponderosa pine, and red and white fir. The grade becomes moderate with occasional steep grades as you ascend along the southwest slopes of the peak. Manzanita and chinquapin congregate in

Views from Lookout Peak reach into the incomparable gorge of Kings Canyon and beyond to lofty High Sierra peaks.

Lookout Peak

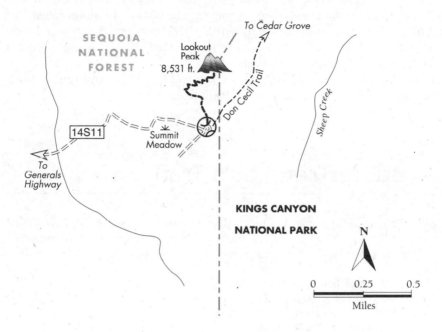

clumps on the peak's steep slopes, and a forest of pines and large granite boulders add to the beauty of the scene.

The trail approaches the peak's steep west ridge and then begins a series of moderately steep switchbacks that ascend the south slopes. About 100 yards below the boulder-stacked summit, adjacent to one of two low radio repeaters, the trail becomes obscure among granite boulders. Acrophobic hikers may choose to end their ascent at the first radio tower and enjoy the view into Kings Canyon from there.

Other hikers will want to continue, scrambling the final 100 yards and gaining about 50 feet, among boulders via a very steep path to the summit blocks above the second radio tower. Find a perch and enjoy the breathtaking vista, or scramble class 2 to 3 rock to the summit.

A knife blade granite ridge juts northeast from the summit into the abyss, pointing toward the alpine heights of Comb Ridge and the Monarch Divide, a lofty crest of 11,000-foot summits. On the northern skyline rises the landmark spire of Mount Harrington in the Monarch Wilderness, with the verdant slopes of Happy Gap notching the Monarch Divide west of that peak. The incomparable U-shaped trough of Kings Canyon, lying 4,000 feet and 2 miles below your perch, stretches eastward toward lofty crests notched with great cirques and punctuated by bold crags.

Mounts Gardiner, Cotter, and Clarence King are especially prominent on the eastern skyline. North Dome and Grand Sentinel guard the entrance to the vast Sequoia–Kings Canyon Wilderness at the road's end far below in Kings Canyon. The view also extends up the valley of Bubbs Creek and southeast past the Roaring River drainage to the peaks of Sphinx Crest and the Great Western Divide. In the foreground, the cavernous defile of Sheep Creek falls away at your feet, with the fir-forested north slopes of Sentinel Ridge marching off toward the east.

You must eventually abandon these far-reaching vistas and retrace your route from Lookout Peak back to the trailhead.

18 Boole Tree Loop Trail

Highlights:	This scenic half-day hike features far-ranging vistas and visits the largest giant sequoia on national forest land.
General location:	Southern Sierra Nevada, Sequoia National Forest, 45 miles east of Fresno.
Type of hike:	Half-day loop trip.
Distance:	2.5 miles.
Difficulty:	Moderately easy.
Elevation gain and loss:	700 feet.
Trailhead elevation:	6,240 feet.
High point:	6,800 feet.
Best season:	Mid-June through October.
Water availability:	None available; bring your own.
Maps:	Sequoia National Forest map; USGS Hume 7.5-minute quad (part of loop trail not shown on quad).
Permits:	Not required.

Key points:

- 0.0 Trailhead; turn right (east) onto loop trail.
- 1.0 Boole Tree.
- 1.6 Spanish Mountain viewpoint.
- 2.3 Kings River viewpoint.
- 2.5 Return to trailhead.

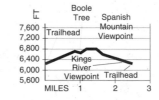

Finding the trailhead: Follow California Highway 180 to the Big Stump Entrance to Kings Canyon National Park, 54 miles east of Fresno. Continue ahead for another 1.6 miles to the Wye, where you turn left toward Grant Grove and Cedar Grove. Pass through Grant Grove Village 1.5 miles from the Wye and proceed northeast to the junction with Forest Road 13S55, 5.8 miles from the Wye. This junction is signed for Converse Basin, Stump Meadow, and the Boole Tree Trail.

Turn left (north) onto this good, but narrow, dirt road, and drive 0.3 mile to a four-way junction. Continue straight ahead where the sign points to the Boole Tree Trail. After 1.9 miles, bear right at the signed junction, dip into Stump Meadow, and ascend to the spacious trailhead parking area at the road's end, 2.6 miles from CA 180. There is ample room for as many as 30 vehicles at the trailhead, plus pit toilets and an information signboard showing a map of the trail.

The hike: Unlike many other giant sequoia trails, the Boole Tree Trail visits only one ancient giant sequoia. Until the 1890s, the sequoias of Converse Basin constituted the largest grove in existence. Today, only giant stumps are left behind, along with renewed growth of young sequoias and the Boole Tree. Standing 269 feet tall, with a diameter of 29 feet, this tree is the largest sequoia standing beyond the boundaries of California's national parks.

This 2.5-mile loop trail is immensely rewarding, passing through a mixed conifer forest that includes a multitude of young sequoias, en route to the Boole Tree. It returns you to the trailhead via the rim of Kings Canyon, featuring outstanding vistas along the way. Although portions of the trail have a moderately steep grade, it is a short hike suitable for all levels of hiking ability.

It is recommended that you take the loop in a counterclockwise direction, climbing to the Boole Tree and then enjoying Kings Canyon vistas along the downhill stretch. Take the right fork of the loop trail at the trailhead and ascend at a moderate grade through an open forest of ponderosa pine, incense-cedar, sugar pine, and young sequoias. The trailside slopes are mantled in a green blanket of fragrant kit-kit-dizze, clumps of manzanita, and bracken fern in shady niches.

The grade steepens, leading you up the course of a verdant draw that drains a trickling seasonal stream. Many of the willows that crowd the bottom of the draw are unusually tall, spreading, and multibranched. White fir also joins the forest ranks within the confines of the draw. Once the grade levels, step across the small stream and exit the draw, heading north. The trail rises via switchbacks and then straightens out as it leads steeply, but briefly, uphill to the crest of a ridge north of Converse Mountain. On this seemingly dry ridge grow thickets of mountain whitethorn and chinquapin, along with clumps of tall willows—a sure sign of moisture just below the surface.

From this ridge, the trail briefly descends its east slopes, re-enters the forest, and soon reaches a trail sign at the junction with the Boole Tree spur trail. Turn right (south) here and stroll 50 yards down to an interpretive sign that explains the history of logging in the Converse Basin Grove in the 1890s. At that time, the Boole Tree was thought to be the largest giant sequoia in existence. This distinction is, perhaps, the reason why it was the only forest monarch spared in this once vast grove. The trail continues on for about 100 yards to the base of the Boole Tree, passing second-growth sequoias along the way. This magnificent old tree, dead and broken at the crown, displays a long, hollow fire scar on its stout bole.

Boole Tree Loop Trail

SEQUOIA NATIONAL FOREST

Spanish Mountain Viewpoint

6,872 ft. X

Kings River Viewpoint

Boole Tree Loop

Boole Tree

6,291 ft. X

Converse Basin Grove

Stump Meadow

Converse Mountain 7,247 ft.

13S55

N

0   0.25   0.5
Miles

To 180

From the Boole Tree, return to the loop trail, turn right, and begin a northbound ascent across open slopes. Vistas to the east are breathtaking from this stretch, reaching into the profound gorge of Kings Canyon and beyond to distant High Sierra crags. The trail levels out as you curve around the south and west slopes of a ridgetop prominence. It then gradually descends westward along the brushy ridge, studded with mixed conifers and granite boulders. Pass an old shed, cross through a gate in the fenceline, and begin descending north.

This ridge is the Spanish Mountain viewpoint shown on the trailhead map, and the vistas are outstanding. Below you to the north is the Grand Canyon–like gorge of Kings Canyon, including a view of the churning river lying 5,000 feet below. Within view is the Kings Canyon Special Management Area, a 49,000-acre roadless expanse adjacent to the north unit of the Monarch Wilderness. You can see from the grassland and oak woodland environment of the Sierra foothills to the high alpine peaks of the Dinkey Lakes country to the north, a view that takes in the entire spectrum of western Sierra environments. Rising high on the northeast skyline is the

Memorable vistas from the Boole Tree Loop Trail include Kings Canyon, one of North America's deepest gorges.

10,051-foot summit of Spanish Mountain. The vertical distance between this peak and the floor of Kings Canyon is 8,200 feet, giving this part of the canyon the distinction of being North America's deepest gorge.

From this viewpoint, the trail begins a steady descent via switchbacks, down north-facing slopes studded with ponderosa pine, white fir, willow, black oak, and young sequoias. After the long series of switchbacks, regain the lower ridge and stroll westward along its crest. The trail eventually curves southwest and passes through another steel gate in the same fenceline. Pause just before passing through the gate and enjoy the superb view north to the churning rapids of the Wild and Scenic Kings River from the Kings River viewpoint. From the gate, the trail gradually descends through fields of aromatic kit-kit-dizze for 0.2 mile to the trailhead parking area.

19 Big Baldy

Highlights:	This pleasant jaunt leads to a rocky viewpoint high above one of the most magnificent giant sequoia groves in the Sierra Nevada.
General location:	Southern Sierra Nevada, Sequoia National Park, 50 miles east of Fresno.
Type of hike:	Round-trip day hike.
Distance:	5.5 miles.
Difficulty:	Moderately easy.
Elevation gain and loss:	611 feet.
Trailhead elevation:	7,600 feet.
High point:	Big Baldy, 8,211 feet.
Best season:	Mid-May through mid-November.
Water availability:	Bring your own.
Maps:	Sequoia–Kings Canyon National Parks map; USGS General Grant Grove 7.5-minute quad.
Permits:	A wilderness permit is not required for day hiking.

Key points:

0.0   Big Baldy Trailhead.
2.0   Big Baldy.
2.75 Point 8,168, end of trail.

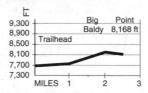

Finding the trailhead: The trailhead, signed for the Big Baldy Ski Touring Trail, lies on the west side of the General's Highway, 0.2 mile north of the Big Meadows turnoff (see driving directions for Hike 16). Parking is available in the wide shoulder a short distance south of the trailhead.

The hike: Recreational opportunities on Big Baldy, ranging from a leisurely hike, to intermediate cross-country skiing, to class 5 rock climbing near this mountain's exfoliating granite crown, combine to make this peak the destination of a variety of outdoor enthusiasts. Add to these opportunities its far-ranging and widely contrasting scenic views, and you have a rewarding excursion that beckons to all.

The Big Baldy Ski Touring Trail heads southwest from the highway through a red fir forest. Lupine, currant, chinquapin, and mountain whitethorn (a ceanothus species) are among the many understory plants decorating this section of trail. After beginning a moderate ascent of north-facing slopes, peer down into the Redwood Creek drainage, where massive, towering sequoias are easily distinguished from other conifers, even at this distance.

Begin a southbound course just west of Big Baldy Ridge after entering Kings Canyon National Park. Sugar and Jeffrey pines quickly make their debut, adding diversity to the fir forest. At times, your trail coincides with the ski route, attested to by the yellow triangles attached to trailside trees. After completing another west-slope traverse, you are confronted with a

Big Baldy • Redwood Mountain Loop

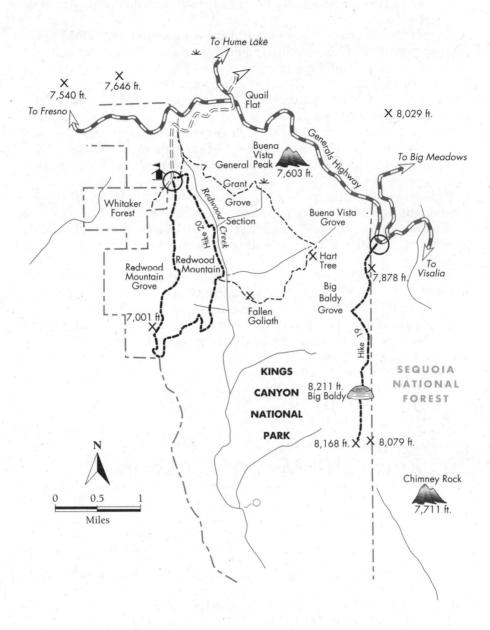

To Hume Lake

7,540 ft.

7,646 ft.

To Fresno

Quail Flat

X 8,029 ft.

Generals Highway

Buena Vista Peak
7,603 ft.

To Big Meadows

Whitaker Forest

General Grant Grove Section

Redwood Creek

Hike 20

Buena Vista Grove

Hart Tree

Redwood Mountain Grove

Redwood Mountain

7,001 ft.

Fallen Goliath

Big Baldy Grove

7,878 ft.

To Visalia

Hike 19

KINGS CANYON NATIONAL PARK

8,211 ft. Big Baldy

SEQUOIA NATIONAL FOREST

N

0   0.5   1
Miles

8,168 ft.   X 8,079 ft.

Chimney Rock
7,711 ft.

view of the dome-like summit of Big Baldy about 1 mile south. Its smooth, granitic northwest face that rises almost 800 near-vertical feet and its crags should stimulate the imaginations of both accomplished and would-be climbers alike.

The trail briefly enters the realm of bare rock, edging very close to the brink of a westward-plunging cliff. It quickly re-enters a fir forest and climbs moderately to the exfoliating granite crown of Big Baldy. A benchmark on the summit indicates that this peak is 2 feet higher than the elevation given on the quad. The trail continues south from Big Baldy for 0.75 mile to Point 8,168 and unobstructed southward views. From Big Baldy itself, views north, west, and east are superb. To the west, huge sequoias are silhouetted against the sky along Redwood Mountain's crest. To the southeast lies the fascinating sheer dome of Chimney Rock. Beyond, the Great Western Divide forms a sawtoothed horizon.

The many cliffs and rock faces surrounding Big Baldy Ridge will entice climbers to return with the equipment and skills necessary to scale these near-vertical environs. Cross-country skiers will be lured back to Big Baldy in winter to experience this fascinating landscape in an entirely different setting.

A pause on the summit allows you time to contemplate the vastness of the sequoia forest in the Redwood Mountain Grove to the immediate west. This area is the largest, and perhaps the finest, of all giant sequoia groves. Those hikers wishing to see more of it will find that the bulk of the grove is accessible only by trail; only one road penetrates its fringes. (See Hike 20, Redwood Mountain Loop.)

From Big Baldy, return to the trailhead the same way you came, only now enriched by nature's gifts of beauty and solitude.

20 Redwood Mountain Loop

See Map on Page 99

Highlights:	This fine loop leads hikers on a grand tour of the most extensive of all giant sequoia groves, well off the beaten track of most sequoia grove hikers.
General location:	Southern Sierra Nevada, Kings Canyon National Park, 50 miles east of Fresno.
Type of hike:	Loop day hike or overnighter.
Distance:	6.1 miles.
Difficulty:	Moderate.
Elevation gain and loss:	1,450 feet.
Trailhead elevation:	6,200 feet.
High point:	6,950 feet.
Low point:	5,450 feet.
Best season:	Mid-May through November.

Water availability: Available from Redwood Creek. If day hiking, bring your own.
Maps: Sequoia–Kings Canyon National Parks map; USGS General Grant Grove 7.5-minute quad.
Permits: A wilderness permit is required for overnight camping in national park backcountry and can be obtained at the Grant Grove Visitor Center.

Key points:

0.0 Trailhead at Redwood Saddle; turn right (south) onto Sugarbowl Trail.
4.5 Junction with southeastbound Hart Tree Trail in Redwood Canyon; bear left (north-northwest).
5.9 Junction with upper end of Hart Tree Trail; stay left (southwest).
6.1 Return to trailhead.

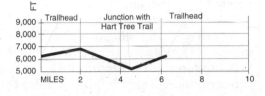

Finding the trailhead: From Fresno, proceed east on California Highway 180 for 55.5 miles to the Wye—the junction of northbound CA 180 and the eastbound General's Highway. Bear right at this junction, drive east 3.5 miles to the junction of a northbound Sequoia National Forest road (signed for Hume Lake) and a southbound Kings Canyon National Park road, and turn right (south); a sign here reads: Kings Canyon National Park. Follow this dusty and often-narrow dirt road for 1.9 miles to Redwood Saddle. Turn left here and proceed for 0.1 mile to the trailhead parking area, shaded by gargantuan sequoias.

The hike: While throngs of tourists pound the sequoia trails of the Giant Forest, only a handful of hikers explore the majesty and solitude of the Redwood Mountain Grove.

Like the coast redwood, the fossil history of the sequoia goes back several million years, indicating that these trees were much more widespread than their present distribution might suggest. In the distant past, California had a wet, mild climate, and precipitation was distributed throughout the year. Beginning in Pliocene times (5.2 million to 1.8 million years ago), California's summer seasons started becoming drier and warmer; now the bulk of precipitation occurs during the winter months.

These climatic changes had a major effect on the distribution of many plant species, eliminating entire species and plant communities and resulting in the evolution of species adapted to California's present-day climate. Extensive glaciation occurred across much of North America during Pleistocene times (1.8 million to 10,000 years ago), as a result of a general cooling trend that affected much of the western portion of North America.

This glaciation in the Sierra Nevada also served to eliminate many plant species and cause the redistribution of others. The sequoia, for example, now inhabits areas on the western slope of the Sierra Nevada that were not scoured by glacial action. These giant trees are found in numerous groves

101

scattered along the Sierra's western slopes. They thrive on all but the steepest well-drained slopes within the montane forests of the Sierra Transition Zone, generally between 5,000 and 7,000 feet—the zone of maximum precipitation in the Sierra.

As California's climate continues its slow evolution (undetectable in a human lifetime), the giant sequoia and the coast redwood will probably, eventually, become extinct. These species are no longer widespread because they have adapted to a specialized environment, dominated by a particular climatic regime. In an evolutionary sense, these species are in their "twilight years." Nevertheless, the giant sequoias are still a viable, regenerating species.

The wood and the bark of the sequoia (the latter growing as much as a foot or more thick) is highly resistant to fire and attack by insects. Most fires in sequoia forests are ground fires, burning only low-lying shrubs and trees and any forest litter. On this hike, you will pass through an area that was "prescription burned" by the National Park Service. Here you can witness how beneficial fire can be for the reproduction of sequoias; at one point, you must even bushwhack through dense sequoia saplings.

Your hike begins on the signed Sugarbowl Trail. The left-branching Redwood Canyon-Hart Tree Trail will be the homebound segment of your loop. Proceed south on the Sugarbowl Trail and ascend gently through a forest of giant sequoias, white firs, and sugar pines. You soon pass a sign proclaiming "Research Area/Ecology of Sequoias/Do Not Disturb." In some areas of Kings Canyon and Sequoia National Parks, prescribed burns are conducted during periods of low fire danger. At certain times of the year, particular areas of these parks may be off-limits to hikers.

The trail heads south along and just east of Redwood Mountain's crest. Rarely are the towering sequoias located in unmixed stands. Most often, they are found with white firs and sugar pines, many of which are also impressively large. As you progress southward, the trail occasionally leads you into sunny openings just east of the crest of Redwood Mountain. In these drier openings, the sequoias are replaced by ponderosa pines, black oaks, incense-cedars, some sugar pines, and white firs. Ground cover in these areas consists of manzanita and the fragrant, lace-leaved kit-kit-dizze. You are treated to superb views into the depths of Redwood Canyon, east to the sheer granite of Big Baldy Ridge, and southeast to the alpine peaks of the Great Western Divide.

Just south of Peak 7,001, re-enter a nearly pure stand of sequoias and begin descending along the crest of Redwood Mountain, quickly reaching a destination and mileage sign. You now begin a descent into the Redwood Canyon via the east slopes of Redwood Mountain. The sequoias give way to a mixed conifer forest on these dry, east-facing slopes. Big Baldy's sheer granite face dominates your eastward view, and you can briefly spy the lookout-capped dome of Buck Rock in the northeast.

As you descend, pass a seasonal creek and approach the bottom of Redwood Canyon. Your trail may be overgrown at times with the regrowth

Giant sequoias, the largest living things on earth, offer abundant shade for hikers taking the unique Redwood Mountain Loop.

that has resulted from the prescribed fires conducted here by the Park Service. As you proceed, giant sequoias rejoin the forest. When you reach a canyon-bottom trail junction, turn left. The Hart Tree Trail heads southeast, eventually looping back to Redwood Saddle. This alternative route would add 2.75 miles and 400 feet of elevation to your hike, but passes the Hart Tree, the tallest known giant sequoia.

Your route now ascends more or less along the course of Redwood Creek, where hikers are dwarfed by the sheer bulk of the sequoias that crowd the canyon. After hiking 1.4 miles from the previous junction, the Hart Tree Trail joins your route on the right. Bear left here and climb the final 150 feet in 0.2 mile back to the trailhead under the protective canopy of giant sequoias.

21 Courtright Reservoir to Dinkey Lakes

Highlights:	This trip leads hikers into the lake-filled high country on the western slopes of the Sierra, featuring a dozen trout-filled lakes and many excellent campsites.
General location:	Southern Sierra Nevada, Dinkey Lakes Wilderness (Sierra National Forest), 50 miles northeast of Fresno.
Type of hike:	Round-trip backpack, 2 to 4 days.
Distance:	12.8 miles or more.
Difficulty:	Moderate.
Elevation gain and loss:	+1,745 feet, -970 feet.
Trailhead elevation:	8,475 feet.
High point:	9,920 feet.
Best season:	July through mid-October.
Water availability:	Abundant after 5 miles.
Maps:	Sierra National Forest map; Dinkey Lakes Wilderness map (topographic); USGS Courtright Reservoir, Dogtooth Peak, Nelson Mountain, and Ward Mountain 7.5-minute quads.
Permits:	A wilderness permit is required for overnight use. Obtain permit at the Pineridge Ranger District office in Prather just off CA Highway168, 22.5 miles northeast of Clovis.

Key points:
- 0.0   Cliff Lake Trailhead.
- 3.0   Junction with trails to Helms Meadow (northeast) and Nelson Lakes (southwest); continue straight ahead (northwest).
- 5.0   Cliff Lake.
- 5.75 Pass at 9,920 feet.
- 6.0   Rock Lake.

6.4   Junction at Second Dinkey Lake; turn right (north) to reach First Dinkey
      Lake in 1 mile or turn left (south) to reach Island Lake in 0.5 mile.

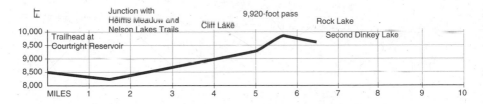

Finding the trailhead: From Clovis, proceed northeast on CA 168 for about 40 miles to the community of Shaver Lake. Turn right (east) near the southern end of Shaver Lake where a sign indicates Dinkey Creek and Wishon Dam. Follow this paved road eastward for 11.6 miles to a junction just south of Dinkey Creek.

Turn right just beyond the pack station, where the sign indicates McKinley Grove, Wishon Reservoir, and Courtright Reservoir. Follow this paved road southeast, passing through the McKinley Grove of giant sequoias and reaching a junction with the right-branching road to Wishon Reservoir after driving another 13.6 miles. Turn left here, following the good paved road toward Courtright Village (no services) and the Cliff Lake Trailhead, about 10 miles from the previous junction.

Memorable vistas of the High Sierra unfold from Dogtooth Peak in the Dinkey Lakes Wilderness.

Courtright Reservoir to Dinkey Lakes

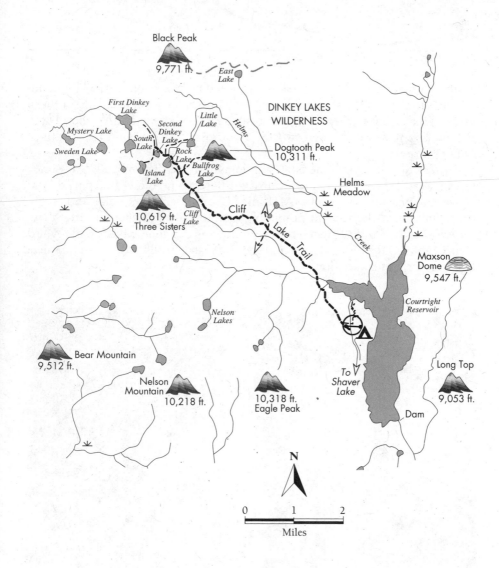

Black Peak
9,771 ft.

East Lake

DINKEY LAKES WILDERNESS

First Dinkey Lake

Little Lake

Mystery Lake

Second Dinkey Lake

South Lake

Helms

Dogtooth Peak
10,311 ft.

Sweden Lake

Rock Lake

Island Lake

Bullfrog Lake

Helms Meadow

10,619 ft.
Three Sisters

Cliff Lake

Cliff

Lake Trail

Creek

Maxson Dome
9,547 ft.

Nelson Lakes

Courtright Reservoir

Bear Mountain
9,512 ft.

Nelson Mountain
10,218 ft.

10,318 ft.
Eagle Peak

To Shaver Lake

Dam

Long Top
9,053 ft.

N

0   1   2
Miles

The hike: Although separated from the true High Sierra by a mid-elevation, forested plateau, this area stands high enough to have hosted mountain-carving glaciers in the distant past. The results can be seen today in the form of numerous subalpine lakes, cirques, smoothed and polished granitic bedrock, and quarried peaks that rise well above timberline.

Not only do fishing opportunities exist in the Dinkey Lakes area, but the two prominent peaks rising above the lakes—10,619-foot Three Sisters and 10,311-foot Dogtooth Peak—can be scaled via class 2 and class 3 routes, respectively. These peaks provide expansive and complementary perspectives, encompassing a large slice of the Sierra Nevada.

From the parking area, your trail heads northwest through a red fir and lodgepole pine forest on a slightly descending grade. You soon pass a doubletrack joining your trail on the right. As you approach the northwest end of the Courtright Reservoir, the forest becomes dominated by lodgepole pine. Hop across the creek draining Cliff Lake and enter the Dinkey Lakes Wilderness. This creek runs high during spring runoff, so early-season hikers may be forced to wade.

The trail then meanders northwestward through a heavy lodgepole pine forest, reaching a four-way junction 3 miles from the trailhead. The northeastbound trail is seldom used, but leads to Helms Meadow and beyond, while the southwestbound trail, equally seldom trod, leads to the Nelson Lakes and beyond. Continue northwest on the Cliff Lake Trail and note the addition of red and white fir to the previously unvaried lodgepole pine forest.

Begin an ascent via switchbacks along a south-facing slope clothed in western white pine and manzanita, encountering views of the Courtright Reservoir and a host of granite domes that surround it. Far to the east, the alpine peaks of the LeConte Divide and other High Sierra summits form a sawtoothed skyline. In the south and southwest rise Brown Peak (10,349 feet), Nelson Mountain (10,218 feet), and Eagle Peak (10,318 feet), all soaring high above their thickly forested basins.

The trail levels off above the switchbacks, and you soon find yourself walking above the northeast shore of beautiful Cliff Lake, 5 miles from the trailhead at 9,500 feet. Numerous possibilities for camping exist above this shore of the lake. With a backdrop of 400-foot cliffs and an open, boulder-dotted forest, this lake is an excellent, justifiably popular campsite.

The trail becomes faint as it passes above the lake, so watch for blazed trees. It becomes easier to follow as you reach a signed junction. The left-branching, descending trail leads to campsites above the upper end of Cliff Lake. Bullfrog Lake lies just over the ridge to the northeast. Continue your northwestbound ascent, though; after 0.75 mile, you reach a pass at an elevation of 9,920 feet.

A possible side trip, 0.75 mile one-way, leads northeast from this pass to the ridge immediately west of Dogtooth Peak. The peak itself is accessible only by a class 3 climb, but the ridgetop provides superb vistas even if you are not inclined to scale the crag. Upon attaining the ridge west of Dogtooth

Peak, amid stunted mountain hemlocks and whitebark pines, a vast sweep of Sierra Nevada terrain unfolds. Some of the better-known peaks and divides include, from northwest to southeast: Kaiser Peak, Mount Ritter, Banner Peak, Silver Divide, Red Slate Mountain, Mount Humphreys, Mount Goddard, LeConte Divide, the Obelisk, Spanish Mountain, and the Great Western Divide country far to the southeast. In the foreground lies the sprawling Courtright Reservoir and its adjacent domes, set amid a dark conifer forest. In the west lies the Dinkey Lakes basin.

From the 9,920-foot pass, descend northwest into the glaciated Dinkey Lakes basin, accompanied by lodgepole pines and mountain hemlocks during your brief jaunt down to Rock Lake. Upon reaching the outlet of this lake at 9,600 feet, you can continue your trail walk to the other lakes in the basin; or, if you desire solitude amid impressive surroundings, follow Rock Lake's outlet creek downstream, cross-country, for 0.9 mile to the isolated Little Lake. Set in a deep cirque at an elevation of 9,250 feet, this lake sits immediately below the precipitous north wall of the Dogtooth Peak ridge. This locale makes an excellent base camp for day hiking jaunts throughout the Dinkey Lakes basin. The remainder of the Dinkey Lakes are accessible by trail or via short cross-country excursions.

From this fine subalpine lake basin, eventually backtrack to the trailhead.

22 Twin Lakes

Highlights:	This short hike to a subalpine lake basin on the western slopes of the Sierra features ice-sculpted landscapes, cool forests, vigorous streams, and good trout fishing.
General location:	Southern Sierra Nevada, Kaiser Wilderness (Sierra National Forest), 55 miles northeast of Fresno.
Type of hike:	Round-trip day hike or overnighter.
Distance:	5.8 miles.
Difficulty:	Moderately easy.
Elevation gain and loss:	+700 feet, -200 feet.
Trailhead elevation:	8,100 feet.
High point:	Upper Twin Lake, 8,601 feet.
Best season:	Mid-July through October.
Water availability:	Abundant along much of the trail; bring your own if day hiking.
Maps:	Sierra National Forest map; Kaiser Wilderness map (topographic); USGS Kaiser Peak 7.5-minute quad.
Permits:	Required for overnight use; obtain at the Pineridge Ranger District office in Prather or at the Eastwood Visitor Center/Ranger Station at the east end of Huntington Lake between Memorial Day and Labor Day.

Key points:

- 0.0 California Riding and Hiking Trailhead.
- 0.5 Junction with Kaiser Creek Trail; bear left.
- 2.3 Junction with George Lake Trail; turn right (southwest).
- 2.9 Upper Twin Lake.

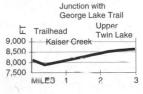

Finding the trailhead: From Fresno, follow California Highway 168 for 71 miles northeast into the Sierra, passing through the town of Shaver Lake, to the east end of Huntington Lake and a signed junction. Turn right (northeast) here onto the paved, two-lane Kaiser Pass Road (Forest Road 80), signed for Mono Hot Springs, Lake Edison, and Florence Lake.

This ascending road becomes a narrow, winding, and steep single lane of pavement (drive with extreme caution) after 6.7 miles. Top out on 9,160-foot Kaiser Pass after 7.4 miles, descend for 2.1 miles to the junction with FR 5 (signed for Sample Meadow Campground), and turn left (west). Follow this good gravel road for 2.2 miles to the spacious trailhead parking area on the east side of the road. There is space here for 15 to 20 vehicles, and an information signboard is located on the west side of the road where the trail begins.

The hike: Kaiser Ridge is a major east-west divide rising north of Huntington Lake on the west slope of the Sierra. Much of this broken, 10,000-foot ridge is protected within the boundaries of the 22,700-acre Kaiser Wilderness, an isolated island of high country rising far west of the High Sierra. This easily accessible wilderness contains two dozen high lakes, alpine crests with far-ranging vistas, and enough backcountry trails to satify both day hikers and long-distance backpackers alike.

This short hike to Upper Twin Lake is suitable as a weekend trip or as a day hike. The subalpine lake basin is one of the most scenic spots in the Kaiser Wilderness, situated beneath the splintered granite crest of Kaiser Ridge. If crowds bother you, avoid this hike on holiday weekends. With three trails leading to Upper Twin Lake, the basin can be downright overcrowded.

The trail begins behind the information signboard on the west side of FR 5 and winds a level course along the edge of a selectively logged forest, staying inside an unlogged forest of lodgepole pine and red and white fir. After a few hundred yards, you enter the Kaiser Wilderness at a Sierra National Forest sign and then begin descending along the sometimes rocky trail. Lodgepole pines dominate the forest that stands among boulder-dotted grassy openings that host sagebrush, aspen, currant, and wildflowers such as aster, yarrow, mule ears, groundsel, and cinquefoil.

The descent ends when you reach the alder-lined banks of Kaiser Creek. Turn left and briefly follow the east bank upstream. Where the trail appears to end, make a hard right turn and cross the large logs spanning the creek. The stock ford lies a few yards downstream from the log crossing. Just a few yards beyond the crossing, you probably won't notice the seldom-used Kaiser Creek Trail joining your trail on the right (north).

Cross back to the east bank of Kaiser Creek at another log/stock ford

Twin Lakes

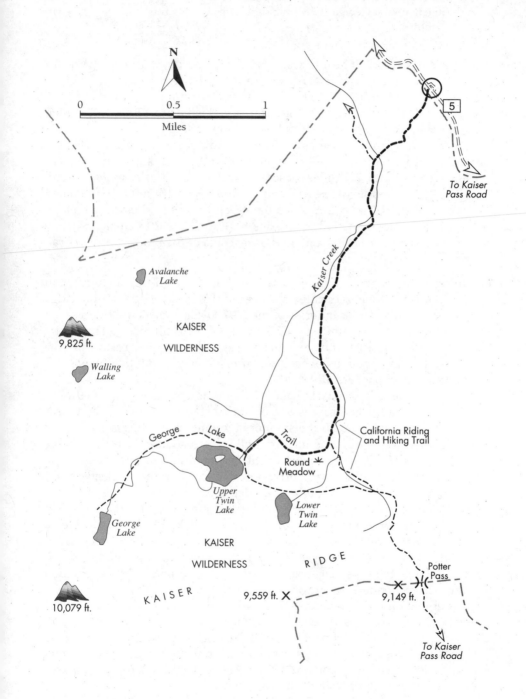

N

0   0.5   1
Miles

To Kaiser
Pass Road

5

Kaiser Creek

Avalanche
Lake

KAISER

WILDERNESS

9,825 ft.

Walling
Lake

George   Lake

Trail

California Riding
and Hiking Trail

Round
Meadow

Upper
Twin
Lake

Lower
Twin
Lake

George
Lake

KAISER

WILDERNESS   R I D G E

Potter
Pass

K A I S E R   9,559 ft. ✕   9,149 ft.

10,079 ft.

To Kaiser
Pass Road

crossing, then resume the pleasant, gradual uphill walk through the pine and fir forest. A rich understory of green shrubs and the verdant foliage of myriad wildflowers complement this shady forest. After 1.9 miles, rock-hop the Round Meadow branch of Kaiser Creek. Beyond this crossing, the trail ascends a steady, moderate to sometimes steep grade, and rises through an increasingly rockbound landscape with extensive areas of bare granite and glacier-deposited boulders (erratics). Red fir and western white pine become the dominant forest trees during this ascent.

At 2.3 miles and 8,480 feet, you reach a junction on a sagebrush-clad slope. The left fork, which you can use to loop back to this junction from Upper Twin Lake, is signed for Badger Flat. For now, turn right onto the fork signed for Twin Lakes (the George Lake Trail). The trail quickly tops a rise and turns west, traversing open slopes studded with lodgepole pine and aspen. Above the verdant spread of Round Meadow, enjoy splendid views along the way of the broken north faces and tree-feathered crests of Kaiser Ridge. This traverse soon curves northwest and crests a minor saddle set beneath a broken slope of metamorphic rocks.

Beyond this saddle, you soon come to another small creek and once again cross its course via logs. On the stream's west bank, turn left (south). After a brief ascent, stroll down to the northeast shore of the lovely, trout-filled waters of Upper Twin Lake. Broken, ice-chiseled granite rises behind the lake to tree-studded Kaiser Ridge, and a bold array of cliffs and 10,000-foot peaks rises immediately west and southwest of the lake.

Ice-polished granite slopes and a scattering of red fir, western white pine, and lodgepole pine add to the beauty of the basin. It lies in a lovely subalpine setting, a miniature version of the High Sierra. Despite the lake's size, there are only a handful of suitable campsites above its west and northwest shores. The heavily impacted sites adjacent to the lakeshore are closed to camping and should be avoided. Fishing is often excellent for the abundant pan-sized trout.

At the trail junction above Upper Twin Lake, the right-branching trail leads west and ascends 500 feet in 1 mile to George Lake. The southbound trail to the left can be taken to loop back to the Round Meadow trail junction in 1.4 miles. If you choose the latter option, follow the trail above Upper Twin Lake's east shore and then curve east after ascending to a pine- and fir-clad saddle (no camping here). The trail then descends past a shallow tarn and soon reaches the north shore of Lower Twin Lake. This lake lies in a more confined basin than its larger "twin" and is long, narrow, fringed by grassy shores, and brimming with trout. Away from its shoreline, a forest of red fir and lodgepole pine shelters many fine camping areas.

Beyond Lower Twin Lake, follow the trail eastward through an open forest of pine, fir, and aspen, gradually descending to a traverse above and south of Round Meadow. Vistas en route stretch northeast to the lofty crest of the Silver Divide and north to the dark peaks of the Ritter Range. After walking 1 mile from Upper Twin Lake, you reach a junction and turn left (northwest) toward Sample Meadow. This narrow, infrequently used trail descends

Upper Twin Lake is a scenic destination for a day hike or overnighter in the Kaiser Wilderness.

above a small, wildflower-decked stream and reaches a step-across ford of that stream alongside the pine- and aspen-fringed margin of Round Meadow. A profusion of colorful wildflowers accent the streambanks here in summer, including red columbine, Richardson's geranium, larkspur, cinquefoil, cow parsnip, and the tall composite mountain helenium.

The trail ahead skirts the eastern margin of the meadow, briefly passing through thorny gooseberry thickets. Step across the same small stream; a fine campsite lies just beyond the crossing. Ahead, you almost immediately rock-hop the stream again at the northeast edge of Round Meadow. From here, ascend slightly to a junction, turn right (north), and backtrack for 2.3 miles to the trailhead.

23 Onion Valley to Whitney Portal

Highlights:	This long backpack traces the highest segment of the John Muir/Pacific Crest Trail (PCT), featuring far-reaching vistas, vast stretches of alpine terrain, and excellent fishing. It traverses what is perhaps the most dramatic high-mountain landscape in the lower 48 states.
General location:	Southern Sierra Nevada, John Muir Wilderness and Sequoia–Kings Canyon Wilderness, 10 miles southwest of Independence and 70 miles east of Fresno.
Type of hike:	Point-to-point backpack, 7 to 10 days.
Distance:	49.5 miles.
Difficulty:	Moderately strenuous.
Elevation gain and loss:	+11,580 feet, -11,020 feet.
Trailhead elevations:	9,180 feet (Onion Valley); 8,361 feet (Whitney Portal).
High point:	Mount Whitney, 14,495 feet.
Best season:	Mid-July through early October.
Water availability:	Abundant.
Maps:	Inyo National Forest map; Sequoia–Kings Canyon and John Muir Wilderness areas map (two sheets, topographic); USGS Kearsarge Peak, Mt. Clarence King, Mt. Brewer, Mt. Williamson, Mt. Kaweah, Mt.Whitney, and Mt. Langley 7.5-minute quads.
Permits:	A wilderness permit is required and can be obtained at the Mt. Whitney Ranger Station in Lone Pine. Daily entry quotas are in effect. Reservations for permits can be made up to six months in advance (see Appendix A for information).

Key points:

0.0   Onion Valley Trailhead.

5.0   Kearsarge Pass.

5.8   Junction above Kearsarge Lakes; bear left (southwest) and descend toward Bullfrog Lake.

7.6   Junction with John Muir/PCT; turn left (south).

9.1   Junction with Bubbs Creek Trail; bear left (east).

9.8   Vidette Meadow.

12.6   Junction with Center Basin Trail; bear right (southeast).

17.1   Forester Pass.

21.4   Junction with westbound Lake South America Trail; stay left (southeast).

22.1   Junction with northeast-branching Shepherd Pass Trail; stay right (south).

22.2   Junction with southbound trail to Kern River; bear left (southeast).

26.7   Ford Wright Creek.

27.8   Ford Wallace Creek.

31.1   Junction of John Muir Trail and PCT above Whitney Creek; turn left (east) onto John Muir Trail.

32.1   Crabtree Ranger Station.

37.2   Junction with Mt. Whitney Trail; turn left (north) to climb Mt. Whitney.

39.0   Summit of Mt. Whitney.

40.8   Return to Mt. Whitney Trail junction; turn left (southeast) onto John Muir Trail.

41.0   Trail Crest.

43.3   Trail Camp.

45.2   Mirror Lake.

46.7   Lone Pine Lake Trail junction; bear left (north).

49.5   Whitney Portal Trailhead.

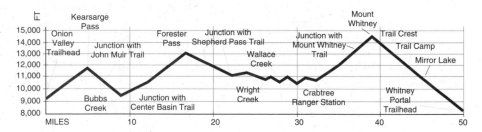

Finding the trailhead: From US Highway 395 in Independence, turn west onto Market Street where a sign indicates Onion Valley. Follow this ascending paved road for 15 miles to the large parking area at the road's end.

To find the Whitney Portal Trailhead, turn west from US 395 in Lone Pine onto the signed Whitney Portal Road and proceed 13 miles to the trailhead just east of the small Whitney Portal Store and Cafe.

The hike: This memorable high-country trek traverses a portion of the John Muir/PCT through some of the most magnificent mountain terrain in the nation. The far-ranging views from the sixteenth-highest mountain in the United States (there are 15 higher summits in Alaska) are only some of the many tremendous views hikers enjoy along this route.

Although portions of this route can be quite popular with hikers, solitude can still be found. Once over Forester Pass, a multitude of opportunities exist for satisfying side trips to some of the most remote and spectacular lake basins in the range. You could spend weeks in the upper Kern River drainage, and encounter few other hikers, while exploring lonely lake basins, climbing peaks, fishing, or simply contemplating the beauty of this glorious land.

Plan at least one week for this hike; two weeks would allow you to fully enjoy the magnificence of this alpine wilderness. Fishing is good in many of the high lakes and in most of the streams along the way. Nights can be quite cool at the very high elevations this hike traverses; overnight lows in the 20s are common at elevations of 12,000 feet and more, even in July and August.

This point-to-point trip requires that hikers either leave another vehicle at the Whitney Portal Trailhead (the recommended alternative) or that they hitchhike 53 miles back to the Onion Valley Trailhead. Contact the Mount Whitney Ranger Station in Lone Pine for information regarding private shuttle service operators.

Bears are increasingly raiding and damaging vehicles at the Onion Valley Trailhead and raiding campsites at some backcountry locations along the route of this hike. Hikers must not leave food, ice chests, or anything that may attract bears inside their vehicles when parked at Onion Valley. The best defense against bears in the backcountry are bear-resistant food canisters. These food canisters are *required* to be used when camping east of Kearsarge Pass. The canisters can be found at many sporting goods stores and are available for rent from the Mount Whitney Ranger Station.

Hikers must also be aware that no campfires are allowed east of Kearsarge Pass, above 10,000 feet in Kings Canyon National Park, or above 10,400 feet in Sequoia National Park. Since most of this trip lies above these elevations, expect to pass many nights without a campfire.

Entry into the Mount Whitney Zone is strictly regulated by a quota system that is in effect between May 22 and October 15. The zone extends from the Lone Pine Lake Trail junction on the east to the outlet of Timberline Lake on the west. Hikers are *required* to have a special stamp on their wilderness permit to enter or exit this zone. The stamp will be issued along with your permit. Due to the extreme popularity of the Mount Whitney Zone, you are strongly advised to make advanced reservations (for a fee), up to six months in advance of the trip. Reservations can be made through the Inyo National Forest Reservation Service, a private contractor, located at the Big Pine Chamber of Commerce. Contact this service by telephone at (888) 374-3773. Permits will be mailed directly to the group leader. Contact any Inyo National Forest ranger station for an information sheet about permit reservations (see Appendix A).

One alternate route that avoids the Mount Whitney Zone would be to follow the PCT south from the John Muir Trail junction above Whitney Creek. This trail leads 11.4 miles to the junction with the Siberian Pass Trail above Rock Creek (see Hike 12), via a 10,900-foot pass northeast of Mount Guyot. Then follow the last half of Hike 12 for 10.3 miles to the Cottonwood Lakes Trailhead above Horseshoe Meadow.

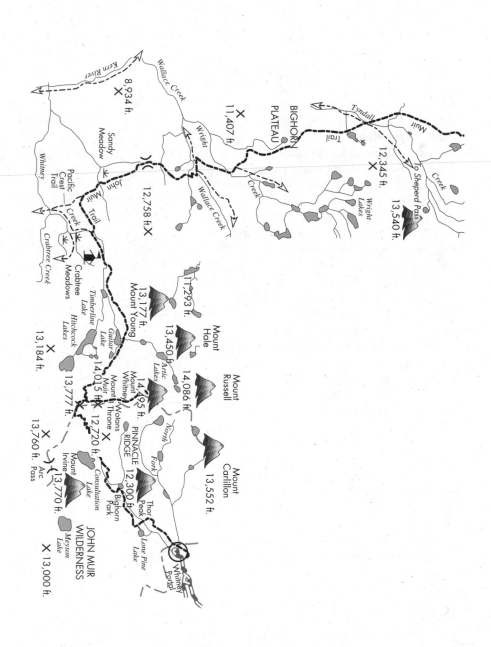

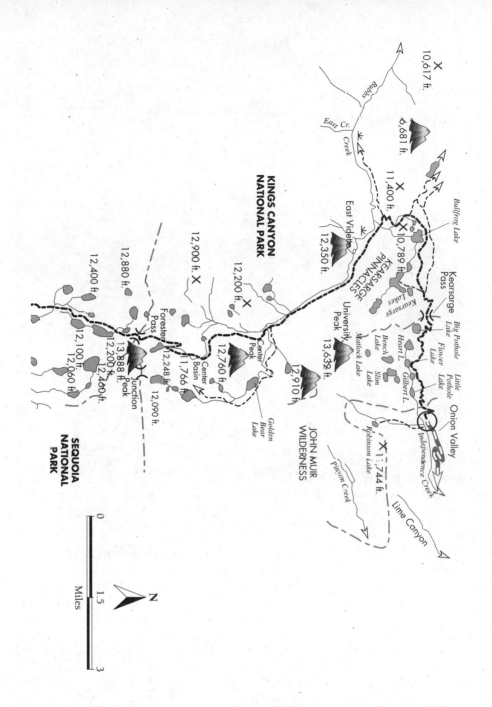

KINGS CANYON NATIONAL PARK

SEQUOIA NATIONAL PARK

JOHN MUIR WILDERNESS

KEARSARGE PINNACLES

X 10,617 ft.

6,681 ft.

East Cr.

Creek

Bubbs

East Cr. Creek

11,400 ft. X

X 10,789 ft.

Bullfrog Lake

East Vidette

12,350 ft.

Kearsarge Pass

Kearsarge Lakes

Big Pothole Lake

Little Pothole Lake

Flower Lake

Bench Lake

Heart L.

Gilbert L.

Slim Lake

University Peak

13,632 ft.

Matlock Lake

Onion Valley

Independence Creek

Robinson Lake

X 11,744 ft.

12,900 ft. X

12,200 ft. X

Center Peak

12,760 ft.

12,910 ft.

Golden Bear Lake

Pinon Creek

Lime Canyon

12,880 ft.

12,400 ft.

Forester Pass

13,888 ft. Junction Peak

12,200 ft.

12,460 ft.

12,100 ft.

12,060 ft.

12,248 ft.

11,766 ft.

Center Basin

12,090 ft.

0   1.5   3

Miles

N

117

Hikers en route to Mount Whitney via the John Muir–Pacific Crest Trail cross the spread of Sandy Meadow and enjoy vistas of Kaweah Peaks Ridge rising above Kern Canyon.

From the Onion Valley Trailhead, head west past an information sign and begin a northwest traverse across open slopes and into a red fir stand. Just before reaching the first switchback, you may notice an unmaintained right-branching trail that leads into Golden Trout Lake's basin. Your path levels off on a small bench, the first of a series of benches in this glacial eastside canyon, and then enters the John Muir Wilderness.

The trail now climbs 500 feet among scattered lodgepole and foxtail pines to tiny Little Pothole Lake. A short, level stretch allows you to catch your breath before another steep ascent of 400 feet to Gilbert Lake. The sky-piercing crag of 13,632-foot University Peak can be seen over a low, tree-covered ridge to the southwest of Gilbert Lake.

After a stroll around the sparsely forested north shore of this overused lake, climb briefly along Independence Creek to the outlet of Flower Lake and a junction with a southbound trail leading into the Matlock Lake basin. If you wish to camp before ascending to Kearsarge Pass, consider the Matlock

Lake area, which sees little use. Bench Lake, nestled in a cirque 350 feet above Matlock Lake, offers very private camping as well as good fishing.

Whitebark pines begin to dominate the forest as you ascend above Flower Lake through the boulder-dotted terrain. You level off briefly on a timberline bench that has a trickle of water—the last easily attainable water before the pass. The route now switchbacks up a rocky slope among stunted whitebark pines, passing high above the isolated Heart Lake. The trail levels off on yet another bench that is sandy and sparsely vegetated with wind- and snowdrift-flattened whitebark pines. The trail from here to the pass is plainly visible and maintains a gentle grade while traversing the south slopes of Mount Gould.

Big Pothole Lake, lying in a 100-foot depression, comes into view as you make the final traverse to surmount the knife-edged Sierra Nevada crest of Kearsarge Pass at 11,823 feet. To the east, the Independence Creek drainage plunges abruptly into Owens Valley, where the town of Independence and US 395 are visible. The Inyo Mountains soar skyward to the east of this valley. To the west, Bullfrog Lake lies below the reddish, glacially scoured slopes of 11,868-foot Mount Bago. To the southwest lie the Kearsarge Lakes, nestled in a high basin below the broken crags of the Kearsarge Pinnacles. Far on the southwestern horizon sit some of the most awe-inspiring mountain peaks in California—the Kings-Kern Divide and the jagged northern peaks of the Great Western Divide.

As you enter Kings Canyon National Park, your route descends rocky slopes for about 0.75 mile to a junction. The right-hand trail traverses high above the basin and meets the John Muir Trail after about 2 miles. Turn left and descend 0.1 mile to a junction with the trail to popular Kearsarge Lakes, where camping is limited to one night and no wood fires are allowed.

Turn right and descend the grassy and rocky basin as the timberline forest cover thickens, contouring above Bullfrog Lake's north shore. The superb view south across the lake's placid waters, dominated by the fluted pyramid of East Vidette, is yet another of the splendid vistas captured along this magnificent high-mountain trek. Bullfrog Lake has been closed to camping for many years due to past overuse and remains so indefinitely. After leaving Bullfrog Lake, your trail passes two small tarns and then descends to meet the John Muir/PCT. This junction marks the first legal camping area on your hike since the Kearsarge Lakes, although campsites here are scarce.

Shaded by lodgepole pines, begin a 1,000-foot descent into Bubbs Creek, crossing two small streams en route and capturing many inspiring views into upper Bubbs Creek and the U-shaped canyon of Center Basin in the southeast. You finally emerge onto the floor of Bubbs Creek Canyon and reach a junction. Turn left here and proceed up the canyon, passing the tree-covered area labeled "Vidette Meadow" on the quad. The heavy lodgepole pine forest and the large stream of Bubbs Creek make this a pleasant, sheltered camping area. Most of the campsites between here and Whitney Portal are at or above timberline.

The trail continues ascending the U-shaped valley of Bubbs Creek, flanked by the towering Sierra crest on the east and the jagged ridge of East Spur on the west. About 3.5 miles from the previous junction you meet—but avoid—the unmaintained Center Basin Trail on your left. That trail ascends Center Basin and crosses the Sierra crest at Junction Pass, descends into the eastside Shepherd Creek drainage, re-crosses the crest at Shepherd Pass, and then descends to the John Muir Trail in upper Tyndall Creek. It was the main route of the John Muir Trail before Forester Pass was opened in 1932. The lakes in Center Basin offer good fishing and secluded camping.

Bearing right at that junction, your trail soon crosses Center Basin's creek and ascends the grassy and rocky slopes clothed in a thinning timberline forest. Passing under the precipitous west slopes of 12,760-foot Center Peak, you have inspiring views up the canyon to some very rugged peaks, dominated by the landmark pyramid of 13,888-foot Junction Peak. After climbing past a few persistent whitebark pines and the last sheltered campsites for miles, you quickly reach the boulder-covered outlet creek of often-frozen Lake 12,248. The gap of Forester Pass can be seen above the rocky slopes southwest of the lake. The smooth northwest wall of Junction Peak soars above the southeast end of the lake, where the Kings-Kern Divide joins the Sierra crest.

From this lake, the trail makes a long switchback while ascending a north-trending ridge. Leaving the ridge and now ascending alpine slopes, your route (often obscured by snow) makes several final switchbacks to surmount the Kings-Kern Divide at Forester Pass. At an elevation of 13,200 feet, it is the highest pass on the John Muir/PCT. As a result, most of the Sierra Nevada crest is visible, from Junction Peak north to the Palisade Crest, in addition to a host of alpine peaks lying west of the crest in Kings Canyon National Park. To the south lie several lakes resting at elevations of 12,000 feet or more, the Great Western Divide, and the deep trench of Kern Canyon. West of Forester Pass, the highest lake in California can be seen nestled in a high cirque on the slopes of Caltech Peak. At an elevation of more than 12,880 feet, it's not surprising that this alpine lake is almost always frozen. A sign at this cold and windy pass informs you that you are entering Sequoia National Park.

Your southbound trail descends from the pass via numerous switchbacks that were dynamited into solid rock. In early summer, this stretch of trail is snow covered and treacherous, at best. After reaching the floor of the basin, skirt the two large lakes lying at the western foot of Diamond Mesa's alpine plateau. Then descend to ford a Tyndall Creek tributary and traverse above a small lake. The pointed crown of 14,018-foot Mount Tyndall can be seen from here, rising 4 miles to the east on the Sierra crest. Circumnavigate an isolated stand of timberline trees and meet a westbound trail that leads to Lake South America and the remote headwaters of the upper Kern River. If time allows, many rewarding side trips can be made via this trail.

Continue south on the John Muir/PCT, enter a lodgepole and foxtail pine forest, and reach a junction, 0.7 mile below the Lake South America Trail, with a northeastbound trail leading to Shepherd Pass. Just over 0.1 mile

Kearsarge Pass Trail.

beyond that junction, you meet yet another trail that branches southwest and descends Tyndall Creek to Kern Canyon. Bear left and a short, forested ascent brings you to two small tarns that are, at times, quite popular with backcountry campers. Now begin a gentle traverse along the west slopes of Tawny Point, passing several impressive, wind-sculptured foxtail pines.

After hiking 1.5 miles from the previous junction, your trail levels off on the alpine expanse of Bighorn Plateau; another glorious vista unfolds, surpassed only by the summit views from Mount Whitney. From this point, obtain your first glimpse of the unmistakable, sloping summit plateau of Mount Whitney, lying on the southeastern horizon. Your trail descends from the plateau to Wright Creek via several grassy benches. A ford of Wright Creek (difficult in early summer) brings you to some good campsites shaded by lodgepole and foxtail pines on this large stream's southern banks. Cross over a low ridge and descend to a ford of Wallace Creek (also difficult in early summer), where you meet the westbound High Sierra Trail on your right and the eastbound trail to Wallace Lake on your left.

Beyond Wallace Creek, begin a moderate 550-foot ascent to a pass at 10,964 feet. If you stop to catch your breath on this steady ascent, you will be rewarded with new inspiring vistas. The broad, sloping plateau of Mount Barnard, rising above the head of Wallace Creek in the northeast, was once labeled a 14,000-foot peak before being resurveyed by the U.S. Geological Service. Now, with an official elevation of 13,990 feet, it is the highest peak in California that is less than 14,000 feet. Its easy southwest slopes beckon peakbaggers and reward them with breathtaking panoramas.

From the foxtail pine–shaded pass, descend to the lush, wildflower-speckled spread of Sandy Meadow. The Kaweah Peaks Ridge and aptly named Red Spur are seen across the meadow on the western horizon, framed by trailside lodgepole and foxtail pines. Beyond Sandy Meadow, cross a small creek, ascend to a low, foxtail pine–covered ridge, and reach a junction. The PCT continues south, but you turn left onto the John Muir Trail. Soon the massive, avalanche-scarred west slope of your destination—Mount Whitney—comes into view.

The trail soon approaches the grassy banks of Whitney Creek, where Mount Chamberlain comes into view on the southeastern skyline, rising near vertically above the Crabtree Lakes basin. The peaks in this region typically have gentle, unglaciated summit plateaus and south-facing slopes that contrast dramatically with their precipitous north faces that were scoured, scarred, and quarried by repeated glacial episodes.

After fording Whitney Creek, meet a southwestbound trail leading to the PCT. This trail drops into Crabtree Meadows, where solitude-seeking hikers can leave the trail and begin hiking east on unmaintained trails into the Crabtree Lakes Basin. Middle Crabtree Lake, labeled "Lake 11,312" on the quad, contains a good population of large golden trout.

Continue east on the John Muir Trail, pass the seasonal Crabtree Ranger Station, and skirt a small pond before re-crossing Whitney Creek. A short, steep climb brings you to the outlet of Timberline Lake (closed to camping), where the bulk of Mount Whitney is framed by low, rocky, sparsely forested hills. Here you enter the Mount Whitney Zone.

Leave the last timberline trees behind, cross over a low rise, and then descend to the inlet stream of appropriately named Guitar Lake. Campsites around this alpine lake are terribly overused and should be avoided. The near-vertical north walls of Mount Hitchcock are partially obscured from view by the rounded, glacially smoothed ridge separating Guitar Lake from the lesser-used Hitchcock Lakes.

From Guitar Lake, the trail ascends past a small lake—the last water until Trail Camp in Lone Pine Creek. Ascend to the head of the basin and begin negotiating a well-designed series of switchbacks that lead up the west slope of the Sierra Nevada crest. This high-elevation ascent will leave even hikers in top physical condition short of breath. As you near the trail junction at the top of this climb, notice that the fragrant blue flowers of the sky pilot are the only visible forms of life at this elevation.

You finally reach the junction with the Mount Whitney Trail at an elevation of 13,480 feet, marked by a metal sign listing various destinations. The deep blue Hitchcock Lakes lie directly below you, while the fluted north face of Mount Hitchcock, soaring 1,400 feet above the lakes, will tempt climbers to return with their gear to challenge this peak's mighty walls. Turn left (north) onto the Mount Whitney Trail. After a few switchbacks, traverse the west slopes of 14,015-foot Mount Muir, a 350-foot class 3 scramble from the trail. Proceed north along the spectacular, windswept Sierra crest, passing several windy notches in the crest and accompanied by continuously inspiring vistas.

Pass just west of Keeler Needle, an easy scramble to the east, and negotiate the final, often snow-covered ascent to the summit plateau. A stroll of 0.3 mile eastward on the plateau brings you to the summit of Mount Whitney. A Park Service sign bolted to the summit slab indicates the exact elevation of the peak within inches. The summit shelter, just west of the peak, was constructed in 1909 by the Smithsonian Institution to provide shelter for astronomers.

Needless to say, the view is a vast one, probably the most spectacular vista accessible by trail in the range. The entire Great Western Divide is visible to the west across the absurdly straight trench of Kern Canyon. To the northwest, the peaks of the western slope fade into distant, forest-covered hills beyond the jagged crest of the Kings-Kern Divide. The Sierra crest is visible as far north as the Palisades.

Kern Peak and portions of the Kern Plateau meet your gaze to the south. To the east, the town of Lone Pine lies more than 10,000 feet below in the Owens Valley, which stretches from Owens Lake in the south to the vicinity of the town of Big Pine in the north. The Inyo-White Mountains rise abruptly east of the valley, with Telescope Peak and the Panamint Range forming the far southeastern horizon.

After reluctantly leaving the often cold and windy summit, retrace your route for 1.8 miles to the trail junction at 13,480 feet, turn left, and ascend 120 feet to Trail Crest's pass at 13,600 feet. The trail then descends via about 100 switchbacks and flattens out at 12,000-foot Trail Camp, usually crowded with Mount Whitney–bound hikers. Beyond Trail Camp, pass above the large Consultation Lake, cross Lone Pine Creek, and then descend briefly to another crossing of Lone Pine Creek at Trailside Meadow, a narrow strip of grassy, wildflower-speckled terrain that is closed to camping.

Next, pass above the shores of Mirror Lake (closed to camping because of previous overuse) and, under foxtail pine shade, stroll through Bighorn Park, also known as Outpost Camp. This area is usually the first overnight stop for Whitney–bound hikers.

Avoid the lateral trail to Lone Pine Lake that is located below the willow-choked meadow of Bighorn Park, where you leave the Mount Whitney Zone. Instead, cross Lone Pine Creek one final time and begin a steep descent. Crossing the boisterous North Fork Lone Pine Creek and passing a west-bound trail, negotiate the final descent through a sparse Jeffrey pine and red fir forest to the trailhead.

Hikers who did not leave another vehicle at this trailhead or arrange for a shuttle will have to hitchhike back to Onion Valley. Due to the summer traffic to and from both trailheads, hitchhiking should present no major problems.

24 North Fork Big Pine Creek

Highlights:	This memorable trip leads you into one of the most majestic east-side canyons in the Sierra Nevada and features productive fishing in numerous timberline lakes, with side trip options that include a visit to the Sierra's largest glacier.
General location:	Southern Sierra Nevada, John Muir Wilderness (Inyo National Forest), 8 miles west of Big Pine.
Type of hike:	Semi-loop backpack, 3 to 5 days.
Distance:	12.7 miles.
Difficulty:	Moderately strenuous.
Elevation gain and loss:	3,100 feet.
Trailhead elevation:	7,700 feet.
High point:	10,800 feet.
Best season:	July through mid-October.
Water availability:	Abundant.
Maps:	Inyo National Forest map; John Muir and Sequoia–Kings Canyon Wilderness areas map (two sheets, topographic); USGS Coyote Flat, Mt. Thompson, and North Palisade 7.5-minute quads.
Permits:	A wilderness permit is required for overnight use and can be obtained at either the White Mountain Ranger District office in Bishop or at the Mt. Whitney Ranger Station in Lone Pine. Reservations for permits can be made up to six months in advance (see Appendix A for information).

Key points:

0.0   Big Pine Creek Trailhead.
1.6   Junction with unmaintained Baker Creek Trail and old trail descending into Big Pine Creek; continue straight ahead (west).
4.5   Junction with Black Lake Trail; turn right (northeast).
5.5   Black Lake.
6.2   Four-way junction below Fourth Lake; turn left (southeast) and begin descending.
6.7   Junction with Glacier Trail; stay left (east).
8.2   Return to Black Lake Trail junction north of First Lake; stay right (east) and retrace your route to the trailhead.
12.7   Big Pine Creek Trailhead.

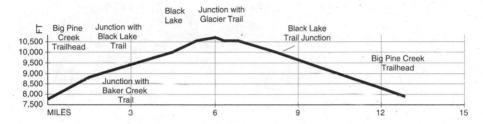

Finding the trailhead: From US Highway 395 in Big Pine, turn west onto Crocker Street where a sign indicates "Big Pine Recreation Area-9." Follow this paved road into the eastern Sierra for 10 miles to the signed parking area, about 0.5 mile below (east of) Glacier Lodge.

The hike: This scenic hike leads you into a deeply glaciated canyon, passing five Big Pine Lakes, providing views of some of the highest peaks in the Sierra, and offering glimpses of the large glaciers (by Sierra standards) that still cling to their flanks. All of the lakes along this hike are fishable, and campsites and water are easy to find. Campfires are prohibited throughout the Big Pine Creek drainage, so be sure to carry a backpack stove. The numerous side trip possibilities can extend this hike from a weekend to a week-long backpack.

The trail begins at the western edge of the parking area where a sign indicates the North Fork Trail. The trail heads west over a low hill, passes just above the pack station, and climbs moderately along a south-facing slope covered with sagebrush, bitterbrush, rabbitbrush, and scattered Jeffrey pines. Over-the-shoulder views are excellent, especially of the U-shaped canyon of Big Pine Creek framing the Inyo Mountains on the eastern horizon. Immediately across the canyon to the south, 11,896-foot Kid Mountain skyrockets more than 4,000 feet directly above Glacier Lodge. In the southwest, your view includes the Middle Palisade Glacier, the Palisade Crest, and 14,040-foot Middle Palisade, soaring above the head of the South Fork Big Pine Creek.

After hiking less than 1 mile, the trail bends northwest and passes above roaring First Falls. You reach a junction after strolling 1.6 miles from the trailhead. The right-hand, or northeast-branching trail, climbs steeply over

North Fork Big Pine Creek

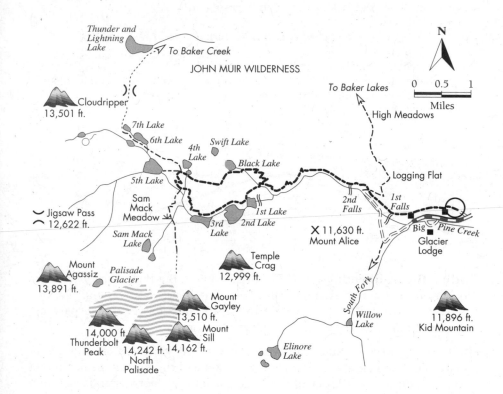

N

Thunder and
Lightning
Lake

To Baker Creek

JOHN MUIR WILDERNESS

To Baker Lakes

0   0.5   1

Miles

High Meadows

Cloudripper
13,501 ft.

7th Lake

6th Lake

Swift Lake

4th
Lake

Black Lake

Logging Flat

5th Lake

Sam
Mack
Meadow

1st Lake

2nd
Falls

1st
Falls

Jigsaw Pass
12,622 ft.

Sam Mack
Lake

3rd
Lake

2nd Lake

X 11,630 ft.
Mount Alice

Big   Pine Creek

Glacier
Lodge

Mount
Agassiz
13,891 ft.

Palisade
Glacier

Temple
Crag
12,999 ft.

South Fork

Willow
Lake

11,896 ft.
Kid Mountain

Mount
Gayley
13,510 ft.

14,000 ft.
Thunderbolt
Peak

Mount
Sill
14,242 ft. 14,162 ft.
North
Palisade

Elinore
Lake

the ridge into Baker Creek and is seldom used. The left-branching trail descends
for 0.3 mile to the end of the old closed road that's visible directly below.

Continue straight ahead toward the cascading Second Falls, and after a
few short switchbacks, enter the John Muir Wilderness. The trail quickly
parallels the noisy North Fork, and lodgepole pines begin mixing into the
Jeffrey pine forest. As you enter the aspen-shaded Cienega Mirth area, the
brush begins to give way to grassy areas with scattered boulders and
wildflowers, watered by springs emanating from the south-facing slopes to
the north.

At the west end of Cienega Mirth, pass a stone cabin and begin a steady
ascent up the canyon for 1.5 miles to the next trail junction, crossing through
a lodgepole, whitebark, and limber pine forest. En route, note the contrast
in vegetation between the south-facing slopes and the north-facing slopes of
Mount Alice and Peak 12,861 to the south. The south-facing slopes are choked
with mountain mahogany, and stands of conifers do not replace the brush
until reaching the 10,600-foot level. Above that point, a moderately thick

forest of lodgepole, whitebark, and limber pine covers the slopes up to an elevation of about 12,000 feet.

In sharp contrast, the trees directly across the creek on the north-facing slopes are stunted, reaching their boundaries of growth only a few hundred feet above the trail, at elevations of 9,800 to 10,000 feet. The timberline on either slope is obviously quite different, not only from each other, but also from the typical elevations of timberline in this region of the High Sierra. This area provides an excellent example of the influence of slope aspect on vegetation types.

After reaching the above-mentioned junction, turn right; a sign here indicates Black Lake. The left-hand trail forms the homebound leg of your loop. Your trail switchbacks up the dry, south-facing slopes, leading you through sagebrush and curl-leaf mountain mahogany, passing a reliable spring, and becoming shaded by lodgepole pine and aspen at around 10,400 feet. You have good views across the canyon to the First and Second Lakes during this ascent.

The trail eventually levels off, crosses the boulder-covered outlet stream of Black Lake, enters a subalpine forest of whitebark and lodgepole pine, and finally reaches Black Lake at 10,600 feet. There are many good campsites from which to choose, and the abundant trout population in the lake should keep anglers busy. From the lake, the trail climbs over a low, forested ridge, where you are likely to be accompanied by the crow-like call of the Clark's nutcracker. This large, gray, black, and white member of the jay family is commonly seen and heard in timberline forests, where it feeds on pine nuts.

From the ridge, descend to cross the small outlet of Fourth Lake just below a small pond. At the four-way junction, the right-hand (northwest) fork leads past Fourth Lake to the Sixth and Seventh Lakes at the head of the canyon. Straight ahead (west) the trail leads to Fifth Lake in 0.25 mile. At an elevation of 10,759 feet, it is arguably the most beautiful lake in the Big Pine chain.

Turn left (southeast) and begin descending numerous switchbacks. After hiking 0.5 mile, pass the signed Glacier Trail which departs on a southerly course. This trail crosses the North Fork, ascends to Sam Mack Meadow, climbs the ridge east of the meadow, and eventually leads to a viewpoint just east of the Palisade Glacier, the largest glacier in the Sierra Nevada. Don't venture out onto the glacier unless you are experienced in glacial travel; even then, never do so alone.

Beyond this junction, the trail approaches the north shore of Third Lake. The western end of this lake is filling up with silt that's carried down the creek from the Palisade Glacier. This active glacier has moved downslope as much as 40 feet in one year. The milky-green waters of First, Second, and Third Lakes attest to the immense grinding power of this slowly moving icefield.

Beyond Third Lake, the trail meanders down to the massive Second Lake, reaching a glorious viewpoint above the lake's northwestern shore. Directly across the lake stands the convoluted mass of pinnacles and buttresses known as Temple Crag, just 1 foot short of 13,000 feet. To the west of Temple Crag are the high peaks looming above the Palisade Glacier, with three rising higher than 14,000 feet. These majestic peaks make an unforgettable reflection in the calm waters of Second Lake.

Continue your descent and traverse above the north shore of First Lake, where the influence of drier conditions begins to show, particularly in the form of scattered mountain mahogany and an occasional Jeffrey pine. Below the lake, cross a small creek, reach the Black Lake Trail junction, turn right, and retrace your route back to the trailhead.

For the adventurous and experienced hiker, a satisfying 19-mile loop trip is possible. From Seventh Lake at the head of the North Fork, a faint trail climbs to the prominent gap north of the lake, descends to Thunder and Lightning Lake, merges with the unmaintained Baker Creek Trail, and intersects the North Fork Trail 1.6 miles from the trailhead.

25 Lake Sabrina to Hungry Packer Lake

Highlights:	This short but memorable backpack leads you into a spectacular peak-rimmed alpine lake basin in the eastern Sierra and features productive fishing and numerous side trip options to more than six alpine lakes.
General location:	Southern Sierra Nevada, John Muir Wilderness (Inyo National Forest), 12 miles southwest of Bishop.
Type of hike:	Round-trip backpack, 3 to 5 days.
Distance:	13.2 miles.
Difficulty:	Moderate.
Elevation gain and loss:	2,140 feet.
Trailhead elevation:	8,960 feet.
High point:	Hungry Packer Lake, 11,100 feet.
Best season:	July through mid-October.
Water availability:	Abundant.
Maps:	Inyo National Forest map; John Muir and Sequoia–Kings Canyon Wilderness areas map (two sheets, topographic); USGS Mt. Thompson, and Mt. Darwin 7.5-minute quads.
Permits:	Wilderness permits are required for overnight use. Seasonal quotas are in effect. Obtain permit at the White Mountain Ranger District office in Bishop. Reservations for permits can be made up to six months in advance (see Appendix A for information).

Key points:

0.0   Lake Sabrina parking area.

0.6   Trailhead.

1.8   Junction with George Lake Trail; stay right (southwest).

2.9   Cross outlet of Blue Lake.

3.2   Junction with southbound trail to Baboon Lakes; turn right (northwest).

5.5   Junction with trail to Midnight Lake; bear left (southeast).

6.6   Hungry Packer Lake.

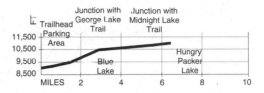

Finding the trailhead: From US Highway 395 in Bishop, turn west onto California Highway 168 where a sign indicates South Lake, North Lake, and Lake Sabrina. Follow this paved road up the canyon of Bishop Creek and into the Inyo National Forest. Bear right after 14 miles where the road to South Lake forks left. Drive 3 more miles to the signed Sabrina Basin parking area at the junction with the westbound North Lake Road.

The hike: The immense glacier-carved bowl of the Middle Fork Bishop Creek, popularly known as Sabrina Basin, boasts three dozen lakes, ranging in elevation from 9,700 to 12,400 feet. Many of these lakes feature excellent fishing, and all have a backdrop of jagged crags that approach 14,000 feet. The lower lakes are typically forest rimmed, while the higher lakes are rockbound. Some may even harbor icebergs throughout the summer.

This basin doesn't see quite as many hikers as the North and South Forks of Bishop Creek, primarily because there is no trail access here to lead over the Sierra crest into Kings Canyon National Park. Moreover, wilderness permit quotas improve your wilderness experience by limiting the number of hikers entering the basin each day during the peak hiking season, from the last Friday in June through September 15.

Since there is no trail leading over the Sierra crest, Sabrina Basin is a hiking destination rather than a hiking corridor. In addition to good fishing, you can spend many days exploring remote cirque basins, many of them harboring high, lonely lakes. The lofty crags of the Sierra crest offer ample challenges to seasoned mountaineers. Campsites and water in Sabrina Basin are plentiful. Be sure to carry a backpack stove since campfires are no longer allowed.

Begin this hike by walking south from the parking area on Lake Sabrina Road. The jagged, snowy peaks of the Sierra crest, piercing the sky to the south, divert your attention from this short section of pavement and give you an exhilarating taste of what lies ahead. Leave the road after 0.6 mile, turning left at the signed trailhead.

The trail traverses mostly open slopes above the east shore of Lake Sabrina. Sagebrush, mountain mahogany, scattered aspen, lodgepole and limber pine, and an occasional Sierra juniper, unmistakable because of its shaggy, reddish bark, clothe these slopes. After hiking 1.8 miles from the parking area, an

Lake Sabrina to Hungry Packer Lake • Lake Sabrina to Tyee Lakes

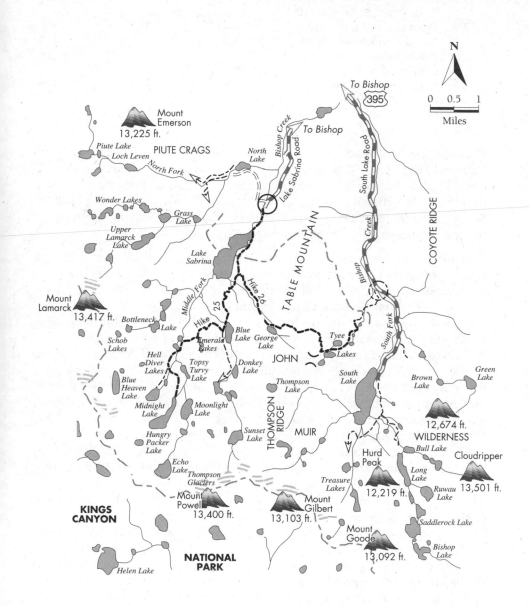

N

To Bishop
395

0   0.5   1
Miles

Mount Emerson
13,225 ft.

Piute Lake
Loch Leven

PIUTE CRAGS

North Fork

North Lake

Bishop Creek

To Bishop

Lake Sabrina Road

South Lake Road

COYOTE RIDGE

Wonder Lakes

Grass Lake

Upper Lamarck Lake

Lake Sabrina

Hike 26

TABLE MOUNTAIN

Bishop Creek

Mount Lamarck
13,417 ft.

Bottleneck Lake

Middle Fork

Hike 25

Blue Lake

George Lake

Tyee Lakes

South Fork

Schob Lakes

Emerald Lakes

JOHN

Hell Diver Lakes

Topsy Turvy Lake

Donkey Lake

Blue Heaven Lake

Midnight Lake

Moonlight Lake

Thompson Lake

THOMPSON RIDGE

South Lake

MUIR

Brown Lake

Green Lake

12,674 ft.
WILDERNESS

Hungry Packer Lake

Sunset Lake

Bull Lake

Cloudripper

Echo Lake

Thompson Glaciers

Hurd Peak

Long Lake

13,501 ft.

Ruwau Lake

Treasure Lakes

12,219 ft.

KINGS CANYON

Mount Powell
13,400 ft.

Mount Gilbert
13,103 ft.

Saddlerock Lake

NATIONAL PARK

Mount Goode
13,092 ft.

Bishop Lake

Helen Lake

eastbound trail leading to George Lake, Table Mountain, and the Tyee Lakes (see Hike 26) leaves your route on the left.

Bear right at this junction and continue south. The trail crosses the outlet creek of George Lake, quickly crosses another small creek, and begins a series of switchbacks under moderate lodgepole pine shade. About 1.1 miles beyond the George Lake Trail, you reach beautiful Blue Lake at 10,398 feet, probably the most heavily used lake in the basin, and with good reason. The view up the canyon across the lake is outstanding. The sparsely timbered talus slopes of Thompson Ridge rise well above the 12,000-foot level east of the lake. Campsites set in moderate forest cover are numerous around its irregular western shores.

The trail crosses the wide outlet of Blue Lake via a log jam and becomes faint along the west shore. Watch for ducks to lead the way when crossing the bare rock stretches. After hiking 0.3 mile from Blue Lake's outlet creek, you reach a junction. Straight ahead, the trail ascends the canyon to Baboon Lakes. A short cross-country jaunt above these lakes brings you to alpine Sunset Lake and the Thompson Glaciers—a highly recommended side trip. For now, turn right, skirt the edge of a small, stagnant pond, and begin a westward course across the basin. The trail is lost across occasional bare rock, but the alert hiker should have no trouble relocating it.

After 1.2 miles of pleasant hiking, pass the largest of the Emerald Lakes chain and then ascend a small ridge that provides excellent vistas of the surrounding terrain. The jagged peaks along the Sierra Nevada crest seem only a stone's throw away; indeed, you will soon be camping in their shadow. A short descent brings you near the shore of the small Dingleberry Lake. From here on up the basin, campsites and water are easy to find. A ford of the Middle Fork Bishop Creek is necessary a short distance above Dingleberry Lake.

You reach the junction with the trail to Midnight Lake after hiking 1.1 miles beyond the Emerald Lakes. This beautiful subalpine gem, with its backdrop of cliffs and rugged peaks, offers superb camping among stunted whitebark pines. Turn left at this junction and ascend a low ridge surrounded by increasingly stunted whitebark pines. The trail rounds the ridge above Topsy Turvy Lake where the upper Middle Fork spreads out in all of its alpine splendor. The alpine meadows, stunted whitebark pines, and breathtaking peaks make this one of the most scenic camping areas in the entire Middle Fork Bishop Creek drainage.

Continue up the trail, hop across the outlet of Hungry Packer Lake just above tiny Sailor Lake, and make the final ascent to the lake along this creek. You quickly reach the north end of Hungry Packer Lake, 6.6 miles from the parking area, where fair campsites among stunted whitebark pines can be found. Fishing is sometimes excellent (rainbow and brook trout, up to 12 inches), but veteran anglers know how temperamental fish can be in these cold, high-elevation lakes. The impressive pinnacle of 13,435-foot Mount

Emerald Lakes in the Sabrina Basin.

Haeckel, a prominent landmark that has guided you from the trailhead, soars above the upper end of the lake.

Moonlight Lake is a short cross-country walk to the east. A seldom-used route, recommended for experienced backpackers only, ascends to Echo Lake, the source of the Middle Fork, and crosses the Sierra crest at Echo Pass. This trailless route involves some class 2 scrambling on the north side; the rest of the route is mainly boulder-hopping. It is an effective means of access to the Muir Pass area of Kings Canyon National Park.

Most of the lakes in this drainage are accessible by short cross-country hikes. If you are searching for solitude, you can, with a little extra effort, have many of these remote lakes to yourself.

26 Lake Sabrina to Tyee Lakes

See Map on Page 130

Highlights. This view packed, up-and-down backpack leads over an alpine plateau to an infrequently visited lake basin in the Bishop Creek drainage of the eastern Sierra.

General location: Southern Sierra Nevada, John Muir Wilderness (Inyo National Forest), 12 miles southwest of Bishop.

Type of hike: Round-trip backpack, 2 to 4 days.

Distance: 12 to 15 miles.

Difficulty: Moderately strenuous.

Elevation gain and loss: +2,640 feet, -559 feet.

Trailhead elevation: 8,960 feet.

High point: Table Mountain, 11,600 feet.

Best season: July through September.

Water availability: Abundant at George Lake at 3.8 miles and at the Tyee Lakes.

Maps: Inyo National Forest map; John Muir and Sequoia–Kings Canyon Wilderness areas map (two sheets, topographic); USGS Mt. Thompson 7.5-minute quad.

Permits: Wilderness permits are required for overnight use. Obtain permit at the White Mountain Ranger District office in Bishop. Reservations for permits can be made up to six months in advance (see Appendix A for information).

Key points:

- 0.0 Lake Sabrina parking area.
- 0.6 Trailhead.
- 1.8 Junction with George Lake Trail; turn left (northeast) and begin ascending.
- 3.8 George Lake.
- 5.0 Crest of Table Mountain
- 6.0 Upper Tyee Lake at 11,041 feet.
- 7.5 Lower Tyee Lake.

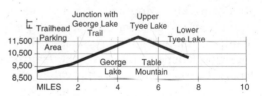

Finding the trailhead: Follow driving directions for Hike 25.

The hike: The vast Bishop Creek drainage boasts a number of lakes that are unsurpassed in all of the eastern Sierra Nevada. About 100 lakes, ranging in size from shallow, 1-acre tarns to deep, 300-acre lakes can be found here. Most are located at, or above, timberline and are backed up against jagged, snow-streaked summits. The three main forks of Bishop Creek are well-known for their scenic grandeur and recreational opportunities, making the area quite popular. Great fishing and awe-inspiring scenery in a backcountry setting are the primary attractions for hikers.

George Lake and the Tyee Lakes lie in remote hanging valleys on the flanks of the broad alpine mesa of Table Mountain. The matchless vista from this mountain to the peaks surrounding the Bishop Creek headwaters is unsurpassed, except, perhaps, by the view from an airplane. This hike is an excellent alternative to popular Sabrina Basin and the South Fork Bishop Creek. The Tyee Lakes are off the beaten path, receive moderate use, and offer good fishing.

When wilderness permit quotas are filled for the other lake basins in the drainage, particularly on busy summer weekends, consider this fine hike to the Tyee Lakes. Here, quotas are only necessary on the July 4th and Labor Day holidays. Campfires are not permitted at the Tyee Lakes, so plan on packing your backpack stove.

From the trailhead parking area, follow Hike 25 for 1.8 miles to the George Lake junction and turn left. Begin a series of fairly steep switchbacks and enjoy increasingly good views northwestward into the North Fork Bishop Creek drainage. After 1 mile of climbing moderately forested slopes dotted with scattered clumps of curl-leaf mountain mahogany, you arrive in the George Lake basin. From here to the lake, the trail is sometimes faint and fades out entirely in some grassy areas. Careful scouting may be necessary to relocate the route.

If you lose the trail, simply follow the creek upstream to George Lake, 2 miles from the previous junction. There are numerous sandy campsites among the whitebark and lodgepole pines lining the northern shore. From the lake, your trail ascends via switchbacks up a steep, sandy slope, with stunted whitebark pines keeping you company. The trail finally surmounts the sandy, open plateau of Table Mountain at 11,600 feet, where the Bishop Creek drainage unfolds below your gaze. The ground-hugging whitebark pines attest to the severity of winters at this elevation.

From Table Mountain, the trail continues in an easterly direction and then swings southward, descending a small gully. If you are inclined to camp on Table Mountain, you may find water in this gully in early summer, but don't depend on it. As the trail descends via switchbacks down the sparsely timbered slope, the valley containing the Tyee Lakes comes into view. This valley lies high above the South Fork Bishop Creek and was created thousands of years ago as a large glacier moved northward down the South Fork. In the process, the lower portion of the Tyee Lakes creek tributary was removed. As a result, the valley containing the lakes ends high up on the wall of the broadened and deepened canyon of the South Fork.

You soon reach the north shore of the second-highest and largest of the Tyee Lakes, Lake 11,041, 6 miles from the trailhead parking area. These lakes are fed by the runoff from a small, permanent snowfield above the upper lake. This lake lies in a bowl at timberline, with stunted whitebark pines offering sheltered camping from the sometimes severe weather. Fishing is good here. The lower lake, 1.5 miles below Lake 11,041, is surrounded by lodgepole pines and aspen, the latter providing a dazzling display of fall color.

The lakes in between offer pleasant camping in a lodgepole and whitebark pine forest, each with its own view from a slightly different setting.

From the lakes, you can either return the same way to Lake Sabrina, or descend the steep, lodgepole pine–clad slope for 1.8 miles from the lower lake to the Tyee Lakes Trailhead (on the paved road to South Lake in Bishop Creek's South Fork canyon). This trailhead lies on the west side of the road, 5 miles from the Lake Sabrina/South Lake junction.

27 North Lake to the Lamarck Lakes

Highlights:	This short hike offers great rewards with a minimum investment of time, features breathtaking vistas of precipitous Sierra crest peaks, and leads to two fish-filled timberline lakes nestled in deep cirques.
General location:	Southern Sierra Nevada, John Muir Wilderness (Inyo National Forest), 16 miles southwest of Bishop.
Type of hike:	Round-trip day hike, or backpack of 2 to 3 days.
Distance:	6.4 miles.
Difficulty:	Moderate.
Elevation gain and loss:	1,600 feet.
Trailhead elevation:	9,300 feet.
High point:	Upper Lamarck Lake, 10,900 feet.
Best season:	July through early October.
Water availability:	Abundant.
Maps:	Inyo National Forest map; John Muir and Sequoia-Kings Canyon Wilderness areas map (two sheets, topographic); USGS Mt. Darwin 7.5-minute quad.
Permits:	A wilderness permit is required for overnight use, and entry quotas are in effect. Obtain permit at the White Mountain Ranger District office in Bishop. Reservations for permits can be made up to six months in advance (see Appendix A for information).

Key points:

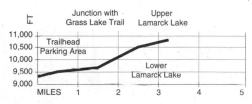

- 0.0 North Lake hiker's parking area; return to North Lake Road and walk southwest to the trailhead at the road's end.
- 0.5 Turn left (south) onto the Lamarck Lakes Trail just beyond the road's end.
- 1.5 Junction with Grass Lake Trail; stay right (west).
- 2.5 Lower Lamarck Lake.
- 3.2 Upper Lamarck Lake.

Finding the trailhead: Follow driving directions for Hike 28.

The hike: This short but fairly strenuous weekender leads you into a magnificent lake basin encircled by bold crags, many of which exceed 13,000 feet. Fishing is often rewarding, and the numerous side trip possibilities (for experienced hikers) should satisfy both veteran and intermediate cross-country hikers. Campfires are prohibited beyond Grass Lake, so be sure to carry a backpack stove.

From the trailhead parking area, follow Hike 28 for 0.5 mile to the Lamarck Lakes Trail and turn left. You quickly begin switchbacking up northwest-facing slopes clothed in aspen and lodgepole pine. Midway, enjoy good views into the classic U-shaped canyon of the North Fork Bishop Creek.

After climbing for 1 mile, the short lateral trail to Grass Lake departs to the left, leading to pleasant, lodgepole-shaded campsites. Fishing for pan-sized trout is usually good in Grass Lake. Turn right at this junction, though, and begin negotiating a series of moderately steep switchbacks. Along the way, views expand to include a host of spectacular alpine peaks in the southeast. You eventually skirt a small tarn to reach the deep-blue oval of Lower Lamarck Lake. There are excellent campsites available here amid stunted timber. The population of large trout in this lake should keep anglers busy, while the early-morning reflections of the rugged peaks in the lake's calm waters will delight photographers. For cross-country enthusiasts, the Wonder Lakes dot the basin to the west, offering a remote and spectacular destination for day-hiking jaunts or remote camping experiences.

Beyond Lower Lamarck Lake, the trail follows the outlet of Upper Lamarck Lake upstream through thinning timber and reaches the oblong lake at 10,900 feet. Good campsites can be found above the northeast corner of the lake amid stunted but shelter-giving whitebark pines. Fishing is also productive in this deep lake.

A moderately strenuous path, worn into the headwall of the basin, leads into the Evolution Basin region of Kings Canyon National Park and begins at Upper Lamarck Lake. From the lake, you may barely make out Lamarck Col on the southwestern skyline, immediately below (left of) Mount Lamarck. The path switchbacks steeply up the headwall of the cirque behind the lake in a southwesterly direction. It then heads southeast into a small drainage and finally jogs southwest to ascend a long, sloping bench all the way to Lamarck Col. A small tarn near the top offers water when it isn't frozen. From the col, the route drops steeply for 1,300 feet to the lakes in upper Darwin Canyon. You must negotiate seemingly endless boulder fields into the Darwin Canyon lakes, until you rediscover a path along the northern shore of the second-lowest lake. Below the lakes, camping is good in an area of alpine meadows, stunted timber, and glacially smoothed rock known as Darwin Bench.

From Darwin Bench, it is an easy hike into the heart of the Evolution Basin. With its dramatic peaks and breathtaking alpine terrain, this area displays some of the most spectacular scenery in all of California—indeed

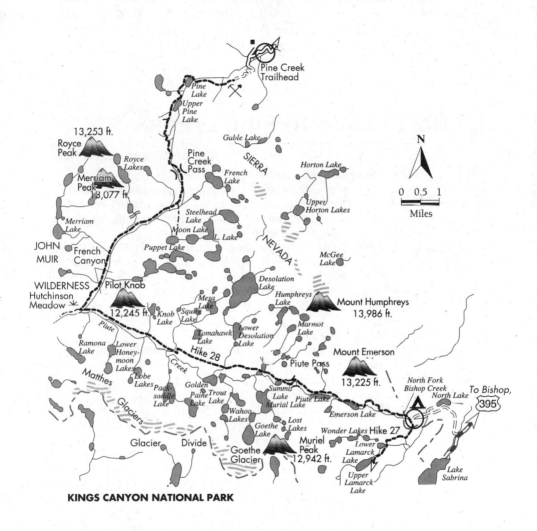

Pine Creek Trailhead

Pine Lake

Upper Pine Lake

13,253 ft.
Royce Peak

Royce Lakes

Guble Lake

SIERRA

Merriam Peak 13,077 ft.

Pine Creek Pass

French Lake

Horton Lake

Merriam Lake

Steelhead Lake

Moon Lake

L. Lake

Upper Horton Lakes

JOHN MUIR

French Canyon

Puppet Lake

NEVADA

McGee Lake

WILDERNESS

Pilot Knob

Hutchinson Meadow

12,245 ft.

Knob Lake

Mesa Lake

Squire Lake

Desolation Lake

Humphreys Lake

Mount Humphreys 13,986 ft.

Marmot Lake

Piute

Ramona Lake

Lower Honeymoon Lakes

Tomahawk Lake

Lower Desolation Lake

Hike 28

Mount Emerson

Creek

Piute Pass

13,225 ft.

Matthes

Lobe Lakes

Golden Paine Lake

Trout Lake

Summit Lake

Murial Lake

Piute Lake

North Fork Bishop Creek

North Lake

To Bishop, 395

Glaciers

Packsaddle Lake

Wahoo Lakes

Goethe Lake

Lost Lakes

Emerson Lake

Glacier   Divide

Goethe Glacier

Muriel Peak 12,942 ft.

Wonder Lakes Hike 27

Lower Lamarck Lake

Upper Lamarck Lake

Lake Sabrina

KINGS CANYON NATIONAL PARK

N

0   0.5   1
Miles

some of the most dramatic alpine country in the lower 48 states. Enough cross-country side trips, ranging from moderate to difficult, exist in this region to keep adventurous hikers busy for many seasons.

Most hikers who cross the Sierra Nevada at Lamarck Col either loop back to North Lake via the northbound John Muir Trail, Piute Canyon, and Piute Pass (a hike of a week or more), or else hike the John Muir Trail southward and hike out to South Lake via Bishop Pass. The latter requires a car shuttle or a hitchhike of about 12 miles to get back to North Lake.

28 North Lake to Pine Creek

See Map on Page 137

Highlights: This memorable backcountry trip leads hikers for miles through timberline and alpine terrain, passes dozens of lakes both large and small, and features good fishing, abundant side trip options, and superb alpine vistas.

General location: Southern Sierra Nevada, John Muir Wilderness (Inyo and Sierra National Forests), 16 miles southwest of Bishop.

Type of hike: Point-to-point backpack, 4 to 7 days.

Distance: 22.1 miles.

Difficulty: Moderate.

Elevation gain and loss: +3,820 feet, -5,700 feet.

Trailhead elevation: 9,300 feet (North Lake); 7,400 feet (Pine Creek).

High point: Piute Pass, 11,423 feet.

Best season: July through mid-October.

Water availability: Abundant.

Maps: Inyo and Sierra National Forest maps; John Muir and Sequoia–Kings Canyon Wilderness areas map (two sheets, topographic); USGS Mt. Darwin, Mt. Tom, and Mt. Hilgard 7.5-minute quads.

Permits: A wilderness permit is required for overnight use, and entry quotas are in effect. Obtain permit at the White Mountain Ranger District office in Bishop. Reservations for permits can be made up to six months in advance (see Appendix A for information).

Key points:

0.0   North Lake hiker's parking area; return to North Lake Road and walk southwest to the trailhead at the road's end.

0.5   Continue straight ahead (west) on Piute Pass Trail.

2.9   Loch Leven.

4.1   Piute Lake.

5.2   Piute Pass.

11.5   Junction with French Canyon Trail at Hutchinson Meadow; turn right (northeast) and ascend French Canyon.

15.3	Junction with southbound trail leading toward Moon Lake; bear left (north).
16.1	Pine Creek Pass.
17.7	Junction with westbound Italy Pass Trail; bear right (north).
18.7	Pine Lake.
20.4	Reach Brownstone Mine Road.
21.5	Junction with trail to pack station; turn right (east).
22.1	Pine Creek Trailhead.

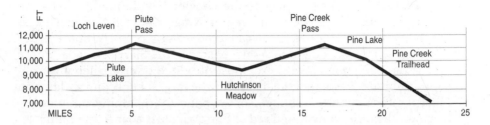

Finding the trailhead: From US Highway 395 in Bishop, turn west onto California Highway 168 where a sign lists mileage to South Lake, Lake Sabrina, and North Lake. Follow this paved road up the Bishop Creek canyon, and after another 14 miles, avoid the left-branching road leading to South Lake. Continue straight ahead for 3 more miles to the signed, right-branching North Lake Road. Follow this dirt road for 1.75 miles to the signed hiker's parking area just above North Lake.

To find the Pine Creek Trailhead, drive 10 miles north of Bishop on US 395, turn west, and proceed 10 more miles up the paved Pine Creek Road to the parking area just east of the pack station.

This trip requires that hikers leave another vehicle at the Pine Creek Trailhead unless they intend to hitchhike 38 miles back to North Lake.

The hike: This moderate, point-to-point trail crosses two Sierra Nevada crest passes higher than 11,000 feet, travels through two of the most lake-filled basins in the range, and surveys vegetation ranging from Jeffrey pine forests to alpine tundra. The scenery on this trip is so majestic that even those dedicated anglers who forget their fishing gear will find consolation in the sheer absorbing beauty of this region.

Campfires are prohibited from the trailhead to Piute Pass, but they are permitted west of the pass in the Sierra National Forest and in the Pine Creek drainage. However, hikers employing zero impact practices will only build fires where firewood is in obvious abundance.

From the parking area, walk back to North Lake Road, turn right, and hike 0.5 mile to the trailhead at the upper end of the campground. A short distance beyond, the southbound Lamarck Lakes Trail (see Hike 27) departs to your left at a large information sign. Turn right and ascend westward through the shade of aspen, lodgepole, and limber pine. After fording the North Fork Bishop Creek twice (which may be difficult in May and June), begin following the switchbacks up talus slopes below the broken red cliffs of the Piute Crags. Above that ascent, you reach Loch Leven, the first lake in this small but highly scenic basin.

From this lake, you can see the notch of Piute Pass on the western horizon. Impressive alpine peaks surround you as you ascend this canyon past several lakes and tarns, the largest being Piute Lake. Beyond Piute Lake, leave the last gnarled whitebark pines behind and ascend the final alpine slopes to Piute Pass.

Your view eastward from the pass takes in the U-shaped valley containing Piute Lake and Loch Leven. Westward, your view is strictly alpine. The jagged, perpetually snowy peaks of the Glacier Divide march off to the west, forming the northern boundary of Kings Canyon National Park. Immediately to the west lies the broad expanse of alpine Humphreys Basin, one of the largest and gentlest lake basins in the Sierra Nevada. There are more than 20 alpine lakes here, most of which offer challenging fishing opportunities. Desolation Lake, one of the largest backcountry lakes in the Sierra, offers superb (although somewhat austere) alpine camping.

North of the pass, convoluted red and brown cliffs soar to the pinnacle-topped summit of 13,986-foot Mount Humphreys, the highest peak this far north in the Sierra. If you wish to partake of the magnificent vistas this peak offers, be prepared for some serious scrambling—the easiest routes are class 4, but well worth the effort.

From the pass, descend westward to round Summit Lake and continue on the trail through the tundra-dominated landscape of Humphreys Basin. All the lakes in this basin are accessible by easy cross-country jaunts and are so numerous that it is easy to have a lake entirely to yourself. Your route soon passes to the north of Golden Trout Lake, at one time, the most heavily used lake in the basin. That heavy use has prompted the Forest Service to restrict camping to no less than 500 feet from the lakeshore.

Lodgepole pines are noted in increasing numbers as you descend along Piute Creek, offering more sheltered camping than in the exposed Humphreys Basin. Fishing is good in this creek for pan-sized golden trout. After a few short switchbacks, the trail levels off in a thick, shady lodgepole pine forest, occasionally passing small, wildflower-decorated meadows. With the pyramidal hulk of Pilot Knob looming directly above to your north, hop across multibranched French Canyon Creek (which can be difficult in June and early July) and meet the French Canyon Trail on your right, just north of the small green spread of Hutchinson Meadow.

Turn northeast onto this trail and begin a long, gentle ascent of French Canyon. You quickly break into the open, following the edge of a narrow, 2-mile-long meadow. Merriam Peak stands majestically above the canyon in the north, and the broken, craggy summits of the Sierra crest lure you onward to the large lakes at the head of this spectacular, U-shaped canyon. Midway up this meadow, avoid a faint westbound trail that climbs to seldom-visited Merriam Lake. At the head of the meadow, hop across the Royce Lakes' outlet creek. Photographers will be tempted to ascend that creek for 0.5 mile to enjoy a magnificent 500-foot waterfall.

From the crossing, quickly pass the last remnants of timber and continue your jaunt through open, alpine meadows. About 0.8 mile below

Royce and Merriam Peaks rise above French Canyon.

Pine Creek Pass, you meet a southbound trail providing access to several large, fishable lakes, including Moon Lake and L Lake. Short cross-country jaunts into this basin lead to many infrequently visited alpine lakes.

After a short, stiff climb beyond that trail, you level off on a large grassy bench. From here a cross-country route of moderate difficulty leads to the Royce Lakes chain, well off the beaten path. These lakes offer good fishing and remote camping if you are willing to forego the comforts of below-timberline camping.

Continue northward, skirt two small tarns and a few persistent whitebark pines, and cross the Sierra crest at 11,120-foot Pine Creek Pass. Views are good southward to the western peaks of the Glacier Divide. The unmistakable spire of Mount Humphreys is visible to the southeast. A host of high peaks surrounding the Pine Creek drainage can be seen to the north, dominated by the jagged crag of 13,713-foot Bear Creek Spire.

Begin a short descent through alpine meadows and along the headwaters of Pine Creek before re-entering timber. You soon pass two small tarns with fair campsites. Continue descending under a thickening canopy of lodgepole and whitebark pines, eventually passing a signed trail leading west to Granite Park and Italy Pass. The starkly beautiful alpine lakes in Granite Park, encircled by several impressive 12,000- and 13,000-foot peaks, make that basin a worthy destination. The Chalfant Lakes, lying just north of Granite Park over a low ridge, reward solitude seekers.

As your descent proceeds, cross a multibranched creek and skirt the western shore of Upper Pine Lake and Pine Lake, both of which offer excellent views across their deep-blue waters. Ford the outlet creek of Pine Lake and pass the last few campsites along Pine Creek, shaded by lodgepole pines. A traverse of north-facing slopes, under the precipitous north wall of Peak 12,280, brings you to a series of short switchbacks where you lose 400 feet in elevation.

Suddenly, your trail emerges onto an access road to the Brownstone Mine. Follow this narrow dirt road as it switchbacks its way to lower Pine Creek. After hiking 1.1 miles along this road, leave it, and proceed eastward on another trail. Your final descent begins immediately across the canyon from the Union Carbide Mill. The trail crosses several small creeks in a Jeffrey pine and red fir forest, with occasional aspen and birch adding trailside company. You eventually come to the pack station, pass a few scattered buildings, and finally reach the Pine Creek parking area at 7,400 feet.

29 South Lake to Dusy Basin

Highlights: This scenic trip ascends the dramatic South Fork Bishop Creek, passing six high lakes en route to the Sierra crest at Bishop Pass. Beyond the pass lie the lakes of Dusy Basin, featuring good fishing and alpine camping among 12,000- to 14,000-foot peaks.

General location: Southern Sierra Nevada, John Muir Wilderness (Inyo National Forest), and Kings Canyon National Park, 12 miles southwest of Bishop.

Type of hike: Round-trip backpack, 3 to 5 days.

Distance: 17.2 miles.

Difficulty: Moderately strenuous.

Elevation gain and loss: +2,200 feet, -600 feet.

Trailhead elevation: 9,800 feet.

High point: Bishop Pass, 11,972 feet.

Best season: Mid-July through early October.

Water availability: Abundant.

Maps: Inyo National Forest map; John Muir and Sequoia–Kings Canyon Wilderness areas map (two sheets, topographic); USGS Mt. Thompson and North Palisade 7.5-minute quads.

Permits: A wilderness permit is required for overnight use, and entry quotas are in effect. Obtain permit at the White Mountain Ranger District office in Bishop. Reservations for permits can be made up to six months in advance (see Appendix A for information).

Key points:
- 0.0 Bishop Pass Trailhead parking area.
- 1.0 Treasure Lakes Trail branches right (southwest); stay left (southeast).
- 2.0 Junction with trail to Bull and Chocolate Lakes; bear right (south).
- 2.9 Junction with southeast-branching trail to Ruwau Lake above Long Lake; bear right (south).
- 4.0 Saddlerock Lake.
- 5.7 Bishop Pass.
- 8.6 Lake 10,734 in lower Dusy Basin.

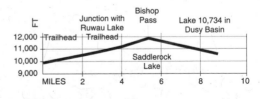

Finding the trailhead: Follow driving directions for Hike 28 and drive 14 miles from Bishop via California Highway 168 to the Lake Sabrina/South Lake junction. Turn left at the junction and drive 7.5 miles to the trailhead parking area above South Lake.

The hike: The headwaters of the Bishop Creek drainage, spread out over some 50 square miles, contain more high lakes than any other drainage on the eastern side of the Sierra. More than 80 sizable lakes, and innumerable

South Lake to Dusy Basin

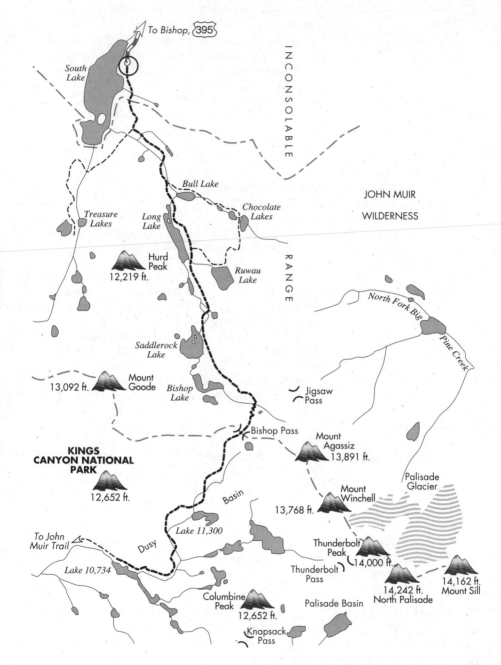

To Bishop, 395

South Lake

INCONSOLABLE

Bull Lake

Chocolate Lakes

JOHN MUIR

WILDERNESS

Treasure Lakes

Long Lake

Hurd Peak
12,219 ft.

Ruwau Lake

RANGE

North Fork Big

Pine Creek

Saddlerock Lake

Mount Goode
13,092 ft.

Bishop Lake

Jigsaw Pass

Bishop Pass

KINGS CANYON NATIONAL PARK

12,652 ft.

Mount Agassiz
13,891 ft.

Palisade Glacier

Mount Winchell
13,768 ft.

Basin

Lake 11,300

Thunderbolt Peak
14,000 ft.

To John Muir Trail

Dusy

Lake 10,734

Thunderbolt Pass

14,242 ft.
North Palisade

14,162 ft.
Mount Sill

Columbine Peak
12,652 ft.

Palisade Basin

Knapsack Pass

smaller tarns, dot the many cirque basins in the forks of Bishop Creek.

This memorable trip ascends the lake-filled basin of the South Fork Bishop Creek, crosses the lofty crest of the Sierra at the alpine saddle of Bishop Pass, and then drops into the broad granite bowl of Dusy Basin in Kings Canyon National Park. A base camp can be established in this alpine basin among six lakes, and days can be spent fishing here or exploring nearby Palisade Basin. The trip can be extended by descending to the John Muir Trail in Le Conte Canyon and following that trail either up or down the Middle Fork Kings River.

From the trailhead at the road's end, follow the well-worn and rocky trail generally southeast, rising at a moderate grade over slopes studded with aspens and lodgepole pines. Good views stretch across the deep waters of South Lake to the bold Sierra crest summits of Mounts Johnson, Gilbert, and Thompson. The lower pyramidal summit of Hurd Peak guards the entrance to the alpine heights of the upper South Fork 2 miles to the south.

As you level off on a bench high above South Lake at 10,250 feet, 1 mile from the trailhead, the Treasure Lakes Trail branches right (southwest). Bear left and ascend steadily through the increasingly rocky, ice-gouged terrain that is studded with lodgepole and whitebark pine for another mile. Cross the South Fork along the way and reach the eastbound trail leading to Bull and Chocolate Lakes. This trail carves a 2.2-mile semicircle around those lakes and Ruwau Lake before returning to the main trail 0.9 mile ahead. If you intend to make the trip to Dusy Basin over the course of two hiking days, you might consider either following that trail in search of campsites, or making an effort to leave the trail between Long and Saddlerock Lakes if you prefer more secluded campsites.

After bearing right at that junction, you soon cross Long Lake's outlet stream to begin a traverse above its eastern shore. This lovely lake, with rock- and meadow-fringed shores, offers some of the best, and most popular, campsites in the South Fork basin. Good campsites are set among lodgepole and whitebark pines above the lake's west shore.

As you approach the lake's south end, the trail descending from Ruwau Lake comes in on your left (east) at 10,800 feet, 2.9 miles from the trailhead. Your trail ascends moderately through timberline stands of whitebark pine, passing beautiful tarns and rich meadows enlivened by the colorful summer blooms of shooting star, lupine, and red heather. Cross the South Fork two more times en route to the timberline gem of Saddlerock Lake, wedged between 13,092-foot Mount Goode to the west and the towering, broken ridge of the Inconsolable Range to the east. Good campsites can be found around this lake and among the tarns above its northwest shore, all in groves of stunted whitebark pines.

The trail traverses Saddlerock Lake's eastern shore and then rises over a rocky shoulder, from where you descend past a scattering of tarns above Bishop Lake, with the last suitable campsites in the basin. The broad saddle of Bishop Pass notches the skyline above to the south while your trail winds past an island of tenacious, ground-hugging whitebark pines to the head of the basin. From here, the trail ascends steeply via a series of tight switchbacks.

Bishop and Saddlerock Lakes from Bishop Pass.

Soon the grade moderates, and you ascend the final talus slopes to the Sierra crest at 11,972-foot Bishop Pass.

The vista from this pass is not as far-ranging as others along the Sierra crest, but it still encompasses some of the wildest and most rugged high country in the range. Southeast are the jagged crags of the Palisades, and below you to the south is the broad, lake-filled cirque of Dusy Basin, inviting despite its stark alpine landscape. Bounding the basin on its east side are Isosceles, Columbine, and Giraud Peaks. Far on the southwestern skyline rise the bold, somber peaks of the Black Divide beyond the barely discernible trough of Le Conte Canyon.

The trail descends southwest from the pass, dropping via granite benches and traversing grassy pockets for 1.1 miles to the northernmost lake in the basin, Lake 11,300, where the trail briefly levels out. After crossing that lake's inlet, scattered clumps of krummholz whitebark pines appear on granite knolls as you descend southward along the lake's outlet stream and enter timberline groves of stunted pines.

After descending about 550 feet from Lake 11,300, the trail reaches the lowest bench in the basin and turns west above the north shore of Lake 10,734, a long and narrow lake with an irregular shoreline. The most sheltered campsites in the basin are found among the lodgepole and whitebark pines above this lake's shoreline. Two more long, narrow lakes and a host of tarns dot the basin southeast of Lake 10,734, where you will find more fine timberline camping. Lake 11,393, the second-highest and largest lake in the basin offers excellent, though austere, alpine camping beneath the ramparts of 14,000-foot Thunderbolt Peak.

For the adventurous, a part cross-country, part boot-worn, cairned trail leads over 11,673-foot Knapsack Pass into Palisade Basin. The pass, an obvious notch in the high ridge south of Columbine Peak, is easily approached from the lakes on the lowest bench of the basin. The way ascends grassy benches and ice-polished granite ledges east from the lower lakes, gaining 900 feet in about 0.8 mile from the southeasternmost lake. From the pass, the cairned route leads northeast to Palisade Basin. There you find the Barrett Lakes, consisting of four lakes and numerous tarns ranging in elevation between 11,300 feet and 11,500 feet. This basin sees far fewer visitors than does Dusy Basin; its campsites are alpine with little protection from the weather. Rising above these icy lakes is the somber crag of 14,242-foot North Palisade, the highest summit in the Palisades group of peaks.

After enjoying the high country of Dusy Basin, retrace your steps to the trailhead.

30 Rock Creek to Upper Morgan Lake

Highlights:	This short but memorable hike begins at the highest trailhead in the Sierra, passes eight timberline lakes, brimming with hungry trout and are set beneath 13,000-foot crags, and offers access to many more lakes via short, cross-country routes.
General location:	Southern Sierra Nevada, John Muir Wilderness (Inyo National Forest), 20 miles northwest of Bishop.
Type of hike:	Round-trip day hike or overnighter.
Distance:	9.2 miles.
Difficulty:	Moderately easy.
Elevation gain and loss:	+854 feet, -200 feet.
Trailhead elevation:	10,250 feet.
High point:	Morgan Pass, 11,104 feet.
Best season:	July through mid-October.
Water availability:	Abundant. If day hiking, bring your own.

Maps: Inyo National Forest map; John Muir and Sequoia–Kings Canyon Wilderness areas map (two sheets, topographic); USGS Mt. Morgan and Mt. Abbot 7.5-minute quads.

Permits: A wilderness permit is required for overnight use, and entry quotas are in effect. Obtain permit at the White Mountain Ranger District office in Bishop or at the Mono Lake Scenic Area Visitor Center at the north end of Lee Vining. Reservations for permits can be made up to six months in advance (see Appendix A for information).

Key points:
0.0   Little Lakes Valley Trailhead.
0.6   Junction with Mono Pass Trail; stay left (south).
2.0   Long Lake.
2.7   Junction with trail to Chickenfoot Lake; bear right (south).
3.0   Junction with trail to Gem and Treasure Lakes; stay left (southeast) and ascend to Morgan Pass.
3.6   Morgan Pass.
3.9   Upper Morgan Lake.
4.6   Lower Morgan Lake.

Finding the trailhead: From Toms Place on US Highway 395, 24 miles north of Bishop and 15 miles south of Mammoth Junction, turn south onto Rock Creek Road where a sign indicates "Rock Creek Lake." Follow this road for 11 miles to the trailhead at the end of the road. The final 2 miles of the road beyond Rock Creek Lake are paved, but narrow, so drive with caution.

The hike: The hike to Upper Morgan Lake follows an old doubletrack that was once the primary access to the Pine Creek Tungsten Mines. It makes an excellent day hike for people who stay at one of the campgrounds on Rock Creek and are interested in some backcountry fishing, with a chance to stretch their legs. It can be undertaken as a backpack, but few campsites are available at Upper Morgan Lake. Lower Morgan Lake, however, boasts several spacious campsites. Little Lakes Valley, west of Morgan Pass, abounds in campsites and subalpine lakes. Families with small children will find the valley to be an excellent choice for a weekend backpack. Backpackers must remember that campfires are prohibited from the trailhead to Morgan Pass, but are allowed at the Morgan Lakes despite the lack of abundant firewood.

From the trailhead, hike south on the old doubletrack and pass the west-branching trail to Mono Pass. The jagged, snow-streaked peaks of the Sierra crest loom boldly at the head of the valley, in constant view as you amble up the trail. Beyond the Mono Pass Trail junction, your route passes four subalpine lakes set within a lodgepole and whitebark pine forest, each with good campsites and good fishing in a breathtaking, high-mountain setting.

As you near the head of the valley, you meet an eastbound trail to

Rock Creek to Upper Morgan Lake • Rock Creek to Pioneer Basin

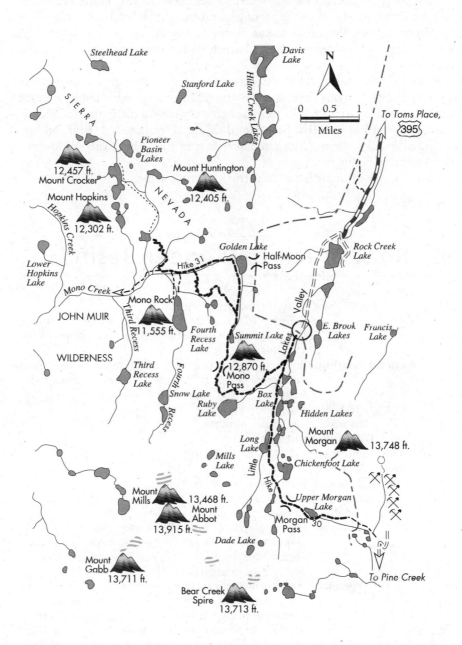

Steelhead Lake

Stanford Lake

Davis Lake

Hilton Creek Lakes

N

0   0.5   1
Miles

To Toms Place,
395

SIERRA

Pioneer Basin Lakes

12,457 ft.
Mount Crocker

Mount Huntington

Mount Hopkins

NEVADA

12,302 ft.

12,405 ft.

Hopkins Creek

Golden Lake

Half-Moon Pass

Rock Creek Lake

Lower Hopkins Lake

Mono Creek

Hike 31

Mono Rock

JOHN MUIR

Valley

E. Brook Lakes

Francis Lake

Third Recess

11,555 ft.

Fourth Recess Lake

Summit Lake

Lake

WILDERNESS

Third Recess Lake

Fourth Recess

12,870 ft.
Mono Pass

Snow Lake
Ruby Lake

Box Lake

Hidden Lakes

Mount Morgan

13,748 ft.

Long Lake

Mills Lake

Chickenfoot Lake

Little

Mount Mills

Hike 30

13,468 ft.
Mount Abbot

Upper Morgan Lake

13,915 ft.

Mount Gabb

13,711 ft.

Dade Lake

Morgan Pass

To Pine Creek

Bear Creek Spire

13,713 ft.

Chickenfoot Lake, one of the most popular lakes in the basin. Shortly thereafter, pass a right-branching trail leading to Gem Lake and the Treasure Lakes, any of which make good base camps to explore the headwaters of Rock Creek.

Your route then makes a few short switchbacks to surmount 11,104-foot Morgan Pass amidst a thick carpet of ground-hugging whitebark pines. Views are superb across the Little Lakes Valley to the alpine peaks of the Sierra Nevada crest. To the east rise the barren peaks surrounding Pine Creek's headwaters.

From the pass, descend boulder-strewn terrain, traversing above the south shore of Upper Morgan Lake. Anglers should have no trouble landing enough rainbow trout for dinner, but backpackers may have a difficult time locating a suitable campsite along the rockbound shores of the lake. The trail continues eastward, passes Lower Morgan Lake, leaves the John Muir Wilderness, and enters an active mining area.

From Upper Morgan Lake, backtrack to the trailhead.

31 Rock Creek to Pioneer Basin

See Map on Page 149

Highlights:	This very scenic trip leads hikers over a 12,000-foot Sierra crest pass and into a lake-filled alpine basin beneath the bold peaks of the High Sierra.
General location:	Southern Sierra Nevada, John Muir Wilderness (Inyo and Sierra National Forests), 20 miles northwest of Bishop.
Type of hike:	Round-trip backpack, 3 to 5 days.
Distance:	15.6 miles or more.
Difficulty:	Moderate.
Elevation gain and loss:	+2,150 feet, -2,000 feet.
Trailhead elevation:	10,250 feet.
High point:	Mono Pass, 12,000 feet.
Best season:	July through mid-October.
Water availability:	Abundant.
Maps:	Inyo or Sierra National Forest maps; John Muir and Sequoia–Kings Canyon Wilderness areas map (two sheets, topographic); USGS Mt. Morgan and Mt. Abbot 7.5-minute quads.
Permits:	A wilderness permit is required for overnight use, and entry quotas are in effect. Obtain permit at the White Mountain Ranger District office in Bishop or at the Mono Lake Scenic Area Visitor Center at the north end of Lee Vining. Reservations for permits can be made up to six months in advance (see Appendix A for information).

Key points:

- 0.0   Little Lakes Valley Trailhead.
- 0.6   Junction with Mono Pass Trail; turn right (southwest) and begin ascending.
- 1.8   Junction with spur trail to Ruby Lake; bear right (southwest).
- 3.2   Mono Pass.
- 4.3   Junction below Summit Lake; continue straight ahead (north), descending toward Golden Lake.
- 5.1   Golden Lake.
- 6.1   Junction along Golden Creek; continue straight ahead (west).
- 6.3   Junction with southbound trail to Fourth Recess Lake; stay right (west).
- 6.6   Junction with Pioneer Basin Trail; turn right (northwest) and ascend into the basin.
- 7.8   Lower Pioneer Basin Lake (10,400).

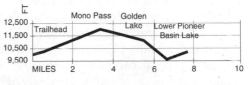

Finding the trailhead: Follow driving directions for Hike 30.

The hike: This moderate backpack trip, beginning at the highest trailhead in the Sierra Nevada, utilizes the northernmost trail to cross the Sierra crest at 12,000 feet. It is probably the easiest pass at that elevation in the entire range. Once over the crest, all the lake basins of upper Mono Creek are readily accessible, most of them by trail. Backpackers should be aware that campfires are prohibited between the trailhead and Mono Pass.

The six peaks of 12,000 feet or more surrounding Pioneer Basin are easily climbed via class 2 scrambles. Mount Stanford, at an elevation of 12,851 feet, is not only the highest but perhaps the easiest to climb. Its central location above the basin offers outstanding, unobstructed views.

The trail begins at the south end of the large parking area. The first 0.6 mile follows the same route as the hike to Upper Morgan Lake, through scattered lodgepole and whitebark pines. Turn right at the signed junction and ascend several small benches in a southwesterly direction. After climbing for 1.2 miles, you pass the southwest-branching trail to Ruby Lake, where excellent scenic campsites can be found.

From this junction, your route switchbacks up sandy, sparsely timbered slopes. Deep, blue Ruby Lake soon comes into view, with a backdrop of impressive Sierra crest crags. Leave the last wind-torn whitebark pines behind, contour into a shallow gully, and labor up the last few switchbacks to the narrow sandy notch of Mono Pass. This Mono Pass rests at 12,000 feet; there is also another Mono Pass on the Sierra crest, 35 miles to the northwest on the eastern boundary of Yosemite National Park.

Views from the pass are good, but somewhat limited. To the north, Summit Lake occupies the sandy bench just below the pass, with flat-topped Peak 12,252 in the background. To the south, several Sierra crest peaks in the 13,000-foot range soar out of the Little Lakes Valley. For a truly panoramic view of this region of the Sierra Nevada, scramble up the easy west slopes of 12,870-foot Mount Starr, immediately to the east.

A descent of 1.1 miles along the sandy trail brings you to a junction with a faint route descending to Golden Lake; the main trail bends northwest. This recommended alternative avoids the Trail Lakes, descends northward along the west side of the small creek, and then contours above Golden Lake's rocky western shore. Good campsites can be found near the outlet of this alpine lake. The trail, more distinct below the lake, descends in a westerly direction along Golden Creek, rejoining the main trail after a total of 1.8 miles.

If you wish to stick to the main trail, bear left 1.1 miles below Mono Pass, descend the sparsely timbered slopes, and pass above the small Trail Lakes and a snow survey cabin. Continue your descent amid thickening timber to a ford of Golden Creek and a juncture with the trail descending from Golden Lake. Turn west and descend along the banks of Golden Creek. Pass a south-bound route leading to the often-overcrowded Fourth Recess Lake, one of the most popular campsites in the area. Continue down through lodgepole pine forest and then turn northwest (right) onto the well-worn trail leading

Pioneer Basin and the Mono Divide.

to Pioneer Basin, just below the contour at the 10,000-foot level.

The trail climbs 400 feet in 1.2 miles to reach the lower lake in Pioneer Basin, at an elevation of 10,400 feet, completely surrounded by a wide, green meadow. The jagged ridge of the Mono Divide rising above the canyon of upper Mono Creek to the south adds to the scenic attraction of this fine lake. A base camp can be established here for climbing peaks, fishing, or simply relaxing amidst one of the most scenic and accessible backcountry lake basins in the range.

You can continue farther into the basin, choosing from ten other alpine lakes for unadorned but breathtaking camping or for day hiking and fishing. To reach the upper lakes, follow the inlet stream of the lower lake, first northeast, then northwest. After 1.5 miles and 500 feet of climbing, you will reach Lake 10,881 in the center of the upper basin.

After enjoying this magnificent area, return the way you came.

32 Duck Pass Trailhead to Tully Lake

Highlights:	This memorable high-country trek leads over a low point in the Sierra crest and follows part of the John Muir/Pacific Crest Trail into Fish Creek, a major San Joaquin River tributary. En route, the trail passes seven timberline lakes and features panoramic vistas of lofty Sierra crags, deep valleys, and wooded plateaus.
General location:	Southern Sierra Nevada, John Muir Wilderness (Inyo and Sierra National Forests), 5 miles south of Mammoth Lakes.
Type of hike:	Round-trip backpack, 5 to 7 days.
Distance:	29 miles.
Difficulty:	Moderately strenuous.
Elevation gain and loss:	+4,100 feet, -2,400 feet.
Trailhead elevation:	9,100 feet.
High point:	Duck Pass, 10,800 feet.
Best season:	July through mid-October.
Water availability:	Abundant.
Maps:	Inyo or Sierra National Forest maps; John Muir and Sequoia–Kings Canyon Wilderness areas map (two sheets, topographic); USGS Bloody Mountain and Graveyard Peak 7.5-minute quads.
Permits:	A wilderness permit is required for overnight use, and daily entry quotas are in effect. Obtain permit at the Mammoth Visitor Center. Reservations for permits can be made up to six months in advance (see Appendix A for information).

Duck Pass Trailhead to Tully Lake

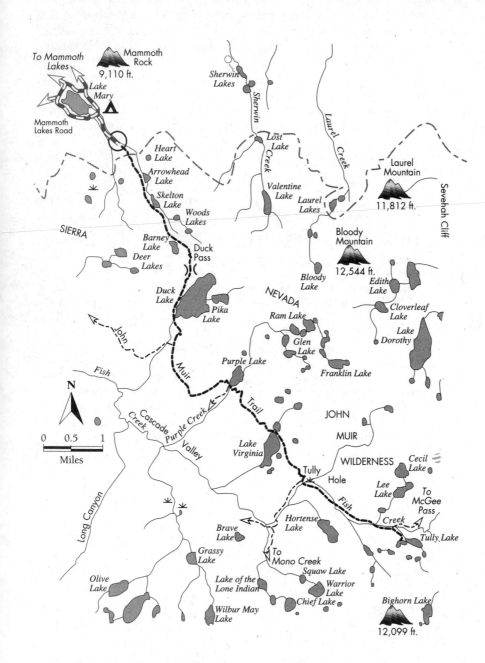

To Mammoth Lakes

Mammoth Rock
9,110 ft.

Lake Mary

Mammoth Lakes Road

Heart Lake

Arrowhead Lake

Skelton Lake

Woods Lakes

Barney Lake

Deer Lakes

Duck Pass

Duck Lake

Pika Lake

SIERRA

John

Muir

Fish

Cascade Creek

Purple Creek

Valley

Long Canyon

Olive Lake

N

0   0.5   1
Miles

Sherwin Lakes

Sherwin Creek

Lost Lake

Valentine Lake

Laurel Lakes

Laurel Creek

Laurel Mountain

11,812 ft.

Sevehah Cliff

Bloody Mountain
12,544 ft.

Bloody Lake

NEVADA

Ram Lake

Glen Lake

Franklin Lake

Edith Lake

Cloverleaf Lake

Lake Dorothy

Purple Lake

Trail

Lake Virginia

JOHN

MUIR

WILDERNESS

Tully Hole

Cecil Lake

Lee Lake

To McGee Pass

Fish Creek

Tully Lake

Brave Lake

Hortense Lake

Grassy Lake

To Mono Creek

Lake of the Lone Indian

Squaw Lake

Warrior Lake

Chief Lake

Bighorn Lake
12,099 ft.

Wilbur May Lake

Key points:

- 0.0 Duck Pass Trailhead.
- 2.0 Skelton Lake.
- 4.3 Duck Pass.
- 5.3 Outlet of Duck Lake.
- 6.0 Junction with John Muir Trail; turn left (south).
- 8.2 Junction with trail to Cascade Valley at outlet of Purple Lake; continue straight ahead (east).
- 10.2 Lake Virginia.
- 12.1 Junction with Fish Creek Trail in Tully Hole; turn left (east) and begin ascending Fish Creek.
- 14.1 Junction with Tully Lake Trail; turn right (southeast).
- 14.5 Tully Lake.

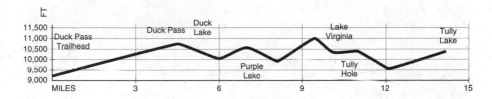

Finding the trailhead: From Mammoth Junction on US Highway 395, about 40 miles north of Bishop and 26 miles south of Lee Vining, turn west onto California Highway 203. Be sure to obtain your wilderness permit at the visitor center, about 3.25 miles west of US 395. Although daily entry quotas are in effect from July 1 through September 15, they are rarely filled except for holiday weekends.

After driving 4.5 miles west from US 395, turn left (south) at the junction with the northbound road to the Devils Postpile National Monument and the ski area. Follow this paved road for 5 miles to the upper end of Lake Mary, where a sign marks the entrance to Coldwater Campground. Drive 0.8 mile through the campground to the large parking area at the road's end.

The hike: This week-long backpack combines a moderate climb over the Sierra Nevada crest and a view-filled traverse on the famous John Muir Trail, with an ascent to the headwaters of the Fish Creek drainage, a major tributary of the Middle Fork San Joaquin River. Fishing in Tully Lake is sometimes excellent, as are the fishing opportunities in all of the lakes en route and in Fish Creek as well. This area is bear country, so hikers must take adequate precautions to protect their food supplies.

Your dusty trail heads southward from the trailhead, climbing to a bench overlooking Arrowhead Lake, where you meet a signed trail leading down to the lakeshore. Continue your southeastward course up the glaciated canyon, pass Skelton Lake after 2 miles, and then ascend several small benches to reach the outlet of the shallow, turquoise Barney Lake. From here, it's a 600-foot climb up to Duck Pass, the obvious gap in the mountains to the southeast. The trail is well graded, but ascends steadily, and closely follows the route indicated on the quad. Subalpine yellow columbine is found

An early-morning reflection in Duck Lake, one of the largest backcountry lakes in the Sierra Nevada.

growing here and there in sheltered nooks on this slope.

After hiking 4.3 miles from the trailhead, surmount the crest of the Sierra Nevada at 10,800-foot Duck Pass, shaded by scattered clumps of stunted whitebark pine. The superb vistas make this pass a worthy destination in itself. The dark pyramids of Banner Peak and Mount Ritter are visible in the northwest, as well as a host of surrounding peaks as far north as the Mount Dana region. You also have an excellent view back down Mammoth Creek to the unmistakable bare, rounded mass of Mammoth Mountain, capped by the summit gondola station. Massive Duck Lake, one of the largest backcountry lakes in the Sierra, lies to the southeast under the jagged peaks that enclose its basin. Smaller and more secluded Pika Lake sits on a bench above Duck Lake, offering more private camping than the often-crowded Duck Lake. Bear in mind that campfires are prohibited in the Duck Lake watershed, and camping within 300 feet of the Duck Lake outlet is not allowed.

A moderate descent past Duck Lake brings you to a signed junction with the John Muir Trail. Turn left and begin a sparsely forested traverse along south-facing slopes, with some of the grandest vistas along the entire hike. The Silver Divide is the east-west ridge of alpine peaks you see to the south across the deep, U-shaped canyon of Fish Creek. You also have good views to the west down the Fish Creek canyon to the peaks on the southeastern boundary of Yosemite National Park.

As you approach Purple Lake, clumps of manzanita and chinquapin appear, attesting to the dry conditions that prevail on these sun-drenched, south-facing slopes. After hiking 2.2 miles from the junction with the John Muir Trail, you reach the outlet of Purple Lake at an elevation of 9,900 feet. Evidence of overuse abounds at this lake—it is probably the most heavily used campsite in this region of the High Sierra. Hikers searching for solitude, and peace and quiet, are advised to move on. If you do stay in this basin, remember that camping and campfires are prohibited within 300 feet of the lake's outlet.

Just before crossing the lake's outlet stream, a southwestbound trail leaves your trail, descending along Purple Creek to the warmer, heavily forested environs of Cascade Valley. Beyond Purple Lake, negotiate a series of switchbacks and pass through a narrow gap just north of the 650-foot, near-vertical northeast face of Peak 11,147. Continuing your eastward course in lodgepole and whitebark pine shade, you soon ford the small creek feeding 10,314-foot Lake Virginia, one of the most beautiful lakes in the Sierra. The view across this large lake to the alpine summits of Silver Divide is superb.

The trail skirts the eastern shore of the lake, passes a small tarn, and then climbs to a low gap, where hikers have whitebark pine–framed views of the craggy peaks that loom majestically at the head of Fish Creek. The impressive sight of these peaks accompanies you as you descend 880 feet via numerous switchbacks into the green expanse of Tully Hole.

Upon reaching Tully Hole, follow the trail downstream for a short distance and turn left (east) onto the Fish Creek Trail. Immediately ford Fish Creek, ascend eastward along its southern banks, and after 0.7 mile, cross to the north banks of the creek, skirting the northern margin of the beautiful green subalpine meadow of Horse Heaven. This part of Fish Creek is usually infested with mosquitoes in early and midsummer.

A series of switchbacks through a lodgepole pine forest avoid the narrow gorge of Fish Creek. After this climb, the trail levels off in a subalpine meadow surrounded by bare, glacially smoothed granite. You soon pass the signed trail branching north to Cecil and Lee Lakes.

After 2 miles of hiking beyond Horse Heaven, meet the signed trail to Tully Lake and turn right. The Fish Creek Trail ascends to McGee Pass and then descends to an east-slope trailhead.

A short ascent along Tully Lake's outlet creek brings you to the shores of this rectangular, blue-green lake. The rocky and grassy shores of the lake are occasionally interrupted by isolated stands of stunted whitebark pine. Sheltered campsites can be found on benches above the lake within these whitebark groves.

A cross-country route of moderate difficulty is possible from Red and White Lake (which is a 1-mile walk east of Tully Lake and has no campsites) to massive Grinnell Lake in the Mono Creek watershed, via an 11,600-foot pass on the Silver Divide directly above (south of) Red and White Lake. Boulder-hopping and exceedingly steep slopes make this a route for experienced backpackers only.

After enjoying this tarn-dotted basin surrounding Tully Lake, eventually make your way back to the trailhead.

33 Agnew Meadows to Devils Postpile

Highlights:	This ambitious circuit, part cross-country and recommended for experienced hikers only, surveys the incomparable crags and high lakes of the Ritter Range. Good fishing and glorious vistas reward hikers who complete this trip.
General location:	Southern Sierra Nevada, Ansel Adams Wilderness (Sierra National Forest), 7 miles west of Mammoth Lakes.
Type of hike:	Loop backpack; 4 to 6 days.
Distance:	21.2 miles.
Difficulty:	Moderately strenuous.
Elevation gain and loss:	+4,140 feet, -4,920 feet.
Trailhead elevation:	Agnew Meadows, 8,340 feet.
High point:	Cecile Lake, 10,300 feet.
Best season:	July through early October.

Water availability: Abundant.

Maps: Inyo National Forest map; Ansel Adams Wilderness map (topographic); USGS Mammoth Mountain and Mt. Ritter 7.5-minute quads.

Permits: A wilderness permit is required and can be obtained at the Mammoth Visitor Center. Daily entry quotas are in effect. Reservations for permits can be made up to six months in advance (see Appendix A for information).

Key points:

0.0	Agnew Meadows Trailhead; proceed north on the Pacific Crest Trail (PCT).
5.6	Junction with Agnew Pass Trail; stay left (west).
6.2	Junction with Middle Fork Trail; continue straight ahead (west).
7.1	Five-way junction at outlet of Thousand Island Lake; turn left (southeast) onto the John Muir Trail.
9.2	Outlet of Garnet Lake.
11.2	Junction with westbound Ediza Lake Trail on north side of Shadow Creek; turn right (southwest) and ascend Shadow Creek.
12.3	Ediza Lake.
13.3	Iceberg Lake.
13.9	Cecile Lake.
14.9	Minaret Lake.
16.4	Junction with northbound trail to Minaret Mine; bear right (southeast).
19.1	Junction with John Muir Trail at Johnston Meadow; turn right (southeast).
19.8	Junction with Holcomb Lake Trail; bear left (south).
20.6	Junction with PCT; continue straight ahead (southeast) on John Muir Trail.
20.8	Junction with Mammoth Trail to Summit Meadow; bear left (southeast).
21.0	Junction with Devils Postpile Trail; turn left (north).
21.2	Reach the road's end at Devils Postpile Campground.

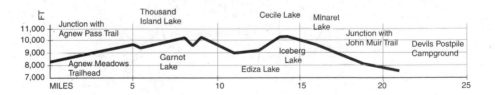

Finding the trailhead: There are two possible ways to reach the trailhead. The first method involves driving your own vehicle—during the summer season, though, you must have a vehicle containing 11 or more people or make the drive before 7:30 A.M. or after 5:30 P.M.

The second alternative, probably the more desirable method, is to park at the Mammoth Mountain Ski Area parking lot and take the Reds Meadow-Devils Postpile shuttle bus. This method minimizes traffic problems, allows you some flexibility in planning hikes in the area, and reduces the wear and tear on your vehicle. The shuttle bus serves all the trailheads in the Devils Postpile area and runs from 7:45 A.M. through 9:30 P.M. every day during

Agnew Meadows to Devils Postpile

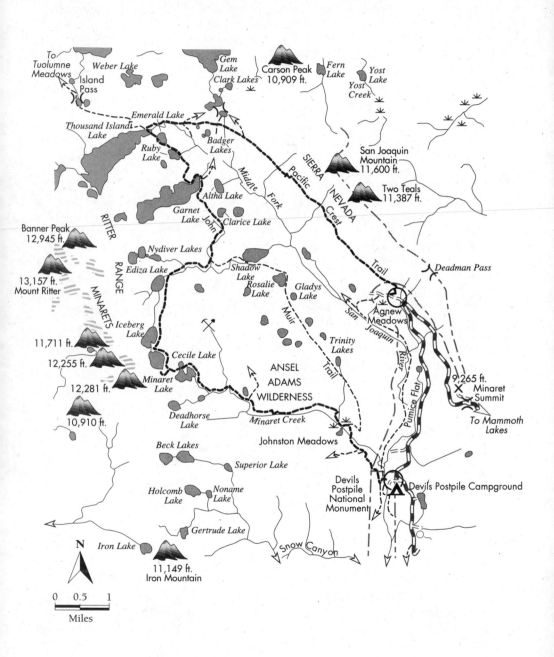

To Tuolumne Meadows

Island Pass

Weber Lake

Gem Lake
Clark Lakes

Carson Peak 10,909 ft.

Fern Lake

Yost Lake

Yost Creek

Emerald Lake

Thousand Island Lake

Ruby Lake

Badger Lakes

SIERRA

Pacific

San Joaquin Mountain 11,600 ft.

NEVADA

Two Teals 11,387 ft.

Banner Peak 12,945 ft.

RITTER

Altha Lake

Garnet Lake

Clarice Lake

Middle

Fork

John

Crest

13,157 ft. Mount Ritter

Nydiver Lakes

RANGE

Ediza Lake

Shadow Lake

Rosalie Lake

Gladys Lake

Trail

Deadman Pass

11,711 ft.

MINARETS

Iceberg Lake

Muir

Trinity Lakes

Agnew Meadows

San Joaquin

12,255 ft.

Cecile Lake

ANSEL ADAMS WILDERNESS

Trail

River

9,265 ft. Minaret Summit

12,281 ft.

Minaret Lake

Pumice Flat

10,910 ft.

Deadhorse Lake

Minaret Creek

Johnston Meadows

To Mammoth Lakes

Beck Lakes

Superior Lake

Holcomb Lake

Noname Lake

Devils Postpile National Monument

Devils Postpile Campground

N

Iron Lake

Gertrude Lake

Snow Canyon

11,149 ft. Iron Mountain

0   0.5   1
Miles

the summer season, beginning operations sometime between May 31 and July 4 (depending upon snow conditions) and ending the weekend after Labor Day. There is a modest per-person fee for the round-trip bus ride.

The Mammoth Mountain Ski Area parking lot can be reached by following California Highway 203 westward for about 7.5 miles from Mammoth Junction on US Highway 395. Mammoth Junction lies 40 miles north of Bishop and 26 miles south of Lee Vining on US 395.

The hike: This backpack trip, which can take as much as a week to complete, samples some of the finest scenery of the majestic Ritter Range. It includes stretches of the John Muir Trail and the PCT, spectacular views of the dark crags of the Ritter Range, and a short cross-country scramble directly under the towering east face of the Minarets.

The popularity of portions of this route attests to its desirability as a hiking area. Crowds are no longer excessive, though, due to daily entry quotas at all trailheads in the area. These quotas are rarely filled except on holiday weekends. If you desire solitude, this hike will be most enjoyable after Labor Day, when you should have this area more or less to yourself. During the summer season, the short cross-country stretch between Iceberg and Minaret Lakes also provides a modicum of solitude, in addition to a challenging route.

There are black bears in the region, so backpackers should take adequate precautions to protect their food supplies, either by hanging food (where trees are available) or by using a bear-resistant canister (the preferred method). Backpackers should be aware of campfire and campsite restrictions in the fragile alpine environment of the Minarets. Camping and campfires are not allowed within 0.25 mile of the outlets of Thousand Island and Garnet Lakes, within 0.25 mile of the north shore of Shadow Lake, or within 0.25 mile of the inlet of Ediza Lake. Campfires are prohibited along this hike between the outlet of Ediza Lake and 0.25 mile below the outlet of Minaret Lake.

Your trail, the permanent route of the PCT, begins north of the Agnew Meadows Campground, initially switchbacking up south-facing slopes clothed in red fir. Above the switchbacks, begin a protracted northwestward traverse across sparsely timbered slopes while obtaining good views into the deep, U-shaped Middle Fork San Joaquin River canyon.

After hiking 2.8 miles from the trailhead, capture a truly magnificent view southwestward across the canyon of the Middle Fork to Shadow Lake and the jagged, snowy ramparts of the Ritter Range. Continue your northwestward traverse and occasionally hop across small, wildflower-cloaked creeks, adding vivid contrast to these drab, otherwise dry slopes.

You pass a northwestbound trail leading to Agnew Pass about 5.3 miles from the trailhead. Shortly thereafter (0.3 mile), cross Summit Lake's outlet creek and then avoid a north-branching trail also leading to Agnew Pass and a south-branching trail descending to the Middle Fork.

A short jaunt beyond that junction leads you to a collection of tarns known as the Badger Lakes. With no inlet or outlet, these shallow, marshy ponds are in a transitional stage between lake and meadow. If you spend time here, you will be amazed by the large population of harmless garter snakes around the marshy shores of these ponds. From Badger Lakes, your mostly lodgepole pine–shaded route heads west to another junction. The right-hand fork ascends to the Clark Lakes, while the left-hand fork descends southeastward along the Middle Fork.

Continue your westward ascent along the upper Middle Fork San Joaquin River and through thinning timber, reaching the northeast end of the large, island-dotted Thousand Island Lake and a five-way junction. Massive Banner Peak soars above the south end of this timberline lake, and 12,311-foot Mount Davis rises to the southwest, where the Ritter Range joins the crest of the Sierra Nevada. A low gap lying between these two peaks offers class 2 access into the Lake Catherine area and the very remote headwaters of the North Fork San Joaquin River.

Turn left (southeast) onto the John Muir Trail. You soon pass the scenic Emerald and Ruby Lakes and then climb to a rocky saddle before descending to the shores of windswept Garnet Lake. The trail skirts the rockbound north shore of the lake, crosses its outlet stream, and turns southward after passing a trail that descends to the Middle Fork canyon.

Following a 400-foot ascent south of Garnet Lake, top a pass at 10,150 feet, where impressive views of Volcanic Ridge and the Minarets unfold. The trail then descends along a tributary of Shadow Creek, re-entering tree cover. Upon reaching a lodgepole pine–shaded junction, turn right (southwest) onto the Ediza Lake Trail. The left-hand fork descends to the overused shores of beautiful Shadow Lake, where camping and campfires are prohibited along the north and east shores.

Your trail ascends along the north bank of Shadow Creek and, after a short switchback, emerges along the eastern shores of Ediza Lake at an elevation of 9,300 feet. The backdrop of the Minarets and the imposing crags of Banner Peak and Mount Ritter make an overnight stay in this lake basin a memorable one. Please remember that camping is not allowed on the fragile terrain along the south side of this lake. Also, campfires are prohibited between the Ediza Lake outlet and just below the outlet of Minaret Lake.

Your route, now on unmaintained trail, ascends southward along the east side of Iceberg Lake's outlet stream, traversing above the east shore of this highly scenic subalpine lake. The demanding route ahead, best hiked in late August or September due to late-melting snow, should be attempted by experienced backpackers only.

The path rises steeply for 400 feet to meet the creek draining Cecile Lake. Scramble up the last, very steep pitch to reach the boulder-littered shores of Cecile Lake (at 10,300 feet and with no campsites), the highest body of water on the east slopes of the Ritter Range. Wedged between the dark wall of the Minarets and the black ramparts of Volcanic Ridge, this area resembles a moonscape.

There is no trail at this point, so boulder-hop around the east shore of this alpine lake to its southern end, where two possible routes descend to Minaret Lake. The first and most popular route descends a short cliff band and follows the obvious trail down to the lake. If you are not familiar with basic rock climbing, or feel uncomfortable descending exposed rock with a backpack, you may elect to take the easier, but slightly longer, route. To find this route, proceed to the extreme southern end of the lake and climb a low, glacially smoothed hill. From here, descend into a talus-covered slope that contains a small creek draining into Minaret Lake. Descend this slope along the small creek and meet the above-mentioned trail leading to the lake. Minaret Lake, with the impressive spire of Clyde Minaret piercing the sky to the west, is an excellent choice for an overnight stay.

The trail skirts the north shore of the lake and begins dropping through sparse forest along meadow-lined Minaret Creek. You shortly enter a thickening forest of lodgepole and silver pine, mountain hemlock, and some red fir. About 1.5 miles below Minaret Lake, you pass a northbound trail leading to the abandoned Minaret Mine, high on the south slopes of Volcanic Ridge. This mine operated between 1928 and 1930 and depended on dog teams coming from Old Mammoth for supplies during its two winters of operation.

Proceed down the canyon along the long-abandoned access road to the mine; your trail soon passes a series of Minaret Creek cascades. The now-dusty, pumice-covered trail descends through heavy timber to a junction with the John Muir Trail just north of marshy Johnston Meadow. Bear right at this junction, cross to Minaret Creek's south bank, and after 0.7 mile, stay left where the westbound trail to Beck and Holcomb Lakes joins your route.

After another 0.8 mile of steady descent through the forest, you meet the PCT. Continue straight ahead, and within 0.2 mile, reach another junction—take the middle fork straight ahead. After another 0.2 mile, at yet another junction, bear left, quickly crossing the Middle Fork San Joaquin River via a bridge.

Once across the river, you meet a southbound trail leading a short distance to Devils Postpile, a unique formation consisting of six-sided columns of basalt. The molten, basaltic lava is believed to have flowed down from a vent somewhere near Mammoth Pass, filling the Middle Fork canyon from Pumice Flat south to the vicinity of Rainbow Falls at a depth of 700 feet. As the flow cooled, it fractured, forming the hexagonal columns. The top of the Postpile was scoured by a large glacier flowing down the Middle Fork, quarrying away much of this basaltic flow. Only small remnants of the flow, of which the Postpile is the most impressive, exist today. Evidence of glaciation, in the form of glacial polish, can be seen by taking the short trail to the top of the Devils Postpile.

From the junction with the Devils Postpile Trail, turn left (north) and hike the final 0.2 mile to Devils Postpile Campground. Catch the next shuttle bus back to your car.

34 Lillian Lake Loop

Highlights:	This short but scenic backpack leads to several high, fish-filled lakes lying in the shadow of the stark alpine peaks that border the southeast edge of Yosemite National Park.
General location:	Southern Sierra Nevada, Ansel Adams Wilderness (Sierra National Forest), 60 miles northeast of Merced.
Type of hike:	Semi-loop backpack, 2 to 4 days.
Distance:	11.2 to 11.8 miles.
Difficulty:	Moderate.
Elevation gain and loss:	2,600 feet.
Trailhead elevation:	7,600 feet.
High point:	9,050 feet (or Shirley Lake, 9,200 feet, if cross-country route is taken).
Best season:	July through mid-October.
Water availability:	Abundant.
Maps:	Sierra National Forest map; Ansel Adams Wilderness map (topographic); USGS Sing Peak and Timber Knob 7.5-minute quads.
Permits:	A wilderness permit is required for overnight use and can be obtained at the Clover Meadow Ranger Station near the trailhead.

Key points:

- 0.0   Norris Creek Trailhead.
- 0.1   Turn left at junction on north bank of Norris Creek and proceed west.
- 0.3   Junction with Jackass Lakes Trail; turn right (northwest) onto Norris Trail.
- 1.25 Junction on ridge with descending trail leading to Fernandez Trailhead; stay left (west).
- 1.5   Junction with return leg of loop trail; bear left (southwest).
- 3.6   Vandeburg Lake.
- 4.1   Junction with southbound Lady Lake Trail; bear right (northwest).
- 4.7   Junction with westbound trail in Stanford Lakes Basin; either continue straight ahead (north) to reach Lillian Lake in 1.2 miles or turn left (west) to follow cross-country route to Shirley Lake.
- 5.7   Reach Shirley Lake via cross-country route; proceed northeast across basin and descend to Lillian Lake.
- 6.5   Outlet of Lillian Lake; turn left onto eastbound Lillian Lake Trail.
- 8.0   Junction with Fernandez Trail; bear right (southeast).
- 9.7   Junction with Timber Creek Trail; stay right (southeast) and continue descending.
- 9.9   Junction with Walton Trail on north bank of Madera Creek; bear right (south) and ford Madera Creek.
- 10.3 Junction on ridge with your inbound trail; bear left and retrace your route to the trailhead.
- 11.8 Norris Creek Trailhead.

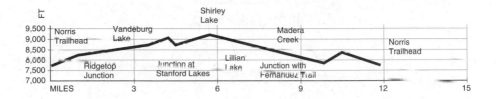

Finding the trailhead: There are two possible ways to reach the trailhead:
(1) from the town of North Fork, or (2) from Bass Lake.

(1) To reach North Fork, drive north from Fresno for 28.5 miles via
California Highway 41. Turn right (east) where a sign points to "Road 200,
O'Neals, North Fork National Forest Scenic Byway." Follow this road for
about 17 miles to North Fork and turn right where a sign points to South
Fork and Mammoth Pool. Stay right just past the sawmill in South Fork
where the sign indicates Rock Creek and Mammoth Pool. Drive this two-
lane paved road, Forest Road 81 (the Sierra Vista Scenic Byway), into the
western Sierra, following signs for Mammoth Pool and Clover Meadow.

After driving 35.8 miles from South Fork, stay left where a right-branching
road descends to Mammoth Pool Reservoir. A sign here points left to Minarets
Station—continue driving this good paved road through a magnificent western
Sierra Nevada conifer forest. You eventually pass the Minarets Work Center
on your left and reach a three-way junction after driving 13.8 miles from
the Mammoth Pool turnoff.

A sign here points left to the Minarets Pack Station and Beasore Meadows.
Turn right and drive 1.8 miles to the Clover Meadow Ranger Station, where
you can obtain your wilderness permit. After picking up your permit, return to the above-mentioned three-way junction, turn right (west) onto FR
7, and bear right in less than 0.25 mile to avoid the pack station turnoff. Stay
left after 2 more miles where a right-branching road leads to the Fernandez
Trailhead. About 100 yards beyond that turnoff, turn right at the sign for
Norris Trailhead. Follow this fairly rough, sometimes steep dirt road for
about 1.9 miles to the trailhead along Norris Creek.

(2) From the north shore of Bass Lake, turn north onto Beasore Road (FR
7) and follow signs pointing to Beasore Meadows and Clover Meadow. This
road is narrow, winding, steadily ascending, and paved, with signs along
the way pointing to Clover Meadow. Just before reaching the turnoff to
Upper Chiquito Campground, the road narrows to one lane; its surface
becomes very rough, with broken pavement and potholes. You reach the
signed turnoff to Norris Trailhead after driving 27.6 miles from Bass Lake.
Turn north and follow the directions given above. Don't forget to pick up
your wilderness permit at the Clover Meadow Ranger Station.

The hike: The high ridge forming the southeastern boundary of Yosemite
National Park marches southwest for 14 miles from its juncture with the
Sierra Nevada crest at Rodger Peak before fading into the forest south of
Madera Peak. Dozens of alpine and subalpine lakes lie in glacially sculpted
cirques on either side of this ridge, nestled below peaks that become

Lillian Lake Loop

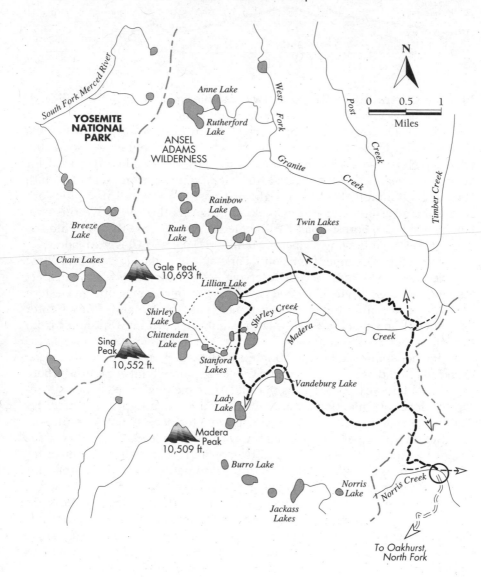

Shirley Lake, at 9,200 feet, mirrors a landscape scraped bare by glacial ice in the Ansel Adams Wilderness.

progressively higher from south to north, reaching a climax at 12,978-foot Rodger Peak. This ridge stands tall, collecting considerable moisture from Pacific storms. You will notice that timberline is much lower here than it is at points east in the Sierra.

Forming a loop near the southern terminus of this alpine ridge, this trip of at least two days visits several subalpine lakes, wanders through magnificent forests, and occasionally rewards hikers with expansive vistas of splendid mountain scenery. The short off-trail stretch from Stanford Lakes to Shirley Lake, and then down to Lillian Lake, should appeal to seasoned hikers. In addition to spectacular scenery, this hike features good fishing and abundant campsites. Locating water is no problem once you reach Vandeburg Lake.

From the parking area, immediately descend to and hop across Norris Creek and turn left onto the Norris Trail. A short westward jaunt along Norris Creek under a canopy of red fir and lodgepole pine brings you to the Jackass Lakes Trail junction. Turn right here; the sign indicates the Norris Trail and points to Fernandez Pass and Lillian Lake.

Your trail now climbs a moderately steep slope and enters the Ansel Adams Wilderness. It levels off under red fir shade before rising once again to meet a trail on your right that descends southeast to the Fernandez Trailhead and Clover Meadow. Bear left at this junction and crest an east-west ridge. Here you meet the return leg of your loop on the right.

From this point, you can see the peaks of the Silver Divide soaring above Fish Creek in the east and the dark, sawtoothed crags of the Ritter Range gnawing at the sky in the northeast. In the northwest, several alpine peaks at the head of the Granite Creek drainage lure hikers onward toward their glaciated environs.

Turn left onto the trail signed for Lillian Lake at this ridgetop junction. The level trail proceeds west through a forest of red fir, lodgepole pine, and a scattering of western white pine. En route, pass below a lovely meadow that may contain grazing cattle in the summer, cross two small creeks draining that meadow, immediately cross another small, cold creek, and then begin ascending through increasingly rocky terrain. Pass another soggy meadow and then enter a shallow, rocky basin.

Now the trail climbs over a low, rockbound ridge and descends to a boulder crossing of Vandeburg Lake's outlet creek that sits under a canopy of mountain hemlock, lodgepole and western white pine, and red fir. The trail avoids the shores of that lake, staying well within the forest; you won't see much of Vandeburg Lake unless you hike to it.

You soon meet the signed turnoff to Lady Lake after climbing a low, granite-bound ridge. Jog northwest, only to crest another low, rocky ridge that's sparsely forested with lodgepole pines. A descent to the Stanford Lakes follows, with accompanying views of impressive alpine peaks that rise above the basin in the west and northwest. Shortly after the trail levels off on the floor of the Stanford Lakes basin, you reach an unsigned junction with a rock-lined, westbound trail.

You have two options at this point. You can continue down the Stanford Lakes basin on the Lillian Lake Trail, reaching Lillian Lake in 1.2 miles. If you are more adventurous and experienced in routefinding, you may elect to turn left on the rock-lined trail. This often-faint trail crosses Shirley Creek and ascends northwest up the glaciated basin along the course of that creek.

The Stanford Lakes are generally too shallow to support a trout population, but anglers will be compensated farther on at Shirley and Chittenden Lakes. As you ascend this basin, notice the abundant evidence of past glaciation. The polished rock, gouges, striations, and step-like benches give mute testimony to the incredible grinding and scouring action of glacial ice in this area.

One mile of mostly cross-country hiking and 400 feet of ascent along Shirley Lake's outlet creek bring you to the shores of this small, but beautiful, lake at an elevation of 9,200 feet. Set at timberline in a granite-bound cirque under the alpine crags of 10,552-foot Sing Peak and 10,693-foot Gale Peak, this fine lake rewards all who visit its shores with sheer beauty and an isolated location. Fishing is good here for pan-sized trout. Chittenden Lake, an easy southward jaunt from Shirley Lake around a truncated spur ridge, provides even more solitude, as well as good fishing for brookies as large as 12 inches. Sing and Gale Peaks add to the attraction of this high basin and can be scaled via class 2 and class 3 routes, respectively.

From Shirley Lake, proceed across the basin in a northeasterly direction to cross a low rise. Descend to Lillian Lake via a steep, rocky gully.

Pick up the trail along the northwest shore of the lake and follow it to the outlet stream. The excellent campsites you pass on this side of the lake are off-limits to backpackers. The Forest Service has closed this shore to camping due to past overuse.

Upon reaching the dam-regulated outlet creek of Lillian Lake, the largest lake in the Granite Creek drainage, meet the Lillian Lake Trail and turn left, descending along the creek. Hop across a Madera Creek tributary, briefly climb over a low ridge, and meet the Fernandez Trail on your left, descending from the lakes in the northwest. Turn right here and begin a thickly forested descent. The trail soon breaks into the open along a dry ridge that's sparsely forested with juniper, lodgepole and Jeffrey pine, and white fir. From here, views are good back up into the Madera Creek headwaters and east across a thickly forested landscape to jagged High Sierra summits.

Your trail soon switchbacks down into heavy timber, passing the rarely used, northeastbound Timber Creek Trail at the bottom of your descent. The nearly level trail now leads toward Madera Creek. Avoid the left-branching Walton Trail. Just beyond that, you are confronted with the wide, swift waters of Madera Creek. To avoid wet feet, detour downstream for about 100 yards, where you will find a log crossing.

From the south side of the creek, begin a 500-foot ascent up the boulder-dotted north-facing slopes that are cloaked in lodgepole and silver pine and red fir. After this moderate ascent, you reach the boundary of the Ansel Adams Wilderness and a junction with the Lillian Lake Trail. From here, retrace your route back to the Norris Trailhead.

35 Isberg Trailhead to Hemlock Crossing

Highlights:	This demanding, seldom-used trail leads into a deep, ice-scoured canyon beneath the towering Ritter Range, featuring productive stream fishing and broad vistas.
General location:	Southern Sierra Nevada, Ansel Adams Wilderness (Sierra National Forest), 65 miles northeast of Merced.
Type of hike:	Round-trip backpack, 4 to 7 days.
Distance:	17.2 miles.
Difficulty:	Moderately strenuous.
Elevation gain and loss:	+1,900 feet, -1,300 feet.
Trailhead elevation:	7,000 feet.
High point:	8,900 feet.
Best season:	July through September.
Water availability:	East Fork Granite Creek from 2.1 to 2.4 miles; North Fork San Joaquin River at 8.6 miles.
Maps:	Sierra National Forest map; Ansel Adams Wilderness map (topographic); USGS Cattle Mountain, Mt. Lyell, Mt. Ritter, and Timber Knob 7.5-minute quads.
Permits:	Required for overnight use; obtain at Clover Meadow Ranger Station en route to the trailhead.

Key points:
- 0.0 Isberg Trailhead.
- 2.1 The Niche, boundary of Ansel Adams Wilderness.
- 2.4 Junction with Cora Lakes Trail; bear right and ford East Fork Granite Creek.
- 2.7 Junction with Cora Creek Trail; stay left.
- 3.0 Unsigned junction with northbound trail; bear right.
- 6.7 Begin descent into North Fork San Joaquin River canyon.
- 8.6 Hemlock Crossing.

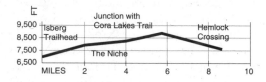

Finding the trailhead: Follow driving directions for Hike 34 to the Clover Meadow Ranger Station, where you can obtain wilderness permits. The ranger station is open daily during the summer season, and there is a telephone available for emergency use. Drinking water is also available.

Continue straight ahead past the ranger station for 0.5 mile to a junction with a northwestbound road signed for Isberg Trail and Mammoth Trail. Turn left and follow this road for 1.2 miles to a junction alongside the West Fork Granite Creek; turn right (east) toward the Isberg Trail. Follow this graded dirt road for another 1.3 miles to the signed Isberg Trailhead and continue ahead for another 200 yards to the parking area on the south side of the road.

The hike: The southwest corner of the Ansel Adams Wilderness encompasses a high divide of 10,000- to 12,000-foot peaks that form the boundary of Yosemite National Park and divide the headwaters of both the Merced River to the north and the North Fork San Joaquin River to the south. Carved out of either side of the divide are dozens of timberline and alpine lake basins. Much of the backcountry along this divide is served by an excellent network of trails, and the four major trailheads in the Clover Meadow area, Norris, Fernandez, Mammoth, and Isberg, receive a steady stream of hikers throughout the summer.

Most hikers to this corner of the Ansel Adams Wilderness hike in to the high lakes along the divide, and some take loop trips over the divide and into Yosemite. The trail to Hemlock Crossing and the North Fork San Joaquin River canyon, by contrast, is a dead-end trail and offers tremendous solitude in a canyon that ranks among the most dramatic in the Sierra. The lakes at the head of the North Fork are not served by trails and are rarely visited. Since much of this trail descends into the canyon, many hikers choose another trail to avoid the long haul back out of the canyon.

The crossing of the North Fork at Hemlock Crossing requires a deep ford of the vigorous river and remains difficult usually until August. After that time, the crossing is knee- to thigh-deep. Once you reach the east bank of the river, a wonderland of high country can be accessed via the North Fork Trail. At the head of the North Fork are lonely lake basins, accessible via cross-country routes, that lie beneath the towering peaks of the Ritter Range.

Isberg Trailhead to Hemlock Crossing

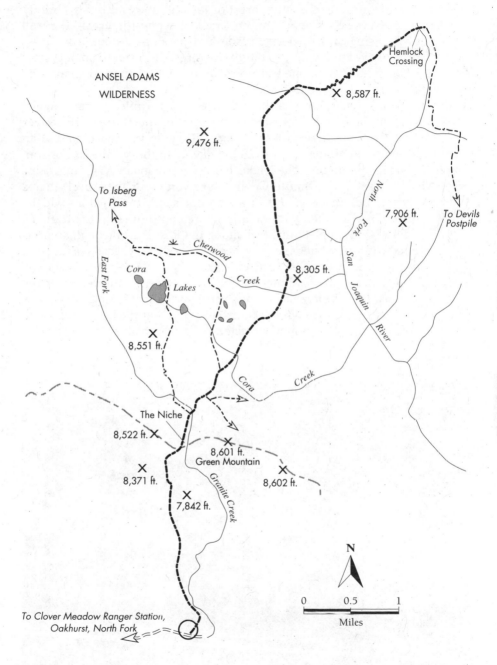

ANSEL ADAMS
WILDERNESS

Hemlock
Crossing

X 8,587 ft.

X
9,476 ft.

To Isberg
Pass

To Devils
Postpile

7,906 ft.
X

Chetwood

East Fork

Cora

Lakes

Creek

X 8,305 ft.

North Fork

San Joaquin

River

X
8,551 ft.

Cora   *Creek*

The Niche

8,522 ft. X

X
8,601 ft.
Green Mountain

X
8,602 ft.

X
8,371 ft.

X
7,842 ft.

Granite Creek

N

0   0.5   1
Miles

To Clover Meadow Ranger Station,
Oakhurst, North Fork

From the parking area, stroll west back down the road to the signed Isberg Trail and turn right (north) onto the wide and dusty singletrack. The trail rises gently at first through a forest of Jeffrey pine and red fir, briefly traversing above the East Fork Granite Creek. Beyond the creek, the trail angles uphill, rising at a moderate grade and passing through a viewless forest. The trail eventually breaks out of the forest onto steep, open granite slopes studded with Jeffrey pine and Sierra juniper, with clumps of manzanita and huckleberry oak at the trailside.

Vistas from this rocky, northeastbound traverse at 1.9 miles are far-ranging. Look out across the densely forested west slopes of the Sierra to the Silver Divide's high peaks to the southeast, Kaiser Ridge to the south, and to an array of ice-chiseled alpine crags stretching away to the southeast horizon. The trail soon leads you into The Niche, a narrow gap in a high granite ridge carved by the East Fork Granite Creek. Here you enter the Ansel Adams Wilderness. Immediately east of the trail is a fine sandy bench alongside the creek, a great place to catch your breath before continuing up the trail.

Beyond The Niche, a pleasant stroll along the East Fork through an open lodgepole and western white pine forest leads 0.3 mile northeast to a junction with a trail leading northwest to Cora Lakes, Isberg Pass, and Yosemite. Turn right (northeast) at this junction and quickly reach the banks of the East Fork. Rock-hop the creek just downstream from the stock ford. The trail ahead rises gently through the forest and past wet meadows rich with the color of shooting star, groundsel, aster, American bistort, and yampah.

Hikers en route to Hemlock Crossing enjoy unforgettable vistas of the Ritter Range and the canyon of the North Fork San Joaquin River.

Soon you arrive at another junction where you continue straight ahead toward Hemlock Crossing. After another 0.3 mile, you come to an unsigned junction and bear right. The trail ahead is uneventful as you proceed across gentle, pine- and fir-forested terrain. After walking 1.1 miles from the previous junction, rock-hop the small Chetwood Creek and begin ascending the slopes of the ridge to the north. It is a steady ascent up this ridge to an 8,900-foot high point, passing through pine and fir forest. Along this stretch, you will begin to enjoy tremendous views of the towering Ritter Range and the deep trough of the North Fork San Joaquin River canyon.

About 2.3 miles north of Chetwood Creek and 6.3 miles from the trailhead, descend east along a small creek and rise to the shoulder of a granite ridge plunging into the North Fork canyon. Descend along the northwest side of the ridge, dropping 1,200 feet in about 2 miles en route to Hemlock Crossing, via a series of tight, rocky switchbacks.

Unforgettable views accompany you for much of the way. The canyon below is nearly devoid of forest, hosting only pockets of pine and fir among an array of ice-polished domes that are composed of the same dark metamorphic rocks as that of the Ritter Range. Numerous large creeks can be seen cascading down the west face of the range. The Ritter Range soars more than 4,000 feet above the canyon and is crowned by 13,157-foot Mount Ritter in the northeast, the high towers of the Minarets in the east, and the dark pyramid of Iron Mountain in the southeast, with an array of 10,000- to 12,000-foot peaks in between.

The plunging trail levels out among the domes and winds down to Hemlock Crossing at 7,600 feet, 8.6 miles from the trailhead. There, beneath Dome 8,286 and the great peaks of the Ritter Range, you will find several fine campsites among a scattering of pine and fir. The crossing itself is a ford immediately below a low waterfall and often remains knee-deep, with a moderate current, throughout the summer.

On the east bank of the vigorous river, trails lead northwest and southeast. The southeastbound trail ultimately leads to Devils Postpile on the Middle Fork San Joaquin River. The northwestbound trail follows the spectacular North Fork up the canyon among an array of domes for 5 miles, where it fades out amidst the rocky terrain in a 9,300-foot valley between the Twin Island and Catherine Lakes basins. This area is an excellent place for experienced hikers to partake in cross-country exploration of the lakes in Bench Canyon, the head of the North Fork beneath Mount Davis and Rodger Peak, and the Catherine Lakes basin beneath Banner Peak and Mount Ritter.

Northern
Great Basin Ranges

East of the Sierra Nevada and north of Death Valley National Park, the arid mountain ranges and valleys of the western Great Basin begin the transition in environmental conditions and landscapes. The basins and ranges begin to rise higher in elevation. Consequently, their heights wring out most of what little moisture is left in storm systems after they have passed over the Sierra Nevada crest.

The higher elevations of these mountains and valleys also translate to a cooler climate, and in winter, snow can accumulate and linger in the valley bottoms, which range from about 4,000 to 6,500 feet in elevation. In the mountains, above 8,000 feet, a moderate snowpack often lingers throughout winter. Of course, the farther north you travel through this region, the more pronounced the winter season becomes. Temperatures as low as 45 degrees below zero have been recorded during winter in the Bridgeport Valley.

In these valleys, the ubiquitous creosote bush of the southern Great Basin and Mojave Desert is replaced by the cold-tolerant sagebrush. In the high mountains, as you travel northward from the vicinity of Big Pine in the Owens Valley, sparse stands of pinyon and juniper are gradually replaced by extensive woodlands. Still higher in the mountain ranges, conifer stands become progressively more extensive as you travel north. In the Sweetwater Mountains, north of the town of Bridgeport on the Nevada state line, forests of lodgepole and whitebark pine, and groves of aspen, cover the range's slopes.

Many of the mountains and a few of the valleys of the northern Great Basin in California are protected within the boundaries of Bureau of Land Management (BLM) wilderness and wilderness study areas (WSAs). Recreational opportunities in this region are limited only by your imagination and by the lack of water. Trails are nonexistent, save for the short paths in the Ancient Bristlecone Pine Forest of the White Mountains. Many trails follow four-wheel-drive roads, but most routes in this region are cross-country.

During the summer months, when most of this region, except for the highest mountains, is too hot and inhospitable for hiking, spend some time poring over U.S. Geological Service and BLM maps of the region to plan a memorable autumn or spring outing in these wild reaches of the California desert. Whenever you visit, always carry an ample water supply and plan on drinking one gallon of water per person, each day.

The hikes described below represent only a small sampling of the recreational opportunities in the region. Since each hike visits a mountain peak, you can view much of the northern Great Basin of California. Hopefully, the views will stimulate your appetite for further exploration.

36 Piper Mountain

Highlights: This trip features an exhilarating ascent of a prominent desert peak via a closed four-wheel-drive road, broad vistas of Great Basin valleys and mountains, and interesting perspectives of the eastern escarpment of the Sierra Nevada.

General location: Great Basin, Chocolate Mountains, Piper Mountain Wilderness (Bureau of Land Management [BLM], Ridgecrest Resource Area), 23 miles northeast of Big Pine.

Type of hike: Round-trip day hike.

Distance: 6 miles.

Difficulty: Moderate.

Elevation gain and loss: 1,425 feet.

Trailhead elevation: 6,280 feet.

High point: Piper Mountain, 7,705 feet.

Best season: March through mid-June, mid-September through November.

Water availability: None available; bring your own.

Maps: USGS Last Chance Range (California-Nevada) 1:100,000-scale map; USGS Chocolate Mountain (California-Nevada) 7.5-minute quad.

Permits: Not required.

Key points:

0.0	Piper Mountain trailhead; proceed south on the closed doubletrack.
0.1	Junction with westbound doubletrack; bear left (south).
0.6	End of doubletrack; continue straight ahead (southwest), cross-country.
0.8	Reach other doubletrack; turn left (south).
2.6	Junction with trail to Piper Mountain; turn right (southeast).
3.0	Summit of Piper Mountain.

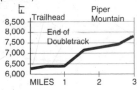

Finding the trailhead: From US Highway 395 at the north end of Big Pine, turn east onto California Highway 168, signed for Ancient Bristlecone Pine Forest, Westgard Pass, Deep Springs, and the US 95 junction. CA 168 is a steep, narrow, and winding road that ascends the west slopes of the Inyo-White Mountains for 13.75 miles to Westgard Pass. The road then descends into Deep Springs Valley, after which you follow another steep and winding grade to Gilbert Summit at 6,374 feet, 18.8 miles from Westgard Pass.

From the large turnout on the right (east) side of the road, turn right onto a southeastbound dirt road. This narrow, seldom-used track, which can be negotiated by carefully driven cars, leads 0.5 mile to a junction with a southbound four-wheel-drive road, which is closed behind the BLM "wilderness" sign. Park at this junction of the two roads beneath the north slopes of Piper Mountain.

Piper Mountain

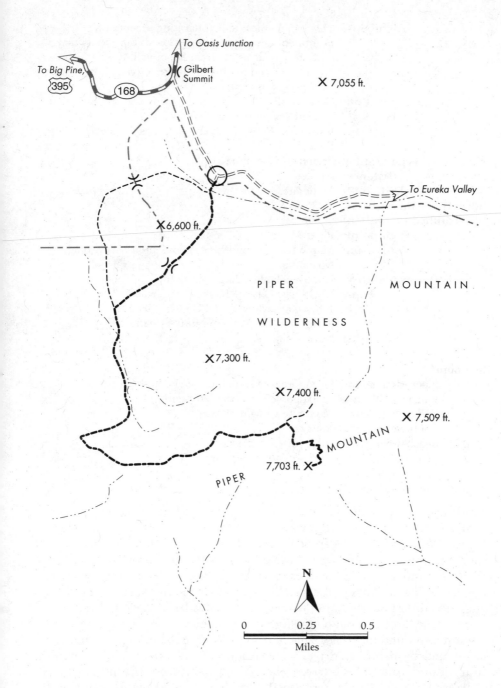

To Oasis Junction

To Big Pine, **395** **168**

Gilbert Summit

X 7,055 ft.

To Eureka Valley

X 6,600 ft.

P I P E R   M O U N T A I N

W I L D E R N E S S

X 7,300 ft.

X 7,400 ft.

X 7,509 ft.

MOUNTAIN

7,703 ft. X

P I P E R

N

0   0.25   0.5

Miles

The hike: Piper Mountain is an isolated high-desert peak, anchoring the north end of the 72,575-acre Piper Mountain Wilderness. The wilderness encompasses a subrange of the Inyo Mountains, commonly referred to as the Chocolate Mountains. Although the topo map labels the peak "Chocolate Mountain," hikers and BLM rangers know the peak as Piper Mountain. Lying east of the Deep Springs Valley and the White Mountains, bounded on the south by the desert trough of Eureka Valley, and rising south of Fish Lake Valley, this desert prominence affords unobstructed, far-ranging vistas.

The route to the peak follows an old four-wheel-drive road that has been closed since the establishment of the wilderness in 1994. A short, 0.2 mile stretch of off-trail walking across an alluvial fan helps relieve the monotony of road walking. Solitude on the peak is almost guaranteed. Judging by the summit register, only a handful of hikers visit the mountain each year; most of them are students from nearby Deep Springs College.

From the parking area, follow the closed doubletrack south, gradually descending into a shallow draw studded with the gnarled shrubs of cliffrose. There, adjacent to three old adits and waste rock dumps, a faint doubletrack turns west. You can follow that route west through a saddle and then south up an alluvial fan. The way described below is shorter and intersects that route 0.7 mile ahead.

Proceed left (south) from the junction, aiming for a low saddle south of Hill 6600. Granite boulders dot the slopes, which are mantled in a coarse veneer of big sagebrush, horsebrush, and native bunchgrasses; in spring, the slopes host an array of colorful wildflowers. After cresting the saddle, begin descending southwest, enjoying fine views of the White Mountains on the western skyline.

The doubletrack soon ends beyond the saddle; make your own way over the corrugated, boulder-littered alluvial fan, following a southwest course. Although there are a few large cairns along this stretch, your best reference point is a solitary, dark-green juniper that lies ahead. When you reach that juniper, you will spy the other doubletrack ascending south into a draw that cleaves the north slope of Piper Mountain. When you reach that track, turn left (south) and ascend its rocky bed. Remember the juniper, and use it for a landmark upon returning from the peak.

Your doubletrack leads steeply into a rocky canyon, eventually passing a pair of old steel gateposts flanking the road. Just beyond, you pass another large cairn where the doubletrack bends southwest. Continue following the old road, first through tall, rich grasses, then among cheatgrass, and ascend the steep slope toward the crest of Piper Mountain. Low mounds of big sagebrush, mormon tea, horsebrush, and hop-sage stud the slopes of the mountain. A pair of switchbacks ease the grade just before you mount the crest, where a broad vista unfolds.

Piper Mountain looms ahead on the eastern skyline, now only 600 feet above you. The now gentle grade of the rocky doubletrack leads eastward over crunchy gray and reddish brown volcanics along or near the mountain's crest. You will enjoy an ever-changing panorama as you proceed. Eventually, the trail levels out upon entering a flat studded with an open woodland of gnarled junipers.

When you reach a point between the granite-capped, juniper-dotted hill of Point 7,400 and the black volcanic summit ridge of Piper Mountain, look for a cairn that indicates a southbound foot trail, 350 feet below the summit. At the cairn, turn right (southeast) onto the trail and follow the switchbacks up a steep grade. Actually, there are two trails here; one is more of a boot-worn path, while the other trail has been constructed by hikers but is incomplete. If you follow the constructed trail, you will need to scramble from its end up to the boot-worn trail to reach the summit ridge.

Both trails pass among scrubby junipers and onto granite slopes, rising 350 feet to the black volcanics capping the summit ridge. From there, follow the winding trail southwest for several yards to the summit. Plan on spending some time here; the vistas are breathtaking and panoramic.

The most dramatic feature, rising in the southwest beyond Deep Springs Lake, Deep Springs Valley, and the Inyo Mountains, is the eastern escarpment of the Sierra Nevada. Stretching some 50 miles from the vicinity of Mounts Williamson and Tyndall, past the Palisade Crest nearly to Mount Humphreys, this snow-streaked crest of 13,000- and 14,000-foot peaks provides a dramatic backdrop to the rugged desert mountains and valleys in the foreground. Closer at hand are the White Mountains, crowned by bristlecone pine–studded hills, that stretch northwest past White Mountain Peak, the highest of all Great Basin summits, to the distant pyramid of Boundary Peak. The Fish Lake Valley sprawls out below to the north in a patchwork of verdant hay fields. On the eastern horizon, the Silver Peak Range in Nevada rises beyond the small, wooded summits of the Sylvania Mountains.

The Last Chance Range, crowned by the barren white dome of Last Chance Peak, marches southeast along the eastern margin of the Eureka Valley. Among the three broad dune fields in this valley are the Eureka Dunes far to the southeast, the tallest dunes in North America. The western margin of Eureka Valley is bounded by the Chocolate Mountains and the Saline Range. Beyond, the lofty spine of the Inyo Mountains marches off into the distance.

Eventually, you must abandon the superb vistas and retrace your route back to the trailhead.

37 White Mountain Sampler

Highlights: This series of four short hikes, totaling 6 miles, leads you through a variety of high-elevation landscapes in the Ancient Bristlecone Pine Forest of the White Mountains.

General location: Great Basin, White Mountains, Inyo National Forest, 10 miles east of Bishop.

Type of hike: Hike No. 1: short loop; Hike No. 2: short loop; Hike No. 3: short loop; Hike No. 4: round-trip day hike, part cross-country.

Distance: Hike No. 1 (Discovery Trail), 1 mile; Hike No. 2 (Patriarch Trail), 0.5 mile; Hike No. 3 (Vista Trail), 0.5 mile; Hike No. 4 (Sheep Mountain), 4 miles.

Difficulty: Hikes Nos. 1, 2, 3, easy; Hike No. 4, moderate.

Elevation gain and loss: Hike No. 1: 160 feet; Hike No. 2: 50 feet; Hike No. 3: 60 feet; Hike No. 4: +1,300 feet, -153 feet.

High point: Hike No. 1: 10,260 feet; Hike No. 2: 11,350 feet; Hike No. 3: 11,360 feet; Hike No. 4: 12,497 feet.

Best season: Late June through mid-October.

Water availability: None available, bring your own.

Maps: Inyo National Forest map; USGS Westgard Pass, Blanco Mountain, and Mt. Barcroft 7.5-minute quads.

Permits: Not required.

Finding the trailhead: From US Highway 395 in Big Pine, turn east onto California Highway 168 where a large sign indicates the Ancient Bristlecone Pine Forest and tells whether the road is open. During the winter, any of a number of gates on the Bristlecone Pine road may be locked, depending on snow conditions. The gate at Sierra View definitely will be locked from late fall until spring. No services are available east of Big Pine, so be sure to have a full tank of gas and plenty of water.

After driving 2.3 miles, pass the southeast-branching Death Valley Road leading to the Eureka and Saline Valleys. Your highway leads through an often-narrow and spectacular canyon while ascending the western slope of the White Mountains. Suddenly, you emerge onto Cedar Flat on the crest of the range amidst a dense forest of juniper and pinyon pine.

Turn left (north) after driving 12.9 miles from Big Pine, where a large sign indicates "White Mountain Road, Bristlecone Pine Forest, White Mountain Research Stations." You soon pass an information booth and continue along this paved road just east of the crest through a thick pinyon pine and juniper forest. Pinyon nut enthusiasts will want to spend time here during the fall to enjoy a harvest of these tasty nuts.

Pass the Grandview Campground 4.5 miles from the highway, and after 2.5 more miles, you reach Sierra View at an elevation of 9,300 feet. A photographic stop here is a must. The Sierra Nevada, from the Cottonwood Creek area near Lone Pine northward to the Mount Dana area in Yosemite

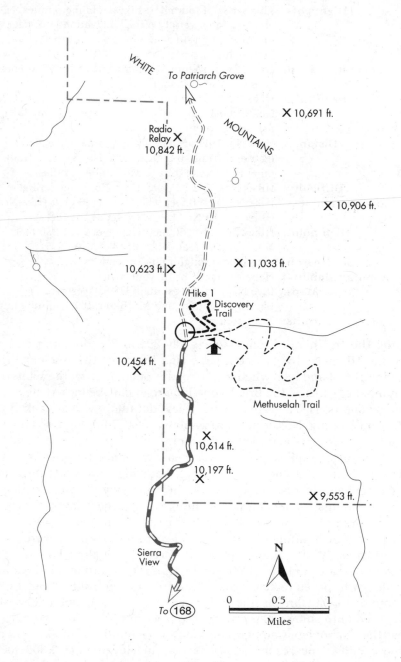

To Patriarch Grove

WHITE

MOUNTAINS

X 10,691 ft.

Radio Relay X
10,842 ft.

X 10,906 ft.

10,623 ft. X

X 11,033 ft.

Hike 1
Discovery Trail

10,454 ft.
X

Methuselah Trail

X 10,614 ft.

10,197 ft.
X

X 9,553 ft.

Sierra View

To (168)

N

0   0.5   1
Miles

National Park, can be seen to the west—undeniably, one of the most majestic mountain chains in the country.

Immediately above you is the first timberline you will encounter on this trip. The pinyon pines are stunted and ground-hugging as they quickly fade into the sagebrush slopes above. Near Patriarch Grove, you pass into above-timberline terrain, where the bristlecone pines diminish into alpine fell fields.

From Sierra View, continue driving north, entering the Ancient Bristlecone Pine Forest after 1 mile. A few limber pines first appear; where a sign indicates the 10,000-foot level, bristlecone pines begin dominating the slopes east of the road. About 10 miles from the highway, you reach Schulman Grove at an elevation of 10,100 feet. There is a visitor center (open during summer) and a picnic area here. There is also a large display case giving information about the bristlecone pines.

The hike: Most people take only a day to drive through the Ancient Bristlecone Pine Forest in the White Mountains, and few do much hiking in the area. The White Mountains are well off the beaten track for most hikers, many of whom wonder about that high, barren-looking range on the east side of Owens Valley as they drive to the High Sierra via US 395. That barren-looking range actually contains extensive subalpine forests of bristlecone and limber pine, perennial streams, and meadows lush enough to support limited cattle grazing. In summer, wildflowers add a touch of color to this high, barren landscape.

These four short hikes are all quite easy and can be completed in a day. If you are staying overnight at the Grandview Campground, you may wish to take two days to fully enjoy this area. There is no overnight camping in the Ancient Bristlecone Pine Forest, so day hikes are the only way to explore this region.

Two trails begin at Schulman Grove. The longer, more rigorous Methuselah Trail heads east, making a 4.25-mile loop while visiting some of the oldest living trees on earth. Some of these bristlecone pines are more than 4,000 years old.

The shorter Discovery Trail leads north. This 1-mile trail switchbacks a short distance northward on limestone slopes, passing some very impressive gnarled and twisted bristlecone pines, many of which are kept alive by a single strip of bark running along their trunks. The dead and downed trees have been weathered to the point of almost being petrified—the wood is like stone and has a beautiful golden appearance.

There is little, if any, ground cover in this area. Consequently, this forest of ancient trees is open and offers fine vistas. Some Sierra Nevada peaks are visible westward across Reed Flat. Where the trail reaches a band of red rock, you will have good views north along the crest of the range as far as County Line Hill and Blanco Mountain. The mostly barren landscape is broken up intermittently by stands of bristlecone pine.

The bristlecones seem to favor limestone—they grow exclusively on such soils, mostly east of the crest. Limestone is an unsuitable habitat for most other conifers, although some limber pine can also be found growing on

White Mountain Sampler

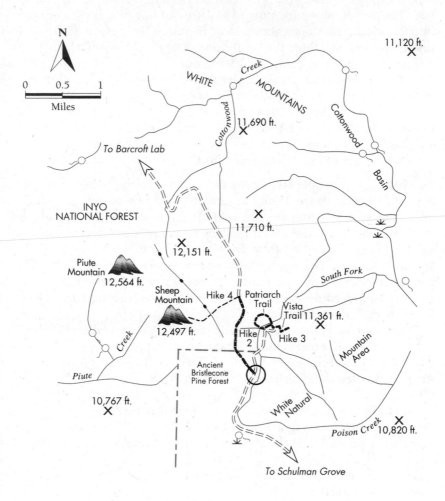

N

0   0.5   1
Miles

11,120 ft.
X

WHITE   Creek   MOUNTAINS

Cottonwood

11,690 ft.
X

Cottonwood

To Barcroft Lab

Basin

INYO
NATIONAL FOREST

X
11,710 ft.

X
12,151 ft.

Piute
Mountain
12,564 ft.

Sheep
Mountain

South Fork

Hike 4   Patriarch
Trail

Vista
Trail 11,361 ft.
X

12,497 ft.

Hike
2   Hike 3

Mountain
Area

Creek

Ancient
Bristlecone
Pine Forest

Piute

White   Natural

10,767 ft.
X

Poison Creek   10,820 ft.
X

To Schulman Grove

these sites. Precipitation here averages about 10 inches per year, so the area supports only a limited variety of plant life.

After enjoying the vista from the northernmost point of Discovery Trail, follow the switchbacks to the south on a lower contour. After 0.5 mile of hiking through some of the most impressive, weather-tortured trees to be seen anywhere, you arrive back at the visitor center and your car.

Now that your appetites for the bristlecone pines and the White Mountains have been stimulated, drive north from Schulman Grove. After the pavement ends, follow the good dirt road along or near the crest, gaining elevation and spectacular vistas along the way. After driving 13 miles, you reach the junction with the road to Patriarch Grove. Turn right and drive 1 mile to the end of

Ancient bristlecone pines, among the oldest living things on earth, have been scarred and sculpted by strong winds and blowing snow for thousands of years here in the Patriarch Grove of the White Mountains.

the road at 11,300 feet. Amidst a weather-beaten subalpine forest, two trails begin. Both hikes are short, easy, and well worth the time and effort.

First, walk west from the parking area and pick up the Patriarch Trail. This short trail makes a 0.5-mile loop through the strange subalpine landscape, passing the Patriarch Tree—not the oldest, but by far the largest bristlecone pine known on earth. This multiple-trunked giant has a circumference of 36 feet, 8 inches.

After this pleasant stroll, head east across the parking area and pick up the short Vista Trail that climbs to the ridgetop at 11,360 feet. From this point, you can see Cottonwood Basin below to the north, where there are vivid green meadows, granite boulders and outcrops, and a good year-round stream. To the west, the alpine peaks of the White Mountains crest rise above the last sparse stand of bristlecones, snow-streaked well into summer.

After returning to your car, drive 1 mile back to the junction with the main road. Park on the edge of the wide dirt road, being sure to stay in the roadbed to avoid crushing the delicate alpine plants. Do not block the road.

Begin hiking north along the road across barren, alpine slopes, passing absolute timberline. After strolling 1.2 miles, you reach a high point at an elevation of 11,850 feet, where the road begins to descend. After having completed the three short hikes back down the road, your body should have acclimatized somewhat, but the elevation and the steepness of this cross-country hike will still take its toll.

Your destination is Sheep Mountain, about 0.8 mile to the southwest. Begin by laboring up the smooth and very steep alpine slopes in a south-westerly direction. It would be difficult to get lost here—simply climb the steep slopes to the first summit, Peak 12,240. Drop into a saddle through which a transmission line passes, supplying power to the University of California's Barcroft Laboratory.

From this saddle, it's 300 feet up the final alpine slopes to 12,497-foot Sheep Mountain, where a magnificent vista unfolds. The view north and east into Nevada is excellent, as is the southward view along the crest of the White Mountains. The great Sierra Nevada rears up majestically beyond Owens Valley, one of the deepest valleys on the continent. To the north is Piute Mountain, Mount Barcroft, and White Mountain Peak. In addition to being the highest in this range, 14,246-foot White Mountain Peak is the highest point in the Great Basin, as well as one of California's 11 peaks with elevations greater than 14,000 feet.

The Great Basin is a vast region, encompassing most of Nevada and parts of Utah, Oregon, Idaho, and California. It is characterized by literally hundreds of mountain ranges aligned in a generally north-south pattern and interrupted by numerous desert valleys. These valleys are generally closed basins where the streams draining the mountain ranges end in "dry" lakes that evaporate in the intense desert sun. The Great Basin has no outlet to the sea. The region contains incredible topographic relief. The crest of the Panamint Mountains, for example, plummets more than 11,000 feet into Death Valley.

Also visible from Sheep Mountain are the buildings of the Barcroft Lab lying at the 12,400-foot level on the east slopes of 13,040-foot Mount Barcroft. It is a barren yet beautiful alpine landscape, accentuated in early summer by numerous snowfields. From the Barcroft Lab, an old doubletrack leads 5.3 miles to White Mountain Peak, a very worthwhile excursion.

After absorbing the superb view, carefully retrace your route back to your car. With these four hikes, you have sampled one of the most unique landscapes in California. There are many more opportunities for hiking in the White Mountains, as a quick glance at the topographic quadrangles reveals. Many involve cross-country walking. Probably the most challenging hike in the range can be made from White Mountain Peak, hiking north along the crest of the range for many miles. You could backpack in this area for a week or more, with solitude virtually assured. Such a no-nonsense cross-country hike, however, should be attempted by veteran hikers only.

Still, all you really need for hiking in this range is a topo map, a compass, and a sense of adventure. This area is also moderately popular with cross-country ski enthusiasts. The excellent network of roads and often superb, dry snow conditions make an expedition into the bristlecones and beyond an unforgettable winter experience.

38 Desert Creek to Mount Patterson

Highlights:	This exciting, seldom-traveled route leads to the alpine crest of an obscure eastern California mountain range and features far-ranging vistas that reach from the Sierra crest to the distant mountain ranges and valleys stretching into Nevada.
General location:	Great Basin, Sweetwater Mountains, Toiyabe National Forest, 13 miles north-northwest of Bridgeport.
Type of hike:	Round-trip day hike or overnighter.
Distance:	8.8 miles.
Difficulty:	Moderately strenuous.
Elevation gain and loss:	+2,773 feet, -100 feet.
Trailhead elevation:	9,000 feet.
High point:	Mt. Patterson, 11,673 feet.
Best season:	July through early October.
Water availability:	Water is available near the trailhead from Desert Creek, but may be fouled by cattle. A more reliable source is the East Fork Desert Creek, but potability is questionable here due to an inactive upstream mine. The best solution is to carry all the water you will need.
Maps:	Toiyabe National Forest map; USGS Mt. Patterson 7.5-minute quad.
Permits:	Not required.

Desert Creek to Mount Patterson

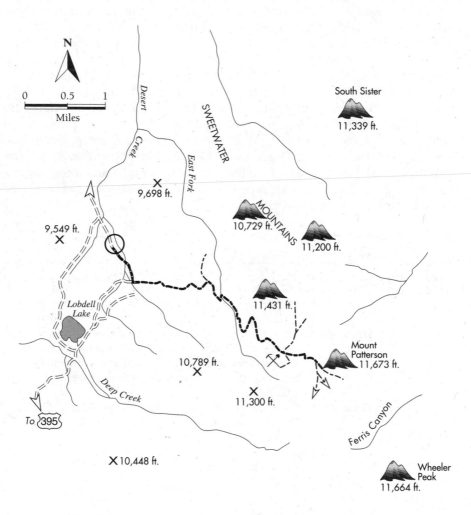

N

0   0.5   1
Miles

South Sister
11,339 ft.

Desert Creek

SWEETWATER

East Fork

X 9,698 ft.

9,549 ft.
X

MOUNTAINS
10,729 ft.

11,200 ft.

11,431 ft.

Mount
Patterson
11,673 ft.

Lobdell
Lake

10,789 ft.
X

X
11,300 ft.

Deep Creek

To 395

Ferris Canyon

X 10,448 ft.

Wheeler
Peak
11,664 ft.

X 9,823 ft.

Key points:

0.0 Begin hiking south on doubletrack along Desert Creek.

0.5 Junction with doubletrack leading south to Lobdell Lake; stay left (east) and begin ascending.

1.6 Junction with northbound doubletrack; bear right (southeast) and descend into East Fork Desert Creek.

2.0 Ford East Fork Desert Creek.

3.5 Four-way junction on crest of Sweetwater Mountains; follow the middle fork east toward Mt. Patterson.

4.1 Junction just below summit; stay left (southeast).

4.3 Leave doubletrack and proceed north, cross-country, to summit.

4.4 Summit of Mt. Patterson.

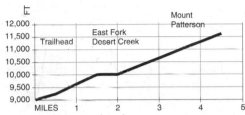

Finding the trailhead: To find the starting point for this hike, you must first locate the Bircham Flat Road, Forest Road 031 (spelled "Burcham" on the map, "Bircham" on the sign). This signed dirt road branches north from US Highway 395 about 14.7 miles northwest of Bridgeport and 2.1 miles southeast of the US 395/California Highway 108 junction. This hard-to-spot turnoff is just beyond a highway sign designating a 50-mph curve and lies just east of a gravel pit.

This good dirt road is wide but develops severe washboards. It heads east for a short distance after leaving the highway, swings north, and ascends to Bircham Flat and on into the Sweetwater Mountains. Where the Bircham Flat Road reaches its high point after 4.2 miles, turn right onto the possibly unsigned Lobdell Lake Road.

Follow this often narrow, sometimes rough dirt road for 6.2 miles to a road junction at Lobdell Lake. Turn left, drive around the south and west sides of the levee-dammed Lobdell Lake, and proceed north across a meadow-covered flat. The road at this point is a rough doubletrack, but only low-clearance vehicles should have trouble negotiating the route. After driving 2 rough miles from the previous junction, you meet a southeastbound doubletrack on your right, designated by a sign depicting a jeep. Turn right onto this doubletrack and proceed southeast along the course of Desert Creek.

After driving about 0.4 mile up this road (which is easier going than the previous 2 miles from Lobdell Lake), you reach a rough segment where large rocks protrude out of the roadbed, forcing all but high-clearance, four-wheel-drive vehicles to park. If you are able to negotiate this extremely rough section, park in another 0.3 mile before the doubletrack crosses Desert Creek.

Hikers with low-clearance vehicles should consider bearing right at the Lobdell Lake road junction and parking near Lobdell Lake. From there, you can follow a northbound doubletrack for about 1 mile to reach the trail 0.5 mile above the Desert Creek Trailhead.

The hike: The Sweetwater Mountains, one of the most well-watered of all the Great Basin ranges, rise high above the West Walker River east of the Sierra Nevada. On their middle flanks are cool stands of lodgepole pine and aspen; above, whitebark pines, twisted and stunted by winter's unobstructed fury, cling tenaciously to life; still higher, conditions become so fierce that only alpine cushion plants are able to survive on the range's highest peaks and ridges. This moderately strenuous trip takes you to the apex of the Sweetwater Mountains to enjoy far-ranging vistas of Nevada and the Sierra Nevada.

From the trailhead, proceed south along the course of Desert Creek. Your doubletrack stays west of meadow-lined Desert Creek, where sagebrush, helenium, lupine, yarrow, cinquefoil, western blue flag, aster, sheep sorrel, rosy everlasting, and a number of grasses thrive. Monkey flowers grow in the wettest areas next to the creek. The open, sagebrush- and aspen-clad slopes on your left contrast markedly with the thick lodgepole pine forest on your right.

You are soon forced to either ford Desert Creek or search downstream for a boulder crossing. Your doubletrack now angles across an open meadow that is often full of cows during the summer, meets another doubletrack on your right coming from Lobdell Lake, and crosses a small Desert Creek tributary. Begin ascending eastward along an open hillside. As you gain elevation, your westward views expand, exposing the jagged, snowy Sierra Nevada crest. You leave most of the cattle behind during this climb.

This eastward ascent terminates at the 10,000-foot level in a subalpine forest of lodgepole and whitebark pine. From here, a brief descent leads

East Fork Desert Creek in the Sweetwater Mountains.

past a "Closed to All Motor Vehicles" sign, intended for the northbound doubletrack. Bear right, head around a spur ridge, and be treated to your first glimpse of the glistening white peaks surrounding Mount Patterson.

The doubletrack now descends to the East Fork Desert Creek. A sign bolted to a whitebark pine indicates that the doubletrack is closed to motor vehicles beyond this point. Unfortunately, some determined (or illiterate) trail bikers ride here despite its closure.

Hop across the small East Fork and proceed upstream near its meadow-clad banks. Sparse whitebark pines survive here and there beneath the stark alpine peaks surrounding this drainage. It is possible to camp here along the East Fork, but level ground is elusive.

Two short switchbacks start you on your climb out of the East Fork. With a moderate to steep ascent just west of Peak 11,431, you eventually pass the last stand of tenacious, stunted, gnarled, ground-hugging whitebark pines, the ground around them littered with the beautifully weathered remains of their ancestors. Continue your climb and negotiate one last, steep switchback.

After a moderately steep traverse, you reach the windswept alpine crest of the Sweetwater Mountains. Pass an old doubletrack leading downslope to your right to the Montague Mine and another set of tracks leading northeast. From this point, get your first view of Mount Patterson, rising abruptly ahead of you. A bulldozed swath, leading up the northwest flank of the peak, detracts from the stark beauty of this alpine landscape.

Head for that steep swath, however, and ascend toward the summit of Mount Patterson. Nearing the peak, another doubletrack branches off to your right. Bear left, continue following the bulldozed route, and soon leave it to scramble a short distance to the summit. Your reward is breathtaking scenery from this 11,673-foot peak.

The Sierra Nevadas compose the westward view, from the Wheeler Crest in the south to the Carson Range in the north. The impressive, glacier-clad Sawtooth Ridge, dominated by Matterhorn Peak and Twin Peaks, is especially striking. The unmistakable, glaciated north face of Mount Lyell in Yosemite National Park is easily distinguished in the south beyond the lower, less impressive Sierra peaks.

Far to the southeast are the White Mountains, crowned by one of only two 14,000-foot peaks in California that lie outside of the Sierra Nevada. To the east, Great Basin ranges gradually dissolve into the vast Nevada desert. To the northwest, Topaz Lake straddles the California-Nevada border, and the Carson Valley sprawls out beyond.

From Mount Patterson, return the way you came. On your way home, consider stopping by the Bridgeport Ranger Station or writing to the Toiyabe National Forest supervisor to express your concern about vehicle (primarily motorcycle) access into the Mount Patterson area. This fragile alpine landscape deserves protection.

Northern Sierra Nevada

For the purposes of this book, the halfway point of the Sierra Nevada separates the range into northern and southern halves. The southern boundary of Yosemite National Park is located at about that halfway point. More importantly, Yosemite represents a transition in the Sierra, from very high and extremely rugged mountains to a more subdued landscape, with generally lower elevations and a well-developed forest cover. The northernmost 12,000- and 13,000-foot peaks of the Sierra punctuate the Yosemite backcountry, and the park is dominated by the last great expanse of granitic rocks in the range, except for the Desolation Wilderness country west of Lake Tahoe. This final expression of granitic terrain in the High Sierra is profound; Yosemite harbors some of the biggest walls in the world and certainly some of the most dramatic spires and domes in the Sierra.

These granitic rocks of the Sierra do continue northward from Yosemite, but they are still buried beneath ancient layers of volcanic rocks. The landscape of the northern High Sierra, as a result, is dominated by volcanic peaks. From the Lake Tahoe region northward to the terminus of the Sierra south of Lake Almanor, the volcanics gradually diminish, and granite once again dominates the landscape. The high country of the Sierra becomes gradually narrower and the elevations lower as you travel north from Yosemite toward Lake Tahoe. Farther north, only isolated pockets of moderately high, subalpine terrain punctuate the Sierra crest.

Although the Northern Sierra doesn't contain the vast, contiguous wilderness the Southern Sierra does, this region can claim more than 1.2 million acres of roadless backcountry in eight wilderness areas, plus several other areas managed as roadless or as potential wilderness additions. A series of eight highways cross the Sierra Nevada crest between Yosemite and Lake Almanor. Though these roads sever many of the Northern Sierra's wild areas, they provide excellent access to the forested west slope, to the high country, and to the drier east side of the range. What's more, many of these highways are kept open during winter, affording access to the high country for cross-country skiers and snowshoers.

The size of the Northern Sierra's wild areas, combined with their easy access, makes backcountry trips here suitable not only for extended backpacks, but for weekend and day hiking trips as well. Furthermore, except for the Lake Tahoe region and parts of Yosemite, you will find much of the Northern Sierra to be surprisingly uncrowded.

39 Hetch Hetchy Reservoir to Rancheria Falls

Highlights:	This scenic, low-elevation hike follows a route above the north shore of Hetch Hetchy Reservoir, passing stark granite cliffs and domes and ending at a beautiful waterfall on a major Yosemite National Park stream.
General location:	Northern Sierra Nevada, Yosemite National Park, 70 miles east-northeast of Modesto.
Type of hike:	Round-trip day hike or overnighter.
Distance:	12.4 miles.
Difficulty:	Moderate.
Elevation gain and loss:	+1,620 feet, -800 feet.
Trailhead elevation:	3,820 feet.
High point:	Rancheria Falls, 4,640 feet.
Best season:	March through November.
Water availability:	Available at 2.2 miles, 4.9 miles, and 6.2 miles. If day hiking, bring your own.
Maps:	Yosemite National Park map; USGS Yosemite National Park map; USGS Lake Eleanor and Hetch Hetchy Reservoir 7.5-minute quads.
Permits:	Wilderness permits are required for overnight camping in the park and are available at the permit station at the Hetch Hetchy Entrance to the park.

Key points:

- 0.0   Hetch Hetchy Trailhead.
- 0.9   Junction of Lake Eleanor Road and Rancheria Falls Trail; turn right (east) onto trail.
- 2.2   Wapama Falls.
- 4.9   Tiltill Creek.
- 5.9   Junction with eastbound spur trail to Rancheria Falls; turn right (east).
- 6.2   Rancheria Falls.

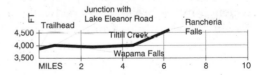

Finding the trailhead: From Oakdale, follow California Highway 120 east for about 84 miles. Just before reaching the Yosemite National Park entrance at Big Oak Flat, turn left (east) onto the signed Evergreen Road. Another sign here indicates Mather Camp and Hetch Hetchy Reservoir.

Follow this paved road for 7.3 miles to a road junction in Mather Camp and turn right (east) onto Hetch Hetchy Road. Follow this paved road for 9 more miles to the parking area at O'Shaughnessy Dam.

The hike: Extensive areas of bare granite, most often in the form of near-vertical cliffs soaring 1,000 feet or more into the California sun, characterize

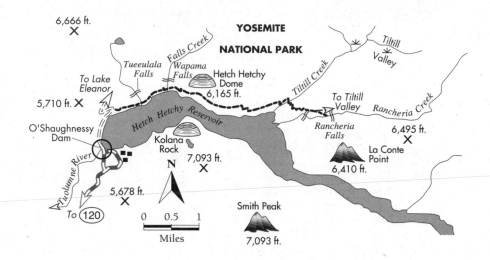

the terrain traversed on this fine hike around Hetch Hetchy Reservoir.

Construction began on O'Shaughnessy Dam in 1914, impounding the Tuolumne River for San Francisco's water supply and flooding the magnificent Hetch Hetchy Valley, once thought to be second only to Yosemite Valley in sheer beauty and grandeur. Hetch Hetchy Valley was carved out of a V-shaped canyon created by the downcutting of stream water. It was then widened into a broad, U-shaped valley by the massive Tuolumne Glacier, flowing tens of miles from its origin at the Tuolumne Ice Field near the Sierra Nevada crest. This ancient glacier attained a maximum depth of about 4,000 feet in the Grand Canyon of the Tuolumne River.

During repeated glacial episodes, ancient soils were removed, leaving vast areas of bare granite bedrock. Over the years, this granite has slowly weathered and decomposed, allowing a few plant species to take hold and gather nutrients from the thin, meager soil. These plants, in turn, continue to break down the rock.

There is still much exposed solid bedrock in this area. The combination of weathering and decomposition of the bedrock continues, enabling more and various plants to persist in establishing themselves. These plants also provide habitat for a variety of wild creatures. Such processes of weathering and plant colonization are in evidence on this hike and provide you with ample food for thought as you visit the reservoir.

From the parking area, proceed north across the dam, with the blue waters of the reservoir to your right and the roaring spillway that feeds the lower Tuolumne River to your left. Views across the reservoir are spectacular, including the white ribbon of Wapama Falls on the north side and the sheer granite of Kolana Rock on the south side of the reservoir.

At the north end of the dam, pass through a tunnel out into the mountain, offering a cool, albeit brief, respite from the penetrating summer sun. Upon exiting the tunnel, pass a destination and mileage sign and continue hiking the old Lake Eleanor Road around the lower end of the reservoir, partially shaded by canyon live oak, California bay, digger pine (a California endemic), ponderosa pine, and black oak. Shrubs like mountain mahogany, manzanita, and some poison oak are also present.

After hiking 0.9 mile from the trailhead, leave the road behind and turn right onto the Rancheria Falls Trail at another destination and mileage sign. Your trail crosses rocky, south-facing slopes and benches above the north shore of the reservoir, shaded at times by canyon live oak, black oak, digger pine, and scattered specimens of California bay and ponderosa pine. Even at this low elevation, the evidence of glacial polish attests to the activity of glaciers in the area.

Pass below Tucculala Falls after about 1.5 miles from the trailhead. These falls tend to dry up as the summer progresses. Beyond, your trail winds its way toward the ribbon of Wapama Falls. This 1,200-foot falls represents the dramatic terminus of Falls Creek, a major Tuolumne River tributary that flows through the backcountry of Yosemite National Park from Dorothy Lake near the Sierra Nevada crest.

Cross the multibranched creek below the roaring falls via the excellent wood-and-steel bridges. To the south, the smooth granite of Kolana Rock plunges 2,000 feet into the depths of Hetch Hetchy Reservoir; directly above to the northeast rises the 2,200-foot walls of Hetch Hetchy Dome. Beyond the falls, begin a shaded ascent along a bench high above the reservoir. Smooth, towering walls are ever-present to your left.

Eventually, leave the shaded bench behind and begin a sunny descent via switchbacks. The trail levels off and begins a traverse into the environs of lower Tiltill Creek. Cross this cascading, gorge-bound creek via another excellent bridge, then immediately begin climbing away from the creek.

With an understory consisting primarily of manzanita, the few digger and ponderosa pines offer only scant shade during this sunny, switchbacking ascent. Along this stretch, glimpse the impressive domes in the northeast, lording over the precipitous canyon of lower Tiltill Creek. The trail levels off around the 4,400-foot level; from here, briefly spy Rancheria Creek where it tumbles and cascades over solid granite. The rocky area below these cascades has been used as a camping area, but is barely shaded by scattered digger and ponderosa pines.

Continue up the trail and branch right onto a faint path that leads to excellent campsites along Rancheria Creek and just below foaming Rancheria Falls, well shaded by ponderosa pine, black oak, and incense-cedar. Fishing for good-sized trout in this creek is challenging.

After enjoying this fine area, you eventually backtrack to the trailhead.

Wapama Falls, plunging 1,200 feet over a resistant granite precipice, is just one of many highlights of the hike around Hetch Hetchy Reservoir.

40 Tioga Road to Ten Lakes

Highlights: This scenic trip follows the headwaters of Yosemite Creek to a lake-filled subalpine basin in central Yosemite National Park.

General location: Northern Sierra Nevada, Yosemite National Park, 80 miles east-northeast of Modesto.

Type of hike: Round-trip backpack, 2 to 4 days.

Distance: 12.6 miles or more.

Difficulty: Moderate.

Elevation gain and loss: +2,180 feet, -730 feet.

Trailhead elevation: 7,500 feet.

High point: 9,680 feet.

Best season: Late June through mid-October.

Water availability: Abundant at Ten Lakes.

Maps: Yosemite National Park map; USGS Yosemite National Park map; USGS Ten Lakes and Yosemite Falls 7.5-minute quads.

Permits: Wilderness permits are required for overnight camping. Obtain at permit stations in Big Oak Flat or Tuolumne Meadows.

Key points:

0.0　Ten Lakes Trailhead; cross Tioga Road and proceed north on the trail.

2.0　Junction with westbound trail to White Wolf; stay right (northeast).

3.8　Half Moon Meadow.

5.25　Junction with Grant Lakes Trail; bear left (northeast).

6.3　Reach Ten Lakes basin.

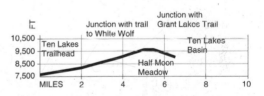

Finding the trailhead: The signed Ten Lakes Trailhead lies just west of the Yosemite Creek bridge on the Tioga Road (California Highway 120). To get there from the west, proceed to Crane Flat, 84 miles from Merced and 90 miles from Modesto. The trailhead can be found 19.6 miles east of Crane Flat. If you are traveling from the east, follow CA 120 west from its junction with US Highway 395 for 12.1 miles to Tioga Pass and then another 27 miles to the trailhead. Permits can be obtained at the Tuolumne Meadows permit station.

The hike: Tucked against the high north slope of the Tuolumne River/Merced River divide, near the geographical center of Yosemite National Park, is an exceptionally beautiful lake basin, featuring excellent fishing and outstanding high-country scenery. John Muir gave the basin its name, but park rangers often refer to it as Seven Lakes, since there are only seven bodies of water large enough to be considered lakes. A host of tarns also dot

Tioga Road to Ten Lakes

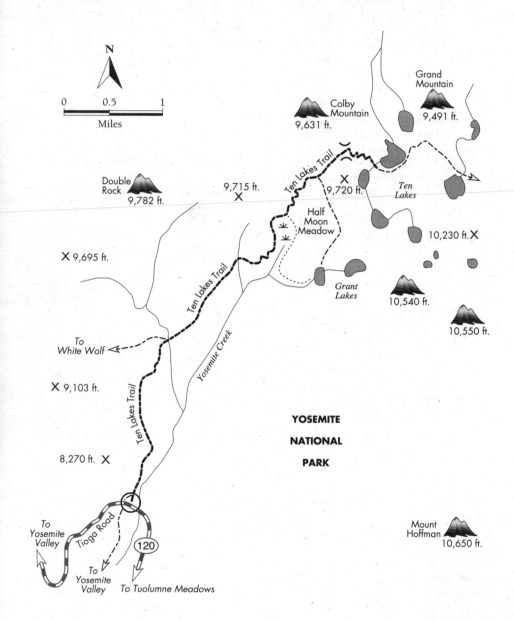

N

0   0.5   1
Miles

Grand
Mountain
9,491 ft.

Colby
Mountain
9,631 ft.

Double
Rock
9,782 ft.

9,715 ft.
X

X
9,720 ft.

Ten Lakes Trail

Ten
Lakes

Half
Moon
Meadow

10,230 ft. X

X 9,695 ft.

Ten Lakes Trail

Grant
Lakes

10,540 ft.

To
White Wolf

Yosemite Creek

10,550 ft.

X 9,103 ft.

Ten Lakes Trail

YOSEMITE

NATIONAL

PARK

8,270 ft. X

Tioga Road

120

To
Yosemite
Valley

To
Yosemite
Valley

To Tuolumne Meadows

Mount
Hoffman
10,650 ft.

the basin. The trail touches only two of the lakes, while the others are accessible either by informal trails or cross-country hikes. This is a fine mid-elevation Yosemite hike, and it is snow-free much earlier than trails in the Tuolumne Meadows and Sierra crest areas of the park.

Yosemite is famous for its glacier carved and ice-scoured terrain, and you will see much of this kind of scenery throughout this hike. In addition, you will witness firsthand the forest transition, from Jeffrey pine and Sierra juniper forest to stunted timberline stands of whitebark pine and mountain hemlock during the 2,000-foot ascent. Primary attractions of this memorable hike include spectacular vistas of Yosemite's remote backcountry and unusually good fishing for brook trout in the Ten Lakes. The nearby Grant Lakes are stocked with rainbows, and also offer good fishing.

Backcountry permits are required for camping in the park, and quotas are in effect on all park trails. The Ten Lakes are a popular destination, but are not as heavily used as are the many backcountry areas that lie close to the primary park roads. Campfires are prohibited above 9,600 feet, but much of the Ten Lakes basin lies below that elevation. Nevertheless, firewood is scarce, so plan to carry a backpack stove. If you must have a campfire, obtain a fire permit in addition to a backcountry permit and camp only in sites with an established fire ring.

The law requires that you protect your food supply from the hungry black bears that roam the park's backcountry. Hanging your food from a tree using the counterbalance method is one way to save your food from the remarkably resourceful bears (see the back of your permit for instructions), but bear-resistant food canisters are the most effective method. It is also a good idea to avoid cooking in your tent or near your campsite. Water is available intermittently en route to Ten Lakes. Once you are in the basin, it is abundant, but must be treated before drinking. Of course, expect mosquitoes to harass you until mid- to late summer.

The trail begins west of the Yosemite Creek bridge on the north side of Tioga Road. For 0.1 mile, it roughly parallels the road among boulders and an open forest of Jeffrey and lodgepole pine and Sierra juniper. After joining another trail coming up from the road, turn right (northeast) and stroll amid white fir, lodgepole pine, and juniper. The moist forest floor here is grassy and bedecked with wildflowers.

This shady canyon bottom stretch, west of the infant Yosemite Creek, is dominated by lodgepole pines, but the forest is soon joined by a scattering of red firs. By contrast, the drier and rockier slopes above host Jeffrey pine and Sierra juniper.

After 0.5 mile, climb the west wall of the canyon and enter that drier forest. The moderately ascending trail offers increasingly good views into Yosemite Creek's headwaters, where you see gentle, forested ridges, abundant ice-scoured bedrock, and, farther on, the glacier-chiseled north face of 10,650-foot Mount Hoffman, high above to the east. Manzanita and huckleberry oak grow thickly among trailside slabs on this sunny slope.

The grade finally eases amid some unusually large junipers, and you hike easily under a shady canopy of red fir and lodgepole pine. The trail crosses a sluggish stream after 1.8 miles, next to a fir-shaded campsite, and then rises gently for another 0.2 mile, where you meet the westbound trail leading 5.5 miles to White Wolf. Immediately after that junction, hop across a larger creek and proceed along the forested margin of a small meadow.

A moderate, tree-shaded ascent ensues, leading past a trickling seasonal stream. The trail continues climbing through pine and fir forest, eventually approaching the corn lily–clad banks of yet another small stream at 3.4 miles. The trail climbs alongside its flower-decked banks, then levels off on a bench boasting several large silver pines among the red firs and lodgepole pines. A brief descent leads to the edge of lodgepole-rimmed Half Moon Meadow after 3.8 miles, a gorgeous spread adorned with colorful wildflowers. Among the blooms are yampah, elephant head, corn lily, aster, groundsel, and monkey flower. You can't help but imagine that this nearly level meadow, lying at the foot of ice-gouged cliffs, may once have been a lake.

The trail skirts the meadow, leading to its northern end, where the final ascent, an 800-foot grind, awaits. An informal trail branches off to the right at this point, leading past possible campsites east of the meadow. An alternate cross-country route to Grant Lakes begins here, heading south from the meadow for 0.5 mile to the lakes' outlet creek and then uphill for another 0.5 mile, gaining 500 feet to get to the lower Grant Lake.

To reach Ten Lakes, follow the steep, switchbacking trail beneath the scattered pines that offer little shade. The initial climb leads past a small, willow-clad stream, your last source of water until you reach the lakes. Views stretch southward, with the green opening of Half Moon Meadow as a foreground to the more distant, heavily forested, and gently rolling mountains and ridges. The grade eventually tapers off as you rise moderately through open slopes thick with lupine, corn lily, groundsel, and monkey flower. Just as you almost attain a ridgetop saddle, jog northeast and rise more steeply once again. Forest cover here consists of a scattered stand of stunted and wind-flagged lodgepole and whitebark pine and mountain hemlock.

After 5.25 miles, you reach a signed junction with a right-forking trail that leads 1 rough mile to Grant Lakes. Bear left at this junction. The final ascent leads through sparse forest that soon gives way to open slopes, which in turn, lead to the broad crest of the Tuolumne River/Merced River divide. Even the most jaded hiker will be awestruck by the vast panorama that unfolds from this 9,680-foot ridge, 5.4 miles from the trailhead. Before you is a dramatic sweep of Yosemite backcountry, from the jagged summits of the Sierra crest, from Tower Peak in the north and Mount Gibbs in the east, to ice-polished domes, thick forests, cirque basins, and impossibly deep canyons.

After reluctantly pulling away from the unforgettable vista, follow the trail down to a saddle and climb briefly upon the slopes of Hill 9600. From here, you gain an incredible view into the depths of Muir Gorge, lying within the Grand Canyon of the Tuolumne River, over 4,000 feet below. Three of the Ten Lakes are visible during the plunging descent from this hill. Finally, after 6.3 miles, you reach the north shore of the second-largest of the Ten Lakes, an island-dotted lake at 8,950 feet. Red firs and lodgepole pines are the predominant trees shading the campsites at this lake and the other lower lakes; at the timberline lakes and tarns, whitebark pines and mountain hemlocks offer only a modicum of shelter.

The main trail climbs 500 feet over the ridge south of Grand Mountain, reaching the largest lake, at 9,400 feet, after 1 more mile. If you are searching for solitude, you can surely find it by expending a little extra effort to reach some of the higher benches and tarns in the basin. Good fishing lakes are still only a short distance away.

41 Tioga Pass to Mount Dana

Highlights:	For hikers in good physical condition, this memorable ascent to the second-highest mountain peak in Yosemite National Park contrasts vast panoramas of the rich forests, verdant meadows, and lofty crags of the Sierra with the arid desert mountains and valleys stretching eastward into Nevada.
General location:	Northern Sierra Nevada, Yosemite National Park, 100 miles east-northeast of Modesto and 5 miles southwest of Lee Vining.
Type of hike:	Round-trip day hike.
Distance:	6.5 miles.
Difficulty:	Strenuous.
Elevation gain and loss:	3,108 feet.
Trailhead elevation:	9,945 feet.
High point:	Mt. Dana, 13,053 feet.
Best season:	Mid-July through September.
Water availability:	Bring your own.
Maps:	Yosemite National Park map; USGS Yosemite National Park map; USGS Tioga Pass and Mt. Dana 7.5-minute quads.
Permits:	Not required for day hikes.

Key points:
  0.0   Tioga Pass Trailhead.
  2.1   Top Sierra crest at
        11,700 feet.
  3.25 Summit of Mt. Dana.

Tioga Pass to Mount Dana

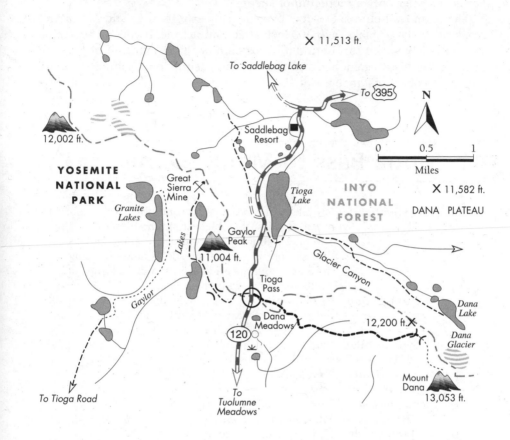

Finding the trailhead: Follow California Highway 120 (Tioga Road) to the Yosemite National Park entrance atop the Sierra crest at Tioga Pass, 12.1 miles southwest of its junction with US Highway 395 or 46.5 miles east of the Crane Flat Ranger Station in the park's western reaches. An entrance fee is collected at the park entrance station. A large parking area is available along the west side of the road just south of the entrance, inside Yosemite National Park.

The hike: Have you ever wanted to scale a lofty Sierra Nevada peak and revel in far-flung panoramas and a sense of accomplishment that is typically reserved for backpacking peakbaggers, but have balked at the long approaches necessary to gain access to such summits? If so, consider the short hike to 13,053-foot Mount Dana, perhaps the easiest, and certainly one of the highest, Sierra peaks accessible to day hikers, provided they are in good physical condition and acclimated to the thin, High Sierra atmosphere. Consider spending a day or two in one of the nearby high-elevation campgrounds along CA 120 in the Inyo National Forest or in the park's Tuolumne Meadows Campground to help you acclimate.

There are numerous challenging routes leading to Dana's summit, but the informal trail worn into the mountainside from Tioga Pass is certainly the easiest. By following this trail, you will, more or less, follow in the footsteps of William Brewer and Charles Hoffman, members of the famous Whitney Survey who mapped much of the High Sierra in the nineteenth century and first scaled the peak on June 28, 1863. Be sure to pack along plenty of water, sunglasses, and sunscreen. Also, plan on the possibility of strong winds and cold temperatures.

The trail begins immediately east of the Tioga Pass Entrance atop the Sierra crest, heading eastward past a prominent lodgepole pine. A grand view of Mount Dana, looming boldly on the skyline more than 3,000 feet above, is enjoyed at the start but soon fades from your view.

Proceeding eastward just north of the low crest, the trail leads through a forest of lodgepole and whitebark pine, past meadows adorned with lupine, groundsel, and Indian paintbrush, and along the shores of numerous small, shallow tarns. Views to the north from this glacier-excavated gap are superb, reaching into the headwaters of Lee Vining Creek and including Tioga Lake and the colorful metamorphic peaks that lie east of the mostly granitic Sierra crest. After 0.5 mile, the trail crosses the crest, entering Yosemite National Park and remaining within its boundaries thereafter. Upon reaching the foot of the Mount Dana massif just below timberline, the well-worn path jogs southeast, climbing a west-facing slope at a moderate grade. Shortly thereafter, you cross a trickling stream where a profusion of wildflowers bursts upon the scene. Within this flower garden, discover beautiful cinquefoil, larkspur, lupine, corn lily, aster, groundsel, monkey flower, Indian paintbrush, and fireweed. You will also be delighted by the vistas stretching across the subalpine spread of Dana Meadows to the Kuna Crest and the rugged peaks of the Cathedral Range.

Soon the trail abandons the lush flower gardens and its moderate grade, and zig-zags very steeply into the uppermost stand of stunted timber. This exceedingly steep grind continues, without respite, to the summit of Mount Dana.

Upon emerging from the timberline forest, notice the diverse collection of low plants and shrubs blanketing the trailside slopes, including red heather, cinquefoil, yellow columbine, corn lily, gooseberry, elderberry, horsemint, sagebrush, snowberry, phlox, buckwheat, and pearly everlasting. Typical of high mountain ascents, splendid vistas multiply as you toil upward.

As you continue up the boulder-covered slopes, the grade eases briefly where you boulder-hop your way over a rock-buried stream. The stream flows on the surface just upstream and is your last source of water en route. Beyond, the trail once again climbs steeply upon scree slopes where only a scattering of grasses grow.

After 2.1 miles, the grade once again moderates briefly atop a grassy bench at 11,700 feet. You can't help but notice the lovely perfume emanating

Mount Dana, rising far above Tioga Pass, is the second-highest peak in Yosemite National Park.

from the prostrate lupine that thrives here. A welcome pause next to the large trailside cairn not only allows you to catch your breath but gives you time to revel in the vast panoramas of Yosemite's magnificent backcountry. Beyond the cairn, the path becomes increasingly obscure as it leads southeast toward the foot of the final 1,300-foot climb to the summit. The route is straightforward; however, if you lose the trail simply choose your own route up the rocky slopes to the top. The only sign of life above 12,000 feet is a fragrant purple flower, polemonium or sky pilot, that should be familiar to you if you have hiked the trail to Mount Whitney.

The far-ranging vistas from this lofty summit reach across meadows, canyons, peaks, forests, and desert. Gazing southwestward, you see three prominent Yosemite subranges: Kuna Crest, Cathedral Range, and the Clark Range. You also can't miss Mount Lyell, the highest peak in the park, and its sparkling glacier. That peak and Mount Dana are the only Yosemite peaks exceeding 13,000 feet. Westward are the vast grasslands of Tuolumne Meadows and an array of ice-polished domes surrounding it. Beyond the meadows are the rockbound upper reaches of the Grand Canyon of the Tuolumne River and the Mount Hoffman high country.

The Sierra crest marches northwestward in a series of lofty crags, including Mount Conness, North Peak, and the peaks of Shepherd Crest. These granitic summits contrast with the red and gray metamorphic peaks that dominate east of the crest. You may have noticed by now that Mount Dana and nearby Mount Gibbs, the red peak to the south, are also composed of ancient metamorphic rocks.

Northward, beyond the Sierra Nevada, are the Sweetwater Mountains. To the northeast is ancient Mono Lake, with the relatively recent volcanic formations of the Mono Craters rising south of the lake; beyond them stand 11,000-foot Glass Mountain and the White Mountains. Directly below your vantage point to the east, great cliffs plunge nearly 2,000 feet into the cirque harboring Dana Lake. Above this lake, broken cliffs rise to the broad table-land of the Dana Plateau, a remnant of the ancient, gentle surface of the Sierra Nevada.

Reluctantly pull away from the tremendous panorama and carefully retrace your steps to Tioga Pass. Other trails in the Tioga Pass area offer worthwhile day hikes to a variety of alpine lake basins.

---

42 Saddlebag Lake Road to Gardisky Lake

Highlights:	This short but rigorous hike quickly leads hikers to a pristine timberline lake and dramatic views of the Sierra crest and the northern peaks of Yosemite National Park.
General location:	Northern Sierra Nevada, Inyo National Forest, 3 miles north of Tioga Pass.
Type of hike:	Round-trip day hike or overnighter.
Distance:	2 miles.
Difficulty:	Moderate.
Elevation gain and loss:	750 feet.
Trailhead elevation:	9,750 feet.
High point:	Gardisky Lake, 10,500 feet.
Best season:	Mid-July through September.
Water availability:	Available en route and at the lake. If day hiking, bring your own.
Maps:	Inyo National Forest map; USGS Mt. Dana and Tioga Pass 7.5-minute quads.
Permits:	Not required.

Key points:
- 0.0   Gardisky Lake Trailhead.
- 1.0   Gardisky Lake.

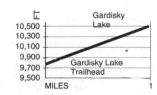

Saddlebag Lake Road to Gardisky Lake

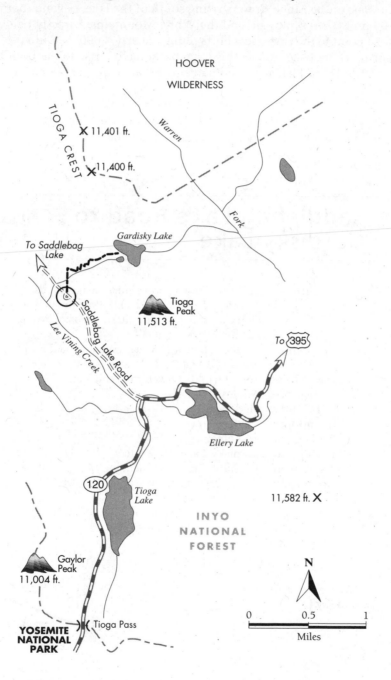

HOOVER
WILDERNESS

TIOGA CREST

✕ 11,401 ft.

✕ 11,400 ft.

Warren

Fork

Gardisky Lake

To Saddlebag
Lake

Saddlebag Lake Road

Tioga
Peak
11,513 ft.

To 395

Lee Vining Creek

Ellery Lake

120

Tioga
Lake

11,582 ft. ✕

INYO
NATIONAL
FOREST

Gaylor
Peak
11,004 ft.

N

YOSEMITE
NATIONAL
PARK

Tioga Pass

0   0.5   1
Miles

Finding the trailhead: Follow California Highway 120 to the signed turn-off to Saddlebag Lake, 2.1 miles northeast of Tioga Pass and 10 miles west of US Highway 395 at Lee Vining. Proceed north on the Saddlebag Lake Road, rough with rocks and washboards, for 1.2 miles to the signed Gardisky Lake Trailhead, located on the left (west) side of the road. There is room for eight vehicles at the trailhead, where you will also find an information signboard, map, and trailhead register.

The hike: Gardisky Lake is an alpine gem, straddling the Tioga Crest above Saddlebag Lake. Though the hike to its shores is short, it is steep enough in places to give you a feeling of accomplishment. Grand alpine scenery and 30-minute access to a lovely alpine basin combine to make this trip one of the best short hikes in the Northern Sierra.

The trail begins with a deceptively gentle grade from the east side of Saddlebag Lake Road, heading northeast into a grass-carpeted lodgepole pine forest. Quite soon, though, the trail angles uphill, and you work your way up a steep grade beneath a canopy of lodgepoles to reach a crossing of a small cascading stream. The trail continues ascending very steeply over varicolored metamorphic rocks above the north banks of the tumbling, willow-bordered stream as it winds through the gradually thinning lodgepole forest. Glorious views open as you ascend, stretching past the towering cone of Mount Dana to the Kuna Crest in the south and westward across upper Lee Vining Creek to the gleaming white granite of the Sierra crest. The view is punctuated by 12,000-foot White Mountain, 12,590-foot Mount Conness, and the sheer east face of 12,242-foot North Peak.

Gardisky Lake lies near the top of the Tioga Crest, immediately south of the Hoover Wilderness.

As the lodgepoles diminish in numbers, spreading whitebark pines, along with a scattering of gnarled Sierra junipers, begin to dominate the forest scheme. After ascending about 700 short but breathtaking feet, the grade moderates as the trail opens up into a lovely timberline meadow fringed by stunted whitebarks. It then rises gently up to a broad, 10,500-foot saddle, where the tread disappears in the turf. A pair of beautiful tarns lie just ahead; stay to their left (north) and reach Gardisky Lake within a few hundred yards.

The basin surrounding the lake is exceptionally beautiful, surrounded by turf, meadows, and picturesque stands of stunted whitebark pines. The red alpine summit of 11,513-foot Tioga Peak rises immediately south of the lake, and its rubbled slopes can be scaled for boundless vistas via a class 2 scramble up the northwest ridge. The lake drains eastward into the Warren Fork of Lee Vining Creek. Like so many lakes in this part of the Sierra, it straddles the crest of the high divide.

This fine timberline basin shows virtually no signs of human impact, which is surprising in light of its short distance from the trailhead. Please do your best to leave no trace of your passing while at Gardisky Lake, to help preserve its pristine qualities. You can camp in the basin among groves of whitebark pine, but zero impact practices must be employed to their fullest, and that includes no campfires.

After enjoying the Gardisky Lake basin, stroll back down the short trail to the trailhead.

43 Saddlebag Lake to McCabe Lakes

Highlights:	This trip, part cross-country and suitable only for hikers with ample cross-country and route finding experience, leads over the Sierra crest to a remote lake basin in Yosemite National Park, offering ample solitude, good fishing, and memorable vistas.
General location:	Northern Sierra Nevada, Hoover Wilderness (Inyo National Forest) and Yosemite Wilderness, 7 miles west of Lee Vining and 3.5 miles north of Tioga Pass.
Type of hike:	Round-trip backpack, 3 to 5 days.
Distance:	9.6 miles.
Difficulty:	Moderately strenuous.
Elevation gain and loss:	+1,400 feet, -1,080 feet.
Trailhead elevation:	10,150 feet.
High point:	Sierra crest, 11,300 feet.
Best season:	Mid-July through September.
Water availability:	Abundant.
Maps:	Hoover Wilderness map (topographic); USGS Yosemite National Park map; USGS Dunderberg Peak and Tioga Pass 7.5-minute quads.

Permits: A wilderness permit is required for overnight camping in the Hoover Wilderness and Yosemite National Park. Permits can be obtained at the Mono Lake Scenic Area Visitor Center at the north end of Lee Vining or at the Tuolumne Meadows permit station in Yosemite National Park.

Key points:
- 0.0   Saddlebag Lake Trailhead.
- 1.6   Junction with trail from boat dock; turn left (west) toward Greenstone Lake.
- 1.9   Turn right (northwest) onto old road above north shore of Greenstone Lake.
- 2.5   Turn left at road junction; proceed northwest to south end of Steelhead Lake.
- 2.6   Leave road at Potter Lake's outlet creek and head west across the basin.
- 3.2   Secret Lake.
- 3.8   Begin descending southwest from Sierra crest.
- 4.8   Reach north shore of Upper McCabe Lake.

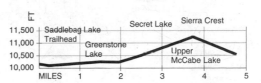

Finding the trailhead: Follow California Highway 120 either 2.1 miles northeast from Tioga Pass or 10 miles west from US Highway 395 to the signed turnoff to Saddlebag Lake and turn northwest. Follow the narrow and rough dirt road for 2.4 miles to the signed trailhead parking area south of the lake. If you choose to ride the boat to the head of the lake rather than hike the shoreline trail, continue up the road for another 0.2 mile to the parking lot at the Saddlebag Lake Resort. Make arrangements for a boat ride to the head of the lake and for a pickup time for the return trip.

The hike: This lofty excursion is an immensely rewarding trek, but due to the trailless alpine terrain near the Sierra crest, it should be attempted only by seasoned backpackers. By offering quick access into the Yosemite backcountry via an obscure route, this trip avoids the crowds typically encountered along trails beginning at Tuolumne Meadows.

The convenience of an inexpensive boat ride across the gull-dotted waters of Saddlebag Lake shortens the distance to the McCabe Lakes by 1.7 miles. If you choose this option, make arrangements for the boat ride and a pickup time of your choice at the store at Saddlebag Lake Resort, located 0.2 mile beyond the trailhead parking area, opposite the campground entrance.

Water is easy to find along much of the route, and mosquitoes should be expected until about mid-August. Wood fires are prohibited between Greenstone Lake and the Sierra crest, and in the Yosemite backcountry above 9,600 feet, which includes the entire McCabe Lakes basin.

From the trailhead parking area, cross Saddlebag Lake Road and follow an old road downhill to Lee Vining Creek below the lake's dam. From there, the road quickly climbs to the dam where the trail begins. Already above

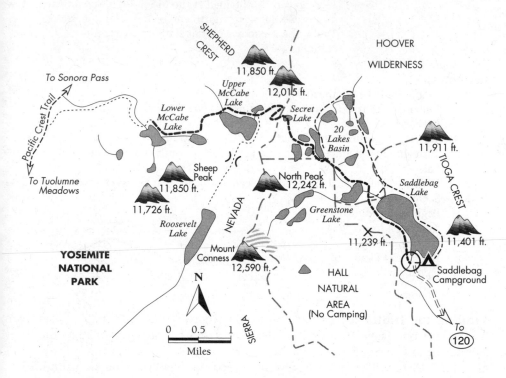

Saddlebag Lake to McCabe Lakes

SHEPHERD CREST

11,850 ft.

HOOVER WILDERNESS

Upper McCabe Lake

12,015 ft.

To Sonora Pass

Lower McCabe Lake

Secret Lake

20 Lakes Basin

11,911 ft.

To Tuolumne Meadows

Sheep Peak

11,850 ft.

North Peak 12,242 ft.

Saddlebag Lake

TIOGA CREST

11,726 ft.

NEVADA

Greenstone Lake

Roosevelt Lake

11,239 ft.

11,401 ft.

YOSEMITE NATIONAL PARK

Mount Conness

12,590 ft.

HALL NATURAL AREA (No Camping)

Saddlebag Campground

N

SIERRA

0   0.5   1
Miles

To 120

Pacific Crest Trail

timberline, the trail undulates above the lake's west shore over the crunchy red and gray metamorphic rocks that dominate the landscape east of the Sierra crest. Only a scattering of krummholz whitebark pines dot the trailside slopes, while red heather, a common alpine plant in the Sierra, is the most prevalent wildflower. About midway around the lake, the granite crags of the Sierra crest come into view, contrasting in color and in character with the metamorphic peaks and ridges nearby.

It is obvious why John Muir so aptly named the Sierra Nevada the "Range of Light," since the nearly white peaks along the crest not only reflect the intense alpine sunshine but almost seem to radiate a light of their own. The lowest point visible on the crest, to the northwest, lies above a grassy slope. That is your pass, and you can begin visualizing a route up to it. As you approach the head of the lake, the pointed summit of 12,242-foot North Peak and its permanent snowfield come into view on the western skyline.

After 1.5 miles, the trail fades into obscurity within an alpine meadow above and west of Saddlebag Lake. Ducks lead you the short distance to the meandering creek that emanates from nearby Greenstone Lake, where a search for a log crossing helps you to avoid wet feet.

Once beyond the creek, you intersect a trail leading west to the shoreline of that lake, one of the many alpine gems in the 20 Lakes Basin. Turn left onto that trail. Proceed to the lake's north shore where the trail and an old

From the rocky shores of glacier-gouged Steelhead Lake, hikers en route to McCabe Lakes in Yosemite National Park pause to absorb the breathtaking beauty of the High Sierra.

mining road, 0.3 mile from Saddlebag Lake's upper boat dock, nearly coalesce. At this point, leave the trail and begin following the old road uphill toward the northwest. The trail ultimately leads to Conness Lakes basin beneath the towering crag of Mount Conness, which is visible to the southwest.

Tree cover in the basin is sparse, but it's still thicker than the stands surrounding Saddlebag Lake, which consist of lodgepole and whitebark pines. Beyond Greenstone Lake, pass a tarn before beginning a moderate ascent that levels off near the trickling outlet of Z Lake. The old road jogs west and, at 2.1 miles from the trailhead, a sign declares that you are entering the Hall Natural Area where camping and open fires are prohibited. Notice that the trailside slopes are now littered with scattered granite boulders—glacial erratics—that rest upon the metamorphic rocks from which the basin was carved.

The brief westward course ends above the rocky, irregular shore of Wasco Lake, where you head northwest, pass a shallow tarn, and leave the Hall Natural Area. The road soon leads past another small tarn and begins descending, now within the Mill Creek drainage. At the north end of this tarn, 2.5 miles from the trailhead and 1 mile from the upper boat dock on Saddlebag Lake, notice another old mining road that branches left. Follow this road downhill to the south end of lovely Steelhead Lake, the largest in the 20 Lakes Basin. From here, the old Hess Mine can be seen above the lake's northwest shore, in a mineralized area at the contact zone between granitic and metamorphic rocks.

Upon reaching the deep lake, the road leads west before climbing a south-trending gully. The nearby cascading creek plunges into Steelhead Lake from invisible Potter Lake. At this point, leave the road and begin following an obscure route, climbing over a bedrock knoll just south of the cascade.

You quickly reach 10,300-foot Potter Lake, 2.75 miles from the trailhead. Hop across its outlet creek above the cascade and head northwest over bedrock and grassy pockets to the slightly smaller Towser Lake. Imposing North Peak and its snowfield provide an exciting backdrop to the lakes in this high basin.

From here, the route to Secret Lake is readily apparent. Climb northwest along a small creek that spills down the grassy and whitebark pine–dotted slope. After 0.7 mile of steady but easy climbing, you arrive along the shores of 10,900-foot Secret Lake. This lake is unusual in that it is perched on a small, hanging bench rather than in a large, glacier-carved bowl.

From Secret Lake, you can ponder a choice of routes to reach the Sierra crest. The easiest and most obvious route follows an uphill-sloping ledge to the south-southwest. To reach the ledge, scramble up the steep slopes behind the lake for about 0.1 mile. At this point, ducks lead you over bedrock directly to the Sierra crest, which you then follow north to the crest's low point. Vistas from the crest are superb.

A ducked route leads down loose, rocky slopes and past snow-flattened whitebark pines to a shallow alpine lake at 10,500 feet. From here, follow the course of that lake's outlet stream to the northeast shore of Upper McCabe Lake. Fair campsites sit where a strip of whitebark pines hug the north shore and offer only a modicum of shelter.

Ample opportunities for side trips can extend your stay in this area for several days. Remote Roosevelt Lake can be reached by following a trailless route southwest from Upper McCabe Lake and crossing the obvious 11,200-foot pass above the lake. Lower McCabe Lake, set in a timberline forest at 9,900 feet, lies 1.4 miles west of the upper lake.

After enjoying this high-country excursion, retrace your steps back to the trailhead.

44 Green Creek to Summit Lake

Highlights:	This fine backpack, suitable as a weekend trip, follows an eastside canyon to the Sierra crest, features memorable vistas of colorful metamorphic peaks, and passes seven fish-filled lakes, many with excellent campsites.
General location:	Northern Sierra Nevada, Hoover Wilderness (Toiyabe National Forest), 10 miles southwest of Bridgeport.
Type of hike:	Round-trip backpack, 3 to 4 days.
Distance:	15.2 miles.
Difficulty:	Moderate.
Elevation gain and loss:	2,100 feet.
Trailhead elevation:	8,100 feet.
High point:	Summit Lake, 10,200 feet.
Best season:	July through early October.
Water availability:	Abundant.
Maps:	Toiyabe National Forest map; Hoover Wilderness map (topographic); USGS Dunderberg Peak 7.5-minute quad.
Permits:	A wilderness permit is required for overnight use and can be obtained at the Bridgeport Ranger Station.

Key points:
- 0.0 Green Creek Trailhead.
- 1.2 Hoover Wilderness boundary.
- 2.3 Junction with West Lake Trail; bear left (southwest).
- 3.8 Junction with southwestbound trail at East Lake; bear left (southeast) and follow east shore of lake.
- 6.3 Junction with Virginia Lakes Trail; stay right (southwest).
- 7.6 Summit Pass, boundary of Yosemite National Park.

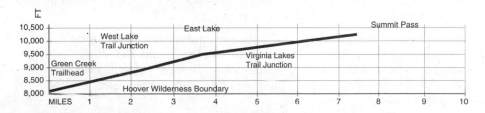

Green Creek to Summit Lake

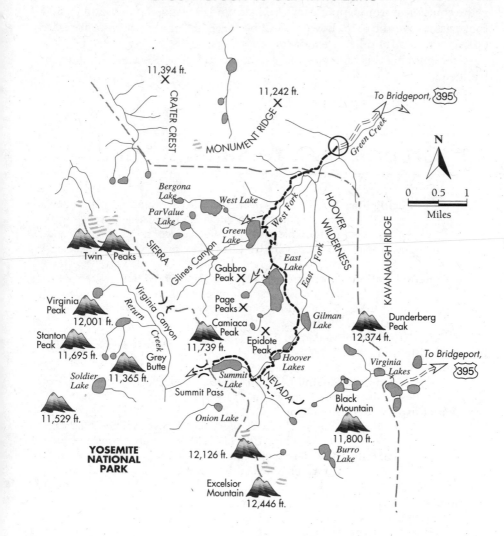

Finding the trailhead: From US Highway 395, 3.8 miles south of the Bridgeport Ranger Station and 85.75 miles north of Bishop, turn southwest onto the signed Green Creek Road. Bear left after 1 mile where a sign points to Green Creek. After another 2.5 miles, turn right; the Virginia Lakes Road continues straight ahead. Proceed another 5.8 miles to the trailhead at the end of the road.

The hike: Visiting a number of subalpine lakes, this interesting eastern Sierra backpack surveys a landscape of colorful peaks that differ in color from the typical white or gray granite found in most eastside canyons. The hike should appeal to angler, photographer, and anyone else who enjoys majestic mountain scenery.

Green Lake in the Hoover Wilderness.

This is bear country, so you are strongly advised to protect your food supply and keep a clean camp. Hang food using the counterbalance method or use bear-resistant canisters. Keep in mind that campfires are not allowed above 9,000 feet in the Green Creek drainage.

The trail begins at the northwest end of the parking area and heads southwest through a forest of lodgepole and Jeffrey pine, aspen, and juniper. Ahead lie the conical alpine peaks encircling the upper West Fork Green Creek and Glines Canyon. Soon you begin negotiating a series of elevation-gaining switchbacks. A pause during this ascent offers over-the-shoulder views down the U-shaped trough of Green Canyon to the Bodie Hills in the eastern distance.

Entering the Hoover Wilderness at a Toiyabe National Forest sign, your trail edges close to Green Creek, dammed at this point by aspen-gnawing beavers. Continue up the canyon and notice the East Fork Green Creek opening up to the south, exposing the massive red flanks of Dunderberg Peak. At 12,374 feet, it is the highest summit in the Green Creek area.

The trail follows the course of the West Fork Green Creek through a forest of aspen and lodgepole pine. Hikers in October will be rewarded not only with solitude but with a colorful display of turning aspens. The trail crosses several creeklets issuing from the lower slopes of Monument Ridge. Along them, you are treated to a variety of colorful wildflowers in season.

After 2.3 miles of steady ascent from the trailhead, you reach a junction with the right-branching trail to West Lake. Turn left, crossing the dam-regulated outlet of Green Lake. You may have to search for a log to get across this swift creek.

Excellent opportunities for camping exist around this large lake at 8,900 feet, and the trout population is abundant and hungry. In the northwest, a white ribbon of water falls over a band of red rock on the flanks of Peak 10,900. Glines Canyon, with its willow-clad meadows and sparse timber, sweeps steadily westward from the lake to Virginia Pass, blocked by semipermanent snow and a 200-foot headwall. Experienced backpackers may be enticed to tackle this pass, descend into Virginia Canyon, and loop back via Summit Lake. However, most hikers will be content to follow the trail to Summit Lake.

From Green Lake, the trail jogs south, begins a series of short switchbacks, and fords the outlet stream of East Lake. Continue climbing under the shade of lodgepole pine and mountain hemlock and ford this creek twice more (crossings will be difficult in early season) before reaching East Lake at the 9,500-foot level. Just before the last ford, avoid a right-branching trail going around the west side of East Lake. Your trail skirts the eastern shore of this fine lake and provides superb views across the deep waters to the triad of Gabbro, Page, and Epidote Peaks. These colorful 11,000-foot peaks offer a change of pace to hikers accustomed to the usual white granite found in most eastern Sierra canyons.

Leaving East Lake behind, your trail passes tiny Nutter Lake, climbs around a low, rocky ridge, and traverses above secluded Gilman Lake. You then ford the East Fork Green Creek below the Hoover Lakes and ascend toward those lakes amid rapidly thinning and increasingly stunted whitebark pines and mountain hemlocks. Scattered willows and red mountain heather add to the alpine feeling of the area.

The trail skirts the eastern shore of the lower Hoover Lake. Hop across the outlet of the upper Hoover Lake before heading around its rocky western shore directly under the precipitous Epidote Peak. A ford of the East Fork is required above upper Hoover Lake; wet feet are difficult to avoid. The sparse, stunted timber, red and gray rocky slopes, alpine peaks, and numerous semipermanent snowfields all combine to make the upper East Fork quite spectacular.

Cross an East Fork tributary after passing the southeastbound trail that leads to the Virginia Lakes Trailhead. Turn right, cross the outlet of Summit Lake, and soon reach the east end of this subalpine gem. To the west, across the low gap of Summit Pass, you are treated to excellent, sky-filling views of the white granite peaks of 11,365-foot Grey Butte and 11,695-foot Stanton Peak, an interesting contrast to the multihued peaks in the Green Creek drainage.

Surrounded by alpine peaks and numerous snowfields, this magnificent lake has a number of campsite possibilities among the stunted lodgepole and whitebark pines and mountain hemlocks that crowd its north shore.

From the Yosemite National Park boundary at Summit Pass west of the lake, views are superb into the densely forested Virginia Canyon and northwest to the soaring, snow-streaked red crag of 12,001-foot Virginia Peak.

After enjoying this fine area, return the way you came.

45 Emma Lake

Highlights:	This short hike quickly leads to a scenic and seldom-visited timberline lake in the eastern Sierra, where fishing is productive and vistas are outstanding.
General location:	Northern Sierra Nevada, Toiyabe National Forest, 15 miles west-northwest of Bridgeport and 10 miles southeast of Sonora Pass.
Type of hike:	Round-trip day hike or overnighter.
Distance:	2 miles.
Difficulty:	Moderate.
Elevation gain and loss:	750 feet.
Trailhead elevation:	8,560 feet.
High point:	Emma Lake, 9,300 feet.
Best season:	Early July through September.
Water availability:	Available at the lake. If day hiking, bring your own.
Maps:	Toiyabe National Forest map; Hoover Wilderness map (topographic); USGS Fales Hot Springs 7.5-minute quad.
Permits:	Not required.

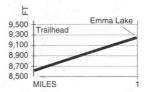

Keypoints:

0.0   Trailhead.
1.0   Emma Lake.

Finding the trailhead: From US Highway 395, 15.1 miles northwest of Bridgeport and 0.7 mile southeast of the US 395/California Highway 108 junction, turn south onto Forest Road 066, signed for Little Walker River and National Forest Campground.

Follow this graded dirt road, rocky with washboards, as it ascends south above the meadows of the Little Walker River. After 3.4 miles, cross the bridge spanning Molybdenite Creek and avoid the left-branching spur road leading to Obsidian Campground (just beyond the bridge). After 3.6 miles, pass the signed Burt Canyon Trail and begin a westbound ascent.

As you continue to ascend, the road becomes much rougher and quite rocky, but remains passable to carefully driven passenger cars. Avoid a right-branching road after 4.5 miles and a left-branching, southbound doubletrack at 6 miles. You reach a loop at the road's end 6.7 miles from the highway, where you find a Hoover Wilderness information signboard and room enough for eight vehicles. Several spurs are used as undeveloped campsites en route to the trailhead.

The hike: Emma Lake is a seldom-visited timberline gem set in a small cirque beneath broad Mount Emma, situated in the volcanic highlands east of the West Walker River and the Sierra crest. This open country, reminiscent of the Rocky Mountains and recommended by the Forest

Emma Lake

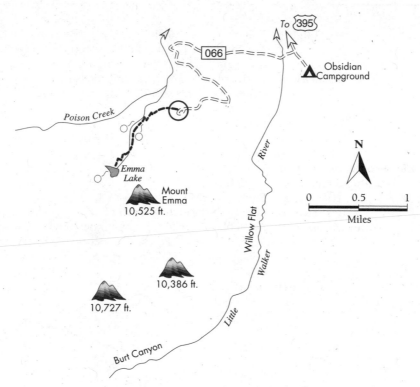

Service as an addition to the Hoover Wilderness, is delightful hiking country that's overlooked by most California hikers. This short hike has a few steep grades, but you won't mind them after reaching the lovely timberline lake in less than one hour.

The trail begins as a long-closed logging road, ascending a moderate grade among stumps and a forest of lodgepole and western white pine and red fir. Fine over-the-shoulder views framed by trailside trees extend northeast to the towering 11,000-foot peaks of the Sweetwater Mountains. This view just might be the incentive for you to return to this region for Hike 38 to the summit of Mount Patterson.

The route quickly narrows to a singletrack. Within minutes, you crest a minor ridge and follow a brief descent across open slopes into a small bowl, enjoying northward views of the West Walker River canyon along the way. After crossing the dry gully on the floor of the bowl, climb the steep slope to gain a low, rocky ridge (a moraine), fringed by whitebark pine and mountain hemlock. Mount Emma towers above the trail here, and the inviting timberline landscapes of the Emma Lake cirque beckon you onward.

The trail descends off the moraine and enters an open, tree-studded basin draining Emma Lake creek. Sagebrush, snowberry, and fields of mule ears carpet the nearby volcanic slopes. Upon entering the basin, the tread becomes more obscure as you head south through a sedge-filled meadow, rich with

Emma Lake.

the yellow blooms of cinquefoil and senecio and the lavender flowers of aster. Jump across the runoff of the spring shown on the topo map, which issues from a grove of lodgepole pine at the trailside.

The trail inclines once again beyond the meadow, leading you out of the timberline forest of whitebark pine and mountain hemlock to Emma Lake's outlet stream. Cross the shallow, multiple branches of the stream just below its emergence from a small, rubbly, terminal moraine. The stream's banks host rich greenery and the vivid blue blossoms of larkspur, as well as the lavender blooms of fireweed.

A final sustained steep grade, moderate in a few places, leads 0.2 mile and 250 feet up past stunted whitebark pines and over the corrugated terrain of glacial moraines to the lovely emerald waters of Emma Lake. Encircled by the light gray–colored volcanic ridges feathered on their crests with spreading, multibranched whitebark pines, this beautiful lake lies in a grand eastern Sierra setting with the broad dome of 10,525-foot Mount Emma rising above its southeast shore. Large springs issue from the talus slopes south of the lake and sustain its waters throughout the summer, long after the snowfields have melted. Scattered groves of whitebark pines and thickets of willow fringe the lake, with an angler's trail also encircling it.

A few small campsites can be found here, making this short hike a good choice for a family weekend of fishing or for simply enjoying the rugged beauty of the High Sierra. The lake is lightly used, even on weekends, making it one of the better easy getaways in the Northern Sierra. If you do camp here, do not build fires and do employ zero impact practices to the fullest.

Eventually, leave Emma Lake and backtrack to the trailhead.

46 Highway 108 to Sardine Falls

Highlights:	This easy, nearly flat hike leads to a foaming veil of whitewater in the volcanic high country east of Sonora Pass.
General location:	Northern Sierra Nevada, Toiyabe National Forest, 1.5 miles southeast of Sonora Pass.
Type of hike:	Round-trip half-day hike.
Distance:	2 miles.
Difficulty:	Easy.
Elevation gain and loss:	200 feet.
Trailhead elevation:	8,800 feet.
High point:	Sardine Falls, 9,000 feet.
Best season:	Early July through September.
Water availability:	Abundant; treat before drinking or bring your own.
Maps:	Toiyabe National Forest map; Hoover Wilderness map (topographic); USGS Pickel Meadow 7.5-minute quad.
Permits:	Not required.

Highway 108 to Sardine Falls

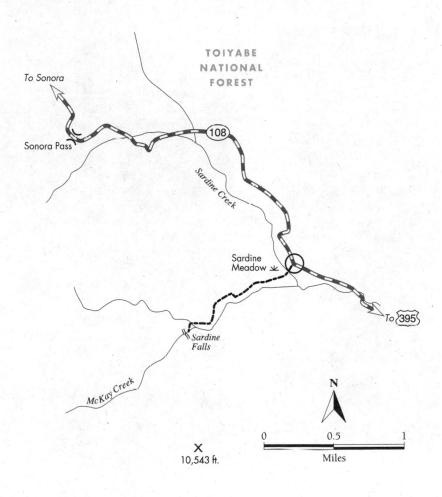

TOIYABE NATIONAL FOREST

To Sonora

Sonora Pass

108

Sardine Creek

Sardine Meadow

To 395

Sardine Falls

McKay Creek

X
10,543 ft.

N

0   0.5   1
Miles

Key points:

0.0	Trailhead on California Highway 108.
1.0	Sardine Falls.

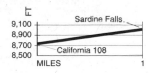

FT
9,100
8,900
8,700
8,500

Sardine Falls

California 108

MILES   1

Sardine Falls.

Finding the trailhead: There is no developed trailhead for this hike, only turnouts on either side of CA 108 on the northern margin of Sardine Meadow and a "Route Closed to Motorcycles" sign on the south side of the highway. Find these turnouts by driving 2.5 miles southeast from Sonora Pass or 12.2 miles west of the CA 108/US Highway 395 junction (1.1 miles west of the signed Soda Creek bridge).

The hike: Anyone who has followed CA 108 over Sonora Pass knows how beautiful the volcanic landscape of the northern Sierra crest is in this area. This short hike to Sardine Falls near Sonora Pass is one of the best ways to enjoy this dramatic landscape without strapping on a backpack and committing to several long days on the trail. Even though the trail is obscured by cattle trails at the start, it is well defined thereafter and is flat and easy enough for you to enjoy if you are willing to spend an hour walking in the mountains.

Begin this hike on the south side of the highway and proceed south past the "Route Closed to Motorcycles" sign into the sagebrush-studded expanse of Sardine Meadow. The large veil of whitewater that is Sardine Falls plunges out of an alpine basin about 1 mile ahead, encircled by 10,000- and 11,000-foot volcanic peaks.

After about 150 yards, you will have to cross the shallow channels of Sardine Creek. This stream is usually less than ankle-deep after August, so you may just get your feet wet. A well-worn trail, maintained by the cattle that graze the meadow in summer, leads into an open lodgepole pine forest alongside willow-bordered McKay Creek. Once you enter that forest, your route follows the doubletrack of a long-closed road, with lupine and scarlet gilia growing profusely along the trailside.

Soon, whitebark pines join the ranks of the forest, and after 0.4 mile, the creek ahead is funneled into a narrow gorge. Here the trail narrows into a singletrack and ascends steeply, but briefly (the only steep grade on the hike), to a low ridge. The trail descends slightly southwest into a small meadow rich with willows and aspens and the blooms of aster, corn lily, meadow rue, tall mountain helenium, cinquefoil, and Indian paintbrush.

In this meadow the trail forks. Be sure to take the rutted, and sometimes muddy and overgrown, right fork. Step across a small creek coming from the west and follow a winding course into a broad open bowl, with stark volcanic peaks rising above, their slopes feathered with tenacious whitebark pines.

As you approach the falls, you must rock-hop one last shallow stream, after which a number of boot-worn trails lead the final several yards to the base of the falls. Sardine Falls, a thundering 50-foot veil of whitewater, plunges over a resistant cliff of gray volcanic rock. A scattering of lodgepole and whitebark pines offer convenient shade for viewing the falls. On a bench just below the falls, on the creek's east side, you will find several excellent campsites set in a grove of lodgepole pines.

From Sardine Falls, retrace your route back to the trailhead.

47 Sonora Peak

Highlights:	This memorable hike leads to an alpine peak on the Sierra crest where 100-mile vistas of awe-inspiring mountain and desert scenery unfold.
General location:	Northern Sierra Nevada, Stanislaus National Forest, 1.5 miles north of Sonora Pass, 45 miles northeast of Sonora, and 22 miles northwest of Bridgeport.
Type of hike:	Round-trip day hike, part cross-country.
Distance:	5 miles.
Difficulty:	Moderately strenuous.
Elevation gain and loss:	2,012 feet.
Trailhead elevation:	9,450 feet.
High point:	Sonora Peak, 11,462 feet.
Best season:	July through early October.
Water availability:	None available; bring your own.
Maps:	Stanislaus National Forest map; Carson-Iceberg Wilderness map (topographic); USGS Sonora Pass 7.5-minute quad.
Permits:	Not required.

Key points:

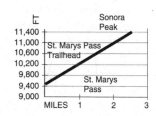

0.0   St. Marys Pass Trailhead.

1.25 St. Marys Pass; turn right and proceed east-northeast, cross-country.

2.5   Summit of Sonora Peak.

Finding the trailhead: The trailhead lies at the end of a spur road, signed for Saint Marys Pass Trailhead, that leads north from California Highway 108 for about 100 yards, about 0.8 mile west of Sonora Pass. This pass is 72.5 miles east of Sonora via CA 108 and 7.75 miles east of the Kennedy Meadows turnoff.

The hike: Sonora Peak's volcanic slopes rise abruptly northward from Sonora Pass. Hikers scaling its alpine summit are rewarded with far-flung vistas of the central and northern Sierra Nevada, the Great Basin, and part of Nevada. The first half of this fairly strenuous hike is on a closed doubletrack and trail; the final half is cross-country. Although routefinding here is no problem for experienced hikers, novices should be content with the views obtained from Saint Marys Pass.

Begin this hike by walking north along the retired doubletrack, past the barrier which blocks it from motor vehicle use. This route leads generally north under the intermittent shade of a scattered timberline forest of lodgepole and whitebark pine. It ascends grassy slopes clothed in sagebrush and splashed with the colors of a variety of wildflowers, including gilia, Indian paintbrush, helenium, cinquefoil, lupine, mariposa tulip, wallflower, aster,

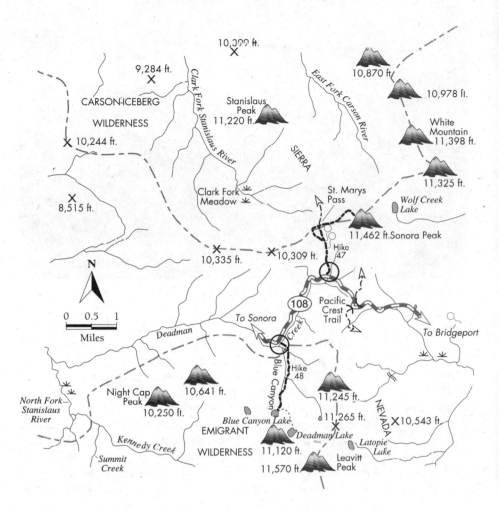

dandelion, pussy paws, and pennyroyal. The massive, reddish alpine mountain that dominates the view ahead is your destination. The closed doubletrack, quite steep at times, leads up to the cold runoff of a wildflower-decorated spring and quickly narrows to a singletrack.

Splash through the runoff of another cold spring, this one decorated by elephant heads and shooting stars. Now ascend the steep, grassy slopes to the west-trending ridge emanating from Sonora Peak. This ridgetop, at 10,400 feet, is known as Saint Marys Pass. The views that have continually expanded throughout this ascent are even more breathtaking at this point and are surpassed only by the view from Sonora Peak itself.

The narrow path you have been following continues northward from here toward the reddish cone of Stanislaus Peak. Another faint path branches

Vistas from Sonora Peak stretch far along the Sierra Crest into Yosemite National Park.

left from here, eventually leading hikers into the upper Clark Fork of the Stanislaus River. Backpackers may want to descend about 2.5 mostly trailless miles into beautiful Clark Fork Meadow after scaling Sonora Peak.

From the pass, leave the trail, turn right (east-northeast) and ascend steep, grassy slopes, leveling off on a bench and passing a last, isolated clump of ground-hugging whitebark pines. At these elevations, where high winds and deeply drifted snow are common, the whitebark grows only to shrub height. In its ground-hugging form, known as krummholz, it is protected by an insulating blanket of snow during the winter. During the extremely short growing season at this elevation, the whitebark pine puts forth little annual growth. Any branches that are able to grow above the snow level will be killed the following winter by the sandblasting effect of wind-blown ice and snow.

At this point, the summit lies dead ahead and from here you simply pick your way up the steep volcanic slopes to the summit. The easiest route ascends to the crest north of the peak, turns southeast, and follows a very faint path to the high point.

Upon completing the ascent to this fine mountain, you are rewarded with a glorious, all-encompassing, 360-degree view. To the east are the Sweetwater Mountains, crowned by the bright white summits surrounding Mount Patterson. Far to the southeast, the White Mountains are easily distinguished from their northern terminus in Nevada and stretch southward. Peaks of the majestic High Sierra are visible as far south as Banner Peak, Mount Ritter, and Mount Lyell. Also visible is Mount Dana, and closer at hand is impressive Tower Peak.

To the south and southwest, immediately across CA 108, is a region of high volcanic peaks, clearly illustrating the depth of the volcanic flows that buried this region before the Sierra Nevada rose to its present height. In the west, the thickly forested western slope of the Sierra is interrupted by the impressive Dardanelles. In the northwest, peaks as far away as the Lake Tahoe region can be seen; in the north, you can see the Carson Valley of western Nevada lying at the foot of the Carson Range. The deep canyon immediately to the north is the East Fork Carson River. Notice the marked difference in the topography north of Sonora Pass compared with that south of the pass. To the north, the character of the landscape is highly scenic, but is more subdued than the magnificent alpine terrain to the south. Consequently, Sonora Pass is often considered the geographical dividing point between the Northern Sierra and the High Sierra.

From the peak, carefully backtrack to the trailhead.

48 Blue Canyon

See Map on Page 223

Highlights: This short but memorable alpine hike leads into a glaciated volcanic canyon where one of the most magnificent floral displays in California can be seen and enjoyed.

General location: Northern Sierra Nevada, Emigrant Wilderness (Stanislaus National Forest), 45 miles northeast of Sonora and 1.5 miles southwest of Sonora Pass.

Type of hike: Round-trip day hike or overnighter.

Distance: 3.6 miles.

Difficulty: Moderate.

Elevation gain and loss: 1,020 or 1,280 feet.

Trailhead elevation: 8,720 feet at the lower trailhead or 8,980 feet at the upper trailhead.

High point: Blue Canyon Lake, 10,000 feet.

Best season: July through early October.

Water availability: Abundant. If day hiking, bring your own.

Maps: Stanislaus National Forest map; Emigrant Wilderness map (topographic); USGS Sonora Pass 7.5-minute quad.

Permits: A wilderness permit is required for overnight camping and can be obtained at the Summit Ranger Station in Pinecrest.

Key points:

0.0   Trailhead on California Highway 108.
0.3   Trails from upper and lower trailhead join; continue ascending Blue Canyon.
0.9   Cross east fork of Blue Canyon's creek.
1.8   Blue Canyon Lake.

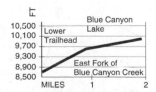

Finding the trailhead: There is no signed trailhead for Blue Canyon hikers. You must park in one of a few turnouts on CA 108. It is wise to use the Sonora Pass quad and the Stanislaus National Forest map to help you identify Blue Canyon so you know when to park.

Just before CA 108 passes the mouth of Blue Canyon, there is parking on the left-hand (northwest) side of the road for about three vehicles. This spot is just above two short switchbacks on the road, and is 2.7 miles southwest of Sonora Pass and 6.5 miles east of the Kennedy Meadows turnoff. From this point, you can see Blue Canyon's creek cascading into Deadman Creek just southeast of the highway, as well as the trail ascending into the canyon.

If this parking area is full, look for the larger parking area 0.2 mile southwest of (below) the upper parking area, 2.9 miles from Sonora Pass and 6.3 miles east of the Kennedy Meadows turnoff. This parking area lies immediately above (east of) a very sharp bend in the highway.

The hike: Blue Canyon is truly one of the most scenic areas in the entire state. This deeply glaciated canyon, surrounded by striking volcanic peaks and ridges, is a natural flower garden containing a vast collection of colorful wildflowers.

At the head of the canyon, lying under impressive 11,000-foot peaks, are two very beautiful alpine lakes. No fish live in these lakes, but the vivid scenery is adequate compensation for the lack of a trout dinner. Campfires are prohibited above 9,000 feet in the Emigrant Wilderness, which includes all of the Blue Canyon.

Starting from the upper parking area on CA 108, descend steeply into Deadman Creek. After hopping across this creek, pick up the good trail ascending into Blue Canyon just north of its creek. If you depart from the lower parking area, however, descend into Deadman Creek and pick up a good path that climbs along the west side of Blue Canyon's creek. Both trails join in Blue Canyon in about 0.3 mile, after avoiding a narrow chasm at the canyon's mouth.

If you started at the upper trailhead, you quickly climb to a lodgepole and whitebark pine–clad bench after crossing Deadman Creek and then enter the Emigrant Wilderness. Follow this sometimes faint path up the canyon toward a pyramidal volcanic peak in the south. The mountains surrounding this canyon are obviously of volcanic origin. This rock was resistant enough that glaciers were able to carve out many deep cirques and excavate the basins that contain these two alpine lakes. Since most volcanic rocks are much less resistant to glacial attack than granite, lake basins are rarely gouged into a volcanic landscape. The resulting glacially sculpted volcanic peaks in this canyon are stunningly beautiful.

Tree cover in the canyon is sparse, restricted to its lower end. Pass by the scattered stands of whitebark pine in the lower canyon, with a few lodgepole and western white pines on the west-facing slopes above. Whitebark pines will accompany you partway up this canyon, often stunted and deformed by years of savage winters.

The variety of wildflowers in this canyon, particularly in its lower half, is truly unbelievable, putting forth a dramatic, colorful display, especially in late July through mid-August. In these natural flower gardens you will find, among a variety of other flowers: red Indian paintbrush, aster, helenium, corn lily, red columbine, green gentian, scarlet gilia, stonecrop, mariposa tulip, monkey flower, larkspur, mule ears, lupine, wallflower, King's smooth sandwort, yampah, buttercup, phlox, shooting star, whorled penstemon, senecio, whitehead, pennyroyal, mountain sorrel, and alpine pynocoma.

Continuing your leisurely walk amid flower gardens and clumps of stunted whitebark pines, approach the cascading creek before climbing steeply beside it on the now-gravelly trail. Care should be exercised along this stretch—walking on volcanic gravel tends to resemble walking on marbles, and a misstep can send you flying. Above this brief climb, you have excellent views of the snow-streaked volcanic crags looming boldly at the canyon's head. Water in Blue Canyon is abundant, issuing forth from the porous volcanic rock and spilling down the steep slopes to feed Blue Canyon's creek.

Hop across the east fork of Blue Canyon's creek, which drains Deadman Lakes and the permanent snowfields cling to the flanks of 11,570-foot Leavitt Peak, the highest in the Emigrant Wilderness. You can ascend this fine canyon to Deadman Lake, or from Blue Canyon Lake, you can hike cross-country to Deadman Lake. From the lake, you can then descend via the east fork for a rewarding and highly scenic alpine loop.

Your trail grows faint beyond the east fork, but quickly reappears ahead. Continue south, passing just west of the colorful landmark pyramid that has guided you from the lower canyon, and descend steeply to cross the creek

Blue Canyon Lake, at 10,000 feet, lies at the head of magnificent Blue Canyon, near Sonora Pass in the Emigrant Wilderness.

in a narrow gorge. Over-the-shoulder views from this vicinity include the Sierra Nevada crest from Sonora Peak north to Stanislaus Peak. As you proceed up the canyon, notice that the variety of wildflowers has diminished markedly, but color is still fairly abundant.

. You eventually end your climb at the incomparable Blue Canyon Lake. This small, turquoise-colored lake lies in a deep cirque at 10,000 feet, surrounded by magnificent volcanic crags soaring more than 1,000 feet above its shoreline. The colorful pinnacle just east of the lake is especially striking.

Unfortunately, backpackers have camped too often on the grassy northwest shore of this alpine gem; the resulting scars abound and may take a century to heal. Please, do not camp at Blue Canyon Lake. Common sense should alert hikers to the fact that camping in a highly fragile alpine environment like this one causes irreparable damage to the delicate alpine vegetation. This trip is better taken as a day hike. If you do plan to camp in Blue Canyon, be sure to exercise zero impact camping practices to the fullest.

Several opportunities exist for side trips from the vicinity of Blue Canyon Lake. Immediately south of the lake, at an elevation of 10,800 feet, is a deep notch. A serious scramble to this notch via unstable volcanic slopes and snowfields yields excellent vistas into Kennedy Canyon and the interior of the Emigrant Wilderness. Also, as previously mentioned, a loop back to the trailhead via the east fork of Blue Canyon is possible for experienced hikers.

From Blue Canyon Lake, most hikers will return to the trailhead.

49 Dardanelles Loop

Highlights:	This scenic loop follows an unmaintained, but easy to follow, trail that circumnavigates the spectacular Dardanelles on the west slope of the Sierra.
General location:	Northern Sierra Nevada, Carson-Iceberg Wilderness (Stanislaus National Forest), 37 miles northeast of Sonora.
Type of hike:	Loop day hike or overnighter.
Distance:	6.6 miles.
Difficulty:	Moderate.
Elevation gain and loss:	1,150 feet.
Trailhead elevation:	7,200 feet.
High point:	8,100 feet.
Best season:	Mid-June through early October.
Water availability:	Available from McCormick Creek at 2.5 miles and at 3.8 miles. If day hiking, bring your own.
Maps:	Stanislaus National Forest map; Carson-Iceberg Wilderness map (topographic); USGS Spicer Meadow Reservoir 7.5-minute quad.
Permits:	A wilderness permit is required for overnight camping and can be obtained at the Summit Ranger Station, located at the Pinecrest Lake-Dodge Ridge turnoff from California Highway 108, about 30 miles east of Sonora.

Key points:

0.0	County Line Trailhead; proceed straight ahead, then turn right (southeast) after 150 yards onto McCormick Creek Trail.
2.5	Junction with faint Dardanelles Spur Trail; bear left (north).
2.7	Junction with faint eastbound trail; bear left (northwest).
3.3	Saddle at 8,100 feet.
5.8	Junction with County Line Trail; turn left (southeast).
6.6	County Line Trailhead.

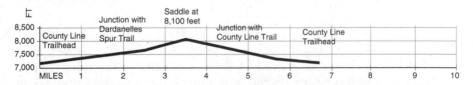

Finding the trailhead: About 17.2 miles west of Sonora Pass on CA 108 and about 49 miles east of Sonora, turn north where a sign indicates Clark Fork Road. This paved road, Forest Road 7N83, crosses the Middle Fork and then the Clark Fork Stanislaus River. After driving 0.9 mile from the highway, turn left onto FR 6N06 where a sign indicates Fence Creek Campground. Follow this dusty dirt road west, avoiding the right-branching spur road to

Dardanelles Loop

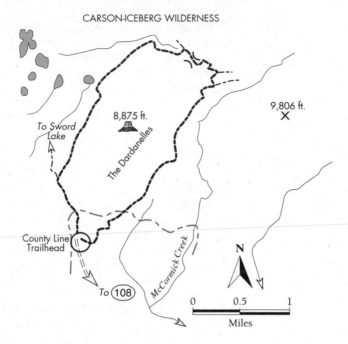

CARSON-ICEBERG WILDERNESS

Fence Creek Campground after 0.2 mile. After driving 6.4 miles from the highway, avoid the right-branching FR 6N06A and continue another 0.7 mile to the County Line Trailhead at the road's end.

The hike: This scenic hike loops around the intriguing Dardanelles, a striking volcanic formation rising well over 1,000 feet above the surrounding heavily forested landscape. The route is vague in places and should appeal to more experienced hikers. The Dardanelles are part of the lava flows that buried this region millions of years ago. Since much of the volcanic material has been removed by repeated episodes of glaciation, the Dardanelles stand like a volcanic island in a "sea" of granite.

From the trailhead, pass amid stumps and other scars of past logging. After 150 yards, branch right (southeast) onto the McCormick Creek Trail, a closed doubletrack, and then head northeast through a forest of Jeffrey pine and white fir, obtaining occasional tree-framed views of the Three Chimneys and Castle Rock in the southeast.

After red fir joins the forest, pass through a small meadow where your route narrows to a singletrack and enter the Carson-Iceberg Wilderness, leaving most of the stumps and logging scars behind. From this point, the Dardanelles loom boldly on the northern skyline, their dark volcanic cliffs contrasting with the greenery that thrives in the rich volcanic soil of their lower slopes.

The Dardanelles typify the volcanic material that buried this region of the Sierra Nevada millions of years ago. The Dardanelles were resistant enough to withstand repeated glacial advances and provide a vivid contrast to the surrounding granite-dominated landscape.

Continuing on a northeasterly course, pass through more small meadows that contain, among the previously mentioned forest trees, lodgepole pines and aspens. As you stroll across an aspen-rich meadow, the fantastic castle-like formation rising in the eastern foreground is Peak 9,070; it lies on the ridge 1 mile southwest of Dardanelles Cone. Your trail passes through more aspen-clad meadows that host corn lilies, willows, currants, and assorted wildflowers. While crossing these meadows, early-morning and late-afternoon hikers are apt to see some of the abundant mule deer that inhabit this region.

You eventually begin climbing and pass an isolated stand of black cottonwood. Soon thereafter, bear left onto a very faint northbound trail, the Dardanelles Spur Trail; if you can't find it, simply head north under a juniper-topped bench of volcanic rock. The McCormick Creek Trail continues east. Your trail climbs steeply at first, leveling off just west of the above-mentioned volcanic bench. Red-painted blazes on rocks and trees help lead the way.

The route soon skirts a corn lily–filled meadow, and you reach a junction at the meadow's eastern end. A faint eastbound trail continues onward, marked by more red blazes. Bear left instead onto a faint northwestbound trail, also marked with red-painted blazes on nearby trees.

Next, begin a series of moderate, ascending switchbacks that lead through a heavy red fir forest and finally top a saddle at 8,100 feet, on the crest of the Dardanelles. From the saddle, begin a northwest descent into a meadow that's often inhabited by cattle during the summer. This part of the trail is where routefinding problems begin.

Take the trail that stays east of and above the meadow, following the red-painted blazes. You soon meet a well-defined cow trail that continues a northwesterly descent, but the blazes turn southwest and the trail disappears. Simply walk out into the sloping meadow and cross to its southwest margin. Pick up the alder-lined outlet creek draining the meadow and follow it downstream, relocating the trail.

Continue your trail walk through a red fir and western white pine forest. Your trail is used frequently by deer and wandering cattle but is seldom traveled by other hikers. Northward views across the granitic-volcanic landscape in the Highland Creek drainage are excellent. Notice that the sheltered northwest slopes of the Dardanelles are thickly forested and less imposing than the dramatic southeast slopes.

The trail passes through several small meadows as you proceed on a southwesterly course through a forest of red and white fir and western white pine. After 2.25 miles of pleasant hiking beyond the cow-inhabited meadow, your trail joins the north-south trail coming from Lost and Sword Lakes and Highland Creek in a broad, grassy saddle. Turn left onto this popular trail from the signed Dardanelles Spur Trail and head south toward the County Line Trailhead. After passing through a stock gate (be sure to close it), you gain 250 feet of elevation before finally descending through pine and fir forest to your car at the trailhead.

50 Gianelli Trailhead to Upper Relief Valley

Highlights:	This scenic subalpine trip on the west slope of the Sierra features broad vistas and spreading meadows, and surveys contrasting landscapes of granitic and volcanic rocks.
General location:	Northern Sierra Nevada, Emigrant Wilderness (Stanislaus National Forest), 30 miles northeast of Sonora.
Type of hike:	Round-trip backpack, 2 to 4 days.
Distance:	16.4 miles.
Difficulty:	Moderate.
Elevation gain and loss:	+1,750 feet, -1,110 feet.
Trailhead elevation:	8,560 feet.
High point:	9,200 feet.
Best season:	July through early October.
Water availability:	Abundant at Whitesides Meadow at 4.7 miles and in Upper Relief Valley at 7.5 miles.

Maps: Stanislaus National Forest map; Emigrant Wilderness map (topographic); USGS Cooper Peak and Pinecrest 7.5-minute quads.

Permits: A wilderness permit is required for overnight camping and can be obtained at the Summit Ranger Station, located at the junction of California Highway 100 and the Pinecrest-Dodge Ridge Road. On weekends, hikers self-issue permits from the dispenser outside of the ranger station.

Key points:

0.0 Gianelli Trailhead.

1.3 Burst Rock.

2.2 Junction with unsigned northbound trail to Powell Lake; continue straight ahead (southeast).

3.0 Junction with trail to Chewing Gum Lake; bear left (east).

4.5 Junction with trail to Y Meadow Dam; stay left (northeast).

5.6 Junction with northwestbound Cooper Meadow Trail in Whitesides Meadow; bear right (east).

5.9 Junction with Upper Relief Valley Trail; turn left (northeast).

7.7 Junction at south end of Upper Relief Valley; bear left (northeast).

8.2 North end of Upper Relief Valley.

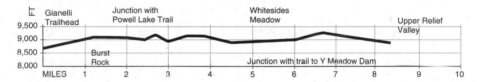

Finding the trailhead: Proceed east from Sonora on CA 108 for about 30 miles and turn right (east) onto the paved two-lane road where a sign indicates "Pinecrest-1." The Summit Ranger Station is located on the east side of the highway at this turnoff. After driving 0.4 mile, turn right again and follow signs to the Dodge Ridge Ski Area. Turn right once again after another 3 miles; a sign here points to Aspen Meadow, Bell Meadow, and Crabtree Camp. This turn is located just before a large sign declaring the entrance to the Dodge Ridge Ski Area.

After turning right here onto Forest Road 4N26, the road leads southwest for 0.4 mile to a stop sign. Turn left (southeast) and ascend to a junction with the southbound road to Bell Meadow, 1.7 miles from the stop sign and 5.5 miles from the highway. Stay left (east) at this junction, drive through the Aspen Meadow Pack Station complex on the dirt road, and follow the one-lane paved road.

The pavement ends 1.3 miles beyond the pack station, and the wide dirt road ahead is rough, with washboards and rocky stretches for the remaining distance to Gianelli Trailhead. After driving 1.4 miles from the end of the pavement, stay left (east) where a signed spur road branches right to the Crabtree Trailhead. Continue ascending, now on FR 4N47, for another 4.1 miles to the trailhead parking area, 12.3 miles from the highway. You will

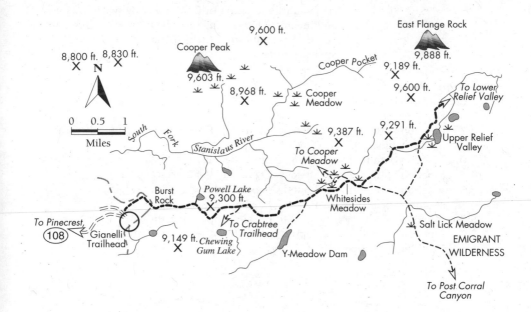

find ample space to park about 15 vehicles, but no signs designating the trailhead parking area.

The hike: Long before the ancestral Sierra Nevada was uplifted to its present height, volcanic eruptions from the east flowed over much of the landscape north of Yosemite National Park. These flows buried most of the exposed granitic bedrock in the region. When the glaciers formed, they began to carry away much of the volcanic debris that buried the landscape, re-exposing this granitic bedrock.

Beyond the northern end of the High Sierra, this glacially re-exposed granite gives way to deep volcanic deposits that weren't completely removed by glaciation, forming a landscape much different than areas farther south in the Sierra. The contrast between the two rock types is often striking, making this hike not only scenic, but offering insights into the geologic history of the region.

The rock-lined trail begins at the north end of the parking area and ascends gradually northeast through a shady forest of red fir, mountain hemlock, and western white pine to a granitic ridge, the Stanislaus River/Clavey River divide. Here, trailside trees filter the northward view across the South Fork Stanislaus River canyon. The trail follows an eastbound course just below the ridge, then turns south at a ridgeline saddle. The trail ahead ascends gently to moderately, making the trip to Burst Rock far more pleasant than on the abruptly rising old trail that hikers once followed.

The trail climbs through a shady pine, fir, and hemlock forest and among granite slabs to the west shoulder of Burst Rock. Pass, and read, a sign that details the brief history of the emigrant trail known as the West Walker-Sonora Road, a very difficult route that gave the Emigrant Wilderness its name. From this point onward, enjoy expansive westward views across the heavily forested western Sierra foothills.

Ascend the sandy slopes south of Burst Rock, then gradually descend to an open saddle. Don't miss the short detour to the granite boulders capping Burst Rock, just northwest of the trail. Superb vistas unfold, some of the most far-ranging on the entire hike. The view north across the South Fork Stanislaus River, with its glacially re-exposed granite, provides a marked contrast to the volcanic peaks rising in odd forms north of the river. These volcanic peaks include 9,603-foot Cooper Peak, 9,600-foot Castle Rock, and the Three Chimneys.

Soaring alpine peaks of the Sierra Nevada crest rise to the east, and in the southeast, a low, heavily glaciated rocky plateau extends toward the eastern boundary of Yosemite National Park. In the south, thickly forested, gentle west-slope terrain contrasts vividly with all of the exposed granite lying immediately to the east. These vistas accompany you through most of this ridgetop journey.

A descent of 250 feet through subalpine forest leads you east from Burst Rock. At the bottom of this descent, in a saddle fringed with stunted trees and red heather, you pass an unmarked trail on your left leading a short distance north to 8,800-foot Powell Lake. Surrounded by bare granite and scattered timber, and with good northward views to volcanic pinnacles, this lake makes a pleasant and quite scenic rest stop.

Next, climb 250 feet over a north-south ridge, topping out at 9,200 feet in a mixed forest of mountain hemlock, red fir, lodgepole and western white pine. Then descend 350 feet to reach a junction in Lake Valley, 3 miles from the trailhead. The signed southbound trail leads to Chewing Gum Lake in 0.7 mile and continues beyond to the trailheads at Crabtree Camp and Bell Meadow. Bear left at this junction to leave tarn-dotted Lake Valley behind.

Begin climbing moderately under a canopy of lodgepole and western white pine and past wildflower-filled openings that are dominated by lupine and senecio. Near the top of this ascent, traverse an open, grassy ridgetop offering great views north and east. This ridge is capped by volcanic deposits, unlike the initial segment of the hike that passed over granitic rock exclusively.

You will notice a difference in the vegetation between the granitic and volcanic slopes. A fairly lush grass and wildflower type of vegetation thrives in the volcanic-enriched soils, whereas only sparse grasses and wildflowers are able to take hold on the meager soils of the granitic slopes. A greater water-holding capacity and the fact that these volcanic rocks have decomposed into fairly deep soil contrast with the often-thin layer of decomposed granite and its lesser water-holding capacity. These differences contribute to the plant variation you see along this hike.

Pass back into the realm of granite and begin another descent of 350 feet. You reach a junction with a southbound trail leading to Y Meadow Dam after hiking 4.5 miles from the trailhead. Bear left here where the sign points to Y Meadow Dam, proceeding northeast through a gradually thinning forest. Break into the open and head east across aptly named Whitesides Meadow, meeting the northwestbound trail to Cooper Meadow near the east end of this large grassland. Staying right at this junction, your trail soon leaves that spread, skirts the edge of a small meadow filled with lupine and senecio, and meanders up to a junction with the popular right-branching trail to Salt Lick Meadow and the lake-filled terrain at the heart of the Emigrant Wilderness.

Bear left here and the trail begins a northeasterly course, first on the north side, then on the south side of the ridge, alternating between volcanic and granitic terrain. About 1.25 miles from the Whitesides Meadow, pass the small meadow and trickling stream forming the headwaters of Relief Creek and begin descending.

You soon skirt the western edge of the Upper Relief Valley's subalpine grassland, gloriously brightened by lupine, senecio, and mountain helenium. Pass a southbound trail leading to Salt Lick Meadow after a short jaunt into the valley. Good campsites can be found around the valley and near the two small, shallow lakes at its northern end. Water isn't as plentiful here as it is in other areas of the Sierra; wherever you obtain water in the backcountry, purification is always recommended.

The view across the valley to the barren, alpine, Sierra Nevada crest peaks, including Sonora Peak, add to the scenic attraction of this grand

Powell Lake lies near Burst Rock in the Emigrant Wilderness and makes a fine destination for a short day hike.

meadow. In the foreground, the volcanic pinnacles of East Flange Rock point their stark fingers into the sky. The valley itself is flanked by dissimilar glaciated slopes. To the east is a low, granite ridge, forested with lodgepole and western white pine and mountain hemlock. To the west lies a volcanic ridge, its dark brown rock contrasting with the greenery that thrives on its slopes.

Experienced cross-country hikers may consider a 2.5- to 3-mile jaunt east from Upper Relief Valley to several remote alpine lakes lying in cirques just north of the 10,322-foot Granite Dome, the large, rounded alpine mountain rising east of the valley. The USGS Cooper Meadow and Emigrant Lake 7.5-minute quads are recommended for this side trip.

Eventually, backtrack to the trailhead.

---

51 Ebbetts Pass to Nobel Lake

Highlights:	This short but scenic trip follows a segment of the Pacific Crest Trail (PCT) leading into a subalpine basin set among volcanic peaks below the Sierra crest near Ebbetts Pass.
General location:	Northern Sierra Nevada, Toiyabe National Forest, 10 miles south-southwest of Markleeville and 50 miles northeast of Angels Camp.
Type of hike:	Round-trip day hike or overnighter.
Distance:	7.4 miles.
Difficulty:	Moderate.
Elevation gain and loss:	+950 feet, -750 feet.
Trailhead elevation:	8,650 feet.
High point:	Nobel Lake, 8,850 feet.
Best season:	July through early October.
Water availability:	Abundant at Nobel Lake. If day hiking, bring your own.
Maps:	Toiyabe or Stanislaus National Forest maps; Carson-Iceberg Wilderness map (topographic); USGS Ebbetts Pass 7.5-minute quad.
Permits:	Not required.

Key points:

0.0 PCT Trailhead.
0.2 Junction with PCT; turn left (east).
2.5 Cross Nobel Creek.
2.7 Junction with northbound trail descending Nobel Canyon; stay right (south).
3.7 Nobel Lake.

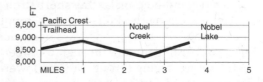

Ebbetts Pass to Nobel Lake

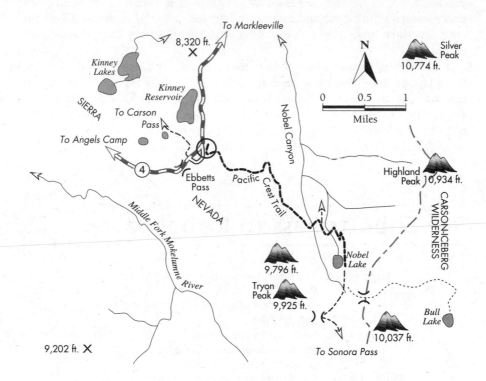

Finding the trailhead: The signed PCT Trailhead lies at the end of a 0.1-mile spur road east of California Highway 4 and about 0.5 mile northeast of Ebbetts Pass. This pass is 125 miles east of Stockton and 12.8 miles west of the CA 4/CA 89 junction southeast of Markleeville. CA 4 is a narrow, winding, and steep paved road with no centerline; drive this road with extreme caution.

The hike: This moderately easy hike utilizes a segment of the PCT to reach the subalpine basin at the head of Nobel Canyon. A base camp can be made in this basin so you can scale Tryon Peak, hike southeast to the remote Bull Lake, or just relax and enjoy the view and magnificent surroundings.

The trail begins at the southwest (upper) end of the parking area and proceeds generally south for 0.2 mile through a forest of lodgepole and western white pine, red fir, and mountain hemlock. Views through the trees across the highway to the glacially smoothed granite and the volcanic pinnacles beyond help make this short stroll pass quickly.

Upon meeting the PCT, turn left, topping out on an open ridge at 8,800 feet, where you have good views north across the upper Silver Creek drainage. Your trail contours through a timberline bowl under striking volcanic cliffs before slicing through a wildflower-dappled meadow. Re-enter a red fir, mountain hemlock, and western white pine forest and contour around a granite spur ridge before beginning a sidehill descent. You have great views along this stretch across the deep, U-shaped trough of Nobel Canyon to 10,774-foot Silver Peak and 10,934-foot Highland Peak.

The gently descending trail leads southeast through a sparse boulder-dotted forest, crossing three small creeklets en route. Just before reaching the bottom of Nobel Canyon, hop across two more small creeks. Notice that the granitic landscape you have been traversing changes into one dominated by volcanic material.

Cross Nobel Creek and swing north briefly to round a spur ridge. The trail soon jogs south around that ridge, enters the shade of red fir and western white pine, and then passes an unsigned trail on your left, descending the length of Nobel Canyon. Soon your trail dips into a gully containing Nobel Lake's outlet stream. Negotiate three long switchbacks to ascend the volcanic hillside, passing an occasional stunted juniper en route.

Above this climb, begin hiking along the outlet of Nobel Lake across increasingly alpine terrain, dotted with a few stunted mountain hemlocks and whitebark pines. You quickly reach the northeastern shore of Nobel Lake. This fine lake lies in a truly "noble" setting, surrounded by a grassy landscape decorated with a variety of wildflowers and scattered stands of whitebark pine and mountain hemlock, with a backdrop of craggy volcanic peaks. In addition to its majestic setting, this lake can be a good producer of pan-sized golden trout.

Good campsites are located throughout this high basin. The area lends itself to cross-country exploration due to its open, gentle terrain. Cattle are only sometimes present in the basin, but water purification is always advised.

From Nobel Lake, return the way you came.

Nobel Lake is a rewarding destination for a day hike or overnighter beginning at Ebbetts Pass on the Sierra Crest.

52 Sandy Meadow Trailhead to Wheeler Lake

Highlights:	This pleasant hike passes through subalpine forests and meadows and features good fishing and scenic campsites with a backdrop of volcanic peaks at Wheeler Lake.
General location:	Northern Sierra Nevada, Mokelumne Wilderness (Stanislaus National Forest), 15 miles southwest of Markleeville and 80 miles northeast of Modesto.
Type of hike:	Round-trip backpack, 2 to 3 days.
Distance:	9.6 miles.
Difficulty:	Moderate.
Elevation gain and loss:	+550 feet, -600 feet.
Trailhead elevation:	7,920 feet.
High point:	8,100 feet.
Best season:	Early July through mid-October.
Water availability:	Available from Sandy Meadow Creek between 1.9 and 2.4 miles, from an unnamed creek at 2.8 miles, and between Jackson Canyon creek at 3.9 miles and Wheeler Lake at 4.8 miles.
Maps:	Stanislaus National Forest map; Mokelumne Wilderness map (topographic); USGS Pacific Valley 7.5-minute quad.
Permits:	Required for overnight use between May 25 and September 15. If you are approaching from the east, you can self-register for permits at the Chamber of Commerce/USFS ranger station at the north end of town in Markleeville. If you are approaching from the west, you can obtain permits from the Alpine Ranger Station (open summer only) on California Highway 4, 1.5 miles east of Bear Valley, or from the Calaveras Ranger Station in Hathaway Pines.

Key points:
- 0.0 Sandy Meadow Trailhead on CA 4.
- 0.3 Enter Mokelumne Wilderness.
- 1.9 Trail junction in Sandy Meadow; bear right (northwest) to reach Wheeler Lake.
- 4.8 Wheeler Lake.

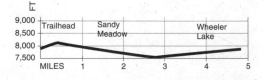

Finding the trailhead: Approaching from the east, follow CA 4 southwest from its junction with CA 89 (5 miles southeast of Markleeville). After 6.2 miles, the centerline on CA 4 disappears, and the road becomes a steep, narrow, and winding, one-lane route stretching southwest as far as Lake

Alpine. The road crests the Sierra at Ebbetts Pass after 13.2 miles, descends to the Middle Fork Mokelumne River, and then rises to Pacific Grade Summit, 21.2 miles from CA 89. The spacious Sandy Meadow Trailhead lies on the south side of the highway, adjacent to stock corrals, 1.1 miles west of Pacific Grade Summit.

If you approach from the west, follow CA 4 for 56 miles northeast from Angels Camp to the trailhead. If you reach Pacific Grade Summit, you've gone 1.1 miles too far.

The hike: This fine hike leads through subalpine forests in the southern reaches of the Mokelumne Wilderness, offering a remote atmosphere, occasional long-range vistas deep into the rugged interior of this wilderness, and a scenic destination. Wheeler Lake features productive fishing, good campsites, and a spectacular setting beneath a crest of high volcanic peaks. The hike is short enough to be taken as a day hike, but is better suited for a two- to three-day trip.

The trail begins on the north side of the highway, several yards west of the trailhead parking area, and is indicated by a "trail" sign. You rise moderately at first through a red fir and lodgepole pine forest and level out just before topping a low saddle. Enter the Mokelumne Wilderness on the north side of the saddle, then begin a steady descent that leads to a long traverse of corrugated slopes, where small meadows and early-season rivulets interrupt the forest of lodgepole and western white pine, red fir, and mountain hemlock—a typical timberline forest of the Northern Sierra.

Wheeler Lake is a scenic destination in the volcanic landscape of the southern reaches of the Mokelumne Wilderness.

Sandy Meadow Trailhead to Wheeler Lake

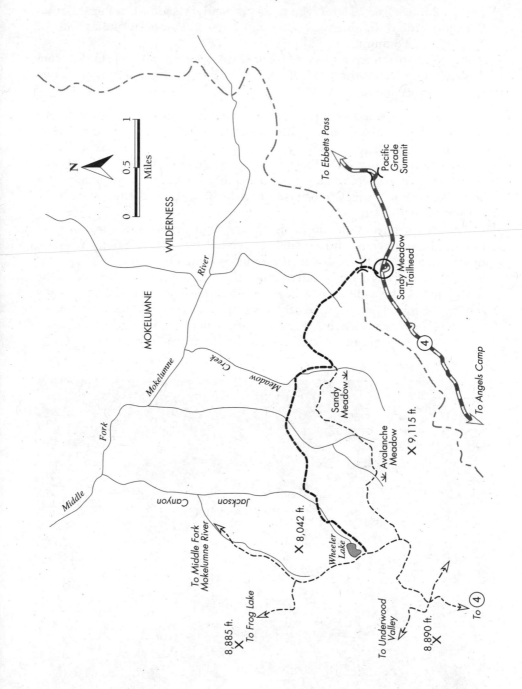

As you continue your descent, occasional views open up to the north across the broad, forested canyon of the Middle Fork Mokelumne River to bold volcanic peaks. This view stretches far to the northeast, to the distant Freel Peak that rises above Lake Tahoe. More lofty peaks, volcanic pinnacles, and broad, verdant alpine fell fields can be seen on the Sierra crest to the east.

After 1.5 miles, you reach the sloping spread of Sandy Meadow, backed up by the volcanic summits of Peak 8,641 to the south and Peak 8,501 to the west. Here a trailside post points left (west) to Avalanche Meadow and right (northwest) to Wheeler Lake. Either trail can be taken to reach the lake; the right-hand trail is more direct and involves less climbing.

After turning right, begin to descend steadily through a viewless forest for about 0.5 mile to a rock-hop crossing of Meadow Creek. Beyond the crossing, the trail heads west and quickly reaches another stream; this one usually requires a shallow ford. Ahead, begin a steady ascent through increasingly rocky terrain, studded with erratic boulders, to a pair of small and shallow, but picturesque, tarns. Just beyond, you will reach Wheeler Lake's outlet stream, where deep holes and pools harbor brook trout up to 12 inches long. Cross this larger stream twice, either by boulder-hopping, crossing a log, or by wading, depending upon the water level.

A steady ascent through a forest of red fir, lodgepole pine, and mountain hemlock follows, leading you on a winding course past ice-polished granite to the east shore of Wheeler Lake. The lake is popular enough to host a few hiking or horse-packing parties on most summer weekends; on weekdays, you may very well have the lake to yourself.

The verdant volcanic slopes of an 8,800-foot ridge rise behind the lake, but the lake basin itself is scooped out of granitic rocks. Fishing is best in the deep water at the north shore and near the lake's outlet. The better campsites in the open, mixed conifer forest surrounding the lake are located among the granite knolls north of the lake. Rangers discourage the use of campsites along the fringe of the meadows beyond the south and west shores. Those sites have been overused in the past, and many are posted as closed to camping.

Few hikers continue on past Wheeler Lake, with the trail around its south and west shores faint and remaining wet and soggy usually until midsummer. North of the lake, trails lead far down to the canyon of the Middle Fork Mokelumne River, to Frog Lake, and to the seldom-visited Underwood Valley. Most likely, though, you will retrace your route from Wheeler Lake back to the trailhead.

53 Carson Pass to Frog, Winnemucca, and Round Top Lakes

Highlights:	This short but spectacular half-day hike takes you to a trio of lovely timberline lakes near Carson Pass on the Sierra crest.
General location:	Northern Sierra Nevada, Mokelumne Wilderness (Eldorado National Forest), 15 miles south of South Lake Tahoe and 85 miles northeast of Stockton.
Type of hike:	Round-trip half-day hike or overnighter.
Distance:	6 miles.
Difficulty:	Moderately easy.
Elevation gain and loss:	730 feet.
Trailhead elevation:	8,573 feet.
High point:	9,440 feet.
Best season:	Mid-July through September.
Water availability:	Available at the lakes. If day hiking, bring your own.
Maps:	Eldorado or Toiyabe National Forest maps; Mokelumne Wilderness map (topographic); USGS Carson Pass and Caples Lake 7.5-minute quads.
Permits:	Required for overnight use between April 1 and November 30. Obtain permit at the Carson Pass Information Station.

Key points:
- 0.0   Carson Pass Pacific Crest Trailhead (PCT).
- 0.6   Junction with spur trail to Frog Lake; bear right (south).
- 0.7   Junction with eastbound PCT; bear right (southwest).
- 2.1   Outlet of Winnemucca Lake and junction with trail descending northwest to Woods Lake; stay left (west) to reach Round Top Lake.
- 3.0   Round Top Lake.

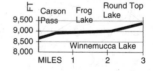

Finding the trailhead: The spacious but often-crowded trailhead parking lot is located alongside California Highway 88 at Carson Pass, 8.8 miles southwest of the CA 88/CA 89 junction and 109 miles east of Stockton. A $3 self-issue parking fee is charged at the trailhead. If the Carson Pass parking lot is full, which it often is during the summer, drive 0.25 mile northwest from the pass to the northbound PCT trailhead. A parking fee is also charged there.

Trailhead facilities include toilets, and interpretive and historical signs. Books, maps, and wilderness permits are available at the Carson Pass Information Station.

The hike: The hike to Frog, Winnemucca, and Round Top Lakes is one of the most popular hikes in the Northern Sierra outside of the Lake Tahoe

Carson Pass to Frog, Winnemucca, and Round Top Lakes

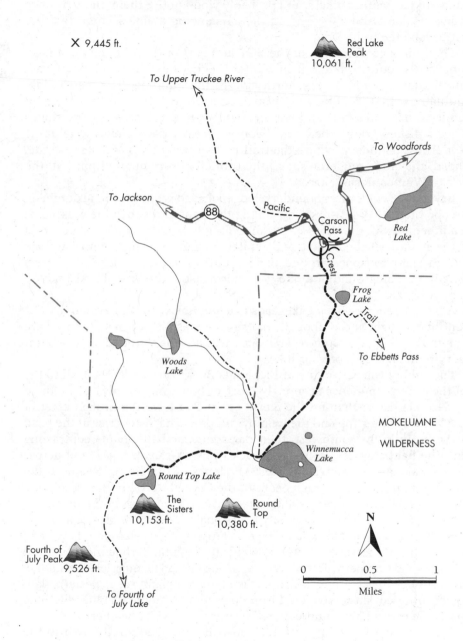

X 9,445 ft.

Red Lake Peak
10,061 ft.

To Upper Truckee River

To Woodfords

To Jackson

88

Pacific

Carson Pass

Crest

Red Lake

Frog Lake

Trail

To Ebbetts Pass

Woods Lake

MOKELUMNE

WILDERNESS

Winnemucca Lake

Round Top Lake

The Sisters
10,153 ft.

Round Top
10,380 ft.

N

Fourth of July Peak
9,526 ft.

To Fourth of July Lake

0   0.5   1

Miles

area, and justifiably so. For a minimal investment of time and effort, you can enjoy some of the finest alpine scenery, broad vistas, and vivid wild-flower displays along the northern crest of the range. Expect to share the trail with many other hikers. You probably won't notice them, though, since your attention will be focused on the outstanding alpine scenery that lies just beyond the trailhead.

The trail, a combination of the PCT and part of the Winnemucca Lake Loop cross-country ski trail in winter, begins next to the Carson Pass Information Station, on the north side of the building. The trail mildly undulates at first, leading you through an open forest of red fir, mountain hemlock, and lodgepole and western white pine, and crossing the slopes of ice-polished granite bedrock. Soon you reach the signed Mokelumne Wilderness boundary, where the trail momentarily rises at a steep grade. Ahead, the grade moderates, and the trail climbs gradually uphill all the way to Winnemucca Lake.

Beyond the wilderness boundary, lodgepole and whitebark pine dominate the open forest. Wind your way among the trees and subalpine grasslands to a junction with the short spur trail to Frog Lake, set a short distance east of the main trail. Lodgepole and whitebark pine and mountain hemlock stud the granite slopes around this beautiful, trout-filled lake, its waters lying in the foreground of a fine view northeast to the Freel Peaks and the Carson Range.

A brief ascent past Frog Lake leads to a junction with the eastbound PCT. Continue straight ahead, though, entering increasingly open slopes that are scattered with stunted pines. This openness affords tremendous vistas for every remaining step of your hike.

The rubbly volcanic dome of Elephants Back rises above the trail to the southeast, a prominence seemingly more at home in the volcanic fields of the Nevada desert than on the Sierra crest. The towering broken crest of 10,380-foot Round Top and the twin pyramids of The Sisters rise at the head of the basin in the southwest, their dark volcanic battlements contrasting with the light gray, ice-scoured bedrock below. Westward, gaze out across Caples Lake and far down the western slopes of the Sierra. Rising in the northwest are the distant high peaks of the Crystal Range in the Desolation Wilderness; Red Lake Peak stands guard over Carson Pass in the north.

The trail ahead, gentle with only occasional moderate grades, is a classic walk through a High Sierra landscape. It crosses slopes clad in willows and laced with early season rivulets and winds through timberline meadows and fields of vivid summer wildflowers. Among the myriad blooms, look for lupine, sulphur buckwheat, groundsel, alpine gold, Indian paintbrush, western wall-flower, whorled penstemon, Davidson's penstemon, mountain bluebells, blue flax, mule ears, phlox, buttercup, red heather, and white heather.

After about 1.9 miles, you crest a low moraine and stroll down to the shores of large and deep Winnemucca Lake, resting at an elevation of 9,000 feet. There are few places in the Sierra where such a timberline gem as this lake can be reached by such a short and easy hike. This kind of timberline landscape is normally reserved for backpackers deep in the backcountry areas of the range. Only a scattering of stunted, tenacious whitebark pines and mountain hemlocks cling to the granite shores of this round, island-studded lake. Bold volcanic cliffs rise 800 feet from the lakeshore, forming the dramatic headwall of the basin. Numerous creeks tumble and cascade into the lake from the lingering snowfield that clings to the walls above. Fishing for pan-sized brook, rainbow, and golden trout can be productive in this deep lake.

If you find Winnemucca Lake to be a bit too crowded, or if you simply want to stretch your legs some more, follow the westbound trail, signed for Round Top Lake, at the log crossing of Winnemucca Lake's outlet stream. This good trail ascends the west wall of the basin with occasional, moderately steep grades. Round Top towers overhead while you cross alpine fell fields studded with wind-flagged whitebark pines. After topping out on a 9,440-foot ridge among mats of krummholz, gradually descend through fields of wildflowers and sagebrush to the willow-bordered shores of Round Top Lake at 9,300 feet.

With a backdrop of the somber volcanic cliffs of The Sisters, this beautiful, heart-shaped lake hosts a timberline forest of whitebark pines around its shores that offer much more shelter than can be found at windswept Winnemucca Lake. Fine views reach to the volcanic summits of Covered Wagon and Thimble Peaks, and far to the Crystal Range in the north.

As you return to the trailhead, briefly spy a sliver of Lake Tahoe in the north as you cross the broad, open slopes just below Winnemucca Lake.

Frog Lake is a popular destination for a short day hike from Carson Pass.

54 Schneider Camp to Showers Lake

Highlights:	This view-packed timberline trip circumnavigates a section of the northern Sierra Nevada crest at the headwaters of the Upper Truckee River, where you enjoy panoramic vistas of the Lake Tahoe region.
General location:	Northern Sierra Nevada, Eldorado National Forest, 4 miles northwest of Carson Pass and 13 miles southwest of South Lake Tahoe.
Type of hike:	Loop day hike or overnighter.
Distance:	8.2 miles.
Difficulty:	Moderate.
Elevation gain and loss:	1,450 feet.
Trailhead elevation:	8,300 feet.
High point:	Sierra crest, 9,200 feet.
Best season:	July through early October.
Water availability:	Available at Showers Lake at 2.2 miles, and at 3.2 miles. If day hiking, bring your own.
Maps:	Eldorado National Forest map or Lake Tahoe Basin Management Unit map; Mokelumne Wilderness map (topographic); USGS Caples Lake 7.5-minute quad.
Permits:	Not required.

Key points:

0.0	Schneider Camp Trailhead; proceed left (northeast) on trail.
1.1	Reach Sierra crest at 9,200 feet and junction with eastbound trail descending Dixon Canyon; bear left (north) and begin descending.
2.2	Junction with Pacific Crest Trail (PCT) at Showers Lake; turn left (north).
4.2	Leave PCT at junction with southbound trail to Schneider Cow Camp; turn left (south) here.
7.7	Junction with doubletrack west of Schneider Camp; turn left (east).
8.2	Return to trailhead.

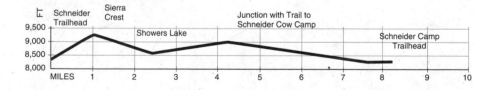

Finding the trailhead: From California Highway 88 above the north shore of Caples Lake, about 102 miles east of Stockton and 3 miles west of Carson Pass, turn north where a sign indicates the CalTrans Caples Lake Maintenance Station. Drive past the maintenance station and, after 0.4 mile, turn right (north) onto Forest Road 10N13 where a sign points to Schneider. The road turns to dirt at this point. Follow this occasionally rough and dusty road for 1.7 miles to the upper end of a broad meadow and park here. The road continues on beyond a stock gate, but it is only a poor doubletrack.

The hike: Anyone who has hiked in the Lake Tahoe area knows how popular this region can be. In fact, some hiking areas in the region are downright overcrowded and for good reason. The scenery here is often spectacular, and the hiking is generally easy.

This hike, traversing subalpine terrain for the entire distance, is by far the least-used trail in this area, except for the Showers Lake environs. Subalpine Showers Lake is often crowded, especially on summer weekends. Solitude-seeking backpackers may have to consider locating their campsites in the Upper Truckee River basin or in one of the westside bowls along the latter part of the hike. Consider establishing a dry camp on the Sierra crest for utter solitude and a glorious sunrise.

From the east end of the large meadow known as Schneider Camp, your trail leads northeastward past a sign indicating that the route is closed to motor vehicles. You quickly pass through a stock gate and begin ascending volcanic slopes clothed in sagebrush and a variety of wildflowers. As you near the top of the climb, pass a few stunted whitebark pines and, after hiking 1.1 miles from the trailhead, reach the high point atop the alpine Sierra Nevada crest.

Vistas from this point are excellent. Below to the east lies the wide valley of the Upper Truckee River. Meiss Lake glistens in the middle of this subalpine valley. Beyond are the southernmost summits of the Carson Range—Red Lake and Stevens Peaks—both of which rise to 10,061 feet. Views from here also include the American River drainage in the west, the Freel Peak environs in the north, and the jagged peaks of the Ebbetts Pass region in the southeast, with higher peaks fading into the distance beyond.

Just after reaching this high point, pass an eastbound trail descending Dixon Canyon and proceed north along the wildflower-clad east slopes of the Sierra Nevada crest. Soon, Round Lake and the Four Lakes come into view in the Upper Truckee River basin; beyond, Lake Tahoe begins to dominate your northward gaze. The contouring trail now begins a descent toward Showers Lake, visible in a shallow basin to the north.

Upon entering a subalpine forest, your steep, gravelly route joins the PCT before reaching Showers Lake. Turn left and begin skirting the numerous east-shore campsites set amid a forest of mountain hemlock, red fir, and lodgepole and western white pine. On any given summer weekend, unoccupied campsites around this lake may be hard to find. This fine lake, surrounded by glacially smoothed granite, lies just below the contact zone between the granitic rock and the volcanic material that buries that bedrock. Fishing here is poor, but the scenery is superb.

Pass a sign pointing to Echo Summit, descend northward to cross the dam-regulated outlet creek below Showers Lake, and double back up that creek, jogging west into a willow-cloaked meadow. Your trail, the north-bound PCT, soon passes another sign pointing to Echo Summit. It then begins traversing a timberline bowl flanked by volcanic mudflow boulders on the left and glacially re-exposed granite on the right.

Exiting this bowl, the trail passes into a drier forest of mountain hemlock and lodgepole pine, with a few whitebark and western white pines adding diversity. Pass through another one of the many stock gates (which you

Schneider Camp to Showers Lake

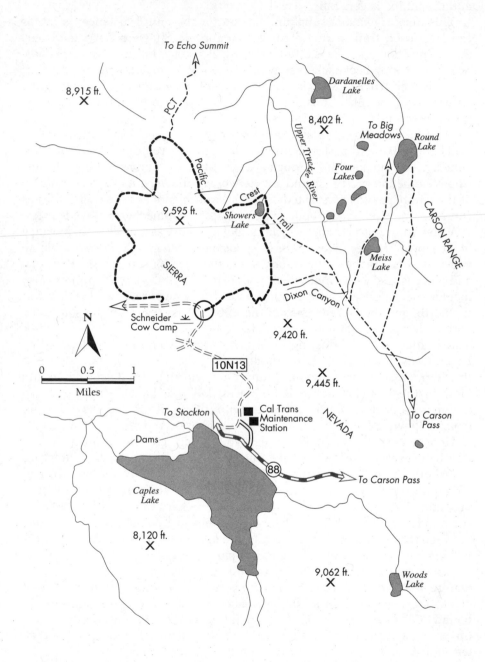

To Echo Summit

8,915 ft.
X

PCT

Pacific

Crest

Trail

9,595 ft.
X

Showers
Lake

SIERRA

Schneider
Cow Camp

N

0   0.5   1
Miles

10N13

9,420 ft.
X

9,445 ft.
X

To Stockton

Cal Trans
Maintenance
Station

NEVADA

88

To Carson Pass

Dams

Caples
Lake

8,120 ft.
X

9,062 ft.
X

Woods
Lake

Dardanelles
Lake

8,402 ft.
X

To Big
Meadows

Round
Lake

Four
Lakes

Upper Truckee River

CARSON RANGE

Meiss
Lake

Dixon Canyon

To Carson
Pass

250

should be sure to close) encountered along this hike. Meet the homebound segment of your loop on the wildflower-speckled Sierra crest, about 1.75 miles from Showers Lake.

Turn left at this junction and part company with hikers on the PCT. A sign here points south to Schneider Cow Camp. Enjoy an excellent northwestward view across a meadow (often occupied by cattle) at the head of Sayles Canyon to Pyramid, Jacks, and Dicks Peaks in the Desolation Wilderness.

The trail passes drift-bent lodgepole pines and shelter-giving stands of mountain hemlock before you encounter a sign bolted high on a lodgepole pine informing northbound motorcyclists (who are rarely seen on this trail) that the terrain north of the sign is closed to motorized forms of recreation.

Your southbound course leads through two timberline bowls west of the Sierra crest. Avoid drawing water from the northernmost bowl unless you have the means to purify it; cattle graze in this area. Occasional views northward into the Desolation Wilderness country, westward across the conifer-clad western slope of the Sierra, and southward to the volcanic divide separating the American and Mokelumne Rivers, help pass the time during your southbound trek.

As you begin an eastward traverse, break into the open to enjoy superb vistas of the Carson Pass region, Elephants Back, impressive Round Top, and Caples Lake. This view clearly displays the vivid contrast between the character of the bedrock granitic rocks and the deep volcanics that bury them. Descend amid a thickening forest, amble out onto a doubletrack, turn left, and hike 0.5 mile back to the trailhead.

Showers Lake lies near the head of Upper Truckee River south of Lake Tahoe.

55 Luther Pass to Freel Meadows

Highlights:	This uncrowded hike, part of which is open to mountain bikes, leads to a pair of lovely subalpine meadows in the Carson Range, high above Lake Tahoe.
General location:	Northern Sierra Nevada, Carson Range, Lake Tahoe Basin Management Unit, 8 miles southeast of South Lake Tahoe.
Type of hike:	Semi-loop day hike or overnighter.
Distance:	7.6 miles.
Difficulty:	Moderate.
Elevation gain and loss:	1,750 feet.
Trailhead elevation:	7,716 feet.
High point:	9,280 feet.
Best season:	Late June through early October.
Water availability:	Water is usually available at lower Freel Meadow until late summer, and a more reliable source is found at Tucker Flat. If day hiking, bring your own.
Maps:	Lake Tahoe Basin Management Unit or Eldorado National Forest maps; USGS Freel Peak 7.5-minute quad.
Permits:	Not required.

Key points:
- 0.0 Tahoe Rim Trailhead.
- 0.3 Lower junction with Tucker Flat Trail; bear left (northwest), staying on Tahoe Rim Trail.
- 2.9 Upper junction with Tucker Flat Trail; continue straight ahead (east).
- 3.9 Lower Freel Meadow.
- 4.3 East end of Upper Freel Meadow; backtrack from here to Tucker Flat Trail.
- 5.7 Junction with Tucker Flat Trail; turn left (southwest) and begin descending.
- 7.3 Junction with Tahoe Rim Trail; turn left and return to trailhead.
- 7.6 Tahoe Rim Trailhead.

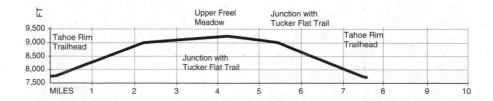

Luther Pass to Freel Meadows

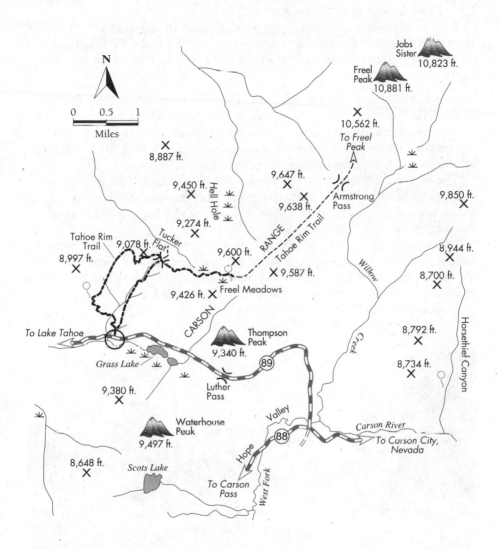

N

0   0.5   1
Miles

Jobs Sister 10,823 ft.

Freel Peak 10,881 ft.

10,562 ft.
To Freel Peak

8,887 ft.

9,450 ft.

9,647 ft.

9,638 ft.

Armstrong Pass

9,850 ft.

Hell Hole

9,274 ft.

Tucker Flat

RANGE

Tahoe Rim Trail

8,944 ft.

8,700 ft.

Tahoe Rim Trail
8,997 ft.

9,078 ft.

9,600 ft.

9,587 ft.

Willow

Freel Meadows

9,426 ft.

CARSON

8,792 ft.

To Lake Tahoe

Thompson Peak

Creek

8,734 ft.

9,340 ft.

Horsethief Canyon

Grass Lake

89

9,380 ft.

Luther Pass

Waterhouse Peak

Valley

Carson River

9,497 ft.

88

To Carson City, Nevada

8,648 ft.

Scots Lake

Hope

West Fork

To Carson Pass

Finding the trailhead: The trailhead lies on the north side of California Highway 89, near the west end of a very large meadow, about 1.75 miles northwest of Luther Pass and about 6.6 miles southeast of the junction of CA 89 and westbound US Highway 50.

Park in the turnout on the south side of the highway at the west end of the above-mentioned meadow. Walk east along the highway for about 100 yards and turn onto the signed, westbound Tahoe Rim Trail on the highway's north side.

The hike: Utilizing a segment of the 150-mile-long Tahoe Rim Trail, this Carson Range hike leads to two lovely meadows. Although once seldom visited by hikers, they are gradually gaining popularity with both hikers and mountain bikers alike. A return via the old Tucker Flat Trail offers an alternative to hikers not wishing to retrace the entire route.

The isolated character of the Freel Meadows-Tucker Flat area offers a welcome change of pace from the many overcrowded trails of the Lake Tahoe region. Be aware, though, that you will be sharing this segment of the Tahoe Rim Trail with mountain bikers.

The trail begins by following blazed trees west as it parallels the highway before bending north into a forest of Jeffrey pine and red and white fir. Cross a small, alder-lined creek and notice the Tucker Flat Trail branching right and ascending along the course of this creek. That trail forms the homebound segment of this hike.

Freel Meadows along the Tahoe Rim Trail offers an uncrowded destination for hikers and mountain bikers in the Lake Tahoe region.

254

Continuing along the Tahoe Rim Trail, you eventually cross a larger stream before following switchbacks up toward Peak 8,997 through a pleasant pine and fir forest. When the trail levels off, cross a small creek that's hidden under large, granitic boulders below an aspen-covered meadow. Your route bends into another gully and crosses a small creek amid aspens, lodgepole pines, and red firs.

After hiking 1.8 miles from the trailhead, you top a boulder-strewn ridge amid western white pines and red firs, briefly glimpsing Lake Tahoe in the northwest and the snowy Sierra Nevada summits in the southeast. The trail then leads generally east while climbing up and around Peak 9,078, almost touching its rocky summit. Occasional openings in the forest reveal the Crystal Range and other Desolation Wilderness peaks to the northwest.

East of Peak 9,078, the trail descends to the Tucker Flat Saddle at 8,800 feet. The old Tucker Flat Trail crosses Tahoe Rim Trail at this point, branching right to descend back to CA 89 (your return route) and branching left to descend into Tucker Flat, where backpackers may elect to spend the night. You, however, work your way east along the wide ridge through a lodgepole and western white pine forest. After hiking 0.75 mile from Tucker Flat Saddle, begin traversing above the west, or lower, Freel Meadow.

This small but beautiful spread is dotted with boulders and brightened by a variety of wildflowers. Its margins are forested with lodgepole and whitebark pines and a few mountain hemlocks. The small creek flowing through the southern edge of the meadow, the headwaters of Saxon Creek, usually contains water until late in the summer.

Proceeding east, your trail passes over a low divide and skirts the northern margin of upper, or east, Freel Meadow. The conical, 10,023-foot Hawkins Peak is framed by the forest in the southeast across this vividly green grassland. The trail crosses above the meadow, providing good views as far south as Stanislaus Peak. Secluded camping is usually the rule in these seldom-visited meadows, but the new Tahoe Rim Trail has increased foot and mountain bike traffic in this area. Once all but unknown, it still rarely seems overcrowded.

Eventually, retrace your route back to Tucker Flat Saddle, turn left, and begin a steep southbound descent. About 0.4 mile below the saddle, just before crossing a small tributary creek on your left, you are treated to southward views of Sierra Nevada crest Peak 9,595 and the Showers Lake basin.

Your route follows the main creek downstream, crossing it twice before leaving it behind to angle through a meadow-floored flat where the trail becomes muddy at times. Aspen joins the pine and fir forest as you descend along the course of the small creek. The creek quickly leads you back to the Tahoe Rim Trail, where you turn left and backtrack to the trailhead.

56 Alpine Meadows Road to Five Lakes

Highlights:	This short hike leads from one of Tahoe's famous ski resorts to an attractive timberline lake basin tucked beneath the Sierra crest.
General location:	Northern Sierra Nevada, Granite Chief Wilderness (Tahoe National Forest), 5 miles west of Lake Tahoe and Tahoe City.
Type of hike:	Round-trip half-day hike.
Distance:	3.8 miles or more.
Difficulty:	Moderately easy.
Elevation gain and loss:	1,000 feet.
Trailhead elevation:	6,560 feet.
High point:	7,550 feet.
Best season:	July through September.
Water availability:	Available at the lakes; treat before drinking or bring your own.
Maps:	Tahoe National Forest map; USGS Tahoe City and Granite Chief 7.5-minute quads.
Permits:	Not required.

Key points:

0.0   Alpine Meadows Road, Five Lakes Trailhead.
1.4   Granite Chief Wilderness boundary.
1.7   Junction with spur trail to Five Lakes; turn left (southwest).
1.9   Lower lake in Five Lakes basin.

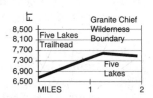

Finding the trailhead: From California Highway 89, 3.8 miles northwest of Tahoe City or 10 miles south of the West Truckee Exit off of Interstate 80, turn west onto the prominently signed Alpine Meadows Road. Follow this paved, two-lane road for 2.1 miles to the trailhead, indicated by a small destination and mileage sign on the right (north) side of the road. Park here in the turnouts on either side of the road.

The hike: Resting atop the Sierra Nevada crest between the famous ski areas of Squaw Valley and Alpine Meadows, the shallow basin of Five Lakes sits in an easily accessible corner of the Granite Chief Wilderness. Although the trail gains 1,000 feet of elevation in about 2 miles, it is still a fairly easy and popular hike and usually not as crowded as many of the trails in the Lake Tahoe region.

Not only is the hike to Five Lakes a good leg stretcher, it surveys contrasting landscapes, ranging from granitic bedrock to volcanic rocks, and from the development of ski resorts to pristine wilderness areas. Swimming is a major attraction at the lakes, but the waters remain cold until late summer. The

Forest Service strongly discourages the bringing of dogs to Five Lakes, so heed to the principles of zero impact and leave your dog at home.

The inconspicuously signed trailhead is located on the north side of Alpine Meadows Road, where the trail begins next to a Granite Chief Wilderness information signboard. The trail immediately begins ascending a moderately steep grade across slopes of brown volcanic rocks. Jeffrey pines offer occasional pockets of shade, but for the most part, you hike across sun-drenched slopes that are mantled in a blanket of manzanita, mountain whitethorn, and huckleberry oak.

During the first 0.5 mile, you gain 300 feet of elevation at a steep grade; thereafter, the trail's grade moderates. As you ascend, fine views open up into the broad volcanic bowl of the Alpine Meadows Ski Area, punctuated at its head by 8,637-foot Ward Peak. Notice the number of granite boulders—erratics—strewn across the volcanic slopes. Soon you will see the source of those boulders, after the grade abruptly levels off and you begin a long traverse. A large body of granite rises on the slopes of the Sierra crest ahead. The broken, ice-chiseled cliffs contrast with the more subdued volcanic landscape in the nearby ski bowl.

After the trail levels out, the pine and fir forest thickens and casts more shade, but you continue across sunny openings filled with mule ears and a variety of other summer blossoms. Mount the granite, begin to pass smooth, ice-rounded outcrops, and engage in a steady but moderate ascent via switchbacks. Jeffrey, western white, and lodgepole pine are much more

Five Lakes basin is a justifiably popular destination in a wild corner of the Granite Chief Wilderness, between the Alpine Meadows and Squaw Valley Ski Areas.

Alpine Meadows Road to Five Lakes

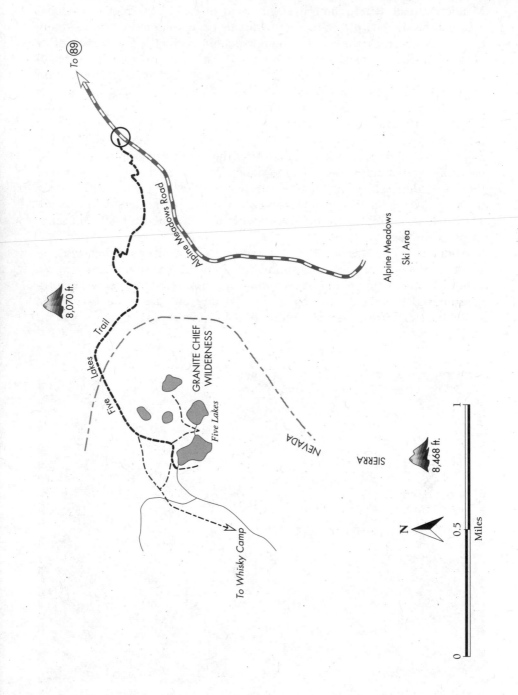

widely scattered on these granitic slopes than they are on the richer volcanic soils below.

At 1 mile, the shoulder of a ridge affords more fine views and gives you your last good look at Ward Peak and the ski bowl. The trail bends northwest, and you face only another 200 feet of climbing above a red fir–clad flat, gradually rising toward the small bowl above this flat. En route, pass an interesting dike of dark basalt, cutting through the granite toward the ridge above to the north. A pair of switchbacks leads across the dike; from there you have a better view of the contrast between the dark volcanics and the nearly white granite.

After perhaps one hour of hiking, at 1.4 miles and 1,000 feet above the trailhead, you enter the Granite Chief Wilderness at the head of a shallow basin in a cool stand of red fir. The trail is now nearly level and proceeds southwest through a forest of red fir and lodgepole and western white pine, crossing a gentle, boulder-studded landscape. You reach the well-worn spur trail to Five Lakes at 1.7 miles and 7,550 feet. A sign here declares that no camping or stock are allowed within 600 feet of the lakes (at least 200 paces).

The westbound trail continues ahead for 0.5 mile to the Pacific Crest/Tahoe Rim Trail, and beyond for 2 miles to Whisky Creek Camp in the canyon far below. Turn left instead onto the spur trail and quickly descend to the lowest and largest of the Five Lakes. Various boot-worn trails branch left (southeast) to the upper lakes in the basin and lead partway around the lower lake.

The basin is a fine place for wandering and exploring, spending a few hours visiting all the lakes, swimming, or simply relaxing in the quiet beauty of the Northern Sierra. The gentle, granite-bound basin supports a timberline forest of mountain hemlock, western white pine, and red fir. Unfortunately, the chair lifts of Squaw Peak are painfully visible on the northern skyline.

After enjoying the Five Lakes basin, retrace your steps back to the trailhead.

57 Grouse Ridge to Glacier Lake

Highlights:	Typical of the far Northern Sierra, this trip provides ample rewards with minimal effort, following a good trail into a glacier-carved, lake-filled subalpine basin and featuring far-ranging vistas, productive fishing, and refreshing late-season swimming.
General location:	Northern Sierra Nevada, Tahoe National Forest, 22 miles west of Truckee and 70 miles northeast of Sacramento.
Type of hike:	Round-trip day hike or overnighter.
Distance:	9.2 miles.
Difficulty:	Moderately easy.
Elevation gain and loss:	+650 feet, -600 feet.
Trailhead elevation:	7,500 feet.
High point:	Glacier Lake, 7,550 feet.
Best season:	July through early October.
Water availability:	No reliable source is available until Glacier Lake. If day hiking, bring your own.
Maps:	Tahoe National Forest map; USGS Graniteville and English Mountain 7.5-minute quads.
Permits:	Not required.

Key points:

0.0 Grouse Ridge Trailhead; proceed northeast on trail.
0.1 Trail from campground joins on the right; continue straight ahead (northeast).
0.8 Junction with westbound trail to Milk and Island Lakes; bear right (north).
1.7 Junction with northbound trail to Sawmill Lake; stay right (northeast).
1.8 Junction of Sand Ridge and Glacier Lake Trails; bear right (east).
4.6 Glacier Lake.

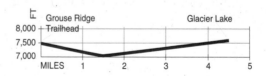

Finding the trailhead: From Interstate 80, 73 miles northeast of Sacramento, take the westbound California Highway 20 exit and proceed west for about 4.1 miles, turning right (north) where a sign points to Bowman Lake. (This turnoff can also be reached by following CA 20 east from Marysville for 60 miles.)

Your road, Forest Road 18, has a good paved surface. As you proceed, follow signs at all junctions pointing to Grouse Ridge Lookout. After driving 6.2 miles from CA 20, turn right where a sign indicates that the Grouse Ridge Lookout is 6 miles ahead. On FR 14 (dirt surfaced), proceed east and, after 1.3 miles, bear right where a sign indicates Grouse Ridge Campground. After another 4 rough and dusty miles, bear left, passing the campground entrance, and follow signs pointing to "Trail Parking Area." You reach the

Grouse Ridge to Glacier Lake

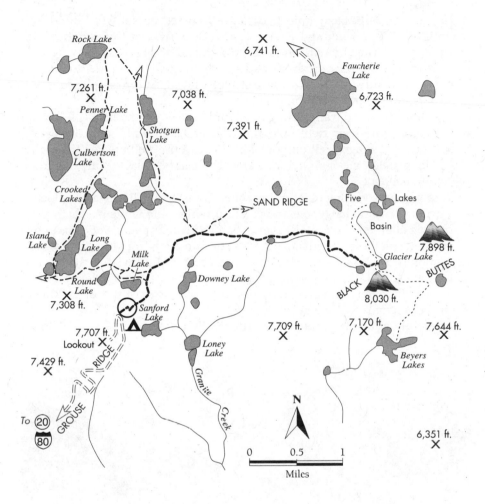

parking area after another 0.2 mile, just beyond the left-branching spur road leading up to the Grouse Ridge Lookout.

The hike: An abundance of glaciated, subalpine scenery awaits you on this easy hike to the Glacier Lake area. Side trips to Five Lakes Basin and Beyers Lakes offer some cross-country challenges and a good chance for solitude.

From the ridgetop trailhead, you are treated to a superb, sweeping panorama, encompassing the North Coast Ranges in the west, Lassen Peak in the northwest, the craggy Sierra Buttes in the north, English Mountain in the northeast, Black Buttes in the east, and the peaks of the Granite Chief–Lake Tahoe region in the southeast. Your route, closed to motorized vehicles, immediately begins descending northeastward through scattered western white pines. The trail from the campground quickly intersects your route on the right. As you continue descending, red firs join the pines along this open ridge.

Just east of Milk Lake amid a thickening forest, pass a westbound trail leading to Milk, Island, and Feeley Lakes. Bear right at this junction and continue wandering through the forest, now joined by an occasional lodgepole pine. In early summer, pine drops add a dash of red to the lupine-dominated understory found along this forested stretch of trail. At times, spiraea is also a fairly common understory plant.

Pass a northbound trail leading to Sawmill Lake, via the lake-filled basin to the north, and bear right onto the Glacier Lake Trail. Soon thereafter, avoid the Sand Ridge Trail on your left, instead proceeding east through a small, lodgepole pine–rimmed meadow. The somber Black Buttes loom on the skyline ahead.

Your gently ascending trail presently heads east through a meadow-floored forest of red fir and lodgepole and western white pine while passing rocky, glacially smoothed knolls at the foot of Sand Ridge. En route, you pass above a small lake that is in the advanced stages of transition from lake to meadow. Lodgepole pines, willows, and corn lilies are rapidly invading its shores. Continue through the lodgepole pine and red fir forest that's decorated by various wildflowers and steadily work your way toward the Black Buttes via increasingly rocky, glaciated terrain.

After hiking about 4 miles from the trailhead, the trail levels off on a

Rockbound Glacier Lake makes a fine destination in one of the largest roadless areas remaining in the Sierra Nevada north of Interstate 80.

subalpine flat before climbing briefly over an open, rocky hill. From this locale, gaze northeast to the rounded mass of 8,373-foot English Mountain, contrasting with the stark black crags of the Black Buttes to the immediate south. Snow patches cling to the Buttes long into summer.

Wind up and over another low hill, this one well forested, then quickly reach Glacier Lake at 7,550 feet. This small but deep glacial tarn, set in a rockbound cirque at the very foot of the Black Buttes and fed by lingering snow patches, has excellent campsites shaded by red fir, mountain hemlock, and western white pine above its rocky west shore. A few rewarding side trips are possible from Glacier Lake.

For the average hiker, a 0.75-mile descent along Glacier Lake's outlet creek via a faint path suffices to get you into the scenic, rockbound Five Lakes Basin. For the more adventurous and experienced hiker, a southeastward ascent of 350 feet takes you over the steep rock and grass slopes above Glacier Lake to the obvious mountain hemlock–clad saddle on the skyline. From there, you may wish to scale, via class 3 rock, the 8,030-foot point of Black Buttes. Otherwise, descend, first southeast, then southwest, for 1.25 miles from that saddle to the remote Beyers Lake.

From Glacier Lake, return the way you came, or turn north onto the Sawmill Lake Trail (1.7 miles from the trailhead), looping back via Penner, Crooked, Island, Long, Round, and Milk Lakes for a grand tour of the area.

58 Feather Falls National Recreation Trail

Highlights:	This pleasant hike through the Northern Sierra foothills leads through pine and oak woodlands to the fourth-highest waterfall in California.
General location:	Northern Sierra Nevada, Feather Falls Scenic Area (Plumas National Forest), 15 miles northeast of Oroville.
Type of hike:	Round-trip or loop day hike.
Distance:	6.7 to 7 miles.
Difficulty:	Moderately easy.
Elevation gain and loss:	+500 feet, -1,000 feet.
Trailhead elevation:	2,500 feet
High point:	2,500 feet.
Low point:	1,600 feet.
Best season:	March through November.
Water availability:	Bring your own.
Maps:	Plumas National Forest map; USGS Brush Creek and Forbestown 7.5-minute quads.
Permits:	Not required.

Key points:
- 0.0   Feather Falls Trailhead.
- 1.3   Cross Frey Creek.
- 3.5   Feather Falls overlook.

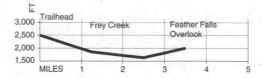

Finding the trailhead: From California Highway 70 in Oroville, turn east onto Oroville Dam Boulevard (CA 162) and, after 1.4 miles, turn right onto Olive Highway. After driving 6.5 miles on this road, turn right onto Forbestown Road. A sign here points to Feather Falls. After another 6 miles, turn left onto Lumpkin Road, where another sign indicates Feather Falls. After driving 10.8 miles on this paved but narrow and winding road, turn left just before reaching the small village of Feather Falls. A sign here indicates that the Feather Falls Trailhead is 2 miles north. After 0.2 mile of north-bound travel, turn right and proceed 1.5 miles to the trailhead at the road's end, where there is adequate parking space under the shadow of towering Douglas-firs and ponderosa pines. There is a developed campground here, with drinking water and toilets.

The hike: With a drop of 640 feet, Feather Falls is the fourth-highest waterfall in California and the sixth-highest in the contiguous United States. This foothills hike on the western slope of the northern Sierra Nevada leads you through well-watered ponderosa pine forests and oak woodlands. The excellent trail maintains a gentle grade throughout. A new trail has been constructed here that follows an even more gentle route to the falls; follow both trails for a rewarding loop. Be aware that you may be sharing the trail

Feather Falls, on the western slope of the Northern Sierra, is the fourth-highest waterfall in California. The Fall River plunges 640 feet into the Middle Fork Feather River.

264

Feather Falls National Recreation Trail

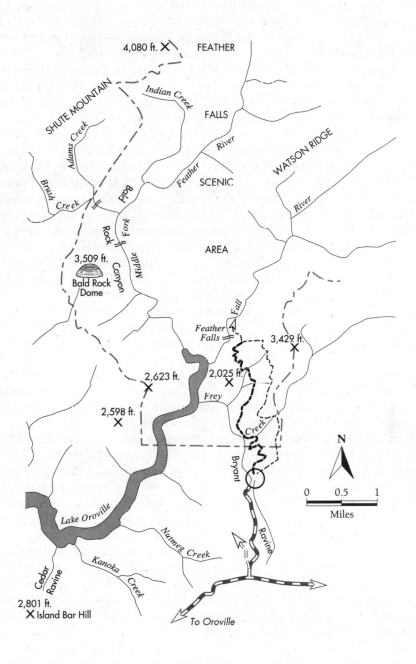

4,080 ft. X   FEATHER

SHUTE MOUNTAIN

Indian Creek

Adams Creek

FALLS

River

Feather

WATSON RIDGE

Brush

SCENIC

River

Creek

Bald

AREA

Rock

Middle Fork

Canyon

3,509 ft.
Bald Rock
Dome

Fall

Feather
Falls   3,429 ft.
X

2,623 ft.
X   2,025 ft.
X

Frey

2,598 ft.
X

Creek

N

Bryant

0   0.5   1

Miles

Lake Oroville

Nutmeg Creek

Ravine

Cedar
Ravine

Kanoka

Creek

To Oroville

2,801 ft.
X Island Bar Hill

not only with other hikers, but with mountain bikers and equestrians as well.

Your hike into the 15,000-acre Feather Falls Scenic Area begins at the information sign at the trailhead. Bear left at the junction with the loop trail and begin descending toward Frey Creek. The eastern segment of the loop follows a higher contour, losing 700 feet and gaining only 300 feet en route to the falls, and is best suited for the return trip to the trailhead.

Your trail leads north through an open forest of ponderosa pine and Douglas-fir, mixed with specimens of canyon live oak, black oak, and madrone. As you proceed along the gradually descending trail, glimpse occasional forest-framed views of the southeast face of Bald Rock Dome. Its sheer granite facade rises impressively above Bald Rock Canyon on the Middle Fork Feather River and beckons adventurous climbers.

Among the trailside wildflowers that add their color to this foothills jaunt are Indian pink, yarrow, larkspur, and iris. The cool, shady forest of ponderosa pine, incense-cedar, Douglas-fir, and black oak reflects the 70 inches of average annual precipitation this relatively low-elevation area receives. Take notice of the numerous patches of poison oak growing alongside the trail— the plant is unmistakable with its three-lobed, oak-like leaves. As the trail makes its way into the Frey Creek environs, thimbleberry and bracken fern join the understory of this north-slope forest. Handrails along this switchbacking section remind you not to shortcut the trail.

Just beyond the 1-mile marker, the trail descends to the banks of Frey Creek, soon crossing above its boisterous waters via a wooden bridge. The trail then parallels the creek downstream above its east bank. Now on a southwest-facing slope, notice that canyon live oak begins to dominate the forest. Bald Rock Dome comes into view again, and in spring, an impressive waterfall can be seen just north of the dome. As you continue descending high above noisy Frey Creek, notice the introduction of Indian paintbrush, monkey flower, and penstemon among the trailside flora.

After curving northeast, the trail descends into a shady Frey Creek tributary canyon where ponderosa pine and incense-cedar rejoin the forest. In moist areas such as this small canyon, large banana slugs, reaching lengths of 7 inches or more, can sometimes be seen making their way across the trail. Cross two small creeks and ascend beneath a shady canopy of ponderosa pine, tanbark-oak, and black oak. Manzanita, lupine, and monkey flower constitute the understory.

The trail appears to be headed for a low, forested saddle on the northwestern skyline. As you ascend the last small gully toward that saddle, try to spy a few specimens of the seldom-seen California nutmeg. This interesting tree, sometimes confused with a fir, has sharply pointed, fir-like needles.

Just before the trail attains the above-mentioned saddle, it veers eastward and begins traversing sunny, southeast-facing slopes. The trail soon switchbacks west on this open, live oak–clad hillside. The surrounding forest-covered mountains come into view and the trail becomes increasingly rocky.

A few digger pines (a California endemic) are seen just above, attesting to the hot, dry conditions that prevail on this sunny slope. The contrast between this slope and the forested slopes traversed previously provides a good example of the way slope aspect (the direction a slope faces) influences vegetation types at this low elevation.

Soon your trail bends northeast and, because of the precipitous nature of this rocky slope, becomes lined with handrails. The large Middle Fork Feather River and a major tributary, the Fall River, meet your gaze as you progress northeastward. Round a bend and you are confronted with the awesome spectacle of roaring Feather Falls. This magnificent, 640-foot falls plunges over a resistant granite precipice on its way to the Middle Fork Feather River and its impoundment in Lake Oroville. Feather Falls does tend to dry up considerably as the summer wears on.

Following the handrail-lined trail, turn left where a faint trail continues ascending along the course of Fall River, passing just above the brink of the falls. Here the upper segment of the loop joins on your right. Backpackers will want to continue upstream along the Fall River Trail for pleasant riverside campsites and often-good trout fishing.

After turning left, descend via one switchback and a wooden stairway to the fenced-in overlook platform precariously perched above the near-vertical gorge of the lower Fall River. This platform offers a head-on view of the impressive falls. To the southwest, you can see the upper end of the Middle Fork arm of Lake Oroville, 0.75 mile below. Adventurous boaters can even view the falls from that point.

From Feather Falls, either return to the trailhead the same way, follow the 3.2-mile upper segment of the loop trail, or ascend the Fall River for about 2 miles to the trail's end.

59 Lakes Basin

Highlights:	This excellent hike is a grand tour of one of the northernmost glacial lake basins in the Sierra Nevada and features far-ranging vistas, good lake fishing, and refreshing late-season swimming.
General location:	Northern Sierra Nevada, Lakes Basin Recreation Area (Plumas National Forest), 22 miles southeast of Quincy and 35 miles northeast of Grass Valley.
Type of hike:	Loop day hike.
Distance:	9.5 miles.
Difficulty:	Moderate.
Elevation gain and loss:	1,475 feet.
Trailhead elevation:	6,600 feet.
High point:	7,500 feet.
Best season:	July through early October.
Water availability:	Bring your own.
Maps:	Plumas National Forest map; USGS Gold Lake 7.5-minute quad.
Permits:	Not required.

Key points:

0.0   Trailhead at Gold Lake Lodge; proceed southwest on doubletrack.

0.2   Return leg of your loop joins on the right; stay left on doubletrack (southwest).

2.0   Junction with right-branching (northbound) trail to Round Lake; bear left again (south).

2.9   Junction with Pacific Crest Trail (PCT); turn right (north).

3.7   Junction with trail from Oakland Pond; bear right (northwest), staying on PCT.

5.0   Junction with northbound trail into Lakes Basin; turn right (north) onto that trail.

5.6   Junction with southeastbound trail to Silver Lake; bear left (northeast).

5.7   Junction with westbound spur leading to PCT; stay right (north).

6.2   Four-way junction; turn right (south) toward Mud Lake.

7.5   Junction west of Silver Lake; turn left (east).

7.8   Junction at north end of Silver Lake with southbound trail to Round Lake; turn left (northeast).

8.0   Junction with trail leading to Lakes Basin Campground; bear right (southeast).

8.7   Junction with another northbound trail to campground on the north shore of Big Bear Lake; bear right (east).

9.3   Return to doubletrack; bear left (northeast).

9.5   Return to trailhead.

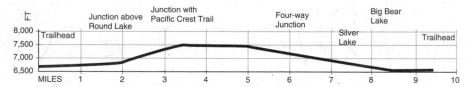

Finding the trailhead: Follow California Highway 89 for 22.3 miles southeast of Quincy, 2.7 miles southeast of the CA 89/CA 70 junction, or 47 miles northwest from Interstate 80 at Truckee, to the prominently signed turnoff to Lakes Basin Recreation Area. Proceed generally southwest on the two-lane pavement of Forest Road 24. Follow this good paved road south for about 7.5 miles.

Just before cresting a low summit on this road and before leaving Plumas County and entering Sierra County (at the signed boundary), turn right (southwest) onto an unsigned paved road. Follow this road a very short distance to the parking area opposite the access road to the Gold Lake Lodge. A southbound road just beyond the parking area leads to Gold Lake.

The hike: This hike through Lakes Basin, an area set aside for day-use only, surveys one of the northernmost glacial lake basins in the Sierra Nevada. Ranging from lakeshores to windswept ridges with panoramic vistas, this trip allows you to experience the contrasting landscapes found in the far Northern Sierra. Fair fishing and cool swimming are always close at hand in the basin, and easy side trips to numerous lakes are made possible by a network of trails in the area. This network of trails links numerous lakes close to the road and makes the area ideally suited for families or anyone else who isn't looking for a hike as strenuous as the one described here.

Lakes Basin

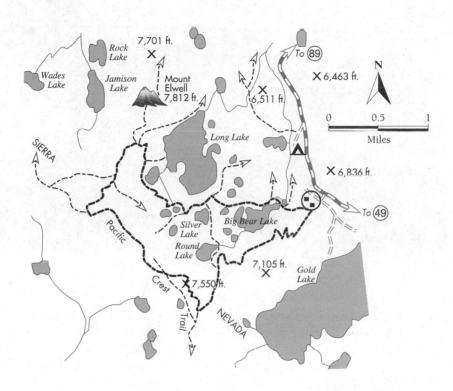

From the parking area, proceed west toward a barrier across a doubletrack and a sign showing a map of the area. Begin hiking southwest along this doubletrack under a canopy of red fir, passing some outlying buildings of the Gold Lake Lodge on your right. After hiking 0.2 mile, meet the return leg of your loop on the right, leading to Big Bear Lake and beyond. Bear left here and proceed along the abandoned doubletrack through a forest dominated by red fir, passing occasional grassy, wildflower-speckled clearings. You sometimes have tree-framed views of Mount Elwell across the basin in the northwest, which, at 7,812 feet, is the highest point in the Lakes Basin area.

Your route becomes increasingly rocky as you work your way up the basin and pass the old Round Lake Mine. Passing a right-branching trail that leads down to Round Lake, the route finally narrows to a singletrack as you approach the Lakes Basin crest, with scattered western white pines, mountain hemlocks, and a few red firs and Jeffrey pines along the way. As you continue climbing, get your first glimpse of immense Long Lake spreading out at the foot of Mount Elwell.

Lakes Basin offers a wide variety of scenic day hikes in the Northern Sierra.

Glacial Gold Lake soon meets your gaze in the southeast, the largest natural lake in this region of the Sierra. After hiking less than 3 miles from the trailhead, you reach a ridgetop junction with the PCT. Note how abruptly the forest has thickened on the deeper soils of this slope, as compared to the sparse forest growing on the meager soils in the glaciated basin through which you have been hiking.

Turn right (north) onto the PCT. From here, you have a superb view east across the island-dotted Gold Lake, and in the south, the serrated Sierra Buttes thrust their toothy crags skyward. In the southeast lie distant I-80 peaks; beyond are summits as far away as the Lake Tahoe region.

This view gets even better as the trail nears the summit of Peak 7,550, high on the crest above Lakes Basin. In addition to the above-mentioned landmarks, the view now includes Snake and Little Deer Lakes below to the west, the North Coast Ranges beyond the western slope of the Sierra Nevada, and far-off Sierra crest peaks in the north. The trail contours around the north side of Peak 7,550 just above the headwall of Lakes Basin. From here, the entire lake-filled basin spreads out before you. Far to the northwest, snow-streaked Lassen Peak rises above all else.

Cross over to the west side of the crest and after two descending switchbacks, a trail from Oakland Pond joins your route on the left. Continue on a gentle northwestward traverse through a red fir and western white pine forest. Another trail soon branches right from your route, but stay left on the well-worn PCT.

Enter a dense mountain hemlock forest and reach another ridgetop junction 5 miles from the trailhead. Turn right here and descend northeast through the often-dense forest. After 0.6 mile, pass a right-branching trail leading to Silver Lake and beyond; shortly thereafter, pass a left-branching trail, a westbound spur leading to the PCT.

Continue descending northeastward along the open ridge, spying several Lakes Basin waters in the east before reaching a four-way junction. A few hikers will be tempted to tackle the steep, 0.8-mile-long climb to Mount Elwell for boundless vistas of the surrounding countryside, but most will turn right and descend toward Mud Lake. Avoid the middle trail leading to Long Lake and Gray Eagle Lodge.

The sometimes brushy route begins descending, levels off, and then re-enters a conifer stand where you will notice an unmarked trail branching left and leading to Long Lake. After hiking around the west shore of small Mud Lake, begin laboring up grass- and tree-covered slopes. You edge close to a trickle of water originating from the small lake just above, whose north shore the trail soon skirts. After passing this small tarn, incorrectly signed Helgramite Lake, a westbound trail joins your route on the right as you descend to Silver Lake. This fine lake, whose shores are shaded by scattered timber, has a backdrop of rugged cliffs that make this one of the most scenic spots in Lakes Basin.

At the north end of Silver Lake, avoid a southbound trail leading to Round Lake and proceed northeast along a ridge lined with manzanita and huckleberry oak, briefly sighting Long Lake directly below to your left. Soon, you pass a northbound trail leading to Lakes Basin Campground on your left. Continue past Cub, Little Bear, and Big Bear Lakes, all lying just south of the trail with shorelines that are easily accessible to anglers and swimmers alike.

Stay right at the north end of beautiful Big Bear Lake, avoiding another northbound trail to the campground. From here, a pleasant 0.6-mile jaunt through the forest brings you back to your inbound doubletrack, where you turn left and backtrack 0.2 mile to the trailhead.

60 Mount Elwell Loop

Highlights:	This memorable, view-packed trip leads to the highest point in Lakes Basin, where broad vistas of the Northern Sierra and Southern Cascades unfold. From the summit, the trail loops back to the trailhead, passing Long Lake along the way, the second-largest and perhaps the most beautiful lake in the basin.
General location:	Northern Sierra Nevada, Lakes Basin Recreation Area (Plumas National Forest), 20 miles southeast of Quincy and 35 miles northeast of Nevada City.
Type of hike:	Loop day hike.
Distance:	7.6 miles.
Difficulty:	Moderately strenuous.
Elevation gain and loss:	2,000 feet.
Trailhead elevation:	5,800 feet.
High point:	Mt. Elwell, 7,812 feet.
Best season:	July through September.
Water availability:	Available at Smith Creek at 1 mile; Long Lake at 5 miles; and Gray Eagle Creek at 6 miles; treat before drinking or bring your own.
Maps:	Plumas National Forest map; USGS Gold Lake 7.5-minute quad.
Permits:	Not required.

Key points:

0.0	Smith Lake Trailhead; follow the trail west, then north.
0.8	Junction with Mt. Elwell Trail east of Smith Lake; turn left (south).
1.4	Maiden Lake.
3.5	Junction with short spur to Mt. Elwell summit; turn right (northwest) and scramble to summit.
3.7	Return to Mt. Elwell Trail and turn right (west).
4.5	Four-way junction; turn left (northeast), descending toward Long Lake.
5.2	Outlet of Long Lake.
6.2	Junction with southeastbound trail to Lakes Basin Campground; bear left (north).
7.2	Junction with eastbound trail to Gray Eagle Lodge; stay left (north).
7.4	Junction with another eastbound trail (unsigned) to Gray Eagle Lodge; continue straight ahead (north).
7.6	Return to trailhead.

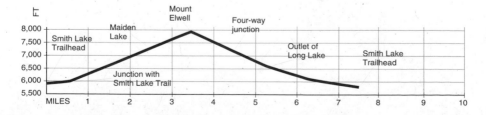

Mount Elwell Loop • Frazier Falls

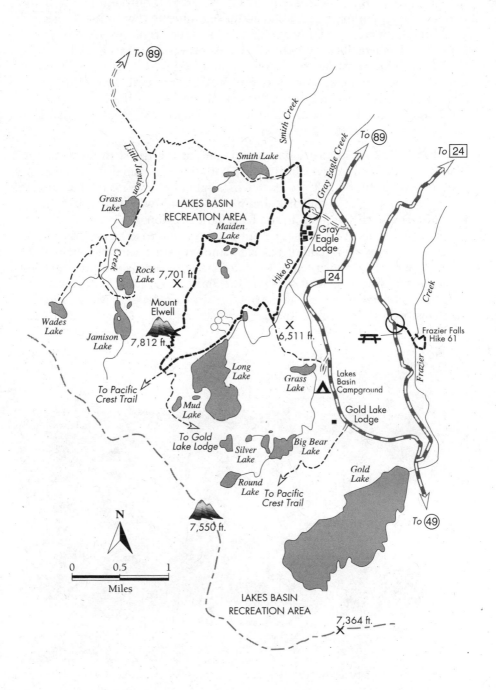

To (89)

Smith Creek

Gray Eagle Creek

To (89)

To (24)

Little Jamison

Smith Lake

Grass Lake

LAKES BASIN RECREATION AREA

Maiden Lake

Gray Eagle Lodge

Creek

Rock Lake 7,701 ft.

Hike 60

24

Mount Elwell 7,812 ft.

6,511 ft.

Frazier Falls Hike 61

Wades Lake

Jamison Lake

Long Lake

Grass Lake

Lakes Basin Campground

Frazier

Creek

To Pacific Crest Trail

Mud Lake

To Gold Lake Lodge

Silver Lake

Big Bear Lake

Gold Lake Lodge

Round Lake

Gold Lake

N

To Pacific Crest Trail

7,550 ft.

0   0.5   1

Miles

To (49)

LAKES BASIN RECREATION AREA

7,364 ft.

273

Finding the trailhead: Follow California Highway 89 for 22.3 miles south-east from Quincy, 2.7 miles southeast from the CA 89/CA 70 junction, or 47 miles northwest from Interstate 80 at Truckee, to the prominently signed turnoff to Lakes Basin Recreation Area. Proceed generally southwest on the two-lane pavement of Forest Road 24 for 5.2 miles to a prominently signed westbound spur road to Gray Eagle Lodge and turn right (west). This paved spur quickly sheds its pavement and becomes a rough gravel road. Cross a bridge spanning Gray Eagle Creek 0.3 mile from FR 24, then turn right onto a northbound spur road, signed for Smith Lake Trail and Gray Eagle Creek Trail at 0.4 mile. The trailhead is located at the loop at the road's end, 0.5 mile from FR 24. There you will find an information signboard with a map and room to park 10 to 12 vehicles.

The hike: This rigorous, all-day hike is one of the finest in all of the far Northern Sierra. Passing beautiful lakes both large and small and traversing cool forests and timberline groves, the highlight of the hike is the far-ranging vistas that open up atop the lofty summit of Mount Elwell, vistas that stretch from the Southern Cascades to the Lake Tahoe region.

The trail begins at the west end of the loop at the road's end, adjacent to a signboard showing a map of Lakes Basin and listing various destinations and mileages. The return leg of the loop branches left (south) just beyond the trailhead. For now, head north on the Smith Lake Trail. Your rocky trail ascends a moderate grade along the hot, brushy east slopes of Mount Elwell's northeast ridge. Manzanita, huckleberry oak, and serviceberry mantle the

The Mount Elwell Loop traverses above Long Lake, one of the largest backcountry lakes in the Northern Sierra.

274

slopes, with only a scattering of white fir and Jeffrey pine to cast small pockets of shade over the trail. Huge erratic boulders dot the slopes, left behind as the last great glacier retreated back into Lakes Basin.

The trail curves around the ridge, then descends slightly into a cool, mixed conifer forest, leading you to the grassy banks of the two small channels of Smith Creek. After a log crossing of the stream, a junction greets you on the west bank. Bear left (south) on the trail signed for Smith Lake and Mount Elwell; follow above the verdant stream banks, where corn lily and leopard lily thrive. The trail gently rises through the forest and you soon reach the westbound trail leading past Smith Lake toward Rock Lake and Jamison Lake. The lakes along that trail lie outside of Lakes Basin and the Frazier and Gray Eagle Creek drainages. They are the only lakes served by the Lakes Basin trail system where overnight backcountry camping is allowed. Smith Lake, lying 0.1 mile west of the junction, makes a fine destination for a short day hike.

Continue heading south from the junction, crossing Smith Creek via logs for the final time. The trail ahead begins a long, steady, moderate to steep ascent via the northeast ridge of Mount Elwell. The trail winds upward, following the often broad ridge beneath a shady canopy of stately red firs. Western white pines join the forest ranks as you rise above 6,800 feet, with the landscape growing increasingly rocky. Suddenly, you emerge from the forest and enter a lovely little basin, covered with a lodgepole pine forest and dotted with shallow, meadow-fringed tarns.

From the open basin, you have your first look up to the rocky summit of Mount Elwell rising in the southwest. At the northwest edge of the basin, the trail leads past beautiful Maiden Lake. During a windy midsummer day, you will likely observe myriad western white pinecones floating across the lake's shallow waters.

As the trail ascends above Maiden Lake, it is ill-defined in places and can be confused with numerous runoff gullies. Careful attention is necessary to stay on course, but the way soon becomes more obvious. Ice-polished bedrock is seen with greater frequency as you ascend the rocky trail at a moderate grade through a red fir, mountain hemlock, and western white pine forest.

You reach a small timberline bowl immediately north and 300 feet below Mount Elwell. The trail ahead ascends the bowl through hemlock forest and often remains buried in snow until mid-July. Top out on a rocky notch in the summit ridge immediately east of the summit. Follow the trail for a few yards west from the notch, then turn right (northwest) onto the summit trail. This path quickly disappears among boulders and slabs, forcing you to scramble among the green and red metavolcanic rocks for the final few yards to the summit.

The promise of far-ranging vistas lures hikers to this peak, and few will be disappointed. All of Lakes Basin spreads out before you to the south, including such prominent waters as Long Lake, Silver Lake, Round Lake, Big Bear Lake, and distant Gold Lake, all set in the broad, ice-scoured basin among many other smaller lakes. Far below in the west and northwest, Jamison Lake, beautiful Rock Lake, and remote Wades Lake lie at the head of Little Jamison Creek canyon.

More distant features in your view include the spires and crags of the Sierra Buttes in the southwest. The Buttes look like what Sierra peaks are supposed to look like, with great cliffs, prominent buttresses, and rocky chutes that are often filled with snow well into the summer months. Distant peaks rise far to the south, soaring to 8,000 and 9,000 feet above either side of the I-80 corridor. On the farthest southeast horizon are peaks of the Tahoe Rim. Eastward you see flat-topped Beckwourth Peak, the sprawling Sierra Valley, and the long, rounded ridges of the Diamond and Dixie Mountains.

The canyon of the Yuba River stretches away to the southwest. Beyond it, the west slope of the Sierra is so broad and gentle it resembles a vast plateau. On a clear day, you can make out the outline of the North Coast Ranges on the distant western horizon. To the northwest, progressively lower Sierra summits stretch away to a view of the snow-streaked cone of Lassen Peak.

To loop back to the trailhead, scramble back down to the trail, turn right (west), and begin a steadily descending course via switchbacks, dropping at a moderate to steep grade. The brushy slopes host clumps of manzanita, tobacco brush, and huckleberry oak, and are studded with a scattering of red fir and western white pine. Fine views of Lakes Basin are enjoyed along the way; especially memorable are the broad, deep waters of Long Lake.

Upon reaching a four-way junction, turn left (northeast), descending toward Long Lake. This descent is steady and very rocky, eventually dropping to the rugged shoreline of the aptly named lake beneath the towering, broken cliffs of Mount Elwell. The tread improves as you follow the shoreline toward the outlet-end of the lake. On a hot day, it may be hard to resist a dip in the cool waters of the lake. Huge erratic boulders and picturesque pines stud the rocky, ice-scoured landscape at the lake's outlet.

Below the lake, wind your way past an area of springs that nurture clumps of willows and an array of wildflowers, including leopard lily, cinquefoil, western wallflower, and meadow rue, as well as dogwood, serviceberry, and elderberry shrubs. The gradual descent proceeds along the lake's cascading outlet stream and past a lovely tarn fringed with grass and lodgepole pines. Beyond the tarn, descend a moderate grade via switchbacks, entering a cool, shady forest of pine, fir, and cedar. Bracken fern grows in profusion at the trailside. Cross two channels of runoff draining the springs above to reach a junction, where you turn left (north) toward Gray Eagle Lodge.

The trail ahead passes through a moist, shady forest for another 0.5 mile, decked with fern and dogwood, to the short spur trail leading to Hawley Falls along Gray Eagle Creek. Bear left and continue northeast, reaching nearly level terrain where you alternate between sunny openings and open forest. Abundant aspens along the nearby creek serenade you with the whisper of their fluttering leaves. Soon you reach another junction. Don't turn right toward Gray Eagle Lodge unless you are a guest there; instead, continue straight ahead on the trail signed for "Smith Lake Trail-1/2."

Your trail ascends a low, brushy moraine, then drops to an unsigned junction with an eastbound trail also leading to the lodge. Avoid that trail and proceed north across the small bowl, stepping across a series of springs along the way. You return to the forest and then drop down to close the loop at the road's end.

61 Frazier Falls

See Map on Page 273

Highlights:	This easy stroll quickly leads to a vigorous 176-foot waterfall in a scenic, ice-sculpted landscape of the Northern Sierra.
General location:	Northern Sierra Nevada, Lakes Basin Recreation Area (Plumas National Forest), 20 miles southeast of Quincy and 35 miles northeast of Nevada City.
Type of hike:	Round-trip half-day hike.
Distance:	1 mile.
Difficulty:	Easy.
Elevation gain and loss:	Negligible.
Trailhead elevation:	6,250 feet.
High Point:	6,250 feet.
Best season:	Mid-June through September.
Water availability:	Bring your own.
Maps:	Plumas National Forest map; USGS Gold Lake 7.5-minute quad.
Permits:	Not required.

Key points:

0.0 Frazier Falls Trailhead and picnic area.
0.3 Bridge Frazier Creek.
0.5 Frazier Falls overlook.

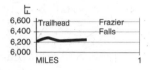

Finding the trailhead: Follow driving directions for Hike 60 to find Forest Road 24, leading from California Highway 89 to Lakes Basin Recreation Area, and turn west. After 1.7 miles, turn left (south) where a sign points to "Frazier Falls-4" and follow the paved one-lane road generally south. This is a narrow, winding, steadily ascending road with occasional turnouts; proceed with caution.

After driving 4.2 miles from FR 24, you reach the Frazier Falls Trailhead, where you find ample parking on either side of the road and a picnic area with tables and pit toilets.

The hike: The Lakes Basin Recreation Area, an ice-sculpted landscape in the far Northern Sierra, offers a wide variety of rewarding recreational opportunities, ranging from scenic drives to boating, swimming, fishing, short walks to myriad lakes, and all-day hikes that survey the spectrum of the basin's landscapes. The short walk to impressive Frazier Falls is one of the best easy hikes in Lakes Basin, and it follows the only trail in the basin that doesn't lead to a lake. The best time to take this hike is during the peak of snowmelt runoff, usually during May and June. Later in the summer, the falls are but a trickle, but the overlook at the trail's end still provides outstanding views of the narrow gorge of Frazier Creek.

The trail begins at the picnic site and is well worn and easy to follow as it begins traversing a series of small benches between outcrops of gray, ice-polished bedrock. Clumps of huckleberry oak are massed at the trailside between bedrock outcrops, and a scattering of lodgepole and Jeffrey pine, white fir, and juniper cast a modicum of shade.

After 0.25 mile of easy walking, you reach the wooden bridge spanning clear Frazier Creek, its banks fringed with dogwoods and white-boled aspens. The trail briefly climbs above the course of the creek, then turns away to gently ascend to an open, brushy ridge. From here, views open up, reaching across a tributary canyon to the ice-sculpted slopes of Mills Peak, featuring broken cliffs, rocky chutes, brushfields, and cool groves of fir on its flanks.

From the ridge, wind your way over the rocky terrain to the fenced-in overlook, 0.5 mile from the trailhead. Your view of the Frazier Falls and Frazier Creek's narrow, exciting gorge is unobstructed. A sign here indicates that the falls begin at an elevation of 6,000 feet, 1.9 miles below Gold Lake, with a cascade of 248 feet, dropping a total of 176 feet. Tall firs in the canyon below and pines on the rim above allow you to judge the scale of the powerful falls and cascades. The falls surge over the brink of the bench above, then plummet down the narrow chute carved by the creek.

Good views reach down Frazier Creek canyon to the distant mountains of the eastern Sierra beyond. It is not hard to visualize this canyon full of glacial ice, as it was 10,000 years ago. The Frazier Creek glacier was hundreds of feet thick, illustrated now by the ice-polished bedrock on the ridges far above the viewpoint.

After enjoying Frazier Falls, retrace your steps back to the trailhead.

Frazier Falls is the destination of the best short hike in the Lakes Basin area.

62 Silver Lake to Gold Lake

Highlights:	This short, scenic hike leads to an ice-sculpted lake basin at the far northern end of the Sierra.
General location:	Northern Sierra Nevada, Bucks Lake Wilderness (Plumas National Forest), 10 miles west of Quincy and 35 miles northeast of Chico.
Type of hike:	Round-trip day hike.
Distance:	3 miles.
Difficulty:	Moderately easy.
Elevation gain and loss:	+300 feet, -150 feet.
Trailhead elevation:	5,800 feet.
High point:	6,100 feet.
Best season:	July through September.
Water availability:	Available at Gold Lake; treat before drinking or bring your own.
Maps:	Plumas National Forest map; Bucks Lake Wilderness map (topographic); USGS Bucks Lake 7.5-minute quad.
Permits:	Not required.

Key points:

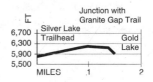

- 0.0   Silver Lake Trailhead; proceed southeast across dam.
- 1.0   Junction with Granite Gap Trail; stay straight ahead (south).
- 1.5   Gold Lake.

Finding the trailhead: From California Highway 70/89 in Quincy, turn west onto the two-lane pavement of Forest Road 119, prominently signed for Meadow Valley and Bucks Lake. After 8.5 miles, turn right (northwest) onto FR 24N29X, signed for Silver Lake. This rough gravel road, with frequent washboards, is narrow and winding, steep in places, and quite rocky over the final 3 miles.

Follow this road for 6 miles, then turn left into Silver Lake Campground. The confined trailhead parking area is located at the road's end, on the northeast shore of Silver Lake, next to the dam. If the trailhead parking area is full, as it often is on summer weekends, park at the campground entrance and walk 0.4 mile to the trailhead.

The hike: This rewarding, easy, and short hike leads you through one of the northernmost lake basins in the Sierra Nevada. The Silver Lake cirque is a broad, mile-wide, ice-sculpted bowl spread out below Spanish Peak and the Sierra crest. The cirque contains numerous small lakes and tarns and is dominated by an expanse of glacier-polished bedrock.

The trail from Silver Lake to Gold Lake is well worn and easy to follow, with only a few moderately steep grades. Vistas are panoramic for much of the way to deep Gold Lake, which offers fair fishing and cool, late-summer

Silver Lake to Gold Lake

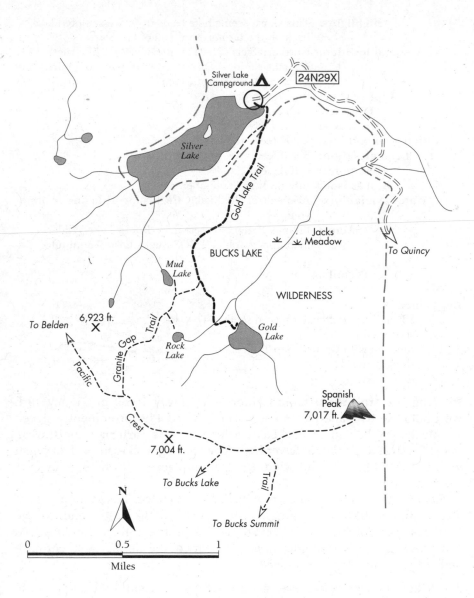

Silver Lake Campground

24N29X

Silver Lake

Gold Lake Trail

Jacks Meadow

To Quincy

BUCKS LAKE

Mud Lake

WILDERNESS

To Belden

6,923 ft.

Granite Gap Trail

Rock Lake

Gold Lake

Pacific

Spanish Peak
7,017 ft.

Crest

7,004 ft.

To Bucks Lake

Trail

To Bucks Summit

N

0   0.5   1

Miles

Gold Lake lies in a deep cirque beneath Spanish Peak in the Bucks Lake Wilderness in the far Northern Sierra.

swimming. Nearby Rock Lake, a small rockbound tarn, offers better diving from its rocky shores, but the trail to it is much more rigorous than the easy trail to Gold Lake.

From the road's end at Silver Lake, the trail begins by following along the Silver Lake Dam, where you enjoy excellent views into the ice-sculpted cirque above. After leaving the dam, the signed Gold Lake Trail branches left, away from the shoreline fishing-access trail. Quickly thereafter, you reach the boundary of the Bucks Lake Wilderness and a trail register.

From here, begin ascending steeply up the rocky moraine, where only a few white firs and Jeffrey pines cast scant shade among the fields of manzanita and huckleberry oak. After two short but steep pitches, crest the huge moraine. Far-flung vistas reach northwest past Silver Lake to distant Lassen Peak, east to the sprawling American Valley, and southeast past Spanish Peak to the bold crags of the Sierra Buttes.

Begin a gentle traverse across the south slopes of the brushy moraine, studded with widely scattered white firs and Jeffrey and sugar pines. Excellent views from the trail stretch across the basin to the broken north buttress of Spanish Peak. In the distant south and southeast rise the rounded, forested ridges of the Northern Sierra; far below the trail lies the soggy spread of Jacks Meadow.

After 1 mile, just after leaving the moraine and bending south, you reach a junction indicated by a trailside post. The Granite Gap Trail turns southwest here, ascending very steeply past Mud and Rock Lakes, 0.5 mile and 200 feet above, and eventually leads to the Pacific Crest Trail. Continue straight ahead (south) toward Gold Lake. The rocky trail follows an undulating course across the ice-gouged basin above the bog of Jacks Meadow. It is a scenic, rockbound landscape, disrupted by only a scattering of Jeffrey pines and white firs.

Eventually spy the cascading outlet stream of Gold Lake and drop down to a crossing of the small stream draining Rock Lake, which is often dry by late summer. Ascend one final, short, and steep pitch to the ridge overlooking Gold Lake. Descend steeply for several yards to the lakeshore.

Gold Lake is a very beautiful, deep, and round lake, fed by several streams cascading from the heights above. A broken headwall of ice-polished bedrock rises behind the lake to the flat, fir-fringed Sierra crest. The dark, metamorphic rock of the north buttress of Spanish Peak forms a dramatic backdrop to the lake. A scattering of brush and pines fringe the lakeshore, but there is little level ground to accommodate backpackers. Mud Lake, along the Granite Gap Trail, offers the only suitable campsites for backpackers in the basin.

After enjoying beautiful Gold Lake, either backtrack to the trailhead or follow the Granite Gap Trail up to Mud and Rock Lakes.

Southern Cascade Range

The Southern Cascade Range covers a broad area of northern California, stretching from Lake Almanor in the south to the Oregon state line in the north, and from Interstate 5 in the west nearly to the Nevada state line in the east. This region not only includes such well-known landmarks as Mount Shasta and Lassen Peak, but lesser-known areas as well, such as the Caribou, Thousand Lakes, and South Warner Wilderness areas.

The Southern Cascades contain the most extensive conifer forests in California. Unfortunately, much of the region has been and is being logged, with roads and timber sales often extending right up to the boundaries of wilderness areas. However, there are abundant areas in which to hike beyond the roads and the boundaries of timber sales.

The contiguous Lassen Volcanic and Caribou Wilderness areas offer outstanding opportunities for both day hiking and extended trips. The Thousand Lakes Wilderness offers exceptional scenery in addition to easy access. Moreover, the South Warner Wilderness in California's northeast corner provides some of the most outstanding landscapes and the best opportunities for solitude in the entire state.

Ranging from the thermal areas and volcano-top vista points of Lassen Volcanic National Park, to the cool, peaceful forests and placid lakes of the Caribou and Thousand Lakes country, and to the open, alpine crest and vast aspen stands of the Warner Mountains, the Southern Cascades offer scenery and destinations for every hiker. All together, there are more than 200,000 acres of designated wilderness in California's Southern Cascades. Combined with several hundred miles of hiking trails, the region offers enough potential backcountry recreation to keep you happy and busy for many seasons.

63 Hay Meadow to Long Lake

Highlights:	This pleasant hike in the southernmost reaches of the Cascade Range leads through peaceful forests and passes several pleasant lakes where generally good fishing and late-summer swimming are major attractions.
General location:	Southern Cascade Range, Caribou Wilderness (Lassen National Forest), 8 miles north of Chester and 55 miles northeast of Red Bluff.
Type of hike:	Loop day hike or overnighter.
Distance:	7.9 miles.
Difficulty:	Moderately easy.
Elevation gain and loss:	650 feet.
Trailhead elevation:	6,400 feet.
High point:	Posey Lake, 7,000 feet.
Best season:	Mid-June through early October.
Water availability:	Available only from lakes.
Maps:	Lassen National Forest map; USGS Red Cinder 7.5-minute quad.
Permits:	A wilderness permit is not required. A California Campfire Permit is required for campfires and backpack stoves.

Key points:
- 0.0 Hay Meadow Trailhead.
- 0.3 Junction at Indian Meadows; bear left (west).
- 1.4 Junction with northeastbound trail to Hidden Lakes; bear left (northwest).
- 1.7 Junction with northbound trail to Long and Cone Lakes; bear left (northwest) again.
- 2.8 Evelyn Lake.
- 3.7 Posey Lake.
- 4.4 Junction with northbound trail at Long Lake; bear right (southeast).
- 4.5 Junction with southbound trail; stay left (east) here and at junction immediately ahead.
- 6.3 Junction with southwestbound trail at Hidden Lake No. 1; stay left (southeast).
- 7.6 Junction with your inbound trail; turn left (southeast) and backtrack to trailhead.
- 7.9 Return to Hay Meadow Trailhead.

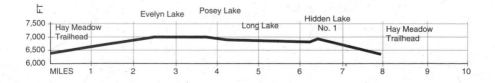

Hay Meadow to Long Lake

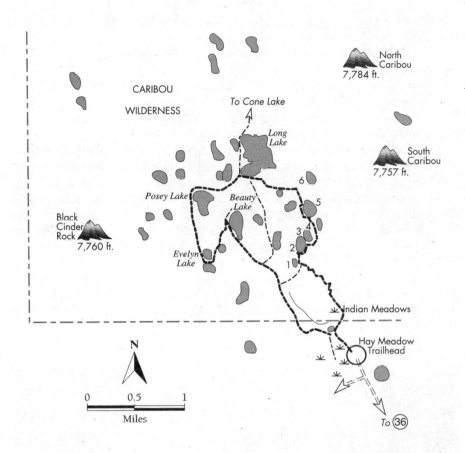

Finding the trailhead: Follow California Highway 36 to its junction with southbound Plumas County Road A13, 5 miles east of Chester and 29 miles west of Susanville. From this junction, turn onto a northbound road directly opposite of CR A13 and proceed north, turning left onto signed Forest Road 10 after 0.2 mile. Avoid the eastbound road to the Chester landfill. Drive west for another 0.4 mile and then turn right, staying on FR 10.

Follow this good paved road north and avoid several signed and unsigned, well-graded spur roads. At major junctions, signs point to the Caribou Wilderness. After driving 9.9 miles from CA 36, turn left onto FR 30N25 where a sign points to "Caribou Wilderness Trailhead-2." Proceed northwest on this narrow, rough, steadily ascending dirt road for 1.4 miles to a junction on a ridge. Bear right and descend for another 0.2 mile to the road's end at the Hay Meadow Trailhead. You will find a stock loading ramp there and space to park 15 or more vehicles.

The hike: The Caribou Wilderness is an area of gentle topography that's interrupted by numerous volcanic cones and lies immediately east of Lassen Volcanic National Park in the Southern Cascade Range. It is a thickly forested area that contains dozens of lakes. The lakes that are able to support fish are stocked with rainbow and brook trout. The numerous shallow lakes unable to maintain trout populations are often good swimming holes, especially in August when their waters have warmed to comfortable levels.

Except during the spring snowmelt period, the only water available to hikers in this area is directly from the lakes. Consequently, you should carry as much water as you will need or else plan to purify any water you obtain in the Caribou Wilderness. Mosquitoes are abundant in early summer and black-tailed deer are likely to be seen throughout the area.

The trail heads northwest from the road's end, past an information sign, and skirts the eastern margin of lush, forest-rimmed Hay Meadow. After a short jaunt through a lodgepole pine and red fir forest dotted with an occasional western white pine, you reach a junction at the south end of wet Indian Meadows. The right fork is the homebound segment of your loop. Stay left here, passing the Caribou Wilderness sign and spying the cone of South Caribou in the northeast as you walk around the south end of Indian Meadows.

The trail jogs west and begins a moderate ascent along a seasonal stream that is usually dry by late summer. After a pleasant stroll through a pine and fir forest, pass an unmarked northeastbound trail leading to the Hidden

Long Lake in the Caribou Wilderness.

Lakes; 0.3 mile beyond that, pass a signed trail on your right leading past Long Lake to Cone Lake. Stay left at both junctions. You are soon traversing above the southwest shore of forest-rimmed Beauty Lake. The trail swings away from the lake after passing a right-branching trail leading to a few lakeshore campsites.

Head southwest and begin crossing above the east shore of the forest- and rock-fringed Evelyn Lake. With a backdrop of volcanic cliffs, this lake is one of the more scenic spots on the hike; just as at Beauty Lake, campsites are somewhat scarce here. After hiking around the south shore of Evelyn Lake, be sure to avoid a well-worn path that hugs the west shore of the lake. Stay left on the less-obvious main trail.

Another pleasant stretch of walking shaded by fir and pine brings you to the meadow-lined shores of Posey Lake. Campsites around this fine lake are fairly abundant, and fishing for pan-sized trout is usually good. A mild descent beyond Posey Lake for 0.5 mile gets you to the shores of Long Lake, the largest lake in the southern Caribou Wilderness. From this lake, you are treated to your first good view of the red cone of 7,784-foot North Caribou and 7,757-foot South Caribou in the northeast. Campsites around this large lake are numerous.

At the lakeshore junction, turn right, quickly passing an unsigned south-bound trail. Almost immediately, you reach a signed junction with another southbound trail, where you bear left and proceed toward the Hidden Lakes. Pass a pond lily–smothered tarn, then jog east to briefly skirt the south shore of Hidden Lake No. 5, where fishing is unpredictable. Garter snakes are fairly common around this lake and the other meadow-fringed lakes in the wilderness.

The trail leads generally south past the lower four Hidden Lakes, of which No. 4 is the deepest. The lower three lakes are ideal for cool dips in August. At Hidden Lake No. 1, meet a southwestbound trail on your right, turn left, and begin a descent. In addition to the other forest trees, white firs join the forest as you negotiate this moderately steep descent.

Leveling off, the trail reaches the upper end of Indian Meadows, where it promptly disappears at the meadow's edge. Walk southeast across this narrow arm of the meadow and find the trail in the lodgepole pines on the other side. It turns south along the east edge of Indian Meadows and intersects the initial segment of the hike. Turn left here and retrace your steps for 0.3 mile to the trailhead.

64 Warner Valley to Boiling Springs Lake and Terminal Geyser

Highlights:	This day hike in the southern reaches of Lassen Volcanic National Park visits fumaroles, hot springs, and an unusual hot-water lake.
General location:	Southern Cascade Range, Lassen Volcanic National Park, 12 miles northwest of Chester and 50 miles northeast of Red Bluff.
Type of hike:	Round-trip day hike.
Distance:	5.6 miles.
Difficulty:	Moderate.
Elevation gain and loss:	+570 feet, -400 feet.
Trailhead elevation:	5,680 feet.
High point:	6,250 feet.
Best season:	Late June through October.
Water availability:	None available; bring your own.
Maps:	Lassen Volcanic National Park map; USGS Lassen Volcanic National Park and vicinity map; USGS Reading Peak and Mt. Harkness 7.5-minute quads.
Permits:	Required only for overnight use.

Key points:

0.0 Warner Valley Trailhead.

0.4 Junction with trail to Drakesbad Resort; bear left here and at junction just ahead.

0.7 Junction with nature trail loop around Boiling Springs Lake; stay left.

1.0 Junction above Boiling Springs Lake; bear left toward Terminal Geyser and stay left again at junction with southbound Pacific Crest Trail (PCT) just ahead.

2.2 Junction with PCT; stay left (south).

2.3 PCT turns southwest toward Little Willow Lake; bear left.

2.6 Descend to closed road; turn left.

2.8 Terminal Geyser.

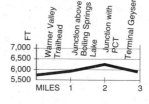

Finding the trailhead: From California Highway 36 in Chester on the north shore of Lake Almanor, turn northwest onto the paved road (Plumas County Road 312) signed for "Juniper Lake-14" and "Drakesbad-17." After 0.7 mile, bear left at the junction, continuing toward Drakesbad. At 6.2 miles, turn right (north) where the sign again points to Drakesbad, staying on the rough two-lane pavement.

The pavement ends after 13.4 miles, where you bear left and follow the very rough, rocky, narrow, and winding road into Lassen Volcanic National Park at 14.1 miles. Pay the entrance fee at the self-service fee station opposite the Warner Valley Ranger Station at 15.2 miles. Continue through the Warner

Warner Valley to Boiling Springs Lake and Terminal Geyser

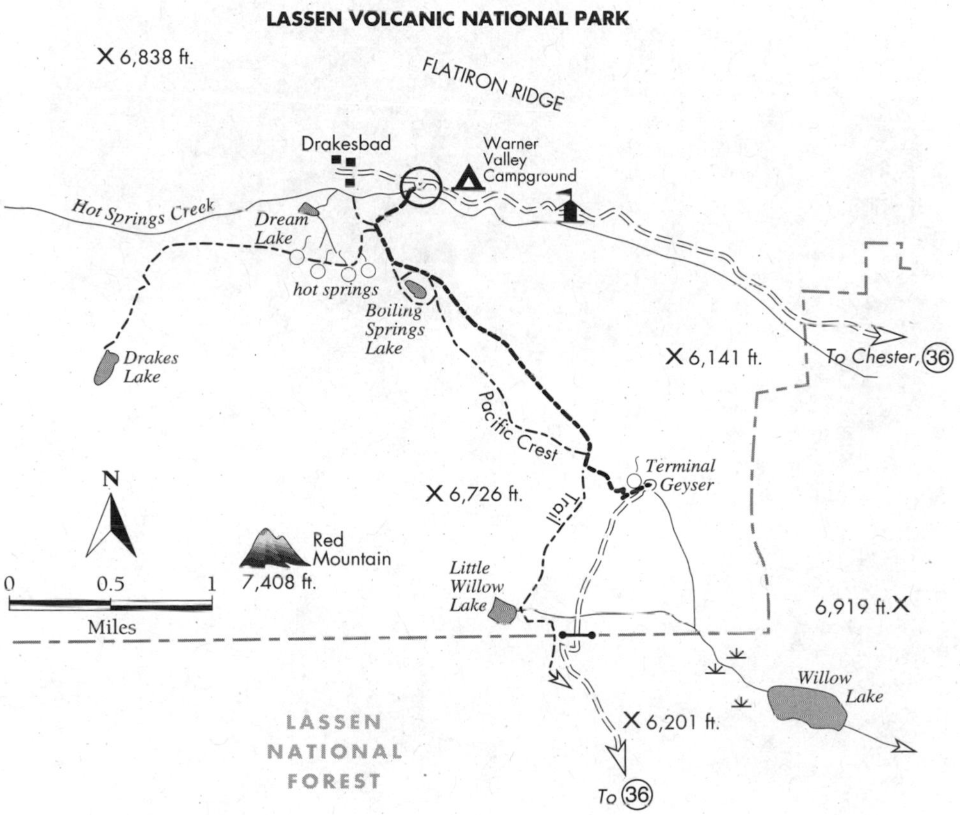

LASSEN VOLCANIC NATIONAL PARK

X 6,838 ft.

FLATIRON RIDGE

Drakesbad

Warner Valley Campground

Hot Springs Creek

Dream Lake

hot springs

Boiling Springs Lake

X 6,141 ft.

To Chester, (36)

Drakes Lake

Pacific Crest Trail

Terminal Geyser

X 6,726 ft.

N

Red Mountain
7,408 ft.

Little Willow Lake

6,919 ft. X

0   0.5   1

Miles

LASSEN NATIONAL FOREST

X 6,201 ft.

To (36)

Willow Lake

Valley Campground to the trailhead parking area, located on the south side of the road, 16.5 miles from Chester. There you will find toilets, picnic tables, an information signboard, and room enough to park about 12 vehicles.

The hike: This trail combines some of the best of the Lassen backcountry, including flower-filled meadows, hushed forests of pine and fir, active thermal features, and dramatic vistas. Following a gradually rising trail that is only lightly to moderately used, this memorable route affords an excellent half-day hike in a remote corner of Lassen Volcanic National Park.

The trail begins behind the destination and mileage sign at the trailhead. Be sure to pick up a copy of the Boiling Springs Lake pamphlet (for a small

Aptly named Boiling Springs Lake, which maintains a constant temperature of 125 degrees F, lies in a remote corner of Lassen Volcanic National Park.

fee) from the dispenser at the trailhead. The pamphlet is keyed to numbered posts along the trail to the lake. It will greatly enhance your appreciation and understanding of the natural processes at work here in the park.

Stroll ahead alongside the large Hot Springs Creek, skirting the edge of a wet meadow among scattered lodgepole pines. Reach the steel bridge spanning the creek and then begin a moderately rising traverse of meadow-clad slopes above Drakesbad Resort. These sloping meadows are drained by numerous very hot springs, so watch your step.

After 0.4 mile, you reach a signed junction and bear left toward Terminal Geyser. After a few paces, bear left again where the trail to Drakes Lake branches right. Ascend into a forest dominated by red and white fir, which also includes lodgepole and Jeffrey pine and incense-cedar. At 0.7 mile, you reach the nature trail loop and bear left again.

At 1 mile, the junction just above Boiling Springs Lake is a good turn-around point for hikers with limited time or energy. This hot (125 degrees F), algae green lake is surrounded by steaming fumaroles and gurgling mudpots. You can hear the echoing cough of the mudpots from above the lake as hydrogen sulfide fumes gather thickly in the lake basin. Heed the warning signs here and do not take the risk of traveling off the trail; thin soil crusts and scalding water surround you. The lake lies in a depression, or crater, with barren red slopes around its shores.

Bear left at this junction and left again at the unsigned junction with the southbound PCT just ahead. You can use the PCT to return from Terminal Geyser. This segment of the PCT is the same length as the trail described below, but it passes entirely through a viewless forest of mixed conifers.

Your trail rises at a steady, moderate grade through a fir forest. Eventually, the grade eases and the forest opens up, with trailside slopes hosting a mantle of evergreen shrubs, including huckleberry oak, a ground-hugging mat of pinemat manzanita, and taller greenleaf manzanita. Good views stretch eastward across the trough of Warner Valley to 7,638-foot Saddle Mountain and 8,045-foot Mount Harkness.

Duck back into the shady fir forest, top a broad ridge, and then gradually descend into a lovely meadow rich with corn lilies, the large, showy blooms of mule ears, arrowleaf balsamroot, larkspur, and pussy paws. This verdant spread lies as a foreground to distant views of the extreme Northern Sierra and part of Lake Almanor.

Descend steadily past the meadow and return to the forest, meeting the PCT at 2.2 miles. Stay left at the junction and follow the PCT south. Within moments, that trail heads southwest, signed for Little Willow Lake. Bear left again and descend steeply along the course of an early-season stream, dropping to a closed Park Service road. Turn left onto the road and proceed several hundred yards to its end at Terminal Geyser.

The soil crust is very thin here, the steaming water just below boiling point, so restrain your urge to approach too closely. Not a true geyser, Terminal Geyser is actually a large fumarole, a hissing cauldron of rising steam that, even on a hot summer day, still rises 20 to 25 feet in the air. On hot days, the site is somewhat uncomfortable as the surrounding air is heated by steam and permeated by hydrogen sulfide fumes.

From the geyser, you can return the way you came, or better yet, follow the PCT back to Boiling Springs Lake. The PCT rises gradually through the forest, paralleling your inbound trail, just farther to the west. After topping the ridge, descend gradually toward Boiling Springs Lake, with occasional glimpses to the heights of Lassen Peak along the way. After you join the loop trail above Boiling Springs Lake, continue north along the east rim of the lake's bowl, from where you enjoy one of the finer backcountry views of Lassen Peak. Rejoin your inbound trail and retrace your steps for another mile back to the trailhead.

65 Lassen Peak

Highlights:	This trip is an exciting day hike to the alpine summit of the southernmost volcano in the Cascade Range, where an all-encompassing vista of northern California unfolds.
General location:	Southern Cascade Range, Lassen Volcanic National Park, 45 miles east of Redding.
Type of hike:	Round-trip day hike.
Distance:	5 miles.
Difficulty:	Moderately strenuous.
Elevation gain and loss:	1,982 feet.
Trailhead elevation:	8,475 feet.
High point:	Lassen Peak, 10,457 feet.
Best season:	Mid-July through early October.
Water availability:	None available; bring your own.
Maps:	Lassen Volcanic National Park map; USGS Lassen Volcanic National Park and vicinity map; USGS Lassen Peak 7.5-minute quad.
Permits:	Not required for day hiking.

Key points:

0.0   Lassen Peak Trailhead.
2.5   Summit of Lassen Peak.

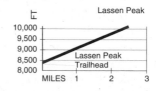

Finding the trailhead: From Red Bluff, follow California Highway 36 east for 47 miles to northbound CA 89. Turn left and drive north into Lassen Volcanic National Park, paying the entrance fee at the park entrance station. Just west of the road's high point in the park, about 1 mile beyond Lake Helen, you reach the signed Lassen Peak Trailhead on the north side of the road.

Lassen Peak • Crags Lake

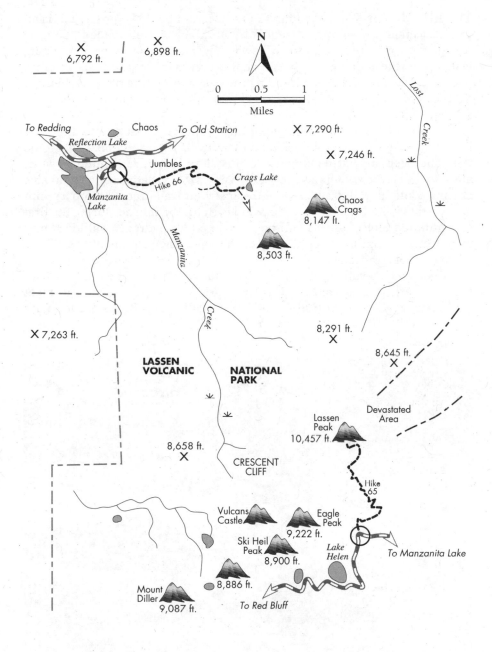

N

0   0.5   1
Miles

X 6,792 ft.   X 6,898 ft.

X 7,290 ft.

X 7,246 ft.

To Redding   Chaos   To Old Station
Reflection Lake
Jumbles
Crags Lake
Hike 66
Manzanita
Lake

Chaos
Crags
8,147 ft.

8,503 ft.

Manzanita

Creek

X 7,263 ft.

8,291 ft.
X

8,645 ft.
X

**LASSEN
VOLCANIC**   **NATIONAL
PARK**

Devastated
Area

Lassen
Peak
10,457 ft.

8,658 ft.
X

CRESCENT
CLIFF

Hike
65

Vulcans
Castle   Eagle
Peak
9,222 ft.

To Manzanita Lake

Ski Heil
Peak
8,900 ft.   Lake
Helen

8,886 ft.

Mount
Diller
9,087 ft.

To Red Bluff

You can also reach the trailhead by driving east from Redding via CA 44 for 48 miles. Turn right onto southbound CA 89 and drive 22 miles through Lassen Volcanic National Park to the well-marked trailhead.

The hike: Lassen Peak, a landmark for emigrant guide Peter Lassen, is an easily attainable goal and is frequently climbed. A well-graded, 2.5-mile trail leads you to its summit for rewarding and remarkably far-ranging vistas of northern California. Although this hike is fairly strenuous, families with children are often seen treading the easy path to the peak. While the trailhead may be warm, the exposed summit is frequently buffeted by strong, cold winds.

The trail heads north from the parking area, switchbacks into a timberline stand of mountain hemlock, and then levels off briefly on a subalpine flat. The deep snowdrifts clinging to this slope, some remaining all year, attest to the severe winters and very deep snows that visit this region annually. Passing a lateral trail to a pair of restrooms, your trail proceeds into a realm of prostrate whitebark pines. If the wind is right, the thin air during the first few hundred feet of ascent will be permeated by hydrogen sulfide fumes from Little Hot Springs Valley, Bumpass Hell, and the Sulphur Works, where there are hot springs and fumaroles.

As you gain elevation, your views continue to expand. The high peaks of southwestern Lassen Volcanic National Park are among the first to meet your gaze. Eagle and Ski Heil Peaks, Mount Diller, and Brokeoff Mountain

The summit region of Lassen Peak, the southernmost volcano in the Cascade Range, was reshaped by eruptions between 1914 and 1917. This popular mountain, offering far-ranging vistas of northern California, is still considered an active volcano.

form a ridge of impressive alpine peaks a few miles to the southwest.

Brokeoff Mountain, the high ridge between it and Lassen Peak, and Mount Conard in the south are all remnants of the former rim of Mount Tehama. Thought to have been 1,000 feet higher than present-day Lassen Peak, Mount Tehama was a composite volcanic cone that existed hundreds of thousands of years ago but eventually collapsed. Lassen Peak is the southernmost volcano in a chain of largely volcanic mountains—the Cascade Range— extending north from Lassen Peak through Oregon and Washington and into British Columbia.

Near the 1-mile point on the trail, a sign points out a terminal moraine just downslope to the southeast. That moraine figures prominently in geologists' estimations that Lassen Peak is approximately 11,000 years old. If Lassen Peak were older, geologists say, it would be extensively glaciated. Since the last ice age began to subside approximately 10,000 years ago, this small path of glaciation was all that the waning glaciers excavated.

Eventually rising above the last wind-tortured whitebark pines, you begin switchbacking up the narrow southeast ridge. Along this stretch, the trail edges close to several dark crags protruding from the talus that mantles the slopes of the peak. These cliffs are composed of dacite and are thought to be part of the original dacite plug dome of Lassen Peak, which was extruded as partially solidified lava from one of Mount Tehama's still-active vents. The fracturing and crumbling of the dome produced the talus slopes you see today.

Above timberline, you are treated to the pungent blue flowers of the showy polemonium as you ascend the alpine slopes via continuous switchbacks, passing another pair of restrooms within 0.75 mile of the peak. The trail levels off on the summit ridge just west of the peak. Notice Davidson's penstemon and the showy polemonium here, demonstrating that life-forms exist even in this incredibly harsh environment. Continue east to the craggy summit of Lassen Peak. Views from the top are breathtaking, encompassing a vast sweep of northern California scenery.

In the northwest stands the gargantuan sentinel of northern California, 14,162-foot Mount Shasta, the largest of the Cascade Range volcanoes. In the foreground between Lassen Peak and Mount Shasta lie the numerous and various volcanoes of the Southern Cascade Range, mantled in dense conifer forests. The Modoc Plateau country lies to the northeast, and beyond are the Warner Mountains in extreme northeastern California.

To the south, the northern Sierra Nevada marches off toward the Lake Tahoe region, punctuated in the foreground by Lake Almanor. The North Coast Ranges line the western horizon, highlighted by Snow Mountain in the southwest and the South and North Yolla Bolly Mountains in the west. View these peaks across the broad plain of the upper Sacramento Valley. This valley is often obscured by an orange haze that is second in California only to the infamous pall that so frequently blankets the Los Angeles Basin.

Lying to the north of the North Coast Ranges are the perpetually snowy Trinity Alps and beyond, the Klamath Mountains march off to the north- west. Below to the east is the thickly forested terrain of Lassen Volcanic National Park and the Caribou Wilderness, interrupted by numerous volcanic features such as cinder cones, composite volcanoes, and lava flows. The impressive dacite domes of the aptly named Chaos Crags lie below to the north. The interesting Devastated Area lies immediately below Lassen Peak on the northeast flank of the mountain.

The Devastated Area is a result of eruptions that took place in the vicinity of the peak between 1914 and 1917. On May 19, 1915, for example, molten lava flowed about 1,000 feet down the west side of the mountain before solidifying. Simultaneously, hot lava and ash flowed down the northeastern slope, where it encountered and melted a deep snowpack, creating a disastrous mudflow that avalanched down the mountain, destroyed the forest in its path, and buried the area under mud and ash. Just a few days later, on May 22, 1915, a terrific explosion sent a giant ash cloud 30,000 feet skyward. A portion of this hot blast of gases and ash settled over the devastated area, regenerating the mudflow and completing the destruction that had begun three days earlier. Today, young trees are slowly reforesting the area.

On the summit region of Lassen Peak, the features you see are largely the result of the volcanic activity that took place between 1914 and 1917. During 1914 and 1915 alone, 150 eruptions of varying intensities were recorded, eruptions which altered the topography of the summit region. Lassen Peak is still considered an active volcano.

A trail just below the summit leads to the north rim of the mountain through an area of small craters and dacite flows. The dacite flows occurred during 1915, and the craters were formed between 1915 and 1917. The northward view from the north rim is unobstructed and worthy of investigation.

After enjoying this magnificent and fascinating mountain, eventually return to the trailhead.

---

66 Crags Lake

See Map on Page 293

Highlights:	This short hike introduces you to some of the volcanic processes that have shaped the Lassen area as the trail ascends to the foot of the spectacular Chaos Crags.
General location:	Southern Cascade Range, Lassen Volcanic National Park, 45 miles east of Redding.
Type of hike:	Round-trip day hike.
Distance:	4.4 miles.
Difficulty:	Moderately easy.
Elevation gain and loss:	+850 feet, -50 feet.
Trailhead elevation:	5,920 feet.
High point:	Crags Lake, 6,720 feet.
Best season:	Mid-June through early October.
Water availability:	None available; bring your own.

Maps: Lassen Volcanic National Park map; USGS Lassen
Volcanic National Park and vicinity map; USGS
Manzanita Lake 7.5-minute quad.
Permits: Not required for day hiking.

Key points:

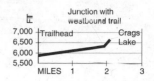

0.0   Chaos Crags Trailhead.
1.8   Junction with westbound
trail; bear left (southeast).
2.2   Crags Lake.

Finding the trailhead: From Redding, follow California Highway 44 east for 48 miles, then turn right onto CA 89 and enter Lassen Volcanic National Park. Proceed past Manzanita Lake and then Reflection Lake. After 1.1 miles, turn right (south) where a large sign indicates Manzanita Lake Campground. Follow this road about 0.1 mile to the signed Chaos Crags Trailhead on the south side of the road, just before the road crosses Manzanita Creek, a signed spawning stream.

The hike: This short hike leads to the depression at the foot of Chaos Crags labeled "Crags Lake" on the quad. Hikers in late summer, however, are likely to find this so-called lake bone-dry. Nevertheless, the area is highly scenic.

From the trailhead, head south through a park-like forest of Jeffrey pine. The trail passes just west of a cluster of buildings comprising the Manzanita Lake Lodge. The lodge area was closed in 1974 because of the probability of massive rock avalanches emanating from the Chaos Crags.

White firs join the forest as you begin hiking along the course of Manzanita Creek, surrounded by dense brush including manzanita and tobacco brush. The trail jogs east into a thick forest, crossing the cold runoff from an upslope spring. Bridge a small spring issuing from beneath the trail and continue east through an increasingly open forest, occasionally spying the bulk of the somber gray Chaos Crags.

The trail approaches the Chaos Jumbles area indicated on the quad. This interesting area consists of loose, angular boulders and is dotted with small conifers. The Chaos Jumbles originated from the Chaos Crags. Some geologists theorize that a sequence of volcanic explosions near the base of the Chaos Crags loosened a large quantity of material that was transported northwest to the flanks of Table Mountain by a succession of avalanches. Scientists believe that these rock avalanches moved at great velocities on a cushion of compressed air, which enabled the rock mass to travel about 2 miles northwest from the base of the Chaos Crags and then about 400 feet up the south slope of Table Mountain. The Chaos Crags are dacite plug volcanoes similar to Lassen Peak, but are composed of four or more plug domes.

After negotiating the second switchback on the trail, you meet a well-worn westbound path on your right. Bear left and continue ascending through a red fir, white fir, and Jeffrey pine forest. The adjacent slopes are smothered with manzanita. Straight ahead loom the bold Chaos Crags, towering almost 2,000 feet above you.

The Chaos Crags in Lassen Volcanic National Park are actually very young (1,200 years old) volcanic plug domes, similar to Lassen Peak.

Soon after lodgepole pines join the forest, you crest a ridge above Crags Lake basin. A faint trail branches right from here and ascends toward the crags. This detour should only be attempted by experienced hikers due to the unstable volcanic slopes.

From this ridge, the Chaos Crags rise in bold relief directly above you, and you have an excellent view down across the Chaos Jumbles. From here, the trail drops steeply via rock and sand slopes into the boulder-filled depression of Crags Lake. Only early-season hikers are likely to find water in this bowl.

A sparse forest of lodgepole, Jeffrey, and western white pine dots the rocky slopes of the basin, with bitterbrush, spiraea, chinquapin, and manzanita forming a brushy understory. The loose rock and often-deep sand makes travel slippery and hazardous in this area.

This basin may appear at first glance to have been glaciated. Considering the age of the Chaos Crags—less than 1,200 years—and the fact that glaciers disappeared approximately 10,000 years ago, glaciation could hardly be responsible for the basin's characteristics. This bowl was formed instead by the same volcanic explosions and resulting avalanches that created the Chaos Jumbles.

From Crags Lake basin, return the way you came.

67 Butte Lake to Snag Lake Loop

Highlights:	This fine hike tours the eastern reaches of Lassen Volcanic National Park, passing through rich forests, visiting two large lakes, and circumnavigating one of the youngest lava flows in the park.
General location:	Southern Cascade Range, Lassen Volcanic National Park, 55 miles east of Redding.
Type of hike:	Loop backpack, 2 to 3 days.
Distance:	11.9 miles.
Difficulty:	Moderate.
Elevation gain and loss:	1,010 feet.
Trailhead elevation:	6,060 feet.
High point:	6,440 feet.
Best season:	Late June through mid-October.
Water availability:	Available from Butte Lake, from Snag Lake between 4.5 and 7.8 miles, and from Grassy Creek and springs near the inlet of Snag Lake at 6 miles.
Maps:	Lassen Volcanic National Park map; USGS Lassen Volcanic National Park and vicinity map; USGS Prospect Peak and Mt. Harkness 7.5-minute quads.
Permits:	A wilderness permit is required for overnight use. Permits can be obtained through the mail by phoning Park Headquarters (see Appendix A) or at the following locations: Loomis Museum, Park Headquarters, Southwest Information Station, Southwest Entrance Station, Manzanita Lake Entrance Station (when Loomis Museum is closed), and at the Hat Creek Information Center (Lassen National Forest), located at the junction of California Highway 44/89 in Old Station.

Key points:

0.0	Butte Lake Trailhead; proceed east on service road to beginning of trail.
2.0	Junction with trail to Widow Lake; stay right (south).
4.5	Snag Lake.
6.0	Junction with southbound trail to Juniper and Jakey Lakes; turn right (southwest).
6.3	Junction with southbound trail to Juniper and Horseshoe Lakes; bear right (north).
6.7	Junction with westbound trail; continue straight ahead (north) along west shore of Snag Lake.
9.5	Junction with southbound trail at west edge of Fantastic Lava Beds; bear right (north).
9.8	Junction with Cinder Cone Trail; bear left (north).
10.0	Junction with Nobles Emigrant Trail; turn right (northeast).
10.5	Junction with north segment of Cinder Cone Trail; stay left, continuing northeast.

11.3 Junction with westbound Prospect Peak Trail; continue straight ahead (northeast).

11.9 Return to trailhead.

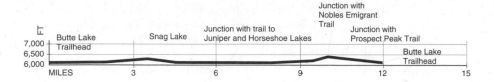

Finding the trailhead: Follow CA 44 east from Redding for 73 miles or west from Susanville for 40.5 miles and turn onto the southbound dirt road signed for Butte Lake, Forest Road 32N21. This road is wide but usually has a rough, washboard surface. As you drive south, avoid various right and left turns, all signed.

After 6.5 miles, you reach the self-pay station at the park boundary and the Butte Lake Campground entrance. Bear left at this junction, and after 0.1 mile, you reach the large trailhead parking area above the north shore of Butte Lake.

The hike: Along the eastern margin of Lassen Volcanic National Park, cinder cones, large lakes, lava flows, and thick forests of pine and fir dominate the landscape. Lacking the exciting backdrop of snowy peaks and crowds of hikers that are prevalent in the western reaches of the park, this fine loop trip takes you through a more peaceful landscape. The gentle grade of the trail, ample campsites, and delightful scenery make this trip a fine choice for a weekender, even for families with children.

The area was not always as peaceful as it seems today. Numerous cinder cones, the tall shield volcano of Prospect Peak, and the Fantastic Lava Beds, a stygian jumble of broken rock, all attest to the region's origin as a land born of fire. Most of the cinder cones you will see along this hike are old and no longer active, now cloaked in forests of pine and fir. Cinder Cone and the Fantastic Lava Beds, though, are nearly devoid of vegetation. The nearly symmetrical aspect of the cone, lacking any obvious effects of erosion, attests to the youthfulness of these features. Geologists believe that Cinder Cone may be less than 2,000 years old.

The Fantastic Lava Beds consist of numerous lava flows that emanated from the cone during this 2,000-year period. One of these flows dammed Grassy Creek, forming Snag Lake. Snag Lake, as a result, is an unusually youthful lake, compared to most mountain lakes that were created by the effects of glaciation 10,000 or more years ago. The most recent volcanic activity in the Cinder Cone area may have taken place as late as 1850 and 1851, although some geologists believe the last eruption occurred about 400 years ago.

The final leg of the loop trip traces Nobles Emigrant Trail, a route that played an important role in the settlement of northern California. This route was pioneered in 1852 by William H. Nobles, who came to California from

Butte Lake to Snag Lake Loop

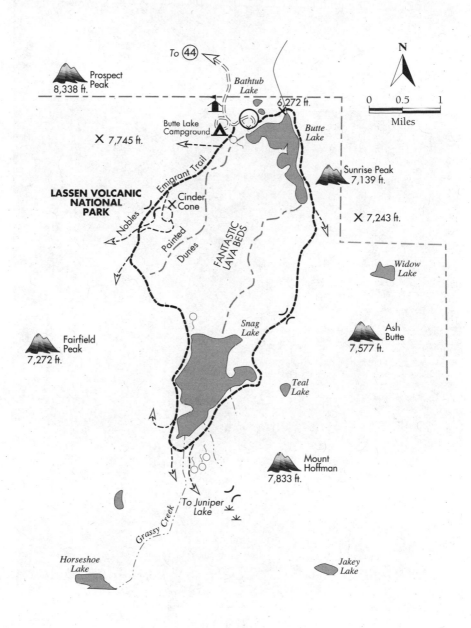

Prospect Peak 8,338 ft.

To (44)

Bathtub Lake

6,272 ft.

Butte Lake Campground

Butte Lake

× 7,745 ft.

Emigrant Trail

Sunrise Peak 7,139 ft.

LASSEN VOLCANIC NATIONAL PARK

Cinder Cone ×

× 7,243 ft.

Nobles

Painted Dunes

FANTASTIC LAVA BEDS

Widow Lake

Snag Lake

Fairfield Peak 7,272 ft.

Ash Butte 7,577 ft.

Teal Lake

Mount Hoffman 7,833 ft.

To Juniper Lake

Grassy Creek

Horseshoe Lake

Jakey Lake

N

0   0.5   1

Miles

Vast lakes, cool, peaceful forests, and gentle volcanic terrain typify the scenery in the far northeastern reaches of Lassen Volcanic National Park.

Minnesota in his quest for gold.

Backpackers should bear in mind the following restrictions when selecting a campsite. Camp at least 100 feet from lakes, trails, and streams, and at least 300 feet from other groups. Camping within 0.25 mile of Butte Lake, except along its south shore, is prohibited. Campfires are prohibited. There are bears in this country, so protect your food supply; bear-resistant canisters work best. Finally, be sure to obtain a backcountry permit if you intend to stay overnight on the trail.

From the parking area, ignore the northbound trail to Bathtub Lake (route of Nobles Trail) and head east, briefly following a service road, to the trail proper. Pass a destination and mileage sign and enter a park-like forest of pine and fir on a smooth tread of volcanic sand. A moderate grade quickly leads you up the slopes of Knob 6,272. Rewarding vistas greet you atop this knob, but quickly fade from view as the trail switchbacks down to an easy log crossing of Butte Creek at the north end of Butte Lake.

Beyond the crossing, the trail hugs the lake's east shore where rainbows leap from its cold, clear waters, inviting anglers to linger. Don't be surprised to see an osprey diving for trout in this lava-rimmed lake. Vistas from the lakeshore stretch across the lava beds to the smooth gray slopes of Cinder Cone and to snowy Lassen Peak.

Approaching the south end of the lake, lodgepole pines and aspens join the forest of pine and fir, accompanying you to a signed junction 2 miles from the trailhead. Bear right here toward Snag Lake and begin climbing southward. This stretch begins in a grassy lodgepole pine forest along an often-dry streambed, but climbs onto drier slopes, where currant and mule ears join the grassy understory. These drier slopes also begin to host pines and firs, which ultimately dominate the forest by the time you reach the top of the ridge ahead. As you gain elevation during this gradual 300-foot ascent, numerous colorful wildflowers join the large yellow blossoms of mule ears on trailside slopes, including penstemon, coyote mint, Indian paintbrush, and aster.

You will probably not realize you have gained the ridge until you begin descending its other side. This gentle descent leads 0.5 mile through thick forest, ending near the east shore of the immense Snag Lake, rimmed on three sides by low, forested ridges, and on the other side by the lava beds that created it. Rainbows and brookies inhabit the lake's vast waters. The trail heads south, across a grassy, aspen-clad slope above the east shore.

Where the trail curves west, you enter a heavy conifer forest, passing beneath benches where campsites might be located. After 4.9 miles, enter a small but wet grassy pocket and cross a trickling stream where the trail briefly becomes obscure. Helping to pass the time on your trek around the park's second-largest lake are tree-framed views of the Fantastic Lava Beds, Cinder Cone, and Prospect Peak. Cross another small stream 0.6 mile from the last, where campsites can be located on the grassy, tree-sheltered benches upstream.

After another 0.5 mile, now high above Snag Lake's south shore, bear right where another trail joins on your left, bound for Juniper and Jakey Lakes. Your trail heads southwest, crosses four springs, and reaches the bridged crossing of Grassy Creek after 0.1 mile. Willows, cottonwoods, lodge-pole pines, and white firs hug the banks of the creek, its abundant moisture nurturing colorful blossoms such as monkey flower, leopard lily, yarrow, aster, and groundsel.

Beyond the crossing, a level trail through lodgepole pine forest (ample opportunities for campsites) leads to another southbound trail heading for Horseshoe and Juniper Lakes. Turn right. Another pleasant 0.4-mile jaunt leads to yet another junction with a left-branching trail bound for more backcountry lakes. Continue straight ahead (north) well above the west shore of Snag Lake.

Soon you enter a charred forest. Lightning in the summer of 1987 ignited this small fire, which fortunately burned itself out at the shore of Snag Lake and along the edge of the lava beds. Here, at the southern edge of the burn, many trees are charred but still living. As you proceed, notice that most of the forest was consumed by the blaze. This "ghost" forest of blackened poles lends an eerie feeling to the landscape. Most of the trees that succumbed to the blaze were thin-barked lodgepole pines, while the thicker-barked white firs and Jeffrey pines survived.

After 0.6 mile from the last junction, cross a small stream and skirt the sandy lakeshore before climbing above a steep, rocky shoreline. Blackened trees frame good views across the lake to red-topped Ash Butte and the prominent cone of Mount Hoffman. You reach the head of the lake opposite the lava beds 1.2 miles from the last junction. Charred forest will accompany you for the next 0.75 mile as you skirt the lava flow, composed of a jumble of jagged, red, gray, and black basalt boulders, barren of vegetation except for a few spindly pines.

Flanked by an intact forest, the trail dips in and out of a small depression, descending gently over gray sand hills that are sparsely forested with lodge-pole pines. Soon, bulky Cinder Cone fills your view as the trail drops into another, deeper depression. The trail is now quite sandy, and progress is much slower.

After strolling 1.6 miles from Snag Lake, a trail joins your route on the left, entering from a slightly higher contour. A sign here advises you to stay on the trail to avoid tracking the cinder fields. Avoiding the visual effect of your passing is another good practice to minimize your impact on the backcountry.

Bearing right at this junction, your trail begins climbing the cinder fields opposite the colorful Painted Dunes. With a view of prominent Cinder Cone ahead of you and snow-streaked Lassen Peak behind, you reach an unsigned junction after 0.3 mile. You can turn right to climb the steep southern slopes of Cinder Cone, its summit offering exceptional views over the Fantastic Lava Beds, Painted Dunes, and much of the route you have traveled so far. You can also bear left, climbing 0.2 mile to the wide track of Nobles Emigrant Trail.

A fine panorama unfolds upon reaching that trail, stretching across the lava beds to Red Cinder Cone, Mount Hoffman, Mount Harkness, and Fairfield Peak. Turning right onto Nobles Trail, climb easily toward a low saddle, flanked on the left by a Jeffrey pine forest and on the right by the smooth, nearly barren slopes of Cinder Cone. Ochre-flowered buckwheat is the only plant seen growing on the cinder fields along the edge of the trail, its yellow blooms brightening the landscape during August.

A 0.1-mile stroll along the trail leads to a junction with a trail climbing out of the cinder cone fields below. Staying to the left, proceed through the long saddle at the forest's edge, where a profusion of round black boulders litters the trailside slopes. Known to geologists as volcanic bombs, these rocks were ejected in a molten state, probably from the main crater atop Cinder Cone.

Descend northeast from the saddle to reach a junction with the trail that climbs 0.5 mile to Cinder Cone's summit, 0.4 mile from the previous junction. Bear left at this juncture and descend into a forest of large Jeffrey pines, from which fine views over the lava beds and Painted Dunes are briefly enjoyed. The trail once again skirts the edge of the lava flow amid pine forest, reaching the left-branching trail to Prospect Peak after another 0.8 mile. Prospect Peak, 2.8 miles away and 2,000 feet above, offers a commanding view and is a worthwhile side trip if time and energy allow.

Continuing ahead, you soon reach a signed spur trail leading 100 yards to the edge of the lava, from which issues the trickling Cold Spring. The remainder of the hike continues along the edge of the lava beds, passing below the campground. Please avoid the use trails leading up to it. Reach the road's end near the ranger station, 0.4 mile from the Prospect Peak Trail, and follow it uphill for the final 0.2 mile to the parking area.

68 Tamarack Trailhead to Everett and Magee Lakes

Highlights:	This memorable trip through rich forests and past numerous lakes forms a grand tour of the best of the Thousand Lakes Wilderness, one of the few wild areas in California's Southern Cascade Range.
General location:	Southern Cascade Range, Thousand Lakes Wilderness (Lassen National Forest), 40 miles east-northeast of Redding.
Type of hike:	Semi-loop day hike, or backpack of 2 to 3 days.
Distance:	12.9 miles.
Difficulty:	Moderate.
Elevation gain and loss:	1,485 feet.
Trailhead elevation:	5,900 feet.
High point:	Magee Lake, 7,215 feet.
Best season:	Late June through early October.
Water availability:	Abundant at the lakes.
Maps:	Lassen National Forest map; USGS Thousand Lakes Valley 7.5-minute quad.

Permits: A wilderness permit is not required. A California Campfire Permit is required to use open fires and backpack stoves.

Key points:

0.0	Tamarack Trailhead.
1.6	Ridgetop junction south of Eiler Butte; bear left (south).
2.5	Junction at Barrett Lake with southbound trail to Durbin Lake; continue straight ahead (north).
3.3	Four-way junction; turn left (west).
3.6	Junction with northbound trail to Cypress Trailhead; bear left (southwest) and begin ascending.
5.9	Everett Lake.
6.1	Junction with Magee Peak Trail; bear left (southwest).
6.3	Magee Lake; backtrack from there to four-way junction.
9.3	Four-way junction; follow middle trail northeast toward Lake Eiler.
9.8	Junction with westbound trail to Cypress Trailhead; turn right (southeast) and follow south shore of Lake Eiler.
11.3	Ridgetop junction; turn left (northeast) and backtrack to the trailhead.
12.9	Tamarack Trailhead.

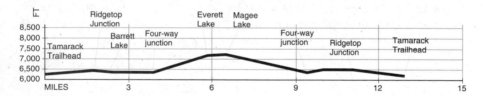

Finding the trailhead: From California Highway 89 in the Hat Creek Valley, turn west onto a dirt forest road signed for "1,000 Lakes Wilderness, Tamarack Trailhead-6." This easy-to-miss turnoff is 14.7 miles south of CA 299 and 3.8 miles south of the Hat Creek Work Center (U.S. Forest Service); it is also 7.2 miles north of Old Station and the junction with eastbound CA 44. The turnoff is 0.1 mile north of signed, eastbound Wilcox Road.

Proceed west on this good dirt road, Forest Road 33N25, which is graveled and graded, with a steady, steep grade much of the way to the trailhead. As you ascend this road, follow the signs pointing to "Wilderness" at major junctions and avoid several spur roads, many unsigned. Follow the "main" road—the wide gravel road that is much more used than others—at unsigned junctions.

After driving 5.7 miles from the highway, turn right (west) onto FR 33N23Y, where a sign points to "Tamarack" and "Wilderness." This road is narrow, often steep, and rocky, and immediately becomes very rough. Hikers driving low-clearance vehicles should drive with care.

After following this rough road for 1.4 miles, you reach the Tamarack Trailhead at the road's end, 7.1 miles from the highway. Parking space is available for eight to ten vehicles. There is an information signboard and trailhead register located at this trailhead.

Tamarack Trailhead to Everett and Magee Lakes

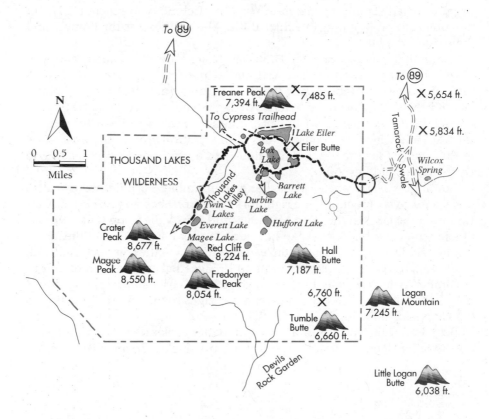

The hike: This interesting semi-loop hike leads through hushed forests, passes four major wilderness lakes, and ends in an impressive cirque surrounded by near-vertical cliffs and alpine peaks. The central feature of the Thousand Lakes Wilderness is a large, lake-dotted bowl, Thousand Lakes Valley, that was excavated by glaciers from the north slopes of Magee Peak, an andesite volcano.

For hikers on the summit of Lassen Peak, Magee Peak and its satellite summits appear unimpressive—simply another sloping, steep-sided feature so typical of the Southern Cascade Range. However, only the north slopes of the mountain were glaciated. Only by ascending the steep trail to Magee Peak's 8,550-foot summit can you experience these contrasting perspectives firsthand.

Except during the spring snowmelt period, the only water usually available in the area comes directly from the lakes. Thus, pack all the water you will need or plan on purifying any that you obtain in the wilderness.

From the trailhead on the eastern boundary of the Thousand Lakes Wilderness, head west past an information signboard and enter a red fir, white fir, and Jeffrey pine forest. As you begin ascending just north of Hill 6300, you enter a dense stand of white fir. After leveling off, the trail skirts the edge of a lava flow, the forest thins, and manzanita and tobacco brush begin to invade sunny openings. After a brief climb, you reach a ridgetop junction just south of invisible Eiler Butte. The right fork is the homebound segment of the hike.

Bear left, descend, and enter Thousand Lakes Valley beneath a canopy of lodgepole and Jeffrey pine and red and white fir. Proceeding southwest through a forest that's becoming increasingly dominated by lodgepole pines, pass north of a shallow pond before skirting the north shore of Barrett Lake. Spying the high summits of Crater Peak, Magee Peak, and Red Cliff soaring skyward at the head of Thousand Lakes Valley, stroll around the west shore of this shallow lake to reach a junction with a southbound trail leading to Durbin Lake and beyond.

Continue straight ahead (north) and then amble 0.8 mile northwest to reach a four-way junction. The right fork leads northeast to Lake Eiler. After exploring the lakes at the head of Thousand Lakes Valley, you will return to this junction and hike past Lake Eiler on the way back to the trailhead.

The middle fork at this junction leads northwest to the Cypress Trailhead. Take the left fork, signed for Everett and Magee Lakes. Cross an often-dry streambed (which usually flows only during the early summer) that drains the upper lakes and quickly meet another right-branching trail leading to the Cypress Trailhead.

Bear left again and begin a series of switchbacks that ascend a shady north-facing slope. As you gain elevation, brush-clad Freaner Peak comes

Ancient glaciers carved a huge bowl—the Thousand Lakes Valley—out of the north slopes of volcanic Magee Peak in the Southern Cascade Range.

into view, the northern sentinel of the wilderness. The massive andesite volcano of Burney Mountain meets your gaze in the northwest; beyond rises the bold, snowy cone of Mount Shasta.

After the trail levels off in a sparse pine and fir forest, cross the same bone-dry streambed you encountered 1.5 miles below. Notice the mountain hemlock now joining the subalpine forest. After a brief climb, the trail passes small, shallow Upper Twin Lake, spectacular with its backdrop of precipitous Red Cliff crags. These cliffs are largely gray, but are streaked with the red volcanic rock (rich in iron) that gave the mountain its name.

Through a subalpine forest of western white and lodgepole pine, red fir, and mountain hemlock, wind your way up to beautiful Everett Lake, where fishing is good for pan-sized trout. Behind the lake rises majestic Red Cliff and the impressive glacial cirque at the head of Thousand Lakes Valley. Campsites are numerous around the shores of this fine subalpine lake.

A short jaunt beyond Everett Lake brings you to a junction with the right-branching trail leading to Magee Peak. The left fork proceeds around the shores of Magee Lake, the highest lake in the wilderness. Lying at the foot of Red Cliff, this lake has numerous excellent campsites shaded by red fir, mountain hemlock, and western white and lodgepole pine; like Everett Lake, it is deep enough to support a healthy population of pan-sized trout. Most of the campsites around the west shore of this lake are too close to the water, however, and should not be used.

From Magee Lake, retrace your route for 3 miles to the above-mentioned four-way junction, this time taking the middle (northeast) fork to Lake Eiler. After 0.5 mile of a very gentle descent, you reach the west end of 6,403-foot Lake Eiler, lying at the foot of Freaner Peak's volcanic slopes. Turn right here and walk around the south shore of the largest lake in the wilderness. Campsites are numerous and trout fishing is good.

After hiking 1 mile around the lake, you reach a junction with a lakeshore path at its southeast end, where you turn right. Quickly topping a short, steep rise, the trail levels off and passes a few ponds in various stages of transition from lake to meadow. After walking 0.5 mile from Lake Eiler, rejoin the initial segment of the hike, turn left, and backtrack 1.6 miles to the trailhead.

69 Patterson Lake via the Summit Trail

Highlights:	This superb, seldom-used, and view-packed trail leads to a deep, subalpine lake in California's northeasternmost mountain range.
General location:	Southern Cascade Range, Warner Mountains, South Warner Wilderness (Modoc National Forest), 15 miles east-southeast of Alturas.
Type of hike:	Round-trip backpack, 2 to 3 days.
Distance:	11.4 miles.
Difficulty:	Moderately strenuous.
Elevation gain and loss:	+2,300 feet, -150 feet.
Trailhead elevation:	6,850 feet.
High point:	Patterson Lake, 9,000 feet.
Best season:	July through early October.
Water availability:	Available from springs at 4.6 and 4.8 miles, from Cottonwood Lake at 5 miles, and from Patterson Lake at 5.7 miles.
Maps:	Modoc National Forest map; South Warner Wilderness map (topographic); USGS Warren Peak 7.5-minute quad.
Permits:	A wilderness permit is not required. A California Campfire Permit is required to use open fires and backpack stoves.

Key points:

0.0	Pepperdine (or Summit Trail) Trailhead.
1.9	Junction with north end of Squaw Peak Trail; stay right (south) on Summit Trail.
5.0	Cottonwood Lake.
5.3	Junction with south end of Squaw Peak Trail; bear right again (south).
5.7	Patterson Lake.

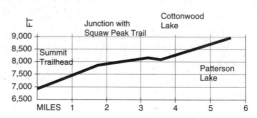

Finding the trailhead: From US Highway 395 at the south end of Alturas, turn east onto County Road 56, signed for "Modoc National Wildlife Refuge Headquarters-3." This turnoff is located immediately north of the Modoc County Historical Museum. Follow the two-lane pavement of CR 56 around Dorris Reservoir and into the foothills of the Warner Mountains.

After 13.1 miles, the pavement ends and you reach a signed junction at 13.6 miles, just after entering the Modoc National Forest. Turn left here onto Forest Road 31, where the sign points to "Pepperdine Camp-7." This good gravel road has a steady, but never steep, grade. Bear left after another 3.3 miles, where southbound FR 42N16 branches right to Jess Valley.

Patterson Lake via the Summit Trail

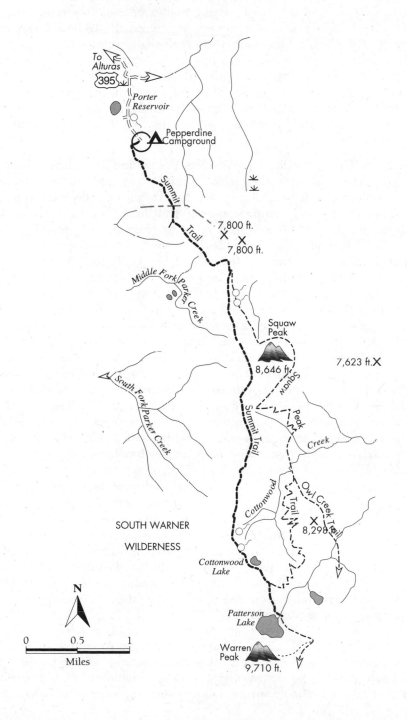

To Alturas
395
Porter Reservoir
Pepperdine Campground
Summit Trail
7,800 ft.
7,800 ft.
Middle Fork Parker Creek
Squaw Peak
8,646 ft.
7,623 ft.
South Fork Parker Creek
Summit Trail
Squaw Peak Creek
Owl Creek Trail
Cottonwood Trail
8,298
SOUTH WARNER
WILDERNESS
Cottonwood Lake
Patterson Lake
Warren Peak
9,710 ft.

N

0   0.5   1
Miles

After driving 20.3 miles from Alturas, turn right where a sign points south to "Modoc National Forest Trailhead, Pepperdine Camp." This turnoff is at the northeast end of a corn lily– and aspen-clad meadow. Proceed south on this dirt road, soon passing marshy Porter Reservoir. After 0.2 mile, stay left, following a narrow road toward the trailhead and campground. After another 0.4 mile, you reach the Summit Trailhead parking area, where there is ample room to park at least ten vehicles, as well as stock corrals, an information signboard, trailhead register, and water faucet. The shady campground, seldom used except during hunting season, is located at the road's end 0.1 mile above the trailhead. It features five camping units, with tables, fire pits and grills, and a pit toilet. Water is available only at the trailhead.

The hike: The South Warner Wilderness, crowning the Warner Mountains in extreme northeastern California, is one of the least-visited wilderness areas in the state. Solitude here is the rule rather than the exception. This backpack on the aptly named Summit Trail leads you to the largest and highest lake in the range, nestled in an impressive, cliff-bound cirque at timberline. Patterson Lake provides for sometimes excellent trout fishing opportunities. A base camp at the lake allows you to scale Warren Peak for far-ranging vistas encompassing portions of three states.

From the trailhead, the trail rises moderately through an open forest of white fir and ponderosa pine. You soon break into the open in a rocky area that's sparsely vegetated with mountain mahogany. From this point, you are treated to the first of many inspiring panoramas along this hike. To the west, seen across the Modoc Plateau, lies Mount Shasta, and to the east are the milky gray Alkali Lakes sprawling across Surprise Valley. Several miles to the south along the crest of the Warner Mountains rises the snowy northeast face of 9,710-foot Warren Peak, towering above your destination.

After a long level stretch of walking, proceed beneath the partial shade of scattered white firs and avoid a right-branching path 1 mile from the trailhead. Your trail soon begins ascending an open, sagebrush-clad slope that affords expansive westward vistas. After hiking 1.9 miles from the trailhead, ascend one switchback (avoiding the shortcut trail) and meet the signed Squaw Peak Trail branching left. Eastward views are good from here, into the Surprise Valley and beyond to the distant northwestern Nevada ranges.

Continuing south along the Summit Trail, you soon spy the snowy cone of Lassen Peak in the southwest. During your mild but steady ascent, the trail alternates between stands of weather-tortured limber pines and open slopes clothed in grasses, sagebrush, some mountain mahogany, and many colorful wildflowers. As you hike along the crest of the range, continuous panoramic vistas accompany you.

As you approach Warren Peak, glimpse an inviting green meadow in the Cottonwood Creek basin immediately downslope to your left (east), and soon thereafter, climb over the crest of the range amid stunted limber pines and enter the upper reaches of that drainage. Avoiding the left-branching trail just above a reliable spring, follow your contouring trail across slopes covered with lupine, horsemint, helenium, and other colorful wildflowers, in addition to some sagebrush. Lodgepole pines join the limber pine forest in this sheltered basin.

The trail proceeds through wildflower-sprinkled meadows and stands of subalpine timber. After a short climb, you reach the small but attractive Cottonwood Lake. This fine lake has no inflow or outflow and is too shallow to support fish, but the stunted timber and vivid wildflowers that surround it, combined with a backdrop of dark, 600-foot cliffs, make this a beautiful spot nevertheless.

Beyond Cottonwood Lake, ascend a moderately steep grade to reach the south end of the eastbound Squaw Peak Trail. This route could be used to loop back toward the trailhead. It is strenuous, however, and involves considerable climbing. Bear right instead and continue south amid stunted lodgepole and limber pines.

Limber pines are quite similar to whitebark pines; both are subalpine species present in the Warner Mountains. They both have needles in bundles (fascicles) of five and are almost indistinguishable except by their cones. The limber pine bears a cone that is open at maturity, is 3 to 10 inches in length, and is characterized by the tips of its cone scales which are quite thick. In contrast, the cone of the whitebark pine is 1.5 to 3 inches in length, closed at maturity, with pointed tips on the scales of its cone.

Nearing Patterson Lake, your view takes in the contrasting scenery of the near-barren desert of Surprise Valley, thousands of feet below to the east, and the subalpine forest and snow-clad cliffs surrounding Patterson Lake a short distance south. Nowhere else in the West but in California do such contrasting environments so often appear in such close proximity to one another.

After topping a slight rise, you reach incredibly beautiful Patterson Lake, set in a deep cirque at timberline, with 700-foot, near-vertical cliffs soaring above it. Campsites are numerous amid stunted timber. Colorful wildflowers garnish the shoreline, including helenium, blue lupine, yarrow, red Indian paintbrush, green gentian, aster, corn lily, shooting star, and elephants head.

Unfortunately, careless backpackers in the past have left their marks at this fine lake in the form of numerous blackened fire rings and trampled campsites too close to the lake. Please tread lightly and fully employ zero impact practices to protect this fragile alpine landscape. Campfires in sparse timberline forests like this one should always be avoided.

Fishing for large trout in Patterson Lake can be excellent but highly variable. The lake is quite deep; during the heat of summer, the trout lurk in the depths and may be hard to catch from the shoreline. Fishing from the banks is best just after ice-off in the spring and after the fall turnover.

The upper Cottonwood Creek drainage lends itself to exploration. Adventurous hikers will want to investigate the glaciated basins of this drainage, characterized by several benches dropping eastward in stairstep fashion from Patterson Lake. These basins have abundant water, are lush with grasses and wildflowers, and host scattered stands of timber which offer sheltered camping.

From Patterson Lake, proceed south on the Summit Trail for 0.5 mile to an east-trending ridge emanating from Warren Peak, where you are rewarded with sweeping vistas. In the northwest lies the Modoc Plateau country, punctuated by massive Goose Lake straddling the Oregon-California border. The Warner Mountains stretch far to the north, plunging eastward for thousands of feet into the Surprise Valley. Within that valley, from north to south, are Upper Alkali Lake, the farmland surrounding the town of Cedarville, and the Middle and Lower Alkali Lakes. Beyond the Surprise Valley, volcanic Great Basin mountain ranges extend eastward into the distant Nevada haze.

To the immediate south lies the headwaters of Owl Creek. Beyond, the crest of the Warner Mountains, mantled with whitebark and limber pines, stretches southward to the apex of that range, 9,892-foot Eagle Peak. Far to the southwest rises Lassen Peak, soaring out of the dense conifer forest that covers the Southern Cascade Range.

Adventurous backpackers could hike the Summit Trail south to its end at the Patterson Ranger Station, a total of 22.5 miles from the Pepperdine Trailhead. Peakbaggers will want to ascend to Warren Peak's lofty crown at 9,710 feet for an all-encompassing vista. To get there, head west from the above-mentioned ridgetop viewpoint along the knife-edged ridge, often passing next to the brink directly above the blue oval of Patterson Lake. At a point just east of the peak, scramble the final pitch to the summit (involving some class 2 climbing).

Upon leaving this magnificent and uncrowded area, backtrack to the trailhead.

Patterson Lake is the highest, largest, and most beautiful lake in the remote South Warner Wilderness.

70 Pine Creek Basin

Highlights: This short hike leads through cool forests to verdant Pine Creek Basin, a lovely, well-watered bowl on the western slopes of the remote and seldom-visited Warner Mountains.

General location: Southern Cascade Range, Warner Mountains, South Warner Wilderness (Modoc National Forest), 15 miles southeast of Alturas.

Type of hike: Round-trip day hike or overnighter.

Distance: 4.5 miles.

Difficulty: Moderately easy.

Elevation gain and loss: 620 feet.

Trailhead elevation: 6,780 feet.

High point: 7,400 feet.

Best season: July through mid-October.

Water availability: Available in Pine Creek Basin; day hikers should treat before drinking or bring their own.

Maps: Modoc National Forest map; South Warner Wilderness map (topographic); USGS Soup Creek and Eagle Peak 7.5-minute quads.

Permits: A wilderness permit is not required. A California Campfire Permit is required to use open fires and backpack stoves.

Key points:
  0.0   Pine Creek Trailhead.
  2.25 Pine Creek Basin.

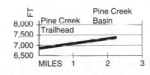

Finding the trailhead: From US Highway 395 at the south end of Alturas, turn east onto County Road 56, signed for "Modoc National Wildlife Refuge Headquarters-3." This turnoff is located immediately north of the Modoc County Historical Museum. Follow the two-lane pavement of CR 56 around Dorris Reservoir and into the foothills of the Warner Mountains.

After 13.1 miles, the pavement ends and you reach a signed junction at 13.6 miles, just after entering the Modoc National Forest. Bear right at this junction onto Forest Road 5, the West Warner Road, heading south toward Soup Springs Campground, Mill Creek Campground, and Jess Valley.

FR 5 is a good, wide, graded gravel road that you follow south for 10.2 miles to a junction with an eastbound dirt road, signed for Pine Creek Trail. Turn left here and reach the trailhead at the road's end, 1.5 miles from FR 5, and 24.8 miles from Alturas. There is ample parking for 12 to 15 vehicles at the trailhead, an information signboard, and a trailhead register. Hikers arriving late in the day will find almost unlimited opportunities for undeveloped camping en route to the trailhead.

Pine Creek Basin

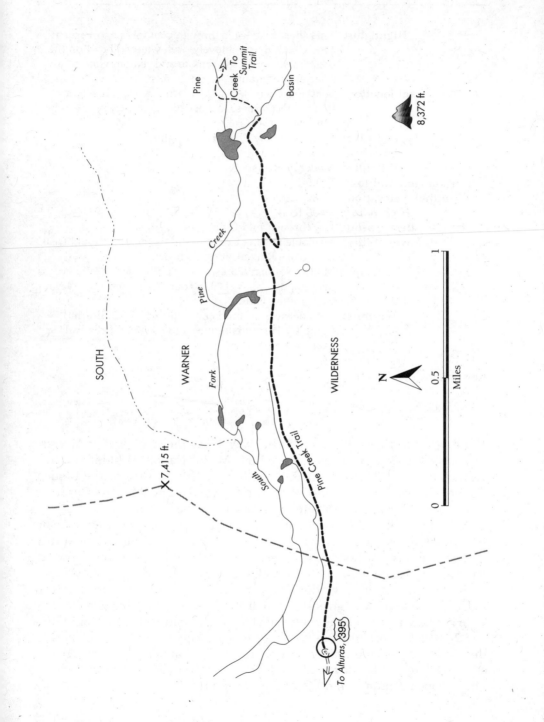

The hike: Following a moderately rising trail through cool, peaceful forests, this memorable short hike leads to the open, verdant bowl of Pine Creek Basin on the west slopes of the Warner Mountains, one of the least-visited backcountry areas of the state. Featuring abundant water, vast stands of aspen, and seemingly endless fields of colorful wildflowers, the basin makes a fine destination for a half-day outing or as a base camp from which to explore the northern reaches of the South Warner Wilderness.

The wide trail begins behind the information signboard and trailhead register, rising gently through a cool forest of white fir, with a scattering of ponderosa pines towering above the shady canopy. Within minutes you begin following a course above the South Fork Pine Creek, a clear, cold, sizable stream. You leave the South Fork and begin following a branch of one of the many spring creeks draining the basin above, soon entering the South Warner Wilderness.

As you work your way up the canyon of the South Fork, mounds of small glacial moraines begin to stud the valley floor. Just beyond those mounds, you pass above a series of shallow tarns that rest amidst the forest at the lower end of Pine Creek Basin. After about 1 mile, the trail traverses high above a deep and sizable tarn. It's fed by the cascading South Fork and by a boisterous spring creek, which you will soon cross.

Beyond the crossing, you have your first look at the broad west slopes of Warren Peak, its broad summit ridge mantled in a blanket of thick, stunted timberline trees that reach nearly to the peak's 9,710-foot summit. After walking 1.75 miles, the basin becomes strewn with a jumble of large volcanic boulders. The trail soon leads you back into a fir forest, where you ascend one switchback. Above that grade, at 2.25 miles and 7,400 feet, skirt another lovely tarn. You then open up into the enchanting upper reaches of Pine Creek Basin, reaching an ankle-deep ford of the South Fork Pine Creek. This creek offers a good turnaround point for a leisurely day hike.

Much of the broad basin affords fine camping, either inside the forest or above the open meadows in groves of conifers and aspen. The nature of the terrain absorbs a number of backpackers, but seldom do many hikers visit the basin at any one time. The Warner Mountains are simply too far from population centers to receive much backcountry use. The range is one of California's most beautiful and unique mountain landscapes, though, blending scenery more typical of the eastern Cascades and Rocky Mountains.

The basin is a large, glacier-carved cirque, but erosion has subdued the volcanic rocks into gentle slopes, with cliffs bounding the bowl on the north and south. Slopes of grass and sagebrush sweep steadily upward to the gentle crest of the range, a long ridge with an average elevation of 8,800 feet, crowned in the southeast by Peak 9,053. The upper reaches of the basin are fringed by stands of fir and whitebark pine, with innumerable springs feeding eight perennial creeks that converge on the basin floor.

Willows border the creeks that course through the basin's rich meadows, and groves of aspen crowd the slopes just above the basin floor. Summer wildflowers are abundant and diverse, including the conspicuous arrowleaf

Verdant Pine Creek Basin is one of the most scenic spots in the South Warner Wilderness.

balsamroot, as well as groundsel, Indian paintbrush, and sticky geranium. Shooting stars nod along the stream banks, and dandelions decorate the meadows through midsummer.

You can continue ahead on the Pine Creek Trail to the Summit Trail and on to Patterson Lake, a tough 2.5-mile grind over the crest, gaining 1,800 feet of elevation en route. Most hikers, however, will turn around at the creek crossing and retrace their steps to the trailhead.

North Coast Ranges

Extending northward from San Francisco Bay to the Oregon state line, the North Coast Ranges contrast markedly with the South Coast Ranges. The farther north you travel from the Bay Area, the greater the precipitation that falls on the North Coast Ranges. Some locations along the far northern California coast *average* up to 100 inches of precipitation annually. As a result, these mountains support rich and diverse forests of conifers and broad-leafed trees. In the most favored locations near the coast are the southernmost extensions of the Pacific Northwest temperate rain forest.

The North Coast Ranges consist of a number of parallel mountain crests aligned in a northwest to southeast pattern. These ranges form a narrow strip in the far north along the western foot of the Siskiyou Mountains in Smith River country. Farther south, the ranges stretch as much as 120 miles in width from the coast at Cape Mendocino to the eastern foothills above the Sacramento Valley near Red Bluff.

In this vast region, only five designated wilderness areas, covering slightly more than 200,000 acres, protect the expansive forests and wild rivers of the North Coast Ranges from development and degradation. Along the coast, dozens of coast redwood groves are protected within the boundaries of various state parks and within Redwood National Park.

There are ample opportunities for hiking in this region, ranging from day hikes to extended backpack trips in places like Point Reyes National Seashore, the Snow Mountain and Yolla Bolly–Middle Eel Wilderness areas, and the King Range National Conservation Area, just to name a few. The hikes described below offer a broad sampling of the hiking opportunities in the region, ranging from windswept coastal peaks to coast redwood forests, and from timberline mountaintops to rich meadows and conifer forests.

71 Mount Wittenberg

Highlights:	This rewarding hike leads you to a windswept coastal peak, featuring colorful wildflowers (in spring), Douglas-fir forests, and ocean vistas.
General location:	North Coast Ranges, Inverness Ridge, Phillip Burton Wilderness (Point Reyes National Seashore), 28 miles north of San Francisco.
Type of hike:	Loop day hike.
Distance:	4.7 miles.
Difficulty:	Moderate.
Elevation gain and loss:	1,365 feet.
Trailhead elevation:	105 feet.
High point:	Mt. Wittenberg, 1,470 feet.
Best season:	All year (avoid stormy weather).
Water availability:	None available; bring your own.
Maps:	USGS Point Reyes National Seashore and vicinity map; USGS Inverness 7.5-minute quad.
Permits:	Not required for day hiking.

Key points:

0.0 Trailhead at visitor center; proceed south on closed road.
0.2 Junction with Sky Trial; turn right (west).
1.6 Junction with path leading to Mt. Wittenberg; turn right (northwest).
1.8 Summit of Mt. Wittenberg.
2.0 Rejoin Sky Trail; turn right (west).
2.4 Junction with Meadow Trail at four-way junction; turn left (east).
3.9 Junction with southbound Bear Valley Trail; turn left (north) onto closed road.
4.5 Junction with Sky Trail; continue straight ahead (north).
4.7 Return to trailhead.

Finding the trailhead: From California Highway 1 in the small hamlet of Olema, about 36 miles north of San Francisco and 20 miles west of San Rafael, turn west where a large sign indicates the Point Reyes National Seashore Headquarters. After driving 0.5 mile from CA 1, turn left where a sign points to the visitor center. You reach the trailhead after another 0.3 mile. Park in the large parking lot opposite the visitor center where a locked gate blocks the road to further travel.

The hike: Point Reyes National Seashore is a land of contrasts. There are densely forested ridges, grassy coastal slopes, surf-battered beaches, rocky headlands plunging into the Pacific Ocean, and several lagoons. This hike

Mount Wittenberg

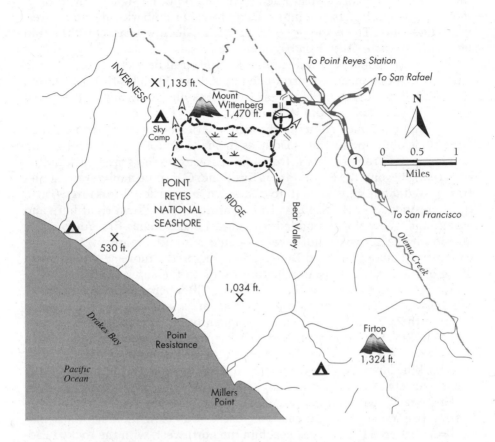

leads you through forests of Douglas-fir and across lush, green meadows. Views from the top of Mount Wittenberg, the high point of the National Seashore, are superb and offer a bird's-eye view of the varied landscapes that characterize the region. A vivid display of wildflowers greets visitors in spring, and black-tailed deer are abundant and are likely to be seen in large herds.

There are several backpacker camps located throughout the area. If you plan on backcountry camping, check with the visitor center for details. The weather in the area is highly variable. During the winter, the area is swept by strong Pacific storms; during the summer, a cold fog often enshrouds the coastal slopes. Careful planning is therefore necessary to thoroughly enjoy this hike.

It is believed that in 1579 Francis Drake, an English explorer, beached his vessel, the *Golden Hinde*, in the protected enclosure of the bay that now bears his name. In 1603 Spanish explorer Don Sebastian Vizcaino bestowed the name La Punta de los Reyes to the peninsula after anchoring in Drakes Bay to wait out a storm.

From the trailhead parking area, head south past the locked gate, avoiding the signed Earthquake Trail that immediately branches left. Stroll 0.2 mile south on the closed road, then turn right onto the signed Sky Trail. A moderate ascent brings you into a shady forest of tanbark-oaks and towering Douglas-firs. The lush understory is dominated by ferns. Once the trail levels off, fragrant California bay joins the forest.

After you negotiate a few switchbacks, your trail breaks into the open in a beautiful green meadow surrounded by a dense Douglas-fir forest. From this point, Inverness Ridge forms the western skyline, crowned by the grassy summit of your goal, Mount Wittenberg.

The trail continues climbing through a series of lovely meadows, then rises moderately and re-enters Douglas-fir shade. Pause to catch your breath and enjoy tree-framed views stretching eastward to the grassy, oak-dotted hills rising beyond the San Andreas Rift Zone. Continue a moderate, sometimes switchbacking ascent to reach an unmarked junction with a northwestbound path. The Sky Trail continues west. Turn right here and ascend the grassy slopes studded with occasional Douglas-firs. You quickly surmount the grassy, wildflower-carpeted summit region of 1,470-foot Mount Wittenberg. Stunted Douglas-firs cling to the more sheltered north slope of the peak, but are unable to prosper on the summit itself.

Mountain peaks, such as that of Mount Wittenberg, lying in immediate proximity to the northern California coast seem remarkably subalpine. Winds of more than 75 miles per hour are frequently recorded between January and May each year at Point Reyes. The effect of these winds is reflected in the stunted Douglas-firs atop Inverness Ridge. In spring a profusion of ferns, grasses, blue lupine, California poppy, and tidy tips carpet this peak and the higher elevations of Inverness Ridge.

The magnificent vista that unfolds from atop Mount Wittenberg offers a superb panorama of the surrounding area. Your view includes the wind- and surf-battered Point Reyes Beach in the northwest, with the rocky headland of Point Reyes jutting into the Pacific Ocean to the west. Closer at hand is Drakes Bay and the shallow lagoons of Drakes Estero and Estero de Limantour. The Pacific Ocean dominates the view from west to south, while the heavily forested Inverness Ridge fills your gaze to the southeast. Beyond the ridge lies Mount Tamalpais and some of San Francisco's skyscrapers. To the east-southeast is the forested valley of the San Andreas Rift Zone, beyond which rise pastoral, grassy hills dotted with stands of oak.

While relaxing on the peak, you are also likely to observe a variety of raptors as they soar on the strong winds that frequently buffet Inverness Ridge. Black-tailed deer are also especially abundant. Because they are protected here, they are more easily observed than in areas where they are hunted.

From the summit, avoid a faint northwestbound path and descend southward, picking up a steep trail that descends to a wide, grassy saddle where you rejoin the Sky Trail. Just before reaching the destination and mileage sign at the saddle, avoid another northwestbound trail. Proceed west on the

Sky Trail. A sign indicates that the Meadow Trail, the return leg of your loop, is 0.4 mile ahead.

Begin descending the wide trail west, then south, around a grassy, above-timberline hill, passing a few stunted Douglas-firs en route. As you proceed, glimpse the grassy clearing of Sky Campground in the northwest. Camping in the National Seashore is restricted to backcountry campsites such as Sky Campground.

When you reach a signed, four-way junction after 0.4 mile, turn left (east) onto the Meadow Trail and re-enter a Douglas-fir forest. Backpackers will want to turn right (northwest) here, hiking 0.5 mile to Sky Campground. After hiking another 0.5 mile east on the Meadow Trail, you break into the open and proceed through a ridgetop meadow before re-entering a forest of Douglas-fir, California bay, and tanbark-oak. The descent moderates as you approach Bear Valley.

Soon you cross the small creek over a wooden bridge, turn left, and stroll down the closed road for 0.8 mile to complete the hike at the trailhead.

72 Summit Springs Trailhead to Snow Mountain

Highlights:	This memorable hike features far-ranging vistas and visits timberline environments en route to a subalpine peak in the North Coast Ranges.
General location:	North Coast Ranges, Snow Mountain Wilderness (Mendocino National Forest), 60 miles northwest of Yuba City and 60 miles southwest of Red Bluff.
Type of hike:	Round-trip day hike or overnighter.
Distance:	7.8 miles to reach both Snow Mountain West and Snow Mountain East.
Difficulty:	Moderate.
Elevation gain and loss:	+1,966 feet, -150 feet.
Trailhead elevation:	5,240 feet.
High point:	Snow Mountain East, 7,056 feet.
Best season:	Late May through mid-October.
Water availability:	Bring your own, since most of the springs and streams in the area are seasonal.
Maps:	Mendocino National Forest map; Snow Mountain Wilderness map (topographic); USGS Crockett Peak, Potato Hill, Fouts Springs, and St. John Mountain 7.5-minute quads.
Permits:	Wilderness permits are not required. A California Campfire Permit is required for open fires and backpack stoves.

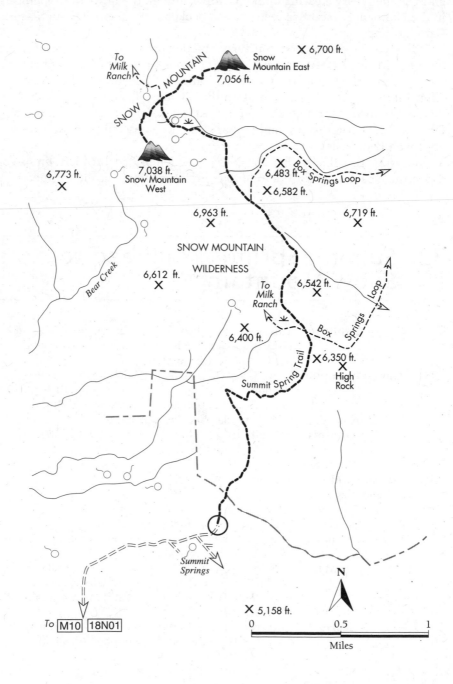

X 6,700 ft.

Snow
Mountain East
7,056 ft.

To
Milk
Ranch

SNOW MOUNTAIN

X
6,483 ft.

Box Springs Loop

X 6,582 ft.

7,038 ft.
Snow Mountain
West

6,773 ft.
X

6,963 ft.
X

6,719 ft.
X

SNOW MOUNTAIN

WILDERNESS

Bear Creek

6,612 ft.
X

To
Milk
Ranch

6,542 ft.
X

Box Springs Loop

X
6,400 ft.

X 6,350 ft.
High
Rock

Summit Spring Trail

Summit
Springs

To M10 18N01

X 5,158 ft.

N

0   0.5   1
Miles

Key points:

0.0　Summit Springs Trailhead.

1.8　Junction with eastbound Box Springs Loop Trail; continue straight ahead (northwest); at junction with northwestbound Milk Ranch Trail, turn right.

2.7　Junction with northbound trail; bear left (northwest).

3.4　Four-way junction on Snow Mountain; turn left (southwest) to reach Snow Mountain West in 0.5 mile; turn right (northeast) to reach Snow Mountain East in 0.5 mile.

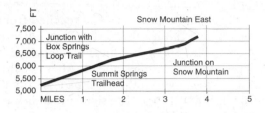

Finding the trailhead: From Interstate 5 in the Sacramento Valley, 70 miles south of Red Bluff and 63 miles north of Sacramento, turn west onto California Highway 20. After 8.6 miles, turn right onto Leesville Road at a hard-to-spot junction where a sign reads "Stonyford-30." Follow this some-times rough and narrow paved county road through peaceful, rolling, grassy and blue oak–covered hills.

After 13.3 miles, bear right where a sign indicates that Lodoga is 9 miles ahead. The left fork leads south to CA 20. Your northbound road brings you to a junction at Lodoga after another 8.9 miles. Bear left, proceeding toward Stonyford and avoiding several signed spur roads en route. After 7 miles, you pass the Stonyford Ranger Station on your right. Turn left onto Market Street in downtown Stonyford 0.5 mile beyond.

Hikers driving from the north via I-5 can take the Maxwell Exit (also signed for Stonyford), located 62 miles south of Red Bluff. Follow the paved county road through the town of Sites, climb over Grapevine Pass, and descend to Lodoga, 23.5 miles from I-5. Follow the aforementioned directions to reach Stonyford.

After driving 0.2 mile from Stonyford, turn left again onto Fouts Springs Road (Forest Road M10/18N0l). A sign here indicates Fouts Springs and Letts Lake. Follow this paved road into the mountains via the Stony Creek drain-age, avoiding several signed spur roads. After 8.1 miles, bear left where the Fouts Springs Ranch Road turns right. A sign here indicates that Letts Lake is 9 miles ahead and the town of Upper Lake is 42 miles ahead.

Your paved road soon leaves the floor of South Fork Stony Creek and begins a mountainside traverse, alternating with short stretches of dirt surface. Pass a left-branching road to Sanborn Cabin after another 4.3 miles and, 1.6 miles beyond that junction, bear right where the Letts Lake Road branches left. Your road, now a good dirt road, crosses forested slopes and reaches a junction with the southbound road leading to Goat Mountain Lookout, 5.1 miles from the previous junction. Turn right here where the sign points to Summit Springs and Bear Creek Station. After 2.1 more miles, turn right onto FR 24N02, leaving FR M10/18N0l. A sign here points to Summit Springs. Quickly bear right again where a sign indicates Blue Slide Ridge. After 1.7 miles from FR M10/18N0l, you reach a four-way junction at the Lake-Colusa county line. Take the northbound road where the sign points to Summit Springs and the Summit Springs Trail. Climb steeply on this good, dirt, ridgetop road for 1.8 miles to the trailhead at the end of the road, avoiding two right-branching roads along the way. This trailhead is 24.7 miles from Stonyford.

The trailhead can also be reached from the town of Upper Lake, which lies above the north end of Clear Lake. From CA 20 in Upper Lake, turn north where a sign indicates the ranger station is 1 mile ahead and Lake Pillsbury is 31 miles ahead. After reaching the ranger station, follow the paved northbound County Road 301 for 15.5 miles, then turn right onto the dirt FR M10/18N0l. The sign here indicates Bear Creek and Snow Mountain. Following this road into the mountains, you pass occasional signs pointing to Bear Creek Station. At one point, the road fords wide and shallow Bear Creek. When FR M10/18N0l branches south, stay left. After passing Bear Creek Station, turn right onto FR 17N16, 7.3 miles from CR 301. Follow this road for 5.5 miles to the above-mentioned four-way junction at the Lake-Colusa county line and drive 1.8 miles to the trailhead. The trailhead is 31 miles from Upper Lake.

The hike: The North Coast Ranges head north from the San Francisco Bay Area into northwestern California, where they merge with the Klamath Mountains. They are made up of numerous mountain ranges aligned in a northwest-southeast pattern.

Remote Snow Mountain lies near the southern end of one such mountain crest that some geologists refer to as the Mendocino Range, one of the longest crests in the North Coast Ranges complex. Its 7,000-foot summit stands at timberline, bearing the brunt of furious Pacific storms and capturing great quantities of moisture. By contrast, the general timberline in the Sierra Nevada to the east lies well above 9,000 feet.

Backpackers should have no trouble locating campsites on this hike. Cedar Camp, 2 miles from the trailhead, and the bowls just east of Snow Mountain offer good possible campsites.

From the trailhead, shaded by ponderosa and sugar pine, white fir, and black oak, your wide, steep trail ascends northeastward, disguised as an old doubletrack. The trail soon leaves the forest and climbs to an open hillside that is sparsely vegetated with grasses and lupines. From here, views instantly expand to include the Sacramento Valley in the east and the uninterrupted, mountainous terrain of the North Coast Ranges in the west.

Upon leaving the doubletrack and branching right onto the trail, you begin traversing oak- and manzanita-covered slopes, accompanied by a 360-degree panorama. In the northwest looms Snow Mountain West. In the south are the forested summits of the Mendocino Range, dominated by the lookout tower–capped summit of 6,121-foot Goat Mountain, the southern sentinel of the range.

Continue crossing the west-facing, oak-clad slopes that are occasionally interrupted by a few white firs and ponderosa pines. When you reach a minor west-trending ridge, the trail enters a white fir stand and turns east. A moderate ascent along this ridge follows, reaching the crest of the range amid a stand of wind-flagged Jeffrey pines, their branches pointing in the direction the prevailing winds blow. The trail then jogs north and again traverses west-facing slopes just below the crest in a Jeffrey pine and white fir forest.

You level off on the flat crest and enter a cool red fir stand before reaching a junction with the eastbound Box Springs Loop Trail. Bear left (straight ahead) at this junction and proceed northwest on the faint trail. Watch for blazes if you lose the route.

After a minor descent, the trail approaches a small but beautiful green meadow surrounded by red firs that are reflected in a vernal pool at the meadow's lower end. Here is another trail junction. The left-branching trail, according to the sign, leads northwest to Milk Ranch and could be used to loop back via the basin just west of Snow Mountain.

For now, turn right. The sign indicates that Snow Mountain is 2 miles ahead. A sign at the meadow's edge calls the area Cedar Camp, although there are no cedars here. Your trail crosses the meadow and heads north, soon crossing over the crest of the range and traversing northeast-facing slopes above the head of the Trout Creek drainage.

You top out on a 6,600-foot saddle and pass into the Dark Hollow Creek drainage, a tributary of the Middle Fork Stony Creek. In an open, forested bowl, accompanied by a ground-hugging understory of manzanita and ceanothus, your route passes a right-branching (northbound) trail leading to the East Snow Mountain and Box Springs Loop Trails. Bear left here. The trail proceeds on the level through a northeast-facing bowl, passing a few grassy-banked, seasonal streams en route. Your northbound trail crosses a minor spur ridge, bends northwest, and passes an impressive double-trunked western juniper before entering another small bowl. These bowls appear to have originated as a result of glaciation.

From this bowl, you can see your destination, Snow Mountain East, thrusting its tawny flanks into the sky. You soon reach a small creek and climb to a tiny meadow at its source. From here, you get a glimpse of the Sacramento Valley in the east.

The red fir forest becomes sparse as you ascend this increasingly rocky basin. Corn lilies grow in profusion in the wetter meadows in this bowl. The trail bends southwest while ascending a few small, grassy benches and quickly surmounts the crest of the range where there is a four-way junction.

The trail straight ahead (northwest) descends into a north-facing bowl, crosses the ridge just south of 6,684-foot Signal Peak, and then descends to Milk Ranch. As mentioned previously, adventurous hikers may want to utilize that 4.1-mile trail to loop back to Cedar Camp.

The left-branching (southbound) trail climbs 190 feet in 0.5 mile to the open summit of Snow Mountain West. Turn right instead, ascending the faint trail for 0.5 mile to the 7,056-foot summit of Snow Mountain East. The view from the summit, an all-encompassing panorama, is superb. From your vantage point high atop the Mendocino Range, you can gaze northwestward to the Yolla Bolly Mountains near the northern tip of the range. Those mountains and the Snow Mountain area provide the only true subalpine environment in all of California's Coast Ranges.

Your view from the southeast to the northwest is strictly of mountains, taking in a large portion of the North Coast Ranges. In the north-northeast rises the snowy cone of Mount Shasta, *the* landmark of northern California. In the northeast rises an almost equally impressive mountain, Lassen Peak.

In the immediate eastern foreground, the Mendocino Range plummets into the often-smoggy Sacramento Valley. Beyond the valley rise the forested western slopes of the Sierra Nevada. The Sutter Buttes add contrast to the exceedingly flat terrain of the Sacramento Valley in the southeast.

From Snow Mountain East, return to the four-way trail junction and either climb up to Snow Mountain West for more excellent vistas or backtrack to the trailhead.

73 North Yolla Bolly Mountains Loop

Highlights:	This rewarding hike, involving some moderate cross-country travel, tours the high country of the northern Yolla Bolly Mountains.
General location:	North Coast Ranges, Yolla Bolly–Middle Eel Wilderness (Shasta-Trinity National Forest), 38 miles west of Red Bluff.
Type of hike:	Loop day hike or overnighter.
Distance:	11.2 miles.
Difficulty:	Moderately strenuous.
Elevation gain and loss:	2,700 feet.
Trailhead elevation:	6,000 feet.
High point:	7,700 feet.
Best season:	Late June through mid-October
Water availability:	Available from springs at 1.3 miles, 6.1 miles, 8.8 miles, 9.4 miles, 10.3 miles, and 10.8 miles; and from North Yolla Bolly Lake at 7.6 miles.
Maps:	Shasta-Trinity National Forest map; Yolla Bolly–Middle Eel Wilderness areas map (topographic); USGS North Yolla Bolly 7.5- x 15-minute quad.
Permits:	Wilderness permits are not required. A California Campfire Permit is required to use open fires and backpack stoves.

Key points:
  0.0 Rat Trap Gap Trailhead.
  0.1 Junction with westbound Yolla Bolly Lake Trail; continue straight ahead (southeast) on the Cold Fork Trail.
  1.3 Barker Camp.

1.6 Junction with North Yolla Bolly Mountain Trail; turn right (northwest).
3.9 South summit of North Yolla Bolly Mountains.
4.6 Junction on saddle between Black Rock Mountain and North Yolla Bolly Mountains; turn right (northwest) and descend to Pettijohn Basin.
6.1 Junction with eastbound Yolla Bolly Lake Trail in Pettijohn Basin; turn right (east).
7.6 North Yolla Bolly Lake.
11.1 Junction with Cold Fork Trail; turn left (northeast).
11.2 Rat Trap Gap Trailhead.

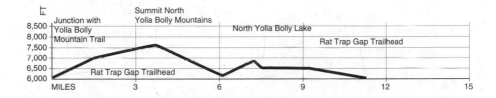

Finding the trailhead: From Red Bluff, follow California Highway 36 west for 38 miles, then turn left (southwest) onto the signed Tedoc Road, Forest Road 45. From Eureka, drive south on US Highway 101 for 22 miles and proceed east on CA 36 for 96 miles to Tedoc Road. This turnoff is about 9.6 miles east of the Harrison Gulch Ranger Station.

Follow this mostly dirt road, with remnant sections of oiled surface, for 12.2 miles to a multisigned junction at Tedoc Gap. Turn right here; a sign indicates that Stuart Gap is 7 miles ahead. Bear left in less than 0.25 mile where the signed right-branching road heads toward Stuart Gap.

Continuing on FR 45, avoid several signed spur roads as you proceed. After driving 5.3 miles from Tedoc Gap, you reach a multibranched road junction and the signed trailhead at Rat Trap Gap.

The hike: The North Coast Ranges, bounded by the Pacific Ocean on the west and the Sacramento Valley on the east, march northward from the San Francisco Bay region to their confluence with the Klamath Mountains in northwestern California. One of the many independent ranges that comprise this mountain complex is known as the Mendocino Range to some geologists. This distinctive crest of mountains is the highest of the North Coast Ranges, reaching above 8,000 feet in the South Yolla Bolly Mountains. The northward location of the Mendocino Range and its proximity to the coast contribute to the considerable precipitation the range receives that nurtures its rich conifer forests. Its western and northern flanks drain the Middle Fork Eel River, the Mad River, and the South Fork Trinity River. Eastside streams eventually empty their waters into the Sacramento, California's mightiest river. The unusual name, Yolla Bolly, is derived from the language of Wintun Indians and means "snow-covered high peak."

The Yolla Bolly–Middle Eel Wilderness lies near the northern terminus of the Mendocino Range high country. Only the highest peaks in the area ever hosted glaciers. Although quite small, they were nevertheless able to

North Yolla Bolly Mountains Loop

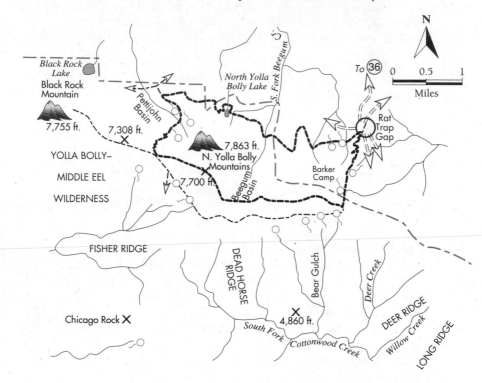

excavate small basins that now add to the attraction of the area. Some of the finest examples of this minor glaciation can be seen in the vicinity of the North Yolla Bolly Mountains. The highest peaks in the wilderness stand at or just above timberline. The remainder of the region is characterized by ridges and canyons covered with thick conifer forests, grassy glades, and mixed conifer and oak woodlands.

Many trails in the area are faint, owing to light use by backcountry enthusiasts and minimal maintenance. Here in this highly scenic area, you can roam for days and see few, if any, other hikers. The exception is during hunting season, when forest roads surrounding the wilderness, trailheads, and backcountry trails are busy with black-tailed deer hunters. Water can be scarce in the summer, forcing you into the lower canyon bottoms to find it, unless you rely on the numerous springs emanating from the slopes of the highest peaks.

From Rat Trap Gap, follow the Cold Fork Trail south, passing the homebound segment of your loop on the right. The route then climbs moderately under a shady canopy of Douglas-fir and red and white fir.

Negotiate a few elevation-gaining switchbacks and pass just above a reliable spring after leaving the last Douglas-firs behind. Another moderately steep ascent follows, bringing you to a small creek draining the area labeled "Barker Camp" on the quad. Campsites can be located here, and it is the last reliable water source until Pettijohn Basin, more than 4.5 miles ahead.

Beyond Barker Camp, you enter the Yolla Bolly–Middle Eel Wilderness at a Shasta-Trinity National Forest sign. Just beyond that sign, an opening in the forest allows you to view the Sacramento Valley and Lassen Peak in the east. Not far beyond, you reach a junction on a major east-west ridge at 7,027 feet.

Turn right here onto the faint North Yolla Bolly Mountain Trail. This route heads west through a corridor in the red fir forest; it soon breaks into the open on grassy, south-facing slopes that are interrupted by scattered stands of stunted red fir. On these open slopes, you are treated to unobstructed southward views into the heavily forested interior of the Yolla Bolly–Middle Eel Wilderness. The trail is often faint on these grassy slopes, where lupine and pussy paws add color during midsummer.

The trail briefly re-enters a red fir stand, and you may notice some foxtail pines joining the sparse forest just southwest of Peak 7,531. Your ridge route passes above the glacier-carved valley of Beegum Basin. The trail then disappears altogether. Continue your grassy, ridgeline jaunt where occasional ducks (piles of stones used as markers) guide you.

Vistas improve as you progress, and now include the Sacramento Valley, Mount Shasta, and the glacier-clad peaks of the Trinity Alps. Lassen Peak meets your gaze in the east, and south of it, the west slope of the Sierra Nevada fades away into the distant haze. In the southeast, across the deep, forested canyon of South Fork Cottonwood Creek, the South Yolla Bolly Mountains rise to their highest point at 8,092-foot Mount Linn. In the west, the heavily forested ridges of the North Coast Ranges march off toward the distant, invisible Pacific Ocean.

Your trail briefly reappears long enough to get you into a stand of foxtail pines just east of the south summit of the North Yolla Bolly Mountains before disappearing for good. The foxtail pine is endemic to California. It is found in two general areas separated by more than 300 miles. The southern population occurs from the high elevations surrounding the Kern River drainage north to Kings Canyon National Park, where it often forms extensive timberline forests. The northern population occurs here in the Yolla Bolly Mountains, the Marble Mountains, the Salmon Mountains, and the Trinity Alps-Scott Mountains area, where it most often occurs in mixed stands with other conifers at high elevations.

From the foxtail pine stand, scramble a short distance west to the rocky high point of the south summit of the North Yolla Bolly Mountains, Peak 7,700. The north summit, Peak 7,863, lies due north, separated from the south peak by a low gap, and is an easy 0.3-mile cross-country jaunt. Vistas from the south peak are excellent. From this vantage point, the Trinity Alps are especially striking. To the northwest rises the summit of 7,755-foot Black Rock Mountain, crowned by a lookout tower and separated from the south peak by a low saddle. Head for that saddle, first scrambling down the steep

A rewarding hike over the North Yolla Bolly Mountains offers solitude and challenge in the seldom-visited Yolla Bolly–Middle Eel Wilderness.

and often-loose rocks west of the south peak. Once that obstacle is behind you the going is easier, although you are still forced to go over and around some rocky sections on the ridge.

Upon reaching the saddle after less than 1 mile, you can continue west up the ridge via a faint trail to Black Rock Mountain for more boundless vistas, or you can turn right on the Pettijohn Trail and descend a series of switchbacks into Pettijohn Basin. As you descend into Pettijohn Basin, notice the black crag of the north peak of the North Yolla Bolly Mountains soaring impressively above the basin. Pass several springs forming the headwaters of the East Fork of the South Fork Trinity River, jog northwest, and begin traversing high above meadow-floored Pettijohn Basin, where secluded campsites can be located. Splash through the runoff of several cold, reliable, but cattle-trampled springs, and within 0.25 mile, begin watching for an unmarked right-branching trail, the Yolla Bolly Lake Trail. When you locate this trail, turn right.

From this point, you can see the imposing Black Rock Mountain and its associated cliffs rising above Pettijohn Basin in the west. After turning right, proceed east through a fir forest while steadily ascending to a ridge above the deep, cliff-bound cirque containing North Yolla Bolly Lake. From this ridge you have unobstructed views east to the Sacramento Valley and the west slopes of the Sierra Nevada.

You will need to negotiate a number of switchbacks before leveling off and reaching the lake. This small, fishable lake, with a backdrop of precipitous

700-foot cliffs, makes an excellent rest spot or campsite, although the latter may be somewhat scarce within the red and white fir forest.

The trail traverses to the east side of the lake, crosses its seasonal outlet, and descends into another small basin lying below a group of striking black pinnacles. As you continue through that basin, notice the presence of western white pines and a few sugar pines. If you fail to notice the trees themselves, you will at least notice their large cones littering the ground.

Your route soon curves south to reach a hop-across fork of South Fork Beegum Creek. A cross-country scramble up the course of this creek leads to the rarely visited Beegum Basin and the opportunity for isolated camping in the shadow of the North Yolla Bolly Mountains. Beyond that crossing, Douglas-fir joins the red and white fir forest as you contour along north-facing slopes toward another small creek. You then pass a spring issuing from beneath a large boulder, cross another small creek, and reach the initial leg of your loop. Here, turn left and stroll back to the trailhead.

74 Lightning Trailhead to Kings Peak

Highlights:	This rewarding trip leads to a remote Coast Range peak, towering above northern California's Lost Coast, and features broad vistas of rugged mountains and coastline.
General location:	North Coast Ranges, King Range, King Range National Conservation Area (Bureau of Land Management [BLM], Arcata Resource Area), 15 miles west-northwest of Garberville and 40 miles south of Eureka.
Type of hike:	Semi-loop day hike or overnighter.
Distance:	6.1 miles.
Difficulty:	Moderate.
Elevation gain and loss:	+2,053 feet, -150 feet.
Trailhead elevation:	2,184 feet.
High point:	Kings Peak, 4,087 feet.
Best season:	April through October.
Water availability:	Available at Big Rock Camp at 0.8 mile and at Maple Camp at 2 miles. If day hiking, bring your own.
Maps:	King Range National Conservation Area BLM map (topographic); USGS Honeydew and Shubrick Peak 7.5-minute quads.
Permits:	A California Campfire Permit is required for the use of open fires and backpack stoves.

Lightning Trailhead to Kings Peak

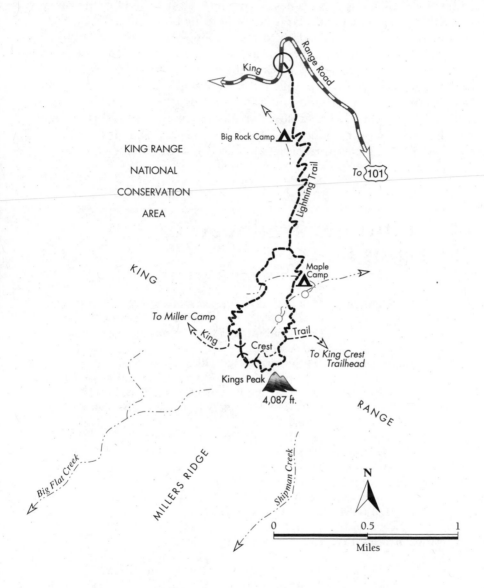

King

Range Road

Big Rock Camp

KING RANGE

NATIONAL

CONSERVATION

AREA

To 101

Lightning Trail

KING

Maple
Camp

To Miller Camp

King

Trail

To King Crest
Trailhead

Crest

Kings Peak

4,087 ft.

RANGE

Big Flat Creek

MILLERS RIDGE

Shipman Creek

N

0   0.5   1
Miles

Key points:

0.0   Lightning Trailhead.
0.8   Junction with spur trail to Big Rock Camp; bear left (east).
1.8   Junction with return leg of loop; bear left (southeast).
2.0   Maple Camp.
2.6   Junction with King Crest Trail; turn right (southwest).
2.7   Junction with Kings Peak Trail; turn left (south).
3.1   Kings Peak.
3.3   Junction with King Crest Trail; turn left (west).
3.9   Turn right (north) at junction and descend.
4.3   Junction with Lightning Trail; turn left (north).
6.1   Lightning Trailhead.

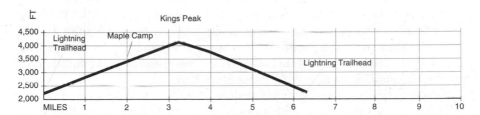

Finding the trailhead: Follow US Highway 101, either 63 miles south from Eureka or 91 miles north from Ukiah, to the Redway Exit. Proceed west into the small town of Redway and then turn west onto the Briceland Road, heading toward Briceland and Shelter Cove. After 1 long mile from Redway, bridge the Eel River and proceed through the Whittemore Grove of redwoods.

Pass through the small town of Briceland 5.7 miles from Redway and, after another 4.2 miles, avoid a right turn signed for Honeydew and Petrolia. Ignore a signed left turn to Whitethorn 12 miles from Redway and continue along the steep and winding paved road, avoiding the signed left-branching road leading to Nadelos and Wailaki Campgrounds 17.1 miles from Redway.

The road climbs to another ridge; just before attaining the summit, avoid a left-forking paved road. At the summit, another paved road continues ahead for 4 miles to Shelter Cove, but you should turn right onto a dirt road, indicated by a large BLM sign. Avoid a paved road that forks immediately right. Instead, follow the steep, narrow, and winding dirt road northwest, passing the entrances to Tolkan Campground after 3.7 miles and Horse Mountain Campground after 6.4 miles. Be sure to avoid an unsigned, left-branching dirt road 0.1 mile before reaching Horse Mountain Camp.

After driving 9.3 miles from the pavement, or 26.8 miles from Redway, you reach a prominently signed junction. Turn left here onto King Range Road. This wide and smooth dirt road is a noticeable improvement from the past 9.3 miles. Stay to the right where a signed spur forks off to Saddle Mountain Road after 2 miles, then curve into and out of several drainages to the signed Lightning Trailhead after 6.4 miles. Parking space is available for several cars just north of the trailhead.

The hike: The Coast Ranges of California typically thrust abruptly skyward from the shores of the Pacific Ocean, making them seem much higher than their modest elevations would suggest. The King Range, located along northern California's coast, boasts the greatest relief in the shortest distance of all of the state's Coast Ranges. Its chaparral-clad slopes soar from the ocean's edge to more than 4,000 feet in a lateral distance of only 3 miles.

Despite the dry appearance of the brush-clad seaward slopes of the range, this region is one of the wettest in the continental United States. The small hamlet of Honeydew in the Mattole River valley, northwest of Kings Peak, averages 100 inches of moisture annually. November through March bring heavy rains to the region, while in summer, fog often blankets the coastline.

The shoreline beneath the King Range is known as the Lost Coast, the wildest and most remote coastal strip remaining in California. The Lost Coast Trail is a superb hiking route along this coastline, stretching more than 50 miles from the mouth of the Mattole River in the north to Usal Creek in the south. Much of this trail passes over public lands administered by the BLM and Sinkyone Wilderness State Park.

This hike follows the Lightning Trail, a steadily climbing spur to the 16-mile-long King Crest Trail, which leads to the apex of the King Range. En route, you pass through coastal forests of Douglas-fir, madrone, tanbark-oak, and coastal chaparral. Two delightful trail camps along the way invite you to stay overnight. Despite the elevation gain, the trail is wide and smooth, making the hike a fine outing for almost any hiker.

From the crest of the King Range, vistas of much of the Lost Coast and access to an extensive trail system in the BLM's 60,000-acre King Range National Conservation Area and the 6,000-acre Sinkyone Wilderness State Park south of Shelter Cove give you ample incentive for planning future hiking vacations in this remote coastal region.

From the destination and mileage sign at the trailhead, the smooth tread of the Lightning Trail climbs quickly past a trailhead register, then switchbacks at a moderate grade to a ridgeline. Climbing steadily southward, salal joins the understory and, after 0.8 mile, you meet a signed spur trail branching right to Big Rock Camp. There is only one campsite here, just a few feet off the main trail, next to a small stream.

Beyond the trail camp, enjoy occasional tree-framed views of the rolling hills of the lower Mattole River valley to the northwest and eastward over the vast forested hills of the North Coast Ranges as you switchback steadily for 1 mile among stately Douglas-firs to a signed junction. Here, trails fork right and left, both leading to Kings Peak and forming a pleasant loop.

Maple Camp lies along the left-branching trail which descends for 150 feet from the junction. Once the trail begins to rise again, you enter a Douglas-fir forest, reaching signed Maple Camp 2 miles from the trailhead. Backpackers will find seven campsites carved into the steep trailside slopes. A spring issues from the draw just below the camp. This spot is a fine choice for an overnight stay. It lies close enough to Kings Peak that you can scale the summit after dinner and enjoy a memorable sunset over the ocean. Be sure to bring a flashlight for the return trip.

Beyond Maple Camp, the trail climbs up the draw before leaving it to ascend brush-clad slopes, gaining the shoulder of a minor ridge after 0.5 mile. The trail then winds upward for 0.1 mile, reaching the crest of the King Range and a junction with its namesake trail. A 0.1-mile traverse across slopes thick with manzanita and scrub oak brings you to another junction.

The crest trail continues the traverse, but to reach the peak, you must take the left fork, which climbs steeply and is noticeably rougher than the previously hiked trails. Just below the peak, another trail branches right, leading back down to the King Crest Trail. You will use that trail for your return trip. First climb the final few feet to the summit, passing a crude shelter just below the high point, 0.4 mile from the King Crest Trail.

The far-reaching vistas from Kings Peak are breathtaking, encompassing mountains, forests, valleys, and the ocean. You can even reach that stretch of Lost Coast beneath the King Crest Trail by following the crest trail and the Smith-Etter Road northwestward to Telegraph Peak. A steep, 10-mile trail leads to the ocean. Consult the BLM's King Range National Conservation Area map for this hike.

Eventually, you must abandon the memorable vistas and begin the trek back to the trailhead. First descend to the aforementioned trail and turn left, following switchbacks through the brush for 0.2 mile to the junction with the King Crest Trail, where you bear left once again. The King Crest Trail drops slightly to another saddle before climbing the east slopes of a minor summit. It then switchbacks steadily downhill to another junction 0.6 mile from the peak. Bear right here, taking this trail to the end of the loop at the junction with the trail to Maple Camp after 0.4 mile. Turn left and retrace your steps for 1.8 miles back to the trailhead.

75 Elk Prairie to Fern Canyon and Gold Bluffs Beach via the James Irvine Trail

Highlights:	This pleasant hike leads through a coast redwood forest and a fern-decked canyon to an inviting northern California beach.
General location:	Northern California coast, Prairie Creek Redwoods State Park, 40 miles north of Eureka and 30 miles south-southeast of Crescent City.
Type of hike:	Round-trip or point-to-point day hike.
Distance:	4.7 miles one way, or 9.4 miles round trip.
Difficulty:	Easy one way, or moderate round trip.
Elevation gain and loss:	+95 feet, -245 feet.
Trailhead elevation:	155 feet.
High point:	250 feet.

Elk Prairie to Fern Canyon and Gold Bluffs Beach via the James Irvine Trail

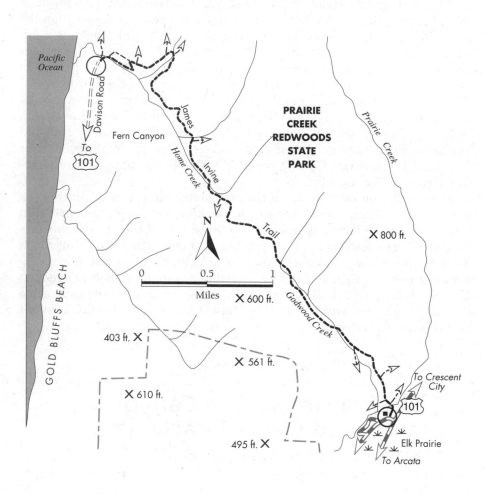

Low point: 20 feet.
Best season: All year (avoid stormy weather).
Water availability: Bring your own.
Maps: Prairie Creek Redwoods State Park map; USGS Orick and Fern Canyon 7.5-minute quads.
Permits: Not required.

Key points:

0.0 James Irvine Trailhead; follow northwest, staying on James Irvine Trail at all junctions (signed).

4.4 Leave James Irvine Trail; turn left (south), descending into Fern Canyon.

4.7 Fern Canyon Trailhead at end of Davison Road on Gold Bluffs Beach.

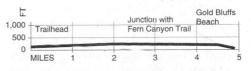

Finding the trailhead: From US Highway 101, 6 miles north of Orick and 34 miles south of Crescent City, turn west at the signed entrance to Prairie Creek Redwoods State Park Campground and Headquarters at the north end of the large Elk Prairie. Drive about 0.1 mile to the large trailhead parking area. A modest day-use fee is charged for parking here.

Some hikers arrange to have a vehicle waiting in the parking area at the end of the hike on Davison Road. That road branches west from US 101 about 3 miles north of Orick and leads 8 miles to its end near Fern Canyon.

The hike: This leisurely hike through forests of towering coast redwoods and sitka spruce follows the James Irvine Trail, formerly a route to a mining camp near the Gold Bluffs. The region is characterized by heavily forested coastal mountains that are cut deeply by numerous streams and rivers. One of the highlights of the hike is spectacular Fern Canyon, a narrow gorge whose walls are encrusted with ferns and mosses. Beyond Fern Canyon lies Gold Bluffs Beach, and hikers with ample time will surely want to explore this rugged coastline. One of the herds of Roosevelt elk (wapiti) that inhabit Prairie Creek Redwoods State Park can often be seen along Gold Bluffs Beach. (If you intend to backpack in Prairie Creek Redwoods State Park, contact the visitor center at the trailhead for details.)

Due to the harvesting of coast redwoods on private lands, California's redwood state parks and Redwood National Park will soon contain some of the only remaining old-growth redwood forests within the original range of this species. The coast redwoods (and their close relatives, the giant sequoias) were once widespread throughout much of the northern hemisphere. Climatic changes over the course of several million years (a relatively recent span in geologic time) have resulted in the elimination of the species from vast areas of its former range. The coast redwoods (*Sequoia sempervirens*) now grow limitedly in the outer Coast Ranges, from sea level to elevations of 2,000 to 3,000 feet, ranging from extreme southwestern Oregon discontinuously southward to Santa Cruz County, California. A few isolated groves exist as far south as Monterey County.

Rainfall within the range of the coast redwood is variable, with annual averages ranging from 35 inches in the south up to 100 inches in the north. The Elk Prairie area receives about 70 inches per year, and along the coast, as much as 100 inches of rain or more falls annually. The climate in Prairie Creek Redwoods State Park is cool and moist. Average temperatures vary by only about 15 degrees annually, generally remaining between 45 and 60 degrees F.

Coast redwoods are among the tallest trees on earth. Their forests are usually quite dense, with trees often exceeding 250 feet in height. The considerable shade cast by these trees and the deep layer of plant debris that accumulates on the forest floor around them tend to reduce the number and variety of herbaceous plants in coast redwood forests. Most commonly, you will see evergreen huckleberry, salal, rhododendron, wax myrtle, sword fern, redwood sorrel, inside-out flower, and trillium. These species are typically found in all coast redwood forests, but in varying degrees of concentration depending on environmental influences.

The trail begins just northeast of the visitor center at a large destination and mileage sign, crossing Prairie Creek via a redwood bridge. This creek is the major watershed of the state park, draining about 25,000 acres, and is a productive fishery for coho and chinook salmon, steelhead, and smaller numbers of cutthroat trout. The salmon and steelhead begin their migrations from the sea to spawn in Prairie Creek during the fall. The creek is closed to fishing during this spawning season.

You reach the first of many trail junctions beyond Prairie Creek. All are well signed; at each junction, simply follow the signs indicating the James Irvine Trail and Fern Canyon. Proceed through a forest of majestic, towering coast redwoods and their understory of ferns, evergreen huckleberry, and redwood sorrel. The trail ascends an almost-imperceptible grade in a northwesterly direction along the course of tiny Godwood Creek.

Salal, a major understory component of coast redwood forests, joins the lush, fern-dominated understory as you progress. Cross Godwood Creek several times in the shadow of coast redwoods, and later, of a few sitka spruces. Large banana slugs are fairly abundant along the entire route, some reaching 8 inches in length.

After leaving Godwood Creek behind, continue your trek through a hushed forest of towering giants and unknowingly cross the divide into the Home Creek drainage. Your route descends into Home Creek. At a point about 3 miles from the trailhead, after passing a lateral trail to Cozzens Grove, the forest becomes dominated by sitka spruce, a coastal species found from this area northward along the Pacific coast into Alaska.

After bearing left where the Zone 5 Grove Trail branches right, continue descending through a sitka spruce forest accompanied by understory plants typical of coast redwood forests (although there are no coast redwoods at this point). About 0.2 mile past the Zone 5 Grove Trail, leave the James Irvine Trail and turn left, descending into Fern Canyon. You soon enter the narrow gorge of Fern Canyon, surrounded by near-vertical walls more than 50 feet high, matted with sword ferns, lady ferns, five-fingered ferns, and mosses. The continuous seepage of water from these walls helps maintain the lush vegetation. During winter and following periods of heavy rainfall, Home Creek often floods the floor of Fern Canyon, forcing hikers to wade their way through the narrow gorge.

Exit the red alder–shaded canyon, crossing Home Creek one last time before reaching the parking area at the end of Davison Road. From here, you can plow through the alders to get to the beach about 0.25 mile west, or hike north to explore Gold Bluffs Beach via the Beach Trail.

If you did not arrange to have a vehicle waiting here, retrace your route through the primeval forest back to Elk Prairie and your car. You can choose from a variety of scenic trails to loop back to the trailhead.

Klamath Mountains

The northwestern corner of California, rugged, remote from population centers, and dotted with only a scattering of small towns, is California's most lightly used and wildest corner. Here, an aggregate of high, very rugged mountain ranges rise above the valleys of some of the state's most outstanding rivers: the Salmon, the Trinity, and the Klamath. These mountains, which extend northward into the southwest corner of Oregon, are known collectively as the Klamath Mountains, and they harbor some of the greatest biodiversity in North America.

Within the Klamath Mountains region are the greatest number of conifer species (30) in all of the temperate conifer forest regions of North America; large areas of ultramafic bedrock and serpentine soils that provide habitat for highly specialized (many endemic) plant species; and significant numbers of endemic freshwater fish and mollusks. The Klamath region also contains one of the largest concentrations of Wild and Scenic Rivers in the nation. Wildlife numbers, especially of black-tailed deer, black bear, and mountain lion, are among the highest in the state.

The ranges that comprise the Klamaths include the Siskiyou, Salmon, Scott Bar, Scott, and Marble Mountains. Within these ranges are five designated wilderness areas protecting nearly 1 million acres of pristine backcountry. Although these mountains top out at "only" 9,002 feet, they represent some of the most significant relief in the state. Some of these mountains rise 5,000 to 7,000 feet from the depths of river valleys, making them seem much higher than their elevations on a map would suggest.

Except for a handful of well-known backcountry destinations in the Trinity Alps and Marble Mountain Wilderness areas, this lonely and wild country sees few backcountry visitors. One of the most seldom-visited areas, the Siskiyou Wilderness, is also one of the most beautiful, featuring dense old-growth forests, high divides composed of the green rocks of serpentinite, and bold peaks. The Russian Wilderness contains a concentration of granite peaks and high lakes that are easily accessible for weekend trips and day hikes. The vast backcountry of the Marble Mountain and Trinity Alps Wilderness areas contain a network of hundreds of miles of trails, rugged peaks, high lakes, and deep, shadowed canyons.

Wherever you hike in the backcountry of the Klamaths, you'll enjoy considerable solitude and a yearning to quickly return to this wild and lonely corner of California.

76 Canyon Creek Lakes

Highlights:	This trip is one of the most scenic in the Trinity Alps Wilderness, following a deep, glacier-carved canyon to a high lake basin beneath the highest peaks of the Klamath Mountains.
General location:	Salmon Mountains, Trinity Alps Wilderness (Shasta-Trinity National Forest), 40 miles northwest of Redding and 60 miles east of Eureka.
Type of hike:	Round-trip backpack, 3 to 4 days.
Distance:	16.2 miles.
Difficulty:	Moderately strenuous.
Elevation gain and loss:	2,606 feet.
Trailhead elevation:	3,000 feet.
High point:	Lower Canyon Creek Lake, 5,606 feet.
Best season:	Mid-June through mid-October.
Water availability:	Abundant after 4 miles.
Maps:	Shasta-Trinity National Forest map; Trinity Alps Wilderness map (topographic); USGS Dedrick and Mt. Hilton 7.5-minute quads.
Permits:	A wilderness permit is required for both day hiking and overnight use and can be obtained from ranger stations in Big Bar or Weaverville.

Key points:
- 0.0 Canyon Creek Trailhead; follow Canyon Creek Trail north.
- 3.8 The Sinks.
- 6.9 Junction with westbound trail to Boulder Creek Lakes; stay right (northwest).
- 8.1 Lower Canyon Creek Lake.

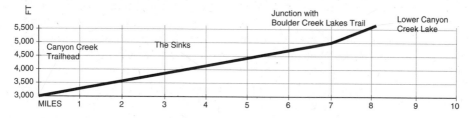

Finding the trailhead: From California Highway 299 in Junction City, 8 miles west of Weaverville and 95 miles east of Arcata, turn north onto Canyon Creek Road. This turnoff lies 0.3 mile west of Junction City and just east of the Canyon Creek bridge on CA 299.

Proceed north on the paved Canyon Creek Road (County Road 401), bearing right after 1.9 miles where a westbound shortcut road to CA 299 joins your road on the left. Continuing up Canyon Creek Road, avoid a left-branching road after another 8 miles. The road turns to dirt after 9.9 miles,

Canyon Creek Lakes

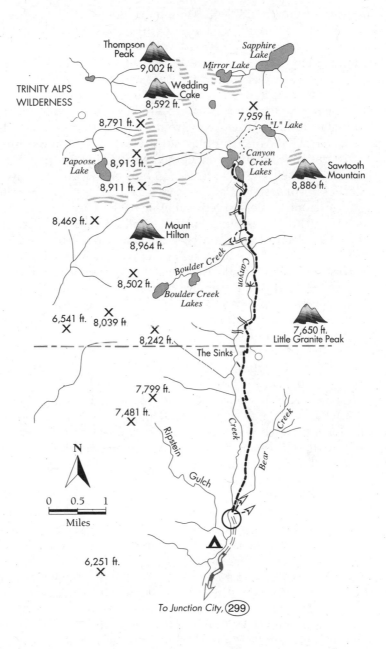

Thompson
Peak
9,002 ft.

Sapphire
Lake

Mirror Lake

Wedding
Cake
8,592 ft.

TRINITY ALPS
WILDERNESS

7,959 ft. X

8,791 ft. X

"L" Lake

Papoose
Lake

8,913 ft. X

Canyon
Creek
Lakes

Sawtooth
Mountain
8,886 ft.

8,911 ft. X

8,469 ft. X

Mount
Hilton
8,964 ft.

Boulder Creek

Canyon

8,502 ft. X

Boulder Creek
Lakes

6,541 ft. X   8,039 ft
X

8,242 ft. X

The Sinks

7,650 ft.
Little Granite Peak

7,799 ft.
X

7,481 ft.
X

Creek

Ripstein

Gulch

Bear   Creek

N

0   0.5   1
Miles

6,251 ft.
X

To Junction City, (299)

343

just beyond Ripstein Campground, and continues 0.8 mile to the large parking area at the trailhead.

The hike: Characterized by precipitous granite and metamorphic peaks and numerous lake-filled glacial basins, the Trinity Alps Wilderness includes portions of the Salmon and Scott Mountains. Along with the Marble and Siskiyou Mountains, these rugged ranges in the northwest corner of California are known collectively as the Klamath Mountains.

The dominating feature in the eastern reaches of this wild area are the Trinity Alps, a cluster of high, jagged peaks whose flanks host numerous permanent snowfields and small glaciers. The highest peak in the region, 9,002-foot Thompson Peak, forms the centerpiece of the Trinity Alps. Canyon Creek, a major drainage originating from several alpine snowfields in the heart of the Trinity Alps, tumbles southward for 17 miles through a remarkably straight canyon to contribute its waters to the Trinity River.

Although well used, this hike takes you into one of the most awe-inspiring regions of northwestern California, where blazing white granite peaks soar skyward from glacier-carved, subalpine lake basins. Trout fishing is unpredictable in the lakes but is usually productive along Canyon Creek below the lakes. Campsites are scarce at the lakes, so it is best to pitch camp on one of the benches below the lakes and make day-hiking excursions into the upper reaches of the basin. Although the lower portion of the canyon can be quite hot during the summer, the upper canyon is cooled by the downslope movement of air from the high peaks in the evening.

From the east side of the loop at the road's end, the trail leads briefly eastward, then curves north as you part company with the Bear Creek Trail. Your northeastbound trail leads through a shady forest of ponderosa pine, incense-cedar, and Douglas-fir. To the west, a high ridge soars more than 4,000 feet above the canyon floor.

The almost-level trail soon bends into Bear Creek, which you boulder-hop beneath the shade of Pacific dogwood and big-leaf maple. The trail then jogs west for a traverse above Bear Creek, leading above Canyon Creek after it jogs north once again. You begin a protracted northward course high on the east wall of the canyon in an oak-dominated woodland mixed with some madrone, Douglas-fir, and ponderosa pine.

After eventually leaving most of the oaks behind, you are treated to occasional views up the canyon toward impressive granite crags and splintered ridges towering thousands of feet above. Partway up the canyon, you begin hiking through a mixed conifer forest consisting of white fir, incense-cedar, ponderosa pine, and Douglas-fir.

After hiking 3 miles, pass a left-forking trail leading down to fair campsites along Canyon Creek in an area known as The Sinks. Negotiate two switchbacks while splashing through the runoff of a cold, reliable spring. Above the spring, you get a glimpse of lower Canyon Creek Falls, but your attention is quickly diverted to the striking mass of pinnacles that comprise 8,886-foot Sawtooth Mountain near the head of the canyon.

The canyon above the falls has the typical U-shape of a glacially excavated

Clear and cold Canyon Creek cascades through a deep mountain valley in the Trinity Alps Wilderness. JOHN RIHS PHOTO.

canyon, distinguishable from the V-shaped profile of the stream-carved lower canyon. Your trail soon approaches Canyon Creek below the upper cascade of Canyon Creek Falls. This upper falls plunges over a low granite ledge into a deep, green pool, an excellent spot for a cool dip on a hot summer afternoon.

Begin hiking next to the wide creek, passing the first, rare weeping spruce. These interesting trees are similar to Douglas-firs but have drooping branchlets and bark similar to that of the familiar lodgepole pine. Weeping spruces are fairly common above the lakes.

The trail becomes hemmed in by tall ferns as you stroll along the eastern margin of the lush Upper Canyon Creek Meadows, passing lateral trails that lead to numerous good campsites. After hiking just over 1 mile from the meadows, pass a left-branching fork that leads to the Boulder Creek Lakes. Good campsites are located on this conifer-clad bench. The trail climbs briefly to another bench just below the lakes. Because camping is limited at the spectacular Canyon Creek Lakes, the best choice for camping is on one of these benches.

The Canyon Creek Lakes are encircled with awe-inspiring white granite peaks pocketed with numerous permanent snowfields. Scattered stands of red fir, Jeffrey pine, and weeping spruce cling to the slopes around these lakes. Fishing for rainbow, brown, and eastern brook trout is fair to good at the lakes, especially in early summer and early autumn.

A recommended side trip to the highest lake in the basin, L Lake at an elevation of 6,529 feet, is a worthwhile excursion. Although campsites may be difficult to locate around this high lake, the views obtained during the cross-country climb above the upper Canyon Creek Lake are superb. You can gaze across the beautiful Canyon Creek Lakes to the rockbound upper basin of Canyon Creek. Several peaks approaching the 9,000-foot level are visible, as well as the apex of the wilderness, Thompson Peak. The numerous permanent snowfields clinging to the sheltered flanks of these alpine crags remind you of the High Sierra.

From this magnificent area, eventually retrace your route back to the trailhead.

77 Long Gulch to Trail Gulch Loop

Highlights:	This memorable, lightly used circuit visits two fish-filled subalpine lakes nestled under the crest of the Scott Mountains in far northwestern California.
General location:	Scott Mountains, Trinity Alps Wilderness (Klamath National Forest), 35 miles south-southwest of Yreka and 70 miles northeast of Eureka.
Type of hike:	Loop day hike, or backpack of 2 to 3 days.
Distance:	8.7 miles.
Difficulty:	Moderate.
Elevation gain and loss:	2,395 feet.
Trailhead elevation:	5,600 feet.
High point:	7,440 feet.
Best season:	July through September.
Water availability:	Abundant.
Maps:	Klamath National Forest map; Trinity Alps Wilderness map (topographic); USGS Deadman Peak 7.5-minute quad.
Permits:	A wilderness permit is required for both day hiking and overnight use in the Trinity Alps Wilderness and can be obtained in several locations. If you are traveling from the north, you can get one at ranger stations in Yreka, Fort Jones, or Etna; if you are traveling from the south, stop at the Weaverville Ranger Station on California Highway 299.

Key points:

0.0	Long Gulch Trailhead.
0.8	Boundary of Trinity Alps Wilderness.
1.4	Junction with spur trail to Long Gulch Lake; turn right to reach lake.
1.7	Long Gulch Lake.
2.0	Return to junction, then turn right (southeast).
3.0	Junction just below crest; turn right (south).
5.0	Outlet of Trail Gulch Lake.
5.5	Junction with Trail Gulch Trail; turn right (northeast).
8.0	Trail Gulch Trailhead; turn right (northeast) and follow road.
8.7	Return to Long Gulch Trailhead.

Long Gulch to Trail Gulch Loop

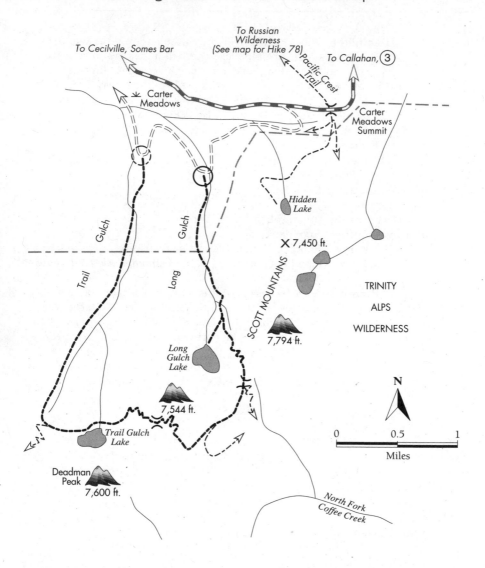

Finding the trailhead: Follow CA 3 to the small town of Callahan on the Scott River, 58 miles north of Weaverville and 45 mile south of Yreka. You can also reach Callahan from Interstate 5, taking the Edgewood-Gazelle Exit 3.5 miles north of Weed, just north of the bridge over the Shasta River. Proceed west from the freeway, following signs to Gazelle, located 7.5 miles northwest of I-5. Turn left (west) in the small town of Gazelle where a sign points to Callahan and Scott Valley. Follow the winding Gazelle-Callahan Road over the mountains for 26.5 miles to Callahan.

At the north end of Callahan, just before bridging the South Fork Scott River, turn west onto a paved road signed for Cecilville, Somes Bar, and

Forks of Salmon. Follow this road as it steadily climbs for 11.6 miles to unsigned Carter Meadows Summit on the Salmon Mountains crest. Continue west, downhill, for 0.75 mile to a left-branching dirt road (Forest Road 39N08), signed for "Carter Meadows Trailheads," and turn left (south). This is a fair dirt road, narrow in places, with a rough washboard surface throughout much of its length. After 1.8 miles, you will reach the Long Gulch Trailhead, just west of a streamside campsite. The Trail Gulch Trailhead is located another 0.7 mile down the road.

The hike: West of I-5 and north of CA 299 lies a rugged stretch of mountainous terrain known to geologists as the Klamath Mountains province. The region actually consists of several mountain ranges interconnected by high divides. Proximity to the Pacific Ocean and a climate not unlike the Pacific Northwest nurture the dense, cool forests that blanket the deep river valleys, mountain slopes, and high divides, with a diversity of tree species unmatched in the state. The southern end of two such Klamath Mountains ranges, the Salmon and Scott Mountains, is embraced by the boundaries of the Trinity Alps Wilderness. Where these two ranges converge is the location of this memorable hike. Here the Salmon and Scott Mountains trend east-west, and evidence of glacial excavation abounds on the ranges' north-facing slopes.

Contrasting cool virgin forests of fir and hemlock with craggy peaks and lake-filled basins, this fine circuit is suitable for either a day hike or a backpack of two to three days. The trail passes through two amazingly straight, north-trending U-shaped glacial valleys, visits two subalpine lakes, and crosses over the lofty crest of the mountains, where far-flung vistas reward you for your efforts.

From the trailhead parking area just west of Long Gulch's creek, a destination and mileage sign points the way south up the long-closed logging road that serves as the initial segment of the trail. Follow this corridor through a white fir forest and pass a small clearcut that's been replanted with ponderosa pines. Beyond, the way is lined with a narrow thicket of young white firs, the result of natural reforestation along this disturbed roadway.

Alternating between gentle and moderate grades for 0.8 mile, a sign announces your entry into the Trinity Alps Wilderness at the northern margin of a boulder-dotted, wildflower-speckled meadow. Jagged pinnacles and the cliff-bound headwall of the Long Gulch cirque meet your gaze for the first time as you proceed through the lovely meadow, now on a trail. At the meadow's upper end, you reach Long Gulch Creek; either hop across its shallow waters or utilize the log crossing just upstream. Beyond that crossing, the trail rises through a meadow before entering a cathedral-like forest of giant white firs.

At 1.25 miles, hop across another small creek to begin meandering, rather steeply, uphill along a rocky moraine amid small white firs, many of which have been killed by a gypsy moth infestation. This ascent brings you to a signed junction 1.4 miles from the trailhead. The left fork, signed for North Fork Coffee Creek, climbs to the Scott Mountains crest, while your right fork leads 0.3 mile to Long Gulch Lake. This trail leads through a fir forest,

Ice-gouged valleys and lake basins and cool forests of hemlock and fir are found in the high country of the Salmon and Scott Mountains along the northern edge of the Trinity Alps Wilderness.

crosses a small, wet meadow, and reaches the lake just beyond its small outlet creek. Pleasant, boulder-strewn, red fir– and western white pine–shaded campsites are scattered along the lake's northwest shore. The lake is deep, clear, and usually boiling with hungry brookies and rainbows. Broken gray cliffs soaring 1,000 feet above the south shore of the 6,390-foot lake provide an exciting backdrop.

To continue the loop, walk back to the aforementioned junction and turn right, heading uphill. The trail rises moderately to steeply under a canopy of red firs to a muddy crossing of an alder-lined creek. As the trail becomes increasingly rocky, mountain hemlocks dominate the forest, where snow patches may linger into July. Views en route are excellent but are enjoyed to their fullest atop the 7,000-foot crest, 1 mile from the Long Gulch Lake Trail junction. A short jaunt westward along the crest reveals a bird's-eye view of Long Gulch Lake and a pleasing vista of the discontinuous forest and hillside meadows on the Salmon Mountains crest to the north, beyond the headwaters canyon of the East Fork of South Fork Salmon River. Russian Peak, the apex of its namesake wilderness, is the prominent, tree-covered knob in the center of your view.

The trail descends southward from the crest for about 50 yards, then forks. Take the right fork, signed for Trail Gulch Lake. Descending first south, then southwest, occasional views through the tall trailside firs into the vast wilderness of high peaks and deep, forested canyons pass the time en route. The trail splits a few times into paths worn by hikers choosing the line of least resistance, but these pathways ultimately rejoin the main trail.

Upon entering a sloping meadow clad in alders, corn lilies, and bracken ferns, hop across a small creek and reach a signed junction 0.6 mile from the crest, along the forested margin of the meadow. Fine campsites surround the meadow, and there is water nearby.

Turn right here and re-enter the meadow. The trail becomes obscure in the grassy spread. Widely spaced ducks lead you into the southwestern lobe of the meadow where you begin to skirt an alder thicket, first west, then northwest. The trail briefly reappears in the forest, but it fades again for a short time as you ascend a sloping meadow in a westerly direction. Ducks lead you up into the red fir forest where the trail becomes apparent and climbs steeply to the high point atop the crest of the range at 7,420 feet. A sign on a stunted trailside hemlock points to Trail Gulch Lake, only a sliver of which is visible in the basin far below.

Vistas from this point are outstanding, including the high country of the Russian Wilderness to the north and the deep, arrow-straight trough of Trail Gulch below to the west. Granite boulders litter the crest here, 1 mile from the last junction. A jaunt either north or south offers more fine vistas and a chance to scale 7,600-foot Deadman Peak, 0.75 mile to the south.

The trail descends very steeply, switchbacking amid a red fir, mountain hemlock, and western white pine forest. Near the bottom of this knee-jarring descent, the trail reaches the head of a sloping, alder-choked opening, where it once again becomes obscure amid fallen trees. With ducks to lead the way, you should have no trouble reaching a rock-strewn meadow that slopes down to the northeast shore of Trail Gulch Lake. Here the trail fades entirely, but the way to the lake's north-trending outlet is obvious.

After hopping across the outlet stream, you may see some lodgepole pines mixing with the red and white fir forest. Follow the trail westward along the 6,450-foot lake's shore. Rainbow and brook trout are abundant in this deep lake. You pass several good campsites, but most are located too close to the shore. However, there are satisfactory sites nearby. Remember to select a campsite at least 100 feet from the lakes, trails, and streams in the Trinity Alps Wilderness.

The trail skirts the foot of a talus slope beyond the lake and reaches a signed junction, 0.5 mile from the lake's outlet and 1.3 miles from the crest. The left fork climbs to the divide, bound for Coffee Creek. Take the right fork, angling downhill. Much of the trailside terrain is sloping, but potential campsites can still be found. You will notice that mosquitoes are more of a nuisance in Trail Gulch than they are in Long Gulch.

Exit the wilderness 1.5 miles from the previous junction and continue descending, eventually using a long-closed logging road. Another 0.5 mile brings you to the small Trail Gulch Creek. Step across it and quickly rise to a bouldered meadow. The old road, descending once again, hugs the east side of the gulch. The Trail Gulch Trailhead is 0.5 mile past the meadow at 5,290 feet.

To complete the circuit, turn right and stroll along the road, gaining 310 feet in 0.7 mile, to your car at the Long Gulch Trailhead.

78 Forest Road 39N48 to Bingham Lake

Highlights:	This view-packed trip, following the Pacific Crest Trail (PCT) through the Salmon Mountains, leads to a remote, seldom-visited lake high in the Russian Wilderness.
General location:	Salmon Mountains, Russian Wilderness (Klamath National Forest), 35 miles south-southwest of Yreka and 70 miles northeast of Eureka.
Type of hike:	Round-trip backpack, 2 to 3 days.
Distance:	11.6 miles.
Difficulty:	Moderate.
Elevation gain and loss:	+1,240 feet, -810 feet.
Trailhead elevation:	6,720 feet.
High point:	7,300 feet.
Best season:	Late June through September.
Water availability:	No reliable water is available until reaching Bingham Lake at 5.8 miles.

Maps: Klamath National Forest map; Russian and Marble Mountain Wilderness areas map (topographic); USGS Deadman Peak and Eaton Peak 7.5-minute quads.

Permits: A wilderness permit is not required. A California Campfire Permit is required for the use of open fires and backpack stoves.

Key points:
0.0   Upper trailhead at end of Forest Road 39N48.

4.0   Junction with westbound trail to Russian Lakes; bear right (northeast), staying on PCT.

5.7   Reach outlet creek from Bingham Lake; leave PCT and proceed east, cross-country.

5.8   Bingham Lake.

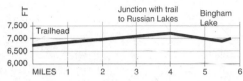

Finding the trailhead: Follow driving directions for Hike 77 to Carter Meadows Summit. The PCT crosses the highway here, heading south and northwest. A trailhead parking area lies 100 yards up the steep spur road just south of the summit (6,200 feet). If you choose to begin here, add 1.1 miles and 520 feet of elevation to the hike.

Immediately west of the summit, FR 39N48 forks right, climbing. A sign here warns: "Dead End Road; Not Maintained for Travel." Despite the lack of maintenance, the road remains passable even to low-clearance passenger cars. It is a little rocky and rough at the start but smooths out farther on.

Turn right here and follow the switchbacks up a forested hillside, first right, then left for 0.4 mile. The PCT crosses the road 75 yards short of the second switchback. After another 0.2 mile, the road switchbacks a third and final time. The PCT is visible just downslope to your left. You may wish to begin here, where there is parking space for about five vehicles. This starting point adds 320 feet of elevation and 0.7 mile to the hike.

To reach the highest starting point, continue along the now smooth road, avoiding two rough, lesser-used spur roads, one that climbs steeply to the left and then another that contours to the right. After the road exits a shady hemlock forest, it almost touches the Salmon Mountains crest. Here, a very short spur road forks left, where you will find parking space to accommodate five vehicles.

The hike: The small 12,000-acre Russian Wilderness embraces the high backbone of the Salmon Mountains and is separated from the Marble Mountain Wilderness to the north and the Trinity Alps Wilderness to the south by only two lightly used mountain roads. Altogether, these three wild areas protect much of the Klamath Mountains high country.

The Russian Wilderness is dominated by a relatively young body of granite intruded into much older metamorphic rocks. These two rock types are of interest to hikers primarily due to their weathering and erosional characteristics, which form very different and contrasting landforms

353

Forest Road 39N48 to Bingham Lake

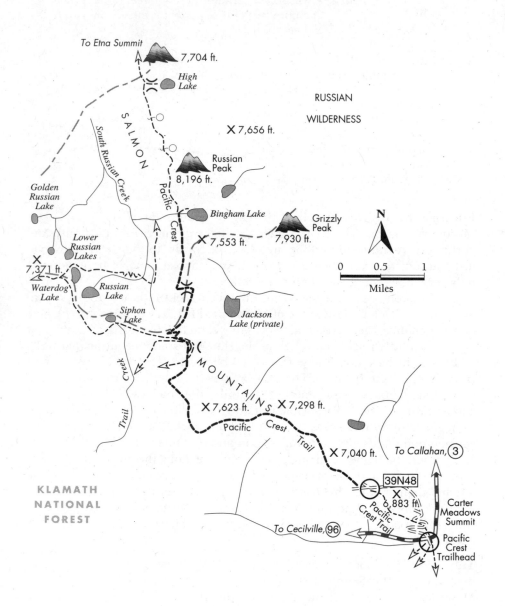

To Etna Summit

7,704 ft.

High Lake

RUSSIAN

WILDERNESS

X 7,656 ft.

S A L M O N

South Russian Creek

Russian Peak
8,196 ft.

Golden Russian Lake

Pacific Crest

Bingham Lake

Grizzly Peak
7,930 ft.

X 7,553 ft.

N

Lower Russian Lakes

0   0.5   1

X 7,371 ft.

Miles

Waterdog Lake

Russian Lake

Siphon Lake

Jackson Lake (private)

Creek

M O U N T A I N S

Trail

X 7,623 ft.   X 7,298 ft.

Pacific   Crest   Trail

X 7,040 ft.

To Callahan, (3)

KLAMATH
NATIONAL
FOREST

39N48

X 6,883 ft.

Carter Meadows Summit

Pacific Crest Trail

To Cecilville, (96)

Pacific Crest Trailhead

throughout the course of this hike. The initial segment of the hike passes along metamorphic-dominated terrain, where smooth but steep slopes harbor discontinuous forests, grass- and wildflower-clad openings, and scree-covered hillsides. Upon entering the Russian Wilderness, though, you may believe you have just entered the Sierra Nevada, with jagged peaks, U-shaped canyons, an abundance of glacier-smoothed bedrock, and nearly two dozen lakes lying in cirque basins carved from this resistant rock.

Few hikers are disappointed by a trek along the famous PCT, and this hike is no exception. Far-ranging panoramas and long traverses near the Salmon Mountains crest offer easy off-trail access to numerous 7,000-foot peaks. Once within the Russian Wilderness, side trips to a half-dozen lakes, many full of hungry trout, could keep hikers and anglers busy for several days.

One notable disadvantage typical of the PCT is the lack of water. You will need to carry a full day's supply to reach the lakes, where water is abundant. This wilderness is not heavily used, so solitude is the rule rather than the exception.

From the ridgetop parking area, the PCT is visible just downslope to the south. To avoid damaging the area's fragile vegetation, restrain your urge to scramble down to it. Instead, return to the forest road and stroll 150 yards west, intercepting the PCT and turning right, or northwest. Rising at an easy grade, the trail parallels an upslope doubletrack just south of the crest.

A variety of conifers clothe the slopes at this point. Incense-cedar, Jeffrey pine, and white fir thrive on these south-facing slopes, while red fir and mountain hemlock hug the crest and the cooler north-facing slopes just over the ridge. Vistas are superb from the start and will accompany you for miles to come. Particularly notable are the U-shaped troughs of Long Gulch and Trail Gulch to the south, above which rise a host of rocky timberline summits.

The doubletrack crosses the PCT twice more, beyond which you begin a traverse beneath Peak 7,040. Here the trail alternates between a white fir forest and grassy openings, resplendent with wildflowers that slope away steeply into the forested canyon of the East Fork of South Fork Salmon River.

The trail undulates along the southern slopes of several 7,000-foot peaks; as you proceed near the 7,000-foot contour, red fir joins the forest. Occasional sun-drenched openings host a variety of mountain shrubs, including manzanita, ceanothus, chinquapin, and ocean spray.

After 2.4 miles, just before the trail curves northwest around a shoulder of Peak 7623, stay alert to notice several foxtail pines growing among the firs a few feet upslope. The foxtail pines of the Klamath region are a subspecies of those found more than 300 miles away in the southern Sierra (see Hike 73 for more about foxtail pines).

The trail heads north, then west, and north again, descending steadily. Your views now include the deep trench of Trail Creek, below to the west. After 3.25 miles, a long-abandoned logging road and the PCT coalesce for 50 yards. The trail then proceeds under a canopy of red fir and mountain hemlock, crosses a gravelly slope below a grassy saddle, and quickly climbs to another old road at 3.75 miles.

Your trail angles uphill beyond the road on a northwesterly course, passing through a lovely sloping meadow just below the crest. En route you cross two small, alder-lined streams. The presence of grazing cattle makes treatment advisable not only for these streams, but also for any other backcountry water source from which you plan to drink.

After 4 miles, you reach an important junction with yet another old doubletrack. You have the option of turning left here to reach a half-dozen high lakes, all but one of which lie within the Russian Wilderness. Siphon Lake, at 7,250 feet, is the first lake, only 0.6 mile west. It is unusual because it lies in a cirque carved into the south side of the crest rather than on the more typical north side. You can find several suitable, tree-shaded campsites here. Follow this trail past the lake and reach Waterdog Lake after another 1.5 miles. This 7,000-foot lake boasts numerous fine campsites. Russian Lake, the largest in the basin, lies just over the ridge to the southeast, where the granite cliffs of Peak 7,731 soar 650 feet directly above. A more difficult cross-country hike, mostly downhill, is required to reach the isolated Lower Russian Lakes and Golden Russian Lake, which lie in the basin just over the low ridge north of Waterdog Lake.

To reach Bingham Lake, bear right on the PCT beyond the doubletrack, climbing northeast past a Russian Wilderness sign. The trail initially rises through firs, then switchbacks onto a grassy slope. As you angle uphill toward the ridge above, you pass beyond metamorphic rocks and onto granitic terrain. Ahead the slope becomes brushy, but it is enlivened by the yellow summer blossoms of buckwheat.

Topping out after 4.5 miles on a 7,300-foot ridge, breathtaking vistas will cause you to linger. Southward, your gaze extends over miles of lofty Trinity Alps Wilderness summits, crowned by glacier-clad Thompson Peak. At 9,002 feet, it is the highest peak in northern California's coast ranges. Looming boldly on the eastern horizon is the immense, snowy bulk of majestic Mount Shasta.

The trail descends northward across the boulder-littered slopes under a shady canopy of red fir and hemlock for 0.5 mile to a 6,730-foot saddle beneath a low but imposing summit. The trail switchbacks once below the saddle before resuming a northerly course. Next, cross a boulder-choked gully beneath which flows a trickling stream. The trail bends slightly into another similar gully. With a more vigorous flow, this stream emanates from Bingham Lake, 5.7 miles from the trailhead.

There are two ways to reach the lake. You can scramble up this gully and alongside the flower-decked stream for 0.1 mile to the lake or follow the PCT a short distance to a faint, ducked route that climbs steep, loose slopes, a slightly longer alternative.

The deep, oblong lake harbors an abundance of pan-sized trout, but campsites along the rocky, forested shore are few and difficult to find. Soaring almost 1,200 feet above the lake to the north, Russian Peak highlights your stop here.

After exploring this remote and spectacular high country, backtrack to the trailhead.

79 South Kelsey Trail to Bear Lake, Little Bear Valley

Highlights: This seldom-used trail features broad vistas and leads to a remote subalpine lake in the lonely Siskiyou Mountains of far northwest California.

General location: Siskiyou Mountains, Siskiyou Wilderness (Klamath National Forest), 15 miles southwest of Happy Camp and 67 miles northeast of Eureka.

Type of hike: Round-trip day hike or overnighter.

Distance: 6.2 miles.

Difficulty: Moderate.

Elevation gain and loss: +850 feet, -800 feet.

Trailhead elevation: 4,750 feet.

High point: 5,600 feet.

Best season: Mid-June through early October.

Water availability: There is no water available along the route until you reach Bear Lake at 3.1 miles.

Maps: Klamath National Forest map; Siskiyou Wilderness map (topographic); USGS Bear Peak 7.5-minute quad.

Permits: A wilderness permit is not required. A California Campfire Permit is required for the use of open fires and backpack stoves.

Key points:

0.0   South Kelsey Trailhead.

2.25 Junction with Bear Lake Trail; turn right (north) and descend.

3.1   Bear Lake.

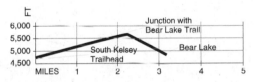

Finding the trailhead: To locate the trailhead, you must first locate Forest Road 15N19, marked by a small sign that indicates "Bear Peak Road" and "Kelsey Trail-11," on the west side of California Highway 96, about 49.4 miles north of Weitchpec and 9.3 miles south of Happy Camp. This hard-to-spot turnoff lies 0.4 mile south of the Clear Creek bridge on CA 96.

After locating the turnoff, proceed west on FR 15N19, a good paved road, avoiding several numbered spur roads. After driving 3 miles, bear left onto FR 15N24, staying on the pavement. Dirt-surfaced FR 15N19 continues ahead to eventually rejoin your paved road.

The pavement ends after another 3.4 miles at a four-way junction. Proceed straight ahead, taking the middle fork where a sign indicates Bear Lake and the Kelsey Trail. Head west on this good dirt road and, 5 miles from the end of pavement, turn right where a sign indicates Bear Lake and the Kelsey Trail. Climb steeply for 0.1 mile to the trailhead, where there is room for at least five vehicles.

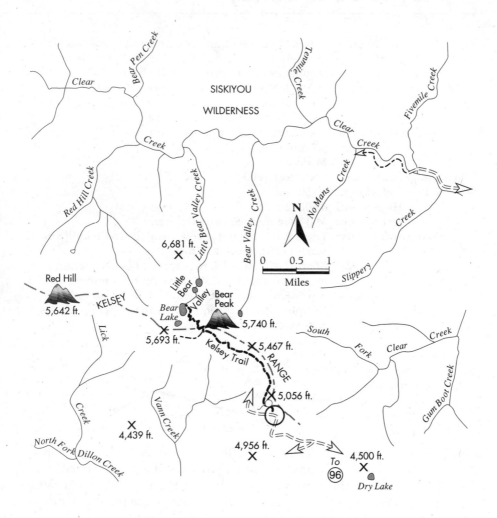

The hike: The southern Siskiyou Mountains rise abruptly westward from the low hills of the North Coast Ranges to a crest of mile-high peaks before plunging eastward into the very deep canyon of the Klamath River. The Klamath River, born in the mountains of southern Oregon, makes a long arc around the east, south, and southwest flanks of the Siskiyou Mountains, effectively delineating the boundaries of the range.

Conifer forests in the range are well developed, owing to its proximity to Pacific Ocean moisture. The Siskiyous bear the distinction of hosting the world's largest concentration of lily species, as well as some 20 species of conifers. Several glacial lakes at rather low elevations dot the cirques that cling to the flanks of many of the peaks.

Vistas of Little Bear Valley, Preston Peak, and Clear Creek canyon unfold from the trail to Bear Lake in the Siskiyou Wilderness.

Lying far from major population centers, this little-known region sees few hikers. The vast Marble Mountain Wilderness that rises eastward beyond the Klamath River is much better known and attracts the majority of hikers visiting this region.

Your trail, an old doubletrack, heads northwest from the trailhead, quickly leading you into a forest of white fir and Douglas-fir, mixed with a few incense-cedars. After a brief climb, your route promptly narrows to a singletrack trail.

After slogging through the mud below the seeping Elbow Spring, head north, with occasional views northwest to brushy Bear Peak and west to the somewhat-rocky east slopes of the Siskiyou Mountains crest, crowned by 5,850-foot Harrington Mountain. Among the varied understory vegetation along this stretch of trail are deer oak, huckleberry oak, manzanita, bear grass, tobacco brush, wild rose, Oregon grape, and bracken fern. After passing above the range of incense-cedar, you may notice an occasional western white pine mixed into the forest.

The trail soon bends northwest while traversing the southwest slopes of Peak 5,467. You are treated to excellent vistas of the wild Siskiyou crest in the west and the glacier-clad crags of the Trinity Alps in the southeast. After reaching a saddle at 5,200 feet, immediately east of Bear Peak, you are further rewarded with superb northward views. Directly below to the northeast lies meadow-bottomed Bear Valley, and beyond rises the spectacular crag of 7,309-foot Preston Peak, the highest summit in California's Siskiyou Mountains. On the far northeastern skyline are Siskiyou Mountain peaks rising just south of the Oregon-California border.

As you climb higher, the vast Marble Mountains meet your gaze to the east across the deep Klamath River canyon. Upon reaching a saddle west of Bear Peak, 2.25 miles from the trailhead, you meet the northwestbound trail leading down to Bear Lake and Little Bear Valley. At this point, a truly magnificent vista emerges, even more all-encompassing than your previous views. In addition to the previously mentioned landmarks, you now see to the north and northwest countless impressive Siskiyou Mountain summits. This is a view reserved for hikers only. From left to right, the prominent high points include: sparsely forested and aptly named Red Hill; Peak 5,631; Prescott Mountain; Peak 5,629; massive Bear Mountain; Twin Peaks; Youngs Peak; and, towering above all else, Preston Peak.

Turn right at this junction and enter the Siskiyou Wilderness. Begin your steep, switchbacking descent to Bear Lake, 800 feet below in the deep cirque of Little Bear Valley. The varied but sparse tree cover consists of red and white fir, Douglas-fir, incense-cedar, western white pine, and the rare weeping spruce, found only in northwestern California and southwestern Oregon.

Spy the pond lily–covered Lower Bear Lake midway during your descent and finally reach deep Bear Lake, where good campsites shaded by fir, spruce, and cedar are located. During the dry season, there is usually no inflow to or outflow from Bear Lake. It nevertheless maintains a healthy trout population, and fishing is best in early summer and early autumn.

80 Shackleford Creek to Summit Lake

Highlights:	This scenic trip affords quick access to one of the Marble Mountain's most dramatic high lake basins, where good fishing and backcountry camping await.
General location:	Salmon Mountains, Marble Mountain Wilderness (Klamath National Forest), 25 miles southwest of Yreka.
Type of hike:	Semi-loop backpack, 2 to 4 days.
Distance:	12.7 miles.
Difficulty:	Moderate.
Elevation gain and loss:	2,200 feet.
Trailhead elevation:	4,400 feet.
High point:	6,600 feet.
Best season:	July through early October.
Water availability:	Abundant.
Maps:	Klamath National Forest map; Marble Mountain and Russian Wilderness areas map (topographic); USGS Boulder Peak and Marble Mountain 7.5-minute quads.

Permits: Wilderness permits are not required. A California Campfire Permit is required for the use of open fires or backpack stoves.

Key points:

0.0	Shackleford Creek Trailhead.
2.5	Junction with southwestbound trail leading to Campbell Lake; bear right (northwest).
3.0	Junction with trail to Calf and Long High Lakes; stay left (west).
3.6	Junction of Shackleford Creek and Campbell Lake Trails; turn left (south) on Campbell Lake Trail.
4.2	Junction with eastbound trail along north shore of Campbell Lake; continue straight ahead (south).
4.4	Junction with southbound Cliff Lake Trail and southeastbound trail following the shore of Campbell Lake; proceed straight ahead (south) to reach Cliff Lake.
5.1	Cliff Lake.
5.8	Return to junction; turn left (west).
7.5	Junction with Shackleford Creek Trail at Summit Lake; turn right (north).
7.9	Junction with northbound trail to Little Elk Lake; bear right (east).
9.1	Return to junction with Campbell Lake Trail; stay left (northeast).
9.7	Junction with trail to Calf and Long High Lakes; bear right (east).
10.2	Junction with southwestbound trail to Campbell Lake; stay left (northeast).
12.7	Return to Shackleford Creek Trailhead.

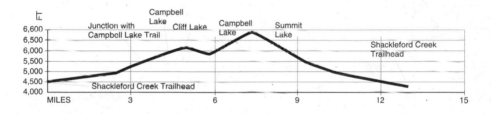

Finding the trailhead: From Interstate 5 at the South Yreka Exit, turn west onto California Highway 3 and drive 15.4 miles to the westbound Scott River Road, just south of Fort Jones. The Scott River Ranger Station is located at this junction, and campfire permits for open fires can be obtained there. Be aware that the Scott River Road is a very narrow, winding paved road, with occasional turnouts. Drive this road with extreme caution.

Proceed west on the Scott River Road for 7.1 miles, then turn south onto the Quartz Valley Road. Follow this road south through forests and farmlands for 3.9 miles; turn right (west) where a sign indicates Shackleford Trailhead. Proceed west on this dirt road, following signs at all major junctions pointing to the Shackleford Trailhead. After 7 miles of dusty travel on this often-narrow road, you reach the trailhead parking area just north of large Shackleford Creek.

If you are approaching from the west, follow CA 96 east for 11 miles from

Shackleford Creek to Summit lake

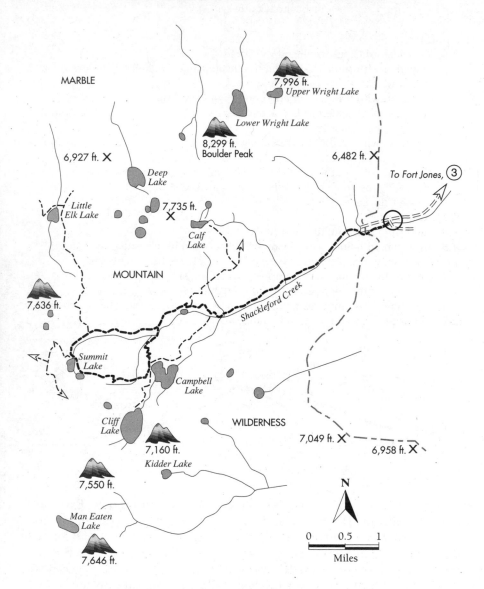

MARBLE

7,996 ft.
Upper Wright Lake

Lower Wright Lake

6,927 ft. X

8,299 ft.
Boulder Peak

6,482 ft. X

To Fort Jones, (3)

Deep Lake

Little Elk Lake

7,735 ft.
X

Calf Lake

MOUNTAIN

7,636 ft.

Shackleford Creek

Summit Lake

Campbell Lake

Cliff Lake

WILDERNESS

7,049 ft. X

6,958 ft. X

7,160 ft.

Kidder Lake

7,550 ft.

N

Man Eaten Lake

7,646 ft.

0   0.5   1
Miles

Seiad Valley. (Seiad Valley is 152 miles northeast of Arcata.) Turn south onto the Scott River Road, following it 23.2 miles south, then east, to the Quartz Valley Road. Follow the above-mentioned directions to reach the trailhead.

The hike: The Salmon and Marble Mountains form a vast region of rugged grandeur in northwestern California, a region protected as the Marble Mountain Wilderness. Due to its remoteness from major population centers, backcountry trails are seldom overcrowded, allowing for an enjoyable and satisfying wilderness experience. Owing to the area's northerly location and proximity to Pacific Ocean moisture, timberline in this wilderness is rather low, at least compared with regions farther south and farther inland. Although the highest peak in the area barely exceeds 8,000 feet, there is an abundance of subalpine scenery.

Shackleford Creek and its headwaters present one of the most spectacular landscapes in the Marble Mountain Wilderness. Its two large, fish-inhabited lakes, rugged cliffs and peaks, subalpine forests, and numerous other lakes which are accessible by lateral trails, all combine to make this area an excellent choice for hikers with less than five days to spend in the backcountry.

Your trail, a closed doubletrack during the first 0.5 mile, heads west from the parking area and leads you into a forest of white fir, Douglas-fir, incense-cedar, and Jeffrey pine, staying within sight and sound of noisy Shackleford Creek. Upon reaching a large wilderness information sign, your route becomes the Shackleford Creek Trail, where you enter the Marble Mountain Wilderness.

The gentle creekside ascent continues, passing numerous potential campsites. Hop across several small streams issuing from the flanks of Red Mountain and proceed through a few small meadows whose margins are being invaded by lodgepole pines. The two-needled lodgepole pine is found in a variety of life zones. Typically, it flourishes on dry, well-drained sites within subalpine forests. Not requiring much oxygen, this tree tends to grow where the local soil and climatic conditions are unsatisfactory to the development of other conifers. You can often find lodgepole pines invading the water-logged environs of meadows, well below their normal elevation range.

After hopping across Long High Creek, enjoy a stimulating view up the canyon to precipitous, rocky crags. After hiking 2.5 miles from the trailhead, your route leaves the main fork of Shackleford Creek after passing a left-branching trail that leads to Campbell Lake in 1 mile. You then begin a moderate ascent along the Summit Lake creek tributary.

After another 0.5 mile, pass a signed junction on your right where a northeastbound trail leads to Calf and Long High Lakes, nestled in a cirque high on the flanks of Red Mountain. Just below this junction, the trail passes between campsites on the right and aptly named Log Lake on the left. This shallow, log-filled, pond lily–covered tarn offers good fishing for rainbow trout.

From Log Lake, the spectacular high country along the crest of the Salmon Mountains fills your southwestward gaze. You soon pass through the cattle-trimmed turf of a meadow infested with sneezeweed. After hiking 0.6 mile from Log Lake, notice the return leg of your loop, just before the trail crosses the seasonal, multibranched Summit Lake creek. It branches right and invisibly makes its way across the meadow in a westerly direction. Cross the creek that will be swollen with runoff in early summer and often-dry by late summer, and begin a series of moderately ascending switchbacks.

After 0.6 mile of climbing, your trail levels off as you enter the realm of red fir, mountain hemlock, and western white and lodgepole pine, quickly reaching the northwest shore of beautiful Campbell Lake. A shoreline trail joins on your left; you may wish to follow that route in search of campsites. That trail eventually returns to the Shackleford Creek Trail in 1.4 miles, 2.5 miles from the trailhead. Fishing in Campbell Lake for rainbow, eastern brook, and brown trout is best in early summer and early autumn.

Continuing straight ahead at this lakeside junction, the trail curves around the west side of this fine lake and joins another trail within 0.2 mile. This hard-to-spot junction is indicated by an old, small sign bolted to a log. Continue straight ahead here, and, after about 100 feet, another log-bound sign points left to Cliff Lake. You can reach Cliff Lake by turning left at this junction and hiking 0.7 mile. At this popular lake and at Campbell Lake, rangers advise you to camp no less than 200 feet from the lakeshore.

Cliff Lake is the second-largest lake in the Marble Mountain Wilderness and the deepest. If you pack in a raft and fish from the middle of the lake, you will probably have good luck during the midsummer slowdown, when the water has warmed and the fish retreat into the depths. Shoreline anglers will find fishing for rainbow, brown, and brook trout is best in early summer and early autumn.

Fall turnover, a common phenomenon affecting the water temperature in lakes, occurs when the water temperature cools. The colder water at the lake's bottom and the warmer water near the surface circulate until the lake attains a uniform temperature throughout. At that point, the fish begin feeding in earnest. Fishing can also be productive just after the ice breaks up in late spring or early summer.

To complete the loop, return to the junction from Cliff Lake and turn left (west), skirting the eastern margin of a small subalpine meadow. You meet yet another trail leading to Cliff Lake on your left. Views improve as you gain elevation, encompassing the precipitous, rocky crags that soar above Campbell Lake.

Your route tops a pass at the 6,600-foot level, then descends westward, passing just north of shallow Summit Meadow Lake. This lake, shaded by mountain hemlocks, lies at the foot of dark, 800-foot metamorphic cliffs. Blue gentian and aster brighten the grassy opening below the lake.

A short jaunt beyond takes you above the east shore of subalpine Summit Lake. Beyond the lake in the northwest soars the reddish crag of Peak 7,636, providing a vivid contrast to the waters of Summit Lake and the dark green conifer forest that surrounds it. Fishing is good here for brookies. As with most lakes in the area, it is best in early summer and early autumn.

After crossing Summit Lake's outlet creek, you meet the Shackleford Creek Trail branching left and right. The left fork leads to the Pacific Crest Trail on the crest of the Salmon Mountains. Turn right, proceeding north, and amble across a lovely subalpine meadow, passing the invisible, unmaintained trail leading to Little Elk Lake on your left. Careful scouting is necessary to find that trail. It crosses the saddle immediately east of Peak 7,636 and descends through a subalpine, glacial basin to Little Elk Lake at the 5,400-foot level, where fishing is only fair for rainbow trout.

Your trail continues east, descending through occasional meadows and mixed conifer forests. It soon fades out entirely just before rejoining the trail to Campbell Lake. Turn left here and backtrack to the trailhead.

Summit Lake lies at the head of Shackleford Creek in the Marble Mountain Wilderness.

Appendix A: For More Information

For additional information regarding California's wildlands, updated information on backcountry conditions, and for information regarding wilderness permits and permit reservations, don't hesitate to contact the following agencies.

Hike 1: Big Sur District, Pfeiffer-Big Sur State Park, Big Sur, CA 93290, (408) 667-2316.

The following hikes are within the Los Padres National Forest:
Hikes 2 and 3: Monterey District, 406 South Mildred, King City, CA 93930, (408) 385-5434.
Hike 4: Park Superintendent, Pinnacles National Monument, 5000 Highway 146, Paicines, CA 95043-9770, (408) 389-4485.
Hike 5: Big Basin Redwoods State Park, 21600 Big Basin Way, Boulder Creek, CA 95006-9050, (408) 338-6132.

The following hike is within the Bureau of Land Management's (BLM) Caliente Resource Area:
Hike 6: BLM, Caliente Resource Area Office, 3801 Pegasus Drive, Bakersfield, CA 93308, (805) 391-6000.

The following hikes are within the Sequoia National Forest:
Hikes 7, 8, 9, and 10: Cannell Meadow Ranger District, P.O. Box 6, 105 Whitney Road, Kernville, CA 93238, (760) 376-2294.
Hike 14: Forest Supervisor, Sequoia National Forest, 900 West Grand Avenue, Porterville, CA 93527, (209) 784-1500.
Hikes 16, 17, and 18: Hume Lake Ranger District, 35860 East Kings Canyon Road, Dunlap, CA 93621, (559) 338-2251.

The following hikes are within Sequoia–Kings Canyon National Parks:
Hikes 15, 16, 19, and 20: Sequoia–Kings Canyon National Parks, Three Rivers, CA 93271-9700, (209) 565-3341.
(**For wilderness permit reservations:** request a copy of *Backcountry Basics*, a wilderness trip-planning guide, from the phone number above or consult the park's website at www.nps.gov/seki. Permit reservations require a fee.)

The following hikes are within the Inyo National Forest:
Hikes 11, 12, 13, and 23: Mount Whitney Ranger District, P.O. Box 8, Lone Pine, CA 93545, (760) 876-6200.
Hikes 24, 25, 26, 27, 28, 29, 30, 31, and 37: White Mountain Ranger District, 798 North Main Street, Bishop, CA 93514, (760) 873-2500.
Hikes 32 and 33: Mammoth Ranger District, P.O. Box 148, Mammoth Lakes, CA 93546, (760) 924-5500.
Hikes 42 and 43: Mono Lake Scenic Area Visitor Center, P.O. Box 130, Lee Vining, CA 93541, (760) 647-6629 or (760) 647-6595.

(For wilderness permit reservations, contact: Inyo National Forest Wilderness Reservation Office, 873 North Main Street, Bishop, CA 93514, or FAX applications to (760) 873-2484. A fee is required for reservations.)
Hike 3G: BLM, Ridgecrest Resource Area, 300 South Richmond Road, Ridgecrest, CA 93555, (760) 384-5400.

For information on the following hikes within the Sierra National Forest, contact: Forest Supervisor, Sierra National Forest, 1600 Tollhouse Road, Clovis, CA 93611-0532, (559) 297-0706, or the appropriate ranger district.
Hikes 21 and 22: Pineridge Ranger District, 29688 Auberry Road, P.O. Box 599, Prather, CA 93651, (559) 855-5360.
Hikes 34 and 35: Minarets Ranger District, 57003 Road 225, P.O. Box 10, North Fork, CA 93643, (559) 877-2218.

The following hikes are located within Yosemite National Park:
Hikes 39, 40, 41, and 43: National Park Service, Yosemite National Park, CA 95389, (209) 372-4461.
(For information regarding wilderness permit reservations, contact: Wilderness Permits, P.O. Box 545, Yosemite National Park, CA 95389, (209) 372-0740. For general wilderness information, phone: (209) 372-0200, press No. 9, then No. 5.)

The following hikes are within the Stanislaus National Forest:
Hikes 47, 48, 49, and 50: Summit Ranger District, 1 Pinecrest Lake Road, Pinecrest, CA 95364, (209) 965-3434.
Hike 52: Calaveras Ranger District, Highway 4, P.O. Box 500, Hathaway Pines, CA 95223, (209) 795-1381.

The following hikes are within the Toiyabe National Forest:
Hikes 38, 44, 45, 46, and 51: Bridgeport Ranger District, P.O. Box 595, Bridgeport, CA 93517, (760) 932-7070; or Toiyabe National Forest, Carson Ranger District, 1536 South Carson Street, Carson City, NV 89701, (775) 882-2766.

The following hikes are within the Eldorado National Forest:
Hikes 53 and 54: Amador Ranger District, 26820 Silver Drive, Pioneer, CA 95666, (209) 295-4251; or Eldorado National Forest Information Center, 3070 Camino Heights Drive, Camino, CA 95709, (530) 644-6048.

The following hikes are within the Lake Tahoe Basin Management Unit:
Hikes 54 and 55: Lake Tahoe Basin Management Unit, 870 Emerald Bay Road, Suite 1, South Lake Tahoe, CA 96150, (530) 573-2669.

The following hikes are within the Tahoe National Forest:
Hike 56: Truckee Ranger District, 10342 Highway 89 North, Truckee, CA 96161, (530) 587-3558.
Hike 57: Nevada City Ranger District, 631 Coyote Street, P.O. Box 6003, Nevada City, CA 95959-6003, (530) 265-4531.

The following hikes are within the Plumas National Forest:
Hike 58: La Porte Ranger District, Challenge Ranger Station, 10087 La Porte Road, P.O. Drawer 369, Challenge, CA 95926, (530) 675-2462.
Hikes 59, 60, and 61: Beckwourth Ranger District, Mohawk Ranger Station, Mohawk Road, P.O. Box 7, Blairsden, CA 96103, (530) 836-2575.
Hike 62: Quincy Ranger District, 39696 Highway 70, Quincy, CA 95971-9607, (530) 283-0555.

For information on the following hikes within the Lassen National Forest, contact: Forest Supervisor, Lassen National Forest, 55 South Sacramento Street, Susanville, CA 95971, (530) 257-2151, or the appropriate ranger district.
Hike 63: Almanor Ranger District, P.O. Box 767, Chester, CA 96020, (530) 258-2141.
Hike 68: Hat Creek Ranger District, P.O. Box 220, Fall River Mills, CA 96028, (530) 336-5521.

The following hikes are within Lassen Volcanic National Park:
Hikes 64, 65, 66, and 67: National Park Service, Lassen Volcanic National Park, P.O. Box 100, Mineral, CA 96063-0100, (530) 595-4444.

The following hikes are within the Modoc National Forest:
Hikes 69 and 70: Warner Mountain District, P.O. Box 220, Cedarville, CA 96104, (530) 279-6116; or Forest Supervisor, Modoc National Forest, 441 Main Street, Alturas, CA 96101, (530) 233-5811.

The following hike is within Point Reyes National Seashore:
Hike 71: Park Superintendent, Point Reyes National Seashore, Point Reyes, CA 94956, (415) 663-8522.

The following hike is within the Mendocino National Forest:
Hike 72: Mendocino National Forest, Stonyford Ranger District, Stites-Lodoga Road, Stonyford, CA 95979, (530) 963-3128; or Forest Supervisor, Mendocino National Forest, 420 East Laurel Street, Willows, CA 95988, (530) 934-3316.

For information on the following hikes within the Shasta-Trinity National Forest, contact: Forest Supervisor, Shasta-Trinity National Forest, 2400 Washington Avenue, Redding, CA 96001, (530) 244-2978, or the appropriate ranger district.
Hike 73: Yolla Bolly Ranger District, Platina, CA 96076, (530) 352-4211.
Hike 76: Weaverville Ranger District, P.O. Box 1190, Weaverville, CA 96093-1190, (530) 623-2131.

The following hike is within the BLM's Arcata Resource Area:
Hike 74: BLM, Arcata Resource Area Office, 1125 16th Street, Room 219, Arcata, CA 95521, (707) 825-2300.

The following hike is within the Prairie Creek Redwoods State Park:
Hike 75: Prairie Creek Redwoods State Park, Orick, CA 95555, (707) 488-2171, or (707) 445-6547.

For information on the following hikes within the Klamath National Forest, contact: Forest Supervisor, Klamath National Forest, 1312 Fairlane Road, Yreka, CA 96097, (530) 842-6131, or the appropriate ranger district.
Hikes 77, 78, and 80: Scott River Ranger District, 11263 South Highway 3, Fort Jones, CA 96032, (530) 468-5351.
Hike 79: Happy Camp Ranger District, P.O. Box 377, Happy Camp, CA 96039, (530) 493-2243.

For road conditions and highway information, call the CalTrans 24-hour information number for northern California: (800) 427-7623.

Appendix B: Hiker Checklist

Too many of us hike into the backcountry and discover we've forgotten something. A successful hike requires ample planning, and one of the first steps to being well prepared is packing the right equipment. Don't overburden your pack with too much equipment and unnecessary items; bring only what you really need. Scan the checklist below before leaving home to help ensure that some essential item has not been forgotten.

- [ ] Extra pack straps
- [ ] Water bottles (1- to 2-quart Nalgene bottles are best)
- [ ] Collapsible bucket (for settling water before filtering)
- [ ] Water filter (with brush to clean in the field)
- [ ] Pocketknife
- [ ] Hiking poles (1 or 2)
- [ ] Foam or self-inflating sleeping pad
- [ ] Sleeping bag
- [ ] Tent, stakes, ground sheet and/or tarp
- [ ] Hat with brim
- [ ] Sunglasses (with UV protection)
- [ ] Sunscreen (with an SPF of 15 or greater)
- [ ] Backpack stove, fuel bottle (full)
- [ ] Signal mirror
- [ ] First-aid kit
- [ ] Medication: prescriptions, anti-inflammatory and/or pain medication
- [ ] Knee and/or ankle wraps (neoprene is best)
- [ ] First-aid tape
- [ ] Moleskin, Second Skin
- [ ] Band-aids, bandages
- [ ] Aspirin (or other pain medication)
- [ ] Lip balm
- [ ] Toothbrush, toothpaste
- [ ] Toilet paper
- [ ] Lightweight trowel
- [ ] Boots (well broken-in)
- [ ] Camp shoes or sandals
- [ ] Extra shirt
- [ ] Extra underwear
- [ ] Extra socks
- [ ] Sweater
- [ ] Pants

- [ ] Hiking shorts
- [ ] Swimsuit
- [ ] Rain gear (Gore-Tex or similar fabric that is both waterproof and windproof)
- [ ] Biodegradable soap, small towel
- [ ] Cookware, cup, pot handle, pot scrubber
- [ ] Spoon and fork
- [ ] Matches in waterproof container
- [ ] Insect repellent
- [ ] Nylon tape or duct tape
- [ ] Pack cover
- [ ] Nylon stuffsacks and nylon cord (for hanging food)
- [ ] Bear-resistant food-storage canister
- [ ] Topo maps
- [ ] Flashlight, with spare bulb and fresh batteries
- [ ] Zipper-lock bags (for packing out trash and used toilet paper)
- [ ] Enough food, plus a little extra
- [ ] Watch
- [ ] Compass
- [ ] GPS unit
- [ ] Binoculars
- [ ] Thermometer
- [ ] Camera, film, lenses, filters, lens brush and paper, tripod
- [ ] Small sewing kit
- [ ] Notebook, pencils
- [ ] Field guidebooks
- [ ] Water
- [ ] Wilderness permit (where required)

Add the following for winter travel:
- [ ] Gaiters
- [ ] Instep crampons
- [ ] Wool or polypropylene cap or balaclava
- [ ] Space blanket
- [ ] Layers of warm clothing
- [ ] Sleeping bag with a rating of at least 0 degrees F
- [ ] Waterproof/windproof clothing
- [ ] Mittens or gloves
- [ ] Thermal underwear (wool or polypropylene)

Index

Boldface-italic locators indicate hiking trips described in the text. *Italic* locators indicate the feature will be found on a map in the text, while **boldface** locators indicate photographs.

About the Author

Ron Adkison, an avid hiker and backpacker, began his outdoor explorations at age six. After more than 30 years of hiking, he has logged more than 8,500 trail miles in ten western states. He has walked every trail in this guide to provide accurate, firsthand information about the trails, as well as features of ecological and historical interest. When he's not on the trail, Ron lives on his family's mountain ranch in southwest Montana. With the help of his wife, Lynette, and two children, Ben and Abbey, he raises sheep and llamas.

Ron shares his love and enthusiasm for wild places in this, his tenth guidebook.

Other FalconGuides by Ron Adkison: *Hiking California, Hiking Grand Canyon National Park, Hiking Washington, Hiking Wyoming's Wind River Range, Hiking Grand Staircase–Escalante and the Glen Canyon Region, Best Easy Day Hikes Grand Canyon, Best Easy Day Hikes Grand Staircase–Escalante and the Glen Canyon Region, Best Easy Day Hikes Northern Sierra.*

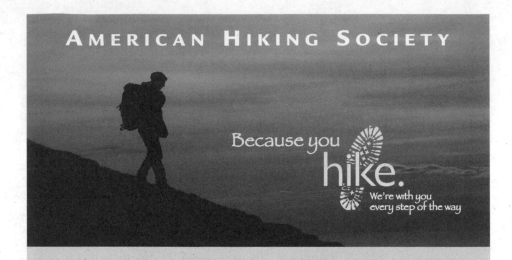